dedication

Mike dedicates this edition to his parents, Ray and JoAnn, and his partner, Barbara, who have provided continued support and encouragement for his writing and other life activities.

Michael dedicates this edition to his wife, Karen, and mother, Mary Ruth, both of whom passed away during the development of the eleventh edition.

Jeanne dedicates this edition to her finance professor, N. D. Quy, to her best friends, Nick Athanassiou and Raven McCrory, and to her research friends, ION.

Don A. Ball

Don A. Ball, a consultant to multinational corporations, was a professor of marketing and international business for several years after leaving industry. He has a degree in mechanical engineering from Ohio State and a doctorate in business administration from the University of Florida. Ball has published articles in the *Journal of International Business Studies* and other publications. Before obtaining his doctorate, he spent 15 years in various marketing and production management positions in Mexico, South America, and Europe.

Wendell H. McCulloch, Jr.

Wendell H. McCulloch, Jr., has been a professor of international business, finance, and law and is the former director of international business programs at California State University, Long Beach. He earned a bachelor's degree in economics at George Washington University and a JD from Yale University. He has published articles in *The Wall Street Journal,* the *Journal of International Business Studies,* and the *Collegiate Forum.* The results of McCulloch's research have appeared in publications by the Joint Economic Committee of the U.S. Congress and the Heritage Foundation. Before beginning his academic career, McCulloch spent 19 years as an executive for American and European multinationals that offered banking, insurance, and investment products in many countries. He was associate general counsel of International General Electric, headquartered in New York; member of the board of directors and general counsel of International General Electric, S.A., headquartered in Geneva; and cofounder and president of Trust of Properties, an investment fund, headquartered in London and Zurich.

J. Michael Geringer

J. Michael Geringer is a professor of strategy and international management at California Polytechnic University in San Luis Obispo. He earned a BS in business at Indiana University and MBA and PhD degrees at the University of Washington. He has authored or edited 14 books and monographs, over 110 published papers, and over 35 case studies; he serves on the editorial boards of several leading international academic journals; he served as the Saastamoinen Foundation Chair at the Helsinki School of Economics in Finland; he was the founding chair of the Strategic Alliances Committee of the Licensing Executives Society; he served as the chair of both the International Business and the Strategy and Policy divisions of the Administrative Sciences Association of Canada; and he is past chairperson of the Academy of Management's International Management division. His research has appeared in the *Strategic Management Journal, Academy of Management Journal, Journal of International Management, Columbia Journal of World Business, Management International Review, Journal of Management Studies, Human Resource Management Journal, Long Range Planning, Organisation Studies,* and *Journal of Applied Psychology,* among others. He has received 11 "best paper" awards for his research, including the Decade Award for most influential article from the *Journal of International Business Studies.* His teaching performance has earned numerous awards in the United States, Canada, Asia, Africa, Australia, and Europe, including the University Distinguished Teacher Award. He was the first recipient of the International Educator Award from Cal Poly, and he endowed a scholarship for students to work and study internationally. He has been active in a range of charitable and service activities, including spearheading the adoption of a school in Soweto, South Africa, and fundraising for public radio. In addition to working with universities around the world, Geringer is active in consulting and executive development for multinational corporations and executives from six continents. His clients have included Nokia; Lucent; Eastman Kodak; Sonera;

Northern Telecom; Rautaruukki; Eastman Chemical; UPM Kymmene; Industry, Science & Technology Canada; Jiangsu Telecom Industrial; California Highway Patrol; Economic Council of Canada; Perlos; YIT; California Department of Transportation; and Okobank, among others. For relaxation, he enjoys daily Stairmaster workouts, along with hiking, camping, gardening, cooking spicy vegetarian foods, and music.

Michael S. Minor

Michael S. Minor is a professor of marketing and international business at the University of Texas, Pan American. He was educated at the University of North Carolina, American University, and Cornell and holds a PhD from Vanderbilt University. His research focuses on comparative consumer behavior, international marketing strategy, political risk, and the consumption of high-technology experiential products. He has published in the *Journal of International Business Studies,* the *Journal of Consumer Marketing, International Studies of Management and Organization,* the *Journal of Services Marketing, International Business Review, Journal of Interactive Advertising,* and elsewhere. He has written for business and popular media from *PCWeek* to *Tennessee Business Magazine.* He is past chairperson of the Consumer Behavior Special Interest Group and past vice chair of the Technology and Marketing Special Interest Group of the American Marketing Association, as well as a former member of the Global Marketing SIG's board of directors. He is active in DOCNET, the association of business doctoral program administrators. He serves on multiple editorial advisory boards and is the coauthor with John C. Mowen of several consumer behavior books. He has won multiple master's-level teaching awards and was recently the doctoral program professor of the year. His consulting experience includes work for UNCTAD's Division on Investment, Technology and Enterprise Development and several U.S. and state government agencies. He has reviewed grant proposals for the Research Council of Norway as well as several U.S. agencies. He lived in Asia for a number of years and speaks Chinese. He relaxes by playing the mandolin and harmonica for the country/classic rock groups RiverRock and Coastlands.

Jeanne M. McNett

Jeanne M. McNett is a professor of management at Assumption College, in Worcester, Massachusetts. She earned a PhD at the University of Massachusetts, Amherst, and an MBA at the Cass School of Business, City University, London. She has had expatriate assignments in Germany, the United Kingdom, Saudi Arabia, Japan, and Korea. Her interests include the role of culture in international business and the pedagogy of international management. Her publications include the *Blackwell Encyclopedia of Management, Vol. VI: International Management,* second edition (Oxford, UK: Blackwell Publishing, 2005), and the *Blackwell Handbook of Global Management* (Oxford, UK: Blackwell Publishing, 2004). Her teaching, research, and presentations have received many awards, including the Roethlisberger Best Paper of the Year Award from the *Journal of Management Education* and the Alpha Phi Alpha Teacher of the Year Award. Her articles have been included in journals and collections focused on teaching in the area of international business. She is an avid master rower and enjoys running, reading, and gardening.

We are pleased to present the eleventh edition of *International Business: The Challenge of Global Competition*.

Purpose and Scope of This Text

Whether students are advanced undergraduates or are in MBA programs, an international business course is an ideal venue for a varied number of questions. Our hope is that this book will answer these questions about business in different cultures, the impact of geography, why products are the same (or different) across cultures, why people have different practices, the effect of the Internet on international business, and many, many more. There are always new questions, and sometimes there are new answers to old questions.

International Business 11/e is organized into four sections in order to maximize its utility to instructors and students alike. The opening section defines the nature of international business and the three environments in which it is conducted. Section Two is devoted to the continuing importance of international organizations and the international monetary system and how both affect business. Section Three focuses on the uncontrollable forces at work in all business environments and discusses their inevitable impact on business practice. We devote the final section of the book to a discussion of how managers deal with all the forces affecting international business. In the eleventh edition, we have continued section opening dialogues to help students better understand what they have learned and are about to learn.

Changes for the Eleventh Edition

With each new edition we have been blessed by an expanding network of those making helpful suggestions. Professors, reviewers, and business professionals who bought the book or received it at a conference and our own graduate and undergraduate students have made useful and constructive comments. We believe that *International Business 11/e* continues to offer you a solid and superior text infused with current topics relevant to current challenges. In this edition, we have extensively revised and updated the material in each chapter to reflect recent world events and new international business issues.

As with every new edition, tables, figures, and graphs have been updated to include the most current data available as of the publication of this text. Keeping an international business text topical and current is a challenge, and we have worked hard to provide you with the most recent information possible. We have also updated examples where relevant and replaced dated examples where appropriate. We have reorganized Chapter 4 to increase its focus on international institutions that influence international business. Chapter 12 ("Labor Forces") and Chapter 20 ("Human Resource Management") have been completely reorganized to avoid redundancies and better focus their respective content. The chapter on organizational design and control (Chapter 14) has been moved so that it follows directly after the discussion of strategy, reflecting suggestions of reviewers and users. As a result, the numbering and ordering of Chapters 15 through 21 have been modified slightly to improve the organization and flow of content. Chapter 21 has been renamed "Financial Management and Accounting" to emphasize an increased emphasis on issues of international accounting in addition to financial management.

Chapter 1   The Rapid Change of International Business

The opening case on the importance of international business experience has been updated and expanded; the popular Worldview box on buying American has been updated; new and updated examples have been added throughout the chapter to enhance understanding of key issues; the discussion of definitions and terminology has been refocused and is now more concise; discussion of the history of international business has been enhanced; the Worldview on the debate on globalization of trade and investment has been revised; and a new mini-case exercise has been added at the end of the chapter dealing with the ownership and nationality associated with many well-known companies and brands.

Chapter 2 International Trade and Foreign Direct Investment

This is a shorter, more focused chapter with an updated introduction and discussion of trade in goods and services. The data on international trade and investment have been updated throughout the chapter, to the most current figures available at the time of publication, and the presentation of these data has been improved to enhance the reader's ability to analyze and understand trends and traits of international trade and investment. Discussion of small and medium-size enterprises and their role in exporting has been updated and enhanced. There is a new Worldview box that examines how trade and investment impact economic and social development, as well as an enhanced Worldview examining why more investment does not flow to Africa. The discussion of maquiladoras has been fundamentally revised and made more concise, and the end-of-chapter minicase on a Mexican company trying to remain competitive in the face of emerging low-cost competition from China has been updated.

Chapter 3 Theories of International Trade and Investment

In Chapter 3 we have revised, reorganized, and clarified the discussion of theories of international trade and added new examples in order to facilitate student comprehension of these topics. Discussion has been added on imperfect competition as a theoretical explanation of trade; the Worldview on comparative advantage and offshoring of service jobs to India has been updated and enhanced; discussion of trade restrictions has been substantially updated, and new examples and discussion of sanctions have been added; and the Worldview on subsidies to the sugar industry has been updated. The discussion of theories of foreign investment has been substantially expanded and reorganized, including new discussion of theories such as financial factors and dynamic capabilities and expanded discussion of internalization and the eclectic theory. A new minicase added at the end of the chapter addresses issues associated with fair trade in cocoa and the use of child labor in Africa.

Chapter 4 International Institutions from an International Business Perspective

Chapter 4 has been renamed to reflect its more focused orientation, including an increased emphasis on the usefulness of international institutions for international business. The chapter's organization has been modified to reflect the political, economic, and shared purposes of the various international institutions. The United Nations' Millennium goals have been included, along with a progress report regarding their attainment. Cooperative military agreements (e.g., NATO) have been included as a type of political institution. Discussion of NAFTA, the World Trade Organization, the European Union, and OPEC has been expanded. A new Worldview has been added on the uneven benefits of trade.

Chapter 5 Understanding the International Monetary System

We have added more discussion on the historical background of the gold standard; added a section on the connection between monetary systems and terrorism; and modified the coverage of the IMF to focus on its contributions to trade growth. We have added an explanation of the Triffin paradox, and there is a new discussion of Jeffrey Sachs's challenges to the IMF. Other changes include additional discussion of the historical background of the emergence of the floating rate system; additional descriptions of the major currency arrangements and their users; and an expanded explanation of balance of payments.

Chapter 6 Sociocultural Forces

Chapter 6 emphasizes the critical area of culture as an uncontrolled force that influences international business. To enhance the chapter's focus, discussion of education has been moved to Chapter 12 ("Labor Forces"). We carefully reedited the section on religion and particularly the material dealing with Islam, after consulting with Muslims from several different national backgrounds. The Worldview on Disneyland has been updated. Information on changes in the South Korean workweek, as well as information on South Korea as an international leader in design, has been added. A new minicase has been added on the wine industry in India.

Chapter 7   Natural Resources and Environmental Sustainability

This chapter has been updated and expanded to better address the increasingly important areas of environmental sustainability and sustainable business. Changes include the use of Porter's diamond as a framework for discussing geographic factor conditions. China, Afghanistan, and Latin America have been added to the chapter's discussion, as well as an expanded section on natural resources. Further additions to the chapter include a consideration of the connection between innovation and factor conditions, a section on environmental sustainability, a review of the stakeholder model for sustainable business, and examples of sustainable businesses.

Chapter 8   Economic and Socioeconomic Forces

This chapter opens with an updated reflection of the reality of India's middle class—increasingly well-to-do and with a penchant for "getting ahead." A new section addresses levels of economic development, to help the reader understand how economic development is categorized by different institutions, and a new Worldview discusses characteristics of developing nations. The discussion of economic development indicators such as gross national income (GNI) and GNI/capita has been updated and expanded. There is a new discussion of the limitations of GNI-based measures, such as the underground economy and currency conversions. A new Worldview has been added that discusses new approaches to the assessment of economic development, such as the human-needs approach and the United Nations' Human Development Index, including a list of the top- and bottom-ranked nations on this index. Figures, tables, and examples have been updated throughout the chapter in order to provide current, relevant support for the concepts being discussed. There are two minicases at the end of the chapter to provide relevant opportunities to apply the concepts in a practical manner.

Chapter 9   Political Forces

In this chapter we examine the renationalization of Bolivia's natural gas industry and discuss the more general leftward turn in several Latin American countries. At the same time, we note the continued shrinkage of communism as, for example, China's millionaires continue to multiply. The section on terrorism reflects recent developments relevant to international business, and a new mini-MNE box discusses the resiliency of businesses and people in the face of hostilities. The material on international debt crises has been removed, and examples throughout the chapter have been updated to enhance comprehension of issues associated with political forces.

Chapter 10   Legal Forces

Chapter 10's discussion of legal forces has been revised to make the content more international and less U.S.-centric. We have eliminated the discussion of the dual court system of the United States. The section on taxation of expatriates has been updated and simplified, and the section on litigation has been made less U.S.-centric and shorter. New material has been introduced on the issue of a harmonized bankruptcy code. Examples in the chapter have been updated as well. A new section explores career prospects for those with a specialization in international law. The emerging issue of "patent trolls" is introduced.

Chapter 11   Financial Forces

Chapter 11 covers the rapidly changing and largely uncontrollable financial forces that are important to international businesspeople. The chapter has been reorganized to focus on exchange rates; their quotation, fluctuation, and forecasting; and then balance-of-payments accounts and other external financial forces. Euro-US$ relationships are used in many of the examples. The chapter contains an expanded discussion of why currencies fluctuate; a new discussion of the law of one price; an added discussion of parity relationships, the Fisher effect, and purchasing power parity; and an expanded section on exchange rate forecasting. We have added discussion of currency exchange controls, tariffs, and taxation and have expanded the discussion on inflation. There is a new Worldview on the effect of foreign aid in developing countries.

Chapter 12 Labor Forces

Labor is a critical element of all business. Labor's role in international business has become increasingly salient as a consequence of globalization and outsourcing. This chapter has been completely reorganized and refocused to avoid redundancies with the chapter on human resource management (Chapter 20) and to update and emphasize key labor issues relevant to international business. There are new examples, as well as new and updated data, throughout the chapter. We have included a new opening case example on differences in labor conditions in Japan and China. The discussion on labor conditions and trends has been revised and refocused, including discussion of the overall size and sector of a nation's work force, aging of populations, the shift of populations from rural to urban areas, unemployment considerations across nations and regions, the issue of immigrant labor and labor mobility, including brain drain, and considerations associated with child labor and forced labor. We have included a new mini-MNE box on the role of small business in generating jobs internationally. We have updated the Worldview on guest workers in Japan; updated and expanded the discussion of sexism in international business; and prepared a more concise and focused discussion of labor unions and their role internationally.

Chapter 13 International Competitive Strategy

Chapter 13 introduces Section Four, on the organizational environment. We have included a new opening case on the use of scenario planning to help manage the strategic uncertainties associated with international business activities. The discussion has been expanded on why firms need to engage in strategic planning if they want to compete successfully in international markets. Throughout the chapter, we have included new and updated examples to promote the reader's comprehension of international strategy concepts and tools. There is an expanded discussion, with examples, of mission, vision, and values statements and their role in international strategy. The use of quantitative and qualitative objectives in international strategic planning activities has been updated. There is an expanded discussion of the typology of multidomestic, global, and transnational strategies for international business, as well as a new section discussing home replication strategies. We have included a new Worldview on regional strategies for competing internationally. The discussion has been revised and expanded on the issue of managing standardization in international strategy, as well as on the use of scenarios in international strategy formulation. We have added a new section on performance measurement in international strategy and have updated the discussion on approaches and trends in the use of strategic planning for international business, including who is involved in the planning and what is incorporated in planning processes. There is an updated discussion of sources and techniques for competitor assessment. The minicase on Wal-Mart's internationalization efforts at the end of the chapter has been updated to include the company's failures in Korea and Germany, its efforts to dramatically expand operations in China through acquisitions and internal growth, and its strategic plans to enter India and other emerging markets.

Chapter 14 Organizational Design and Control

The discussion of organizational design and control in international business has been moved so that it now follows directly after the discussion of international strategy. The opening case on Kraft Foods has been updated to highlight the company's global reorganization of its structure in an effort to enhance Kraft's international competitiveness in a changing marketplace. There are new and updated examples throughout the chapter to help illustrate key concepts associated with the structure and design of international organizations. There are two new Worldviews, one on Accenture's "virtual" global structure and another on structural changes that can help enhance companies' global competitiveness. The minicase at the end of the chapter has been updated as well.

Chapter 15 Assessing and Analyzing Markets

This chapter's material, which addresses the assessment and analysis of markets, was in Chapter 14 in the previous edition. We begin this chapter with a vignette of a wealthy consultant who believes that we cannot consciously express our motivations for purchases but that these motivations can be uncovered in the "reptilian" part of the brain. Further, this insight should apply to national groups as well as individuals. We anticipate lively discussion of this issue in classrooms around the world! We continue to clarify the difference between country and segment screening. We continue our coverage—perhaps the most detailed anywhere—of the methods used in doing market research abroad. The chapter's appendix, "Sources of Information Used in Screenings," has been moved from the text to the book's Web site, www.mhhe.com/ball 11e, hosted by McGraw-Hill Higher Education.

Chapter 16   Entry Modes

This chapter provides an expanded treatment of the critical topic of how businesses make decisions about the best way to enter foreign markets. We have significantly reorganized the material in this chapter to improve coherency and flow and to promote improved student comprehension of this material. Data and examples have been updated throughout the chapter. There is new and expanded discussion of management contracts, contract manufacturing, and other nonequity forms of market entry.

Chapter 17   Export and Import Practices

In this chapter on exporting and importing we have continued to expand our emphasis on services as well as tangible products. We have added an update of export–import terminology and shortened the chapter slightly by reducing some detail on paperwork procedures. A discussion of changes in procedures as a result of security concerns has also been added.

Chapter 18   Marketing Internationally

The international marketing chapter continues to emphasize the standardization-adaptation dilemma. To reflect current trends in international marketing, we have included new and further developed examples, such as the opening case study on Procter & Gamble's path to globalization. All of the data in the chapter have been updated to maintain the currency of the topics being addressed. The discussion of international advertising has been expanded to include consideration of the pervasive impact of culture on advertising decisions at subtle levels. The chapter's Building Your Global Résumé box includes a wide variety of sources of information on career opportunities in international marketing, advertising, and sales. The discussion of international channels and the issue of disintermediation has been updated.

Chapter 19   Global Operations and Supply Chain Management

Chapter 19 focuses on global supply chain management, an increasingly critical part of global operations and a key to the international competitiveness of businesses. The presentation of material in this chapter has been made more concise. The updated opening case examines the Spanish company Zara and the use of operations management capabilities for achieving competitive advantage in the fashion industry. There are new and updated examples throughout the chapter. The mini-MNE box on Cognizant Technology Solutions of India and its global offshoring model has been updated. There is an expanded discussion on the use of mass-customization techniques. The Worldview on Johnson Controls has been updated to emphasize the company's use of design and manufacturing excellence to achieve competitive advantage in global markets for automobile interiors. We have included a new Worldview on Nestlé's GLOBE program for using global standardization of processes and systems to create strategic advantage within and across its worldwide network of food industry operations.

Chapter 20   Human Resource Management

Chapter 20's discussion of HRM issues in international business has been reorganized to reduce redundancies with Chapter 12's discussion of international labor forces. A new opening case addresses issues associated with expatriate positions. The section on the global mind-set of the international human resource management approach, and how that approach links strategy, selection, and training, has been revised. A new Worldview box examines the role of cultural backgrounds and nationality in selecting candidates for international positions. There is also a new Worldview on the appropriateness of women for international assignments, and the section on expatriates has been substantially revised. Another new Worldview considers culture shock and its effect on expatriate and repatriate personnel. The discussion of families of expatriates, including issues faced by trailing spouses and children, has been substantially revised. We have revised the discussion of challenges associated with repatriation, expatriate support services, and compensation and benefits for expatriates and other international personnel. A new minicase at the end of the chapter deals with considerations facing an employee who is deciding whether to accept an international position that has been offered to her.

Chapter 21   Financial Management and Accounting

This chapter has been renamed in order to highlight its increased emphasis on issues of international accounting in addition to financial management. The chapter has been reorganized to move from an emphasis on the capital structure of the firm to an emphasis on cash flow management and discussion of international exposure and hedging. Examples, including Chinese trends in initial public offerings, have been updated throughout the chapter. A new mini-MNE box examines the use of micro-lending in developing country environments. The discussion of multilateral netting has been expanded. Our discussion of financial risk management has been expanded with examples of transaction, translation, and economic exposure and their hedging. A new Worldview examines unintended consequences of U.S. law on repatriated cash flows. The discussion on swaps and derivatives has been expanded, and there is a new section that addresses the importance of networking for financial partners. Discussion of making sales without money has been expanded, and we have added sections on transfer pricing and taxation, international accounting, the role of foreign currency, accounting and culture, convergence of accounting standards, and triple-bottom-line accounting. There is a new Worldview on Sarbanes-Oxley as an unpopular export, and we have expanded the discussion of international finance centers.

Glossary

The Glossary is a very extensive collection of definitions of documents, institutions, concepts, and terms used in international business. The Glossary is an extremely valuable resource for students and instructors.

New Features

With the eleventh edition we introduce an innovative and unique set of Building Your Global Résumé boxes that appear in each of the chapters. Prepared by Bernard Yevin, dean of the Business Informational Technology Division of Forsyth Technical Community College, each box presents valuable tools and insights to help students build a foundation for entering and excelling in international business activities and careers. These boxes cover such topics as finding international job opportunities, building international skills and experience, gaining relevant knowledge and tools to increase success in finding and performing international business jobs, and learning from the practical experience and recommendations of global mentors who have successfully pursued careers involving international business activity.

The eleventh edition also continues to use the innovative globalEDGE™ Research Tasks, created by Tunga Kiyak and Tomas Hult of the CIBER Center at Michigan State. These end-of-chapter exercises challenge students to solve problems similar to those faced by practicing international business managers, and they acquaint students with the tools and data real managers use. The globalEDGE™ Research Tasks are ideal for Web-based courses. For example, in working on a product launch, students may be asked to compile a list of the top 10 countries in terms of their attractiveness for potential return of FDI. Students can access all the Internet resources needed to solve the problems at www.globaledge.msu.edu.

A new video collection features original business documentaries as well as NBC news footage. Featured titles include "Will Rallies Help Immigrants?" "Is China Cheating When It Comes to Trade?" "Cirque du Soleil: A Truly Global Workforce," and "J&J: Creating a Global Learning Organization." Videos correspond to the video cases (with discussion questions) at the end of the book.

Other Useful Elements

- Mini-MNE boxes discuss smaller-size businesses and how they function and compete in the global business world.
- Worldview boxes highlight real-world applications of key concepts to help students relate the material they are learning to their own business careers.
- An extensive set of maps throughout the text gives students important geographic perspectives.
- End-of-chapter tools include Summaries, Key Words, Questions, globalEDGE™ Research Tasks, and Minicases to further help students in their comprehension.

CESIM: Global Challenge Simulation

This online simulation involving international markets for mobile handsets is packaged with new copies of the text. There are three market areas (North America, Europe, and Asia). The simulation presents a range of features that could be offered (impacting product differentiation), a choice of production sites (in Asia or North America), price options, and exposure to exchange rate fluctuations. It can be used with 3 to 12 teams (6 to 50 students per simulation) and can involve teams from more than one class or university, if desired. There is an enhanced online support facility with the eleventh edition, as well as an improved user interface to enhance the performance and appearance of the simulation. The simulation can be used at no additional expense for either instructors or students who use new copies of the text.

Acknowledgments

The departure of Don Ball and Wendell McCulloch from active participation in this book leaves a gap in the field of international business. When Don and Wendell began this project, there were virtually no textbooks on international business. Few textbooks, and virtually none in international business, have reached an eleventh edition and maintained their market leadership as has been the case with this book. We will miss their guidance, and their personalities, as we attempt to fill their shoes. We also note the untimely passing of our colleague and coauthor, Paul Frantz, whose experience and friendship will also be missed. But we welcome the addition of Jeanne McNett, who has displayed abundant energy and valuable insight and contributions during the tenth and eleventh editions of this text.

To the long list of people to whom we are indebted, we want to add Professors Gary Anders, Arizona State University West; Gary Anderson, Bowling Green State University; John Anderson, University of Tennessee, Knoxville; Nicholas Athanassiou, Northeastern University; Robert T. Aubey, University of Wisconsin, Madison; Winston Awadzi, Delaware State University; Mark C. Baetz, Wilfred Laurier University; Bahman Bahrami, North Dakota State University; Rufus Barton, Murray State University; Lawrence Beer, Arizona State University; Joseph R. Biggs, California Polytechnic State University; S. A. Billon, University of Delaware; James R. Bradshaw, Brigham Young University; Sharon Browning, Northwest Missouri State University; Dennis Carter, University of North Carolina, Wilmington; Mark Chadwin, Old Dominion University; Aruna Chandras, Ashland University; John Cleek, University of Missouri, Kansas City; Gerald Crawford, University of North Alabama; Refik Culpan, Pennsylvania State University; Peter DeWill, University of Central Florida; Galpira Eshigi, Illinois State University; Christof Falli, Portland State University; Colette Frayne, California Polytechnic State University, San Luis Obispo; Prem Gandhi, State University of New York, Plattsburgh; Ellen Kaye Gerke, Alliant International University; Kenneth Gray, Florida Agricultural and Mechanical University; Robert Guffey, Elon College; Stanley D. Guzell, Youngstown State University; Gary Hankem, Mankato State University; Baban Hasnat, State University of New York, Brockport; Tom Hinthorne, Montana State University; Veronica Horton, University of Akron; Paul Jenner, Southwest Missouri State University; Bruce H. Johnson, Gustavus Adolphus College; Ahmad Karim, Indiana University–Purdue University, Ft. Wayne; Michael Kublin, University of New Haven; Eddie Lewis, University of Southern Mississippi; Carol Lopilato, California State University, Dominguez Hills; Mingfang Li, California State University Northridge; Lois Ann McElroy Lindell, Wartburg College; Dorinda Lynn, Pensacola Junior College; Lynette Mathur, Southern Illinois University, Carbondale; Hugh J. McCabe, Westchester Community College; Fraser McLeay, University of Montana; Les Mueller, Central Washington University; Gary Oddon, San Jose State University; Darrell Neron, Peirce College; Ebele Oriaku, Elizabeth City State University; Jaimie Ortiz, Florida Atlantic University; Mike Peng, Ohio State University; Susan A. Peterson, Maricopa College; Avin Raj, Assumption College; Jere Ramsey, California Polytechnic State University, San Luis Obispo; Tagi Sagafi-nejad, Loyola College, MD; Rakesh Sambharya, Rutgers University; Eugene Seeley, Utah Valley State College; John Setnicky, Mobile College; V. N. Subramanyam, Lancaster University; Angelo Tarallo, Ramapo College; Jesse S. Tarleton, William and Mary College; John Thanopoulos, University of Akron; Kenneth Tillery, Middle Tennessee State University; Hsin-Min Tong, Redford University; Dennis Vanden Bloomen, University of Wisconsin, Stout; Heidi Vernon, Northeastern University; George Westacott, State University of New York, Binghamton; Terry Witkowski, California State University; Habte Woldu, University of Texas, Dallas; and Bernard Yevin, Forsythe Technical Community College. Attorney Mary C. Tolton, Esq., of the law firm Parker, Poe, Adams & Bernstein of Raleigh, North Carolina, provided valuable supplementary readings for the legal forces chapter; and we acknowledge the help of Denalee Eaton and Kimberly Gainey, students at California State University, Long Beach; Handan Vicdan and Ebru Ulusoy, PhD students at the University of Texas–Pan American; Sandra de los Santos and Elizabeth Reyes, members of the PhD program staff at the University of Texas–Pan American; and Heidi Peterson, Bryan Esterly, Anna Byrd, and Kaley Phillips, students at California Polytechnic University, San Luis Obispo.

We are also indebted to the following reviewers for helping us fine-tune the eleventh edition to better meet market needs: Yeqing Bao, University of Alabama, Huntsville; Macgorine Cassell, Fairmont State University; Scott C. Hammond, Utah Valley State College; Mr. Haryanto, Monmouth College; Gregg Lattier, Lee College; Juan F. Ramirez, Nova Southeastern University; John C. Ruhnka, University of Colorado at Denver and Health Sciences Center; Linda C. Ueltschy, Bowling Green State University; and G. Bernard Yevin, Forsyth Tech Community College.

Hundreds of professors have reviewed this text over its eleven editions and have shaped it into the solid textbook it is. Their suggestions and feedback have been invaluable to us, and we very much appreciate their efforts and time.

We would like to offer our special thanks to Jeffrey Jones for contributing the Critical Thinking Exercises to the instructor's manual. And a special thanks is given to the outstanding editorial and production staff from McGraw-Hill/Irwin who have worked so hard and so well to make this project succeed and stay on schedule, particularly John Biernat, Ryan Blankenship, Laura Hurst Spell, Meg Beamer, Laura Griffin, and Marlena Pechan. We feel honored to work with such a talented and professional team.

A World of Resources . . .

International Business: The Challenge of Global Competition continues to be the most objective and thorough treatment of international business available for students. Enriched with maps, photos, and the most up-to-date world data, this text boasts the collective expertise of three current and three former authors with firsthand international business experience, specializing in international management, finance, law, global strategy, and marketing—a claim no other text can make. Only Ball, McCulloch, Geringer, Minor, and McNett can offer a complete view of international business as diverse as the backgrounds of your business students.

Worldview Examples

Worldview features in every chapter offer compelling examples of how international business is affected by legal, political, economic, and social issues, helping students understand how interrelated these business strategy and policy issues are.

WORLD view

Are You Really Buying American?

Consider the following scenario of a "typical" American family:

The Boltons, Mike and Barbara, live in New York City. Mike is a security consultant with the security services firm Wackenhut Corporation. Barbara is an advertising executive in the Global Head Office of J. Walter Thompson.

On her way home from work, Barbara listens to the new Dixie Chicks CD in her Chrysler van. She stops for gas at the Shell station, then drives to the grocery store. She fills her shopping cart with a variety of items, including Ortega taco shells and salsa, Hellmann's mayonnaise, ReaLemon lemon juice, Ragu spaghetti sauce, Carnation Instant Breakfast drink, a six-pack of Dr. Pepper, a quart of A&W Root Beer, a container of CoffeeMate nondairy coffee creamer, a can of Chicken-of-the-Sea tuna, Lipton tea, Mott's apple sauce, a half-dozen cans of Slim-Fast, frozen Bird's Eye vegetables, some Evian water, and several packages of Stouffer's Lean Cuisine frozen dinners. For a treat, she picks up a pint of Ben and Jerry's ice cream and a Baby Ruth candy bar. She also grabs several cans of Alpo for their dog, Sassy, and a box of Friskies and a bag of Tidy Cat cat

litter for their cat, Millie. She selects a Philip Roth novel and a copy of *Elle* magazine, then goes down the toiletries aisle for some Dove soap and Jergen's moisturizing lotion. Before finishing, she calls Mike on her Samsung cellular phone from T-Mobile to see if there's anything else he needs. He asks her to pick up some PowerBars for him to take to the gym during his lunchtime workouts next week. On her way home, she stops at the bookstore and picks up a book—*The Da Vinci Code*.

After finishing up at work, Mike gets into his Jeep Cherokee and puts the new Ben Harper and the Innocent Criminals CD into the Clarion car stereo. He stops at the Amoco station to fill his gas tank and checks the air pressure in his Firestone tires. He makes a quick stop at Computerland to pick up the newest release of WordPerfect, signing the credit card slip with his Bic pen. Then he goes to the video store to pick up *The Pink Panther* on DVD, before heading to the package store for a bottle of Wild Turkey bourbon. He walks next door to the sporting goods store to pick up some Wilson racquetballs for his workouts next week and then heads home.

Barbara's favorite TV show, *Jeopardy!*, is just starting as Mike comes in the door, so she pours herself a glass of Beringer wine from Napa Valley and changes the Dish TV satellite channel on their Magnavox television so that she can watch her show. Before he prepares dinner, Mike opens a Miller beer and leafs through the day's mail, setting the most recent issue of *Road and Track* magazine aside to read later. Soon, dinner is ready and they sit down for their meal, while watching a show on the National Geographic Channel.

While this may sound like a very typical evening for many Americans, foreign-owned firms produced nearly every item that the Boltons purchased or consumed:

- Wackenhut is owned by Group 4 Falck of Denmark.
- J. Walter Thompson is owned by the WPP Group of the United Kingdom.
- Germany's DaimlerChrysler manufactures Chryslers and Jeeps.
- The British-Dutch company Royal Dutch Shell owns Shell.

mini MNE

>>A Little Guy Makes Global Business Easier for the Little Guys

DE Technologies, a tiny Virginia-based private company with only six employees and offices in the United States and Canada, has patented a technology for using the Internet/intranet to process sales globally. Intended for small and medium-size enterprises, development of the technology was stimulated by the frustrations that DE Technologies' founder encountered while attempting to arrange international trade deals in Russia for his own small company. Traditional systems for international trade, involving multiple, inefficient, and time-consuming layers of vertical service industries, can require 20 or more forms and 60 days to complete and cost 5 to 40 percent of the cost of the total transaction.

With DE's system, which is called the Electronic Commerce Backbone System (ECBS), small and medium-size firms can automatically export and import goods and services without previous international trade experience. The ECBS allows buyers and sellers to buy products in the currency of the destination country, view product descriptions in the language of the destination country, view digital still or motion video displays of the products for sale, and view the calculations and displays of prices for air, land, and sea transportation; it also ensures direct payment of goods via credit cards or documentary credit.

Procedures such as the preparation and filing of export–import documents, freight, insurance, titles, letters of credit, pro forma invoices, and bills of lading are done by the program. This eliminates the necessity of engaging foreign freight forwarders, export and import agents, and

other international channels-of-distribution members. Thus, ECBS reduces the costs of ocean and air freight, banking, and human resources.

Small and medium-size enterprises (SMEs) can become members by paying a small membership fee, which gives them access to the ECBS. A transactional fee of 0.3 percent also is levied. According to the founder of DE Technologies, "the capability of the system will allow thousands of SMEs to compete effectively in the Import/Export business with 'The Big Guys' as the barriers to entry will be lowered tremendously."

The ECBS can be supplemented with the Borderless Order Entry System (BOES), a patented process for electronically managing international trade transactions in an integrated manner. It allows companies to create and file necessary electronic documents (in any currency or language), monitor and track steps in the transaction, calculate applicable freight costs as well as taxes and duties, and perform financial arrangements of a sophisticated nature. The result is a reduction of as much as 30 percent in the costs of conducting international trade transactions. SMEs can export and import products from any nation, using the Internet or Intranets, and thereby expand market share in international markets.

Source: "Cutting through a World of Red Tape," *Business Week On-line*, www.businesswe . . . m/smallbiz/0006/te000628.htm?script Framed (June 30, 2000); "Electronic Commerce Backbone System (ECBS)," *DE Technologies Web site*, www.detechnologies.com/ ecbs.htm (July 1, 2004); "Information Technology and International Trade Position Paper," *DE Technologies Web site*, www .detechnologies.com/ecbs.htm (July 3, 2006); and "Borderless Order Entry Systems," *DETechnologies Web site*, www.detechnologies .com/boes.htm (July 3, 2006).

mini- MNE Examples

These boxed features in every chapter illustrate how small businesses compete for global markets. Students find these examples interesting as they learn that you don't have to be a multinational to sell overseas.

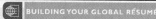

New! Building Your Global Résumé

Each box presents valuable tools and insights to help students build a foundation for entering and excelling in international business activities and careers. These boxes cover such topics as finding international job opportunities, building international skills and experience, gaining relevant knowledge and tools to increase success in finding and performing international business jobs, and learning from practical experience and recommendations from global mentors that have successfully pursued careers involving international business activity.

Visual Format

For the increasingly visual student population, the tables, figures, maps, and photos in the text bring international business to life. Students are better able to absorb ideas and compare and contrast information on different countries when it is presented in a visual format rather than long passages of text.

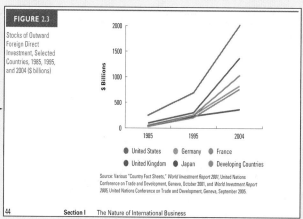

FIGURE 2.3

Stocks of Outward Foreign Direct Investment, Selected Countries, 1985, 1995, and 2004 ($ billions)

● United States ● Germany ● France
● United Kingdom ● Japan ● Developing Countries

Source: Various "Country Fact Sheets," World Investment Report 2001, United Nations Conference on Trade and Development, Geneva, October 2001, and World Investment Report 2005, United Nations Conference on Trade and Development, Geneva, September 2005.

44   Section I   The Nature of International Business

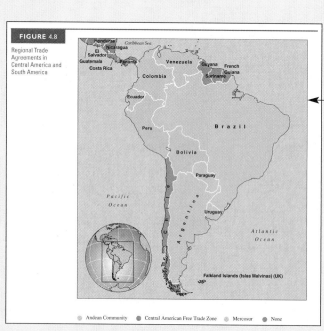

FIGURE 4.8

Regional Trade Agreements in Central America and South America

● Andean Community ● Central American Free Trade Zone ● Mercosur ● None

Instructive Maps

Numerous maps display valuable data and help students grasp geographic implications.

Summary

Explain the significance of culture for international business.

To be successful in their relationships overseas, international businesspeople must be students of culture. They must not only have factual knowledge; they must also become culturally sensitive. Culture affects all functional areas of the firm.

Identify the sociocultural components of culture.

Although experts differ about the components of culture, the following are representative of what numerous anthropologists believe exist: (1) aesthetics, (2) attitudes and beliefs, (3) religion, (4) material culture, (5) education, (6) language, (7) societal organization, (8) legal characteristics, and (9) political structures.

Discuss the significance of religion to businesspeople.

Knowing the basic tenets of other religions will contribute to a better understanding of their followers' attitudes. This may be a major factor in a given market.

Explain the cultural aspects of technology.

Material culture, especially technology, is important to managements contemplating overseas investment. Foreign governments have become increasingly involved in the sale and control of technical assistance. Technology may enable a firm to enter a new market successfully even if its competitors are already established there. It often enables the firm to obtain superior conditions for an overseas investment because the host government wants the technology.

Discuss the pervasiveness of the information technology era.

Businesspeople must keep abreast of the changes in information technology to avoid falling behind their competitors. The Internet enables small firms to compete in the global market, a fact that provides new opportunities for some firms and new competition for others. Businesspeople who can capture information from transaction data have a significant advantage over those who cannot. The opinion in the retailing industry is that this capability is the primary reason for Wal-Mart's success, for example.

Explain the importance of the ability to speak the local language.

Language is the key to culture. A feel for a people and their attitudes naturally develops with a growing mastery of their language.

Discuss the importance of unspoken language in international business.

Because unspoken language can often tell businesspeople something that spoken language does not, they should know something about this form of cross-cultural communication.

Discuss the two classes of relationships within a society.

A knowledge of how a society is organized is useful because the arrangement of relationships within it defines and regulates the manner in which its members interface with one another. Anthropologists have broken down societal relationships into two classes: those based on kinship and those based on free association of individuals.

Discuss Hofstede's four cultural value dimensions.

Geert Hofstede analyzed IBM employees in 72 countries and found that the differences in their answers to 32 statements could be based on four value dimensions: (1) individualism versus collectivism, (2) large versus small power distance, (3) strong versus weak uncertainty, and (4) masculinity versus femininity. These dimensions help managers understand how cultural differences affect organizations and management methods.

End-of-Chapter Learning Tools

At the end of each chapter are a Summary, Key Words, and Questions. The Summary is tied to the Concept Previews that open the chapter. The Key Words list includes page references for easy reference. The Questions test students' ability to retain and apply what they've learned in the chapter.

Key Words

culture (p. 160)	Asian religions (p. 169)	lingua franca (p. 176)
ethnocentricity (p. 160)	caste system (p. 171)	unspoken language (p. 179)
aesthetics (p. 164)	material culture (p. 173)	bribes (p. 181)
demonstration effect (p. 168)	technological dualism (p. 175)	extortion (p. 181)
Protestant work ethic (p. 169)	appropriate technology (p. 175)	extended family (p. 183)
Confucian work ethic (p. 169)	boomerang effect (p. 175)	associations (p. 183)

Questions

1. Why is it helpful for international businesspeople to know that a national culture has two components?

2. A knowledge of culture has been responsible for Disney's success in Tokyo, and ignorance of culture was responsible for the company's large losses in Paris. Discuss.

3. Why do international businesspersons need to consider aesthetics when making marketing decisions?

4. How can the demonstration effect be used to improve productivity? To improve sales?

5. Some societies view change differently than do Americans. What impact does this have on the way American marketers operate in those markets? The way American production people operate?

6. Why must international businesspeople be acquainted with the beliefs of the major religions in the areas in which they work?

7. What Buddhist belief would cause American marketing and production managers to think carefully before transferring their marketing plans or bonus plans to an area where Buddhists are present in large numbers?

8. Why is technological superiority especially significant for international firms?

9. What is the significance of the extended family for international managers?

10. Use Hofstede's four dimensions to analyze this situation: John Adams, with 20 years of experience as general foreman in the United States, is sent as production superintendent to his firm's new plant in Colombia. He was chosen because of his outstanding success in handling workers. Adams uses the participative management style. Can you foresee his having any problems on this new job?

GlobalEDGE™ Research Tasks

Using the text and the globalEDGE™ Web site (www.globaledge.msu.edu), students solve realistic international business problems related to the types of tools and data sources international managers use to make informed decisions.

Research Task

globalEDGE.msu.edu ⊙ globalEDGE

Use the globalEDGE site (http://globalEDGE.msu.edu/) to complete the following exercises:

1. Assume you own an exporting company that specializes in consumer products. You have been selling your products in several different countries but have yet to enter the Asian market. You have chosen South Korea as the first Asian country to enter. Since you have not previously sold your products in any Asian market, you think it would be a good idea to form a strategic alliance with a local firm. You strongly believe that the first impression is important. Therefore, you have decided to collect some information regarding the business culture and local habits of South Korea from the "Kwintessential" Web site. Prepare a short report in terms of the most shocking characteristics that may influence business interactions in this country.

2. The cultural distance of countries in which your firm operates is one of the many explanations of significant differences that your U.S.-based employees face when travelling to different affiliates worldwide. Typically, an index of cultural distance can be determined by summing the differences of country-level scores such as those introduced by Hofstede's cultural dimensions. At the present time, your firm has operations in Austria, Guatemala, Iran, Malaysia, and South Africa. Using the *Hofstede Resource Center* based on studies involving cultural dimensions to assess all five countries, determine which affiliates are located in a culture that is least and most similar to the U.S. As there are four main components of each overall cultural distance score, which component(s) can be considered most influential for each country?

188   **Section 3**   International Environmental Forces

Minicases

Minicases also appear at the end of each chapter. These brief scenarios challenge students to apply concepts discussed in the chapter to a real-world situation.

Minicase 13.1 Wal-Mart Takes On the World

Founded in the U.S. state of Arkansas by Sam Walton in 1962, Wal-Mart has developed into the largest retailer in the world and the largest company on the Fortune 500 list, with sales of $312.4 billion in fiscal 2006. Embodying high levels of service, strong inventory management, and purchasing economies, Wal-Mart overpowered competitors and became the dominant firm in the U.S. retail industry. After rapid expansion during the 1980s and 1990s, Wal-Mart faces limits to growth in its home market and has been forced to look internationally for opportunities.

Many skeptics claimed that Wal-Mart's business practices and culture could not be transferred internationally. Yet, in its first decade of operations outside the United States, the company's globalization efforts progressed at a rapid pace. As of 2006, over 40 percent of Wal-Mart's stores were located outside the United States. Its more than 2,700 international retail units employ over 450,000 associates in 13 international markets. In fiscal 2007, Wal-Mart planned to open at least 220 additional international units. Wal-Mart's sales from international operations are expected to reach $78 billion in 2007, a level that is expected to increase substantially over the next decade. If the international business were an independent chain, it would be the fourth-largest retailer in the world, behind Wal-Mart's U.S. operations, Home Depot, and Carrefour.

Globalizing Wal-Mart: Where and How to Begin?

When Wal-Mart began to expand internationally, it had to decide which countries to target. Although the European retail market was large, to succeed there Wal-Mart would have had to take market share from established competitors. Instead, Wal-Mart deliberately selected emerging markets as its starting point for international expansion. In Latin America, it targeted nations with large, growing populations—Mexico, Argentina, and Brazil—and in Asia it aimed at China. Because [the comp]any lacked the organizational, managerial, and fi[nancial re]sources to simultaneously pursue all of these mar[kets, Wa]l-Mart pursued a very deliberate entry strategy for [emer]ging markets, focusing first on the Americas rather [than the] more culturally and geographically distant Asian [mark]ce.

[Its] first international store, opened in 1991 in Mexico [City, the c]ompany used a 50-50 joint venture. This entry mode [helped Wa]l-Mart manage the substantial differences in cul[ture and i]ncome between the United States and Mexico. Its

Mexican partner, the retail conglomerate, Cifra, provided expertise in operating in the Mexican market and a base for learning about retailing in that country. When it entered Brazil in 1996, Wal-Mart was able to leverage its learning from the Mexican experience to take a majority position in a 60-40 venture with a local retailer, Lojas Americana. When the company subsequently entered Argentina, it did so on a wholly owned basis. After gaining experience with partners, in 1997 Wal-Mart expanded further in Mexico by acquiring a controlling interest in Cifra, which it renamed in 2000 to Wal-Mart de México S. A. de C. V. By 2006, Wal-Mart operated 808 units in Mexico in 30 states, achieving annual sales of $15.8 billion and employing over 130,000. It accounts for over half of all supermarket sales in Mexico.

Still, learning the dos and don'ts was a difficult process. "It wasn't such a good idea to stick so closely to the domestic Wal-Mart blueprint in Argentina, or in some of the other international markets we've entered, for that matter," said the president of Wal-Mart International. "In Mexico City we sold tennis balls that wouldn't bounce right in the high altitude. We built large parking lots at some of our Mexican stores, only to realize that many of our customers there rode the bus to the store, then trudged across those large parking lots with bags full of merchandise. We responded by creating bus shuttles to drop customers off at the door. These were all mistakes that were easy to address, but we're now working smarter internationally to avoid cultural and regional problems on the front end."[5] Wal-Mart's initial entry into Brazil used greenfield store sites and emphasized aggressive pricing to build market share, but the French retailer Carrefour and other Brazilian competitors retaliated, launching a costly price war. Wal-Mart's strength in international sourcing was initially of limited assistance in Brazil, since the leading sales category—food—was primarily sourced locally, where Carrefour and others already had strong relationships with local suppliers. Over time, Wal-Mart changed its competitive emphasis to customer service and a broader merchandise mix than smaller local companies could match. The company also pursued acquisitions to supplement internal growth, buying 118 Bompreço stores in 2004 and 140 Sonae stores in 2005. By 2006, Wal-Mart was the third-largest retailer in Brazil, operating 293 stores and employing 50,000 associates.

The Challenge of China

The lure of China, the world's most populous nation, proved too great to ignore. Wal-Mart was one of the first international

---

 ### Chapter 1 Video Case Cirque du Soleil

In 1984, Guy Laliberté left his home in Canada to make his way across Europe as a circus performer. There he and other artists performed in the street. The troupe was called Cirque du Soleil—"circus of the sun." It started with a simple dream: a group of young artists getting together to entertain audiences, see the world, and have fun doing it.[1] Laliberté and company quickly found that their entertainment form without words—stilt-walking, juggling, music, and fire breathing—transcended all barriers of language and culture. Though he understood that an entertainer could bring the exotic to every corner of the world, Laliberté did not envision the scope to which his Cirque du Soleil would succeed. Today Cirque performs nine permanent shows, such as *Algeria*, which is touring Japan, and *Mystere, O,* and *ZUMANITY,* all with permanent homes at the MGM Mirage resorts in Las Vegas. In 20 years of live performances, 44 million people have seen a Cirque show.[2] Despite a long-term decline in the circus industry, Cirque has increased revenue 22-fold over the last 10 years.[3]

Cirque du Soleil is a family of more than 600 individuals from 40 different countries. Each of Cirque's 3,000 employees is encouraged to make contributions to the group. This input has resulted in rich, deep performances and expansion into alternative media outlets such as music, books, television, Web sites, and merchandising. The company's diversity ensures that every show reflects many different cultural influences. Many different markets will have an exotic experience at a Cirque show, regardless of which show is playing where. Cirque does target specific markets with products designed to engage a particular audience. Yet Cirque has little need to adapt its product to new markets; the product is already a blend of global influences. The result is a presentation of acrobatic arts and traditional, live circus with an almost indescribable freshness and beauty.

Cirque du Soleil's commitment to excellence and innovation transcends cultural differences and the limits of many modern media. Its intense popularity has made Cirque both the global standard of live entertainment and the place for talented individuals from around the world to perfect their talents. The extent of the diversity, however, does pose a host of unique challenges. Every employee must be well versed in various forms and styles. To foster cultural enrichment, Cirque purchases and shares a large collection of art with employees and gives them tickets to different events and shows.

The performers work in the most grueling and intimate situations, with their lives depending on one another. The astounding spectacles they create on stage result from hours of planning, practice, and painstaking attention to

detail among artists from diverse cultures who speak 25 different languages. Sensitivity, compromise, and hunger for new experiences are prerequisites for success at Cirque. The organization has learned the art of sensitivity and compromise in its recruiting. Cirque du Soleil has had a presence in the Olympics for a decade. It works closely with coaches and teams to help athletes consider a career with Cirque *after* their competitive years are over, rather than luring talent away from countries that have made huge investments in athletes. This practice has given Cirque a huge advantage in the athletic community, a source of great talent from all over the world.

Guy Laliberté has not forgotten his own humble beginnings as a Canadian street performer. Now that Cirque du Soleil has achieved an international presence and incredible success—the group expects to be doing $1 billion in annual gross revenue by 2007—it has chosen to help at-risk youth, especially street kids. Cirque allocates 1 percent of its revenues to outreach programs targeting youth in difficulty, regardless of location in the world.[4] Guy understands that to be successful in a world market, one must be a committed and sensitive neighbor. Cirque's headquarters in Montreal is the center of an urban revitalization project sponsored by Cirque. Community participation and outreach bring the company international goodwill and help Cirque du Soleil transcend many of the difficulties global brands often face when spanning cultures.

Questions for Discussion

1. Why is Cirque du Soleil successful throughout the world? How does the product transcend culture differences between countries?

2. How have the five major drivers of globalization influenced Cirque du Soleil?

3. Why is it important for Cirque du Soleil to be a good corporate citizen? How does the organization strive to fulfill this role?

Sources

1. "Founder's Message," www.cirquedusoleil.com.

2. Mario D'Amico, and Vincent Gagné, "Big Top Television," *Marketing* 109, no. 26 (August 9–August 16, 2004), p. 20.

3. Chan Kim and Renee Mauborgne, "Blue Ocean Strategy," *Harvard Business Review,* October 2004, p. 77.

4. "Social Action," www.cirquedusoleil.com.

588   International Business: The Challenge of Global Competition

---

Video Cases

Video cases for most chapters are presented at the end of the book. Each video case illustrates applications of the relevant chapter concepts and has a corresponding video on the Instructor's Video DVD and/or online. These cases feature timely and thought-provoking topics affecting the international business environment—such as "Will Rallies Help Immigrants" and "Is China Cheating When It Comes to Trade"—as well as profiles of successful international businesses and managers—such as "J&J: Creating a Global Learning Organization" and "Starbucks: Building Relationships with Coffee Growers."

Supplements for Instructors

Online Learning Center, www.mhhe.com/ball11e

The Online Learning Center (OLC) with PowerWeb is a Web site that follows *International Business* chapter by chapter with digital supplementary content germane to the book. As students read the book, they can go online to take self-grading quizzes, review material, and work through interactive exercises. OLCs can be delivered multiple ways—through the textbook Web site, through PageOut, or within a course management system such as WebCT or Blackboard.

The following supplements are included on one convenient Instructor's Resource CD:

Instructor's Manual

Written by coauthor Jeanne McNett, the Instructor's Manual will help save you valuable time preparing for the course by providing suggestions for heightening your students' interest in the material. Each chapter-by-chapter section presents concept previews, an overview of the chapter, a detailed chapter outline, suggestions and comments, student involvement exercises, and solutions to end-of-chapter material. The manual also includes video case teaching notes. Special Critical Thinking Exercises, prepared by Jeffrey Jones, St. Louis Community College—ForestPark, are also provided for each chapter.

Test Bank

Written by coauthor Jeanne McNett, the Test Bank contains approximately 100 questions per chapter in multiple-choice, true/false, and short-answer format. Each question is ranked for difficulty level and includes page references to the text.

PowerPoint Slides

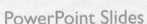

Created by coauthor Jeanne McNett, this PowerPoint presentation includes key points from each chapter, sample figures from the text, and supplemental exhibits that help illustrate the main points in a chapter. Over 600 images are included.

Explosive Growth

- Number of International Companies
  - UNCTAD-United Nations agency in charge of all matters relating to FDI and international corporations.
    - 1995–45,000 parent companies with 280,000 foreign affiliates ($7 trillion in sales)
    - 2004–70,000 parent companies with 690,000 foreign affiliates ($19 trillion in sales)

Videos

A new video collection features original business documentaries as well as NBC news footage. Featured titles include "Will Rallies Help Immigrants?" "Is China Cheating When It Comes to Trade?" "Cirque du Soleil: A Truly Global Workforce," and "J&J: Creating a Global Learning Organization." Videos correspond to the video cases (with discussion questions) at the end of the book.

Supplements for Students

CESIM: Global Challenge Simulation

This online simulation involving international markets for mobile handsets is packaged with new copies of the text. There are three market areas (North America, Europe, and Asia). The simulation presents a range of features that could be offered (impacting product differentiation), a choice of production sites (in Asia or North America), price options, and exposure to exchange rate fluctuations. It can be used with 3 to 12 teams (6 to 50 students per simulation and larger classes can readily be accommodated by using multiple simulations simultaneously) and can involve teams from more than one class or university, if desired. The simulation is also well-suited for many on-line courses. There is an enhanced online support facility with the eleventh edition, as well as an improved user interface to enhance the performance and appearance of the simulation. Use of this online simulation is free with new copies of this text.

Online Learning Center, www.mhhe.com/ball11e

The Online Learning Center (OLC) with PowerWeb is a Web site that follows *International Business* chapter by chapter with digital supplementary content germane to the book. As students read the book, they can go online to take self-grading quizzes, review material, and work through interactive exercises.

Financial Times

McGraw-Hill is pleased to be able to announce a partnership with *The Financial Times.* Order this package and students will receive a 15-week subscription at a specially discounted rate. Students enjoy the full benefits of a *Financial Times* subscription, including access to FT.com In-Depth, an online portal featuring breaking news, special reports, portfolio tools, and more. Free subscription for adopting instructors.

BusinessWeek Edition

Your students can subscribe to *BusinessWeek* for a specially priced rate of $8.25 in addition to the price of the text. Students will receive a pass code card shrink-wrapped with their new text. The card directs students to a Web site where they enter the code and then gain access to *BusinessWeek*'s registration page to enter address information and set up their subscription. Students can choose to receive their subscription in print copy or digital format.

Brief Table of Contents

SECTION ONE The Nature of International Business 3

chapter 1 The Rapid Change of International Business 4
chapter 2 International Trade and Foreign Direct Investment 30
chapter 3 Theories of International Trade and Investment 62

SECTION TWO Cooperation among Nations 101

chapter 4 International Institutions from an International Business Perspective 102
chapter 5 Understanding the International Monetary System 138

SECTION THREE International Environmental Forces 157

chapter 6 Sociocultural Forces 158
chapter 7 Natural Resources and Environmental Sustainability 190
chapter 8 Economic and Socioeconomic Forces 226
chapter 9 Political Forces 254
chapter 10 Legal Forces 278
chapter 11 Financial Forces 302
chapter 12 Labor Forces 322

SECTION FOUR The Organizational Environment 349

chapter 13 International Competitive Strategy 350
chapter 14 Organizational Design and Control 384
chapter 15 Assessing and Analyzing Markets 408
chapter 16 Entry Modes 424
chapter 17 Export and Import Practices 444
chapter 18 Marketing Internationally 472
chapter 19 Global Operations and Supply Chain Management 502
chapter 20 Human Resource Management 540
chapter 21 Financial Management and Accounting 566

Table of Contents

CHAPTER 1

The Rapid Change of International Business 4

Why You Need International Business Experience and How to Get It 5
International Business Terminology 7
  Multinational, Global, International, and Transnational Companies 7

WORLDVIEW
Are You Really Buying American? 8

  Definitions Used in This Text 9
A Brief History of International Business 10

WORLDVIEW
Global Company—By Whose Definition? 11

Building Your Global Résumé
Finding International Job Opportunities and Job Listings or an International Internship 12

Globalization—What Is It? 12
  Globalization Forces 13
  Explosive Growth 15

MINI MNE
A Little Guy Makes Global Business Easier for the Little Guys 16

  The Globalization Debate and You 18
Why Is International Business Different? 20
  Forces in the Environments 20

WORLDVIEW
The Debate on Globalization of Trade and Investment 21

  The Domestic Environment 23
  The Foreign Environment 24
  The International Environment 25
International Business Model 25
Organization of This Book 26

Summary 27
Key Words 28
Questions 28
Research Task globalEDGE™.msu.edu 28

MINICASE 1.1: OWNERSHIP OF COMPANIES AND BRANDS 29

CHAPTER 2

International Trade and Foreign Direct Investment 30

Large International Firms Invest Overseas, and They Also Export 31
International Trade 32
  Volume of Trade 33

MINI MNE
How Important Are Small and Medium-Size Enterprises in Generating Export Sales? 33

  Direction of Trade 37
  Major Trading Partners: Their Relevance for Managers 39
Foreign Investment 41
  Portfolio Investment 41
  Foreign Direct Investment 42

WORLDVIEW
How Do Trade and Investment Impact Economic and Social Development? 42

  U.S. Foreign Direct Investment Abroad 47
  Foreign Direct Investment In The United States 48
Why Enter Foreign Markets? 49
  Increase Profits and Sales 49

WORLDVIEW
Why Doesn't More FDI Flow to Africa? 50

  Protect Markets, Profits, and Sales 53
How to Enter Foreign Markets 56
Multidomestic or Global Strategy? 56
  The World Environment Is Changing 57

Building Your Global Résumé
Setting Realistic Job and Career Objectives 57

  Seven Global Dimensions 58
Summary 58
Key Words 59
Questions 59
Research Task globalEDGE™.msu.edu 59

MINICASE 2.1: JABIL CIRCUIT INC.'S GUADALAJARA FACTORY: GOING UPSCALE TO SURVIVE AGAINST LOW-COST COMPETITION FROM CHINA 60

CHAPTER 3

Theories of International Trade and Investment   62

Free-Market Reforms Revive Chile's Economy   63
International Trade Theory   64
   Mercantilism   64
   Theory of Absolute Advantage   65

Building Your Global Résumé
Adopt a World View   66

   Theory of Comparative Advantage   67
   Heckscher-Ohlin Theory of Factor Endowment   69

WORLDVIEW
Comparative Advantage and Offshoring of Service Jobs
to India   70

   How Money Can Change the Direction of Trade   72
   Some Newer Explanations for the Direction of Trade   73
   Summary of International Trade Theory   79
Trade Restrictions   80
   Arguments for Trade Restrictions and Their Rebuttal   80
   Tariff Barriers   86

WORLDVIEW
Sugar Subsidies: Sweet for Producers,
Not for Consumers   86

   Nontariff Barriers   88
   From Multinational to Globally Integrated Manufacturing
   Systems   91
   Costs of Barriers to Trade   91

MINI MNE
A Small Business Fights the Standards Barrier   92

International Investment Theories   92
   Monopolistic Advantage Theory   93
   Product and Factor Market Imperfections   93
   Financial Factors   93
   International Product Life Cycle   93
   Follow The Leader   93
   Cross Investment   94
   Internalization Theory   94
   Dynamic Capabilities   94
   Dunning's Eclectic Theory of International
   Production   94

Summary   95
Key Words   96
Questions   97
Research Task globalEDGE™.msu.edu   97

MINICASE 3.1: IS YOUR CHOCOLATE THE RESULT
OF UNFAIR EXPLOITATION OF CHILD LABOR?   98

CHAPTER 4

International Institutions from an International Business Perspective   102

The United Nations Millennium Goals: A Call for Change   103
International Political Institutions   105
   The United Nations   105

MINI MNE
Significance of the UN for International Businesspeople   107

   Cooperative Military and Security Agreements   108
International Economic Institutions   110
   World Trade Organization   110

WORLDVIEW
Trade Benefits Uneven   113

Building Your Global Résumé
Tips from Your Personal Global Mentor   116

   Organisation for Economic Cooperation and Development   116
   Other Economic Institutions   117
Economic Integration   120
   North American Free Trade Agreement   120
   European Free Trade Agreement   122
   African Trade Agreements   123
   Mercosur (Mercosul)   124
   Central American Free Trade Agreement   125
   Other Central and South American Trade Agreements   125
   Asia-Pacific Economic Cooperation   125
The European Union   126
   EU Background   126
   EU Growth   127
   Evolving Purpose of the EU   128
   Institutions of the EU   130
   The EU Going Forward   132
   EU Achievements   132
   The EU's Impact   132

Summary   134
Key Words   135
Questions   136
Research Task globalEDGE™.msu.edu   136

MINICASE 4.1: USE OF INTERNATIONAL
INSTITUTIONS—SETTING UP A 100 PERCENT–OWNED
SUBSIDIARY   137

CHAPTER 5

Understanding the International Monetary System   138

Money Laundering, Terrorism, and International
Monetary Institutions   139

The Gold Standard: A Brief History   140
    Bretton Woods   141
International Monetary Fund   142
The World Bank   144

MINI MNE
IFC Supports Small Loans to Entrepreneurs   145

Bank for International Settlements   145
The Emergence of a Floating Currency Exchange
Rate System   146
    Current Currency Arrangements   146

Build Your Global Résumé
Knowing How to Follow the International Money Trail   147

    The Euro   148
Balance of Payments   149
    BOP Accounts   150
    Deficits and Surpluses in BOP Accounts   152

WORLDVIEW
Central Reserve/National Currency Conflict   153

    Special Drawing Right (SDR)   153
Summary   154
Key Words   155
Questions   155
Research Task globalEDGE™.msu.edu   155

MINICASE 5.1: SDR EXCHANGE RISK   155

CHAPTER 6

Sociocultural Forces   158

Six Rules of Thumb for Doing Business across
Cultures   159
What Is Culture?   160
Culture Affects All Business Functions   161
    Marketing   161
WORLDVIEW
Cultural Success and Failure in Disneyland   162

    Human Resource Management   163
    Production and Finance   163
Sociocultural Components   163
Aesthetics   164
    Art   164

Building Your Global Résumé
Tips from Your Personal Global Mentor   165

    Music and Folklore   166
Attitudes and Beliefs   166
    Attitudes Toward Time   166
MINI MNE
Cultural Habits Spread: In Vino, India?   167

    Attitudes toward Achievement and Work   168

Religion   169
    Work Ethic   169
    Asian Religions   169
    Islam   172
    Animism   173
Material Culture   173
    Technology   174
    The Information Technology Era   175
    Material Culture and Consumption   175
Language   175
    Spoken Language   176
    Unspoken Language   179
    The Language of Gift Giving   181
Societal Organization   183
    Kinship   183
    Pedro Diaz Marin   183
    Associations   183
    Entrepreneurial Spirit   184
Understanding National Cultures   184
    Individualism versus Collectivism   185
    Large versus Small Power Distance   185
    Strong versus Weak Uncertainty Avoidance   185
    Masculinity versus Femininity   185
    The Four Dimensions and Management Implications   185

Summary   187
Key Words   188
Questions   188
Research Task globalEDGE™.msu.edu   188

MINICASE 6.1: BE ATTUNED TO BUSINESS
ETIQUETTE   189

CHAPTER 7

Natural Resources and Environmental Sustainability   190

Switzerland, Where Geography Drives Competitive
Advantage: Geography, Watches, Chocolate,
and Cheese   191
Location   192
    Political Relationships   193
    Trade Relationships   194
Topography   195
    Mountains and Plains   195
    Deserts and Tropical Forests   200
    Bodies of Water   202
WORLDVIEW
U.S. Inland Ports Offer Global Shippers a New
Advantage   204

Climate   208
    Climate and Development   208
    Climate Implications   208

Natural Resources 209
 Energy 209
MINI MNE
Small Business: Ocean Mining and Environmental
Impact 215
 Nonfuel Minerals 215
 Innovation and Factor Conditions 215

WORLDVIEW
LOST May Not Be Lost 216

Environmental Sustainability 216

WORLDVIEW
Why Europe Leads the Way: The Environment
and Business 217
 Characteristics of Environmentally Sustainable
 Business 218

Building Your Global Résumé
Be Geo-Savvy: Know About the World in Which You Live
and Will Work 219
 The Stakeholder Model for Sustainable Business 220
 Examples of Sustainability in Business 222

Summary 223
Key Words 224
Questions 224
Research Task globalEDGE™.msu.edu 224

MINICASE 7.1: SUSTAINABILITY AND COLLABORATION:
A NEW WAY OF THINKING 225

CHAPTER 8

Economic and Socioeconomic Forces 226

Of Zippies and the China-India Development Race 227
International Economic Analyses 229

Building Your Global Résumé
Tips from Your Personal Global Mentor 230

Levels of Economic Development 230
 Categories Based on Levels of Economic
 Development 230
Dimensions of the Economy and Their Relevance for
International Business 231
 Economic Dimensions 231

WORLDVIEW
Characteristics of Developing Nations 232

WORLDVIEW
Telephones: An Economic Indicator? 238
 Socioeconomic Dimensions 242

WORLDVIEW
New Approaches to Economic Development 243
 Industry Dimensions 247

MINI MNE
Using the Internet for Economic Research 249

Summary 249
Key Words 250
Questions 250
Research Task globalEDGE™.msu.edu 251

MINICASE 8.1: THE IMPACT OF GALAWI'S
DEVELOPMENT POLICY 251

MINICASE 8.2: WORLD LABORATORIES 251

CHAPTER 9

Political Forces 254

There Are Two Polands—Which One Joined
the EU? 255
Ideological Forces 256
 Communism 256
 Capitalism 257
 Socialism 258
 Conservative or Liberal 258
Government Ownership of Business 259
 Why Firms are Nationalized 259

WORLDVIEW
Getting Nationalization Right 260
 Unfair Competition? 260
 Government–Private Firm Collaboration Difficult 260
Privatization 260
 Airports, Garbage, Postal Services, and . . . ? 260
 Private Buyers do Well, but An American Needs
 a Passport 262
 Privatization Anywhere and Any Way 262
 The Super Bowl: Government Versus Private 263
Government Protection 263

Building Your Global Résumé
Your Understanding of the Impact of Geopolitics
on Business 264
 Terrorism 264
 Security in the Future 268
Government Stability 268
 Stability and Instability: Examples and Results 269
Traditional Hostilities 270
 Arab Countries and Israel 270
 Hutus and Tutsis in Burundi and Rwanda 270
 Tamils and Sinhalese in Sri Lanka 270

MINI MNE
Businesses—and People—Are Resilient 271

International Companies 271
Country Risk Assessment 272
 Types of Country Risks 272
 Information Content for Cra 272
 Who Does Country Risk Assessing? 272

Summary 275
Key Words 275
Questions 276
Research Task globalEDGE™.msu.edu 276

MINICASE 9.1: COMPANY PRIVATIZATION 277

Summary 299
Key Words 300
Questions 300
Research Task globalEDGE™.msu.edu 300

MINICASE 10.1: ITALIAN LAW 301

CHAPTER 10

Legal Forces 278

When a Local Issue Can Have International
Ramifications 279
International Legal Forces 280
    Rule of Law 280
    What Is International Law? 280
    Sources of International Law 280
    Extraterritoriality 281
International Dispute Settlement 281
    Litigation 281
    Performance of Contracts 281
    Despite Legal Uncertainties, International Business Grows 282

Building Your Global Résumé
Earn a Law Degree with Specialization in International
Law 283

Intellectual Property: Patents, Trademarks, Trade Names,
Copyrights, and Trade Secrets 283
    Patents 283
    Trademarks 284
    Trade Names 284
    Copyrights 284

MINI MNE
A New Understanding of Patent Theory 285

    Trade Secrets 285
Common Law or Civil Law? 285
    European Practice 285
    United States Practice 286
    Differences Between The United States and England 286
Standardizing Laws around the World 287
Some Specific National Legal Forces 287
    Taxation 287
    Antitrust Laws 292
    Bankruptcy 293
    Tariffs, Quotas, and Other Trade Obstacles 293
    Torts 294
    Miscellaneous Laws 295

WORLDVIEW
Americans Accused in Film Piracy in China 296

U.S. Laws That Affect the International Business
of U.S. Firms 296
    Federal Employment Laws 297
    Foreign Corrupt Practices Act 297
    Accounting Law 298

CHAPTER 11

Financial Forces 302

U.S. Consumers Credited with Saving the World from
Recession: Heavy Lifting May Be Over 303
Fluctuating Currency Values 304

WORLDVIEW
Other Countries Use the $ Symbol Too 305

Foreign Exchange 305
    Exchange Rate Quotations 305
    Causes of Exchange Rate Fluctuation 307
    Exchange Rate Forecasting 310
Other Financial Forces 311
    Currency Exchange Controls 311
    Tariffs 312

Building Your Global Résumé
A Career in International Finance—Where Do You Look
for a Job? 313

    Taxation 314
    Inflation 315
    Balance of Payments 317

WORLDVIEW
The Financial Force of Foreign Aid for Developing
Countries 318

Summary 319
Key Words 319
Questions 320
Research Task globalEDGE™.msu.edu 320

**MINICASE 11.1: MANAGEMENT FACES A BOP
DEFICIT 321**

CHAPTER 12

Labor Forces 322

Differences in Labor Conditions: Examples of Japan
and China 323
Worldwide Labor Conditions and Trends 324
    Overall Size and Sector of the Work Force 324
    Aging of Populations 325

MINI MNE
Small Businesses and Jobs 326

    Rural to Urban Shift 328

Building Your Global Résumé
Consider International Jobs and Careers Other Than in
Business   329

Unemployment   329
Immigrant Labor   330
Child Labor   331
Forced Labor   333
Brain Drain   333
Guest Workers   335
Considerations in Employment Policies   335

WORLDVIEW
Guest Workers in Japan?   336

Social Status   336
Sexism   336

WORLDVIEW
Social Status in the United Kingdom, India, and Japan   337

Racism   339
Minorities in Traditional Societies   340
Labor in Developing Nations   341
Employer-Employee Relationships   341
Importance of Proper Preparation When Entering
a Market   342
Labor Unions: Europe, United States, and Japan   343
Multinational Labor Activities   344

Summary   345
Key Words   346
Questions   346
Research Task globalEDGE™.msu.edu   346

**MINICASE 12.1: STAFFING YOUR OPERATIONS
ABROAD   347**

CHAPTER 13

International Competitive Strategy   350

Thinking Strategically about the Future in an Uncertain
World   351
The Competitive Challenge Facing Managers of
International Businesses   352
What Is International Strategy, and Why
Is It Important?   353
Global Strategic Planning   353
Why Plan Globally?   353
Global Strategic Planning Process   354

Building Your Global Résumé
Tips from Your Personal Global Mentor   359

WORLDVIEW
Regional Strategies for Competing Globally   363

WORLDVIEW
Scenarios: Improving Strategic Planning by Telling
Stories   366

Strategic Plan Features and Implementation
Facilitators   367
Kinds of Strategic Plans   368
Methods of Planning   368
New Directions in Planning   370
Summary of the International Planning Process   372
Analysis of the Competitive Forces   372
Is Competitor Assessment New?   372
Sources of Information   373
Using Competitor Assessment to Look Forward,
not Back   375
Benchmarking   375

WORLD VIEW
Using Industrial Espionage to Assess Competitors   376

Summary   378
Key Words   379
Questions   379
Research Task globalEDGE™.msu.edu   379

**MINICASE 13.1: WAL-MART TAKES ON
THE WORLD   380**

CHAPTER 14

Organizational Design and Control   384

Kraft Foods—Reorganizing to Become a "Best of Global
and Best of Local" Company   385
What Is Organizational Design, and Why Is It Important
for International Companies?   387
Organizational Design Concerns   387
Evolution of The International Company   388

Building Your Global Résumé
Tips from Your Personal Global Mentor   389

Changes in Organizational Forms   395
Current Organizational Trends   395

WORLDVIEW
Accenture's "Virtual" Global Structure   396

Corporate Survival in the 21st Century   397
Control   397

WORLDVIEW
How to Become More Globally Competitive   398

Subsidiaries   398
Subsidiaries 100 Percent Owned: Where are Decisions
Made?   399
Joint Ventures and Subsidiaries Less Than 100 Percent
Owned   402
Reporting   403
"De-Jobbing"   403
Managing in a World out of Control   404
Control: Yes and No   404

Summary   405

Key Words   405
Questions   406
Research Task globalEDGE™.msu.edu   406

MINICASE 14.1: ELECTREX, INC.—MUST IT REORGANIZE?   407

MINICASE 14.2: COMPETITION WITHIN THE INTERNATIONAL COMPANY   407

CHAPTER 15

Assessing and Analyzing Markets   408

Marketing Research   409
Market Screening   410
   Two Types of Screening   411
   Initial Screening   411
   Second Screening—Financial and Economic Forces   412

Building Your Global Résumé
Acquiring and Using Your Global Analytical Tool Kit   414

   Third Screening—Political and Legal Forces   414
   Fourth Screening—Sociocultural Forces   415
   Fifth Screening—Competitive Forces   416
   Final Selection of New Markets   416

MINI MNE
Some Tips on Market Research   419

WORLDVIEW
"Demon Wife," Blooks, YouTube   420

Segment Screening   420
   Two Screening Methods, Reconsidered   421

Summary   421
Key Words   422
Questions   422
Research Task globalEDGE™.msu.edu   423

MINICASE 15.1: THE SUGAR DADDY CHOCOLATE COMPANY   423

CHAPTER 16

Entry Modes   424

EBay: An Early Entrant in International Markets   425
Entering Foreign Markets   426
   Nonequity Modes of Entry   426

Building Your Global Résumé
Tips from Your Personal Global Mentor   428

MINI MNE
Where Will Your Cargo End Up?   429

   Equity-Based Modes of Entry   431
Channels of Distribution   436

International Channel-of-Distribution Members   437
   Indirect Exporting   437
   Direct Exporting   440

WORLDVIEW
Piracy as Product Diffusion   441

Summary   442
Key Words   442
Questions   443
Research Task globalEDGE™.msu.edu   443

MINICASE 16.1: METHOD OF ENTRY—THE MCGREW COMPANY   443

CHAPTER 17

Export and Import Practices   444

How a Box Transformed the World   445
Export—Why and Why Not?   446

WORLDVIEW
The 12 Most Common Mistakes Made by New Exporters   447

Locating Foreign Markets and Developing a Plan   448
   Sources of Export Information, Counseling, and Support   448

Building Your Global Résumé
Consider a Job in Import–Export Management for Entry into International Business   449

WORLDVIEW
The Long and the Short of Exporting   451

   Export Marketing Plan   451
Payment and Financing Procedures   452

MINI MNE
Experts Help Small Firms Export   453

   Export Payment Terms   453
   Export Financing   456

mini MNE
Dump the L/Cs; Pay with Plastic!   457

Export Procedures   458
   Export Documents   459
   Export Shipments   461

WORLDVIEW
Shoes for People with Two Left Feet   462

Importing   463
   Sources for Imports   463
   Customhouse Brokers   463
   Import Duties   464

Summary   466
Key Words   466
Questions   467
Research Task globalEDGE™.msu.edu   467

MINICASE 17.1: STATE MANUFACTURING EXPORT SALES PRICE 468

MINICASE 17.2: MORGAN GUARANTY TRUST COMPANY CONFIRMATION LETTER 468

Appendix: Sample Outline For the Export Business Plan 469

CHAPTER 18

Marketing Internationally 472

Procter & Gamble's Path to Globalization 473
Added Complexities of International Marketing 474
The Marketing Mix (What to Sell and How to Sell It) 475
 Standardize, Adapt, or Formulate Anew? 475
 Product Strategies 475

WORLDVIEW
On Global Marketing 478

WORLDVIEW
Will "Smart Mobs" Dictate Consumer Trends? 480

 Promotional Strategies 482

Building Your Global Résumé
Consider a Career in International Marketing 490

 Pricing Strategies 492
 Distribution Strategies 494
 Channel Selection 495
 Foreign Environmental Forces and The Marketing Mix Matrix 496

Summary 499
Key Words 499
Questions 500
Research Task globalEDGE™.msu.edu 500

MINICASE 18.1: U.S. PHARMACEUTICAL OF KOREA 500

MINICASE 18.2: AN ETHICAL SITUATION 501

CHAPTER 19

Global Operations and Supply Chain Management 502

Zara: Transforming the International Fashion Industry through Innovative Supply Chain Management 503
Managing Global Supply Chains 505
Design of Products and Services 506
Sourcing Globally 507
 Reasons for Sourcing Globally 507
 Global Sourcing Arrangements 508

Building Your Global Résumé
Consider a Career in Global Logistics and Supply Chain Management 509

 Importance of Global Sourcing 509

 Finding Global Sources 510
 The Increasing Use of Electronic Purchasing for Global Sourcing 510

mini MNE
Cognizant Technology Solutions: Sourcing Low-Cost Talent Internationally to Achieve Global Competitive Advantage 512

 Problems with Global Sourcing 513
Manufacturing Systems 515
 Advanced Production Techniques to Enhance Quality and Lower Costs 515

WORLDVIEW
Chasing the Sun 517

Logistics 521

WORLDVIEW
Johnson Controls: Exploiting Design and Manufacturing Excellence for Global Advantage 522

Standardization and the Management of Global Operations 522
 Organization and Staffing 524
 Control 525
 Planning 525
Impediments to Standardization of Global Operations 526
 Environmental Forces 526

WORLDVIEW
Nestlé: Standardizing Processes and Systems to Exploit Global Opportunity 527

 Some Design Solutions 529
Local Manufacturing System 529
 Basis for Organization 529
 Horizontal and Vertical Integration 530
 Design of The Manufacturing System 530
 Operation of The Manufacturing System 531

Summary 536
Key Words 537
Questions 537
Research Task globalEDGE™.msu.edu 538

MINICASE 19.1: PENWICK–EL PAIS 538

CHAPTER 20

Human Resource Management 540

Becoming an Expatriate, or Expat, as They Are Sometimes Called 541
The International Human Resource Management Approach 542
Recruitment and Selection of Employees 543
 Ethnocentric Staffing Policy 543

WORLDVIEW
Executives with the Right Stuff Are in Big Demand 545

Polycentric Staffing Policy   545
Regiocentric Staffing Policy   546
Geocentric Staffing Policy   547
Training and Development   547
Home or Parent Country National   547

WORLDVIEW
Are Women Appropriate for International Assignments?   548

Host Country National   548
Third Country National   549
Expatriates   550
The Expatriate's Family   551

WORLDVIEW
Culture Shock   552

Language Training   553

Building Your Global Résumé
Speak a Foreign Language   554

Repatriation—The Shock of Returning Home   554
Expatriate Services   554
Compensation   555
Salaries   555
Allowances   556
Bonuses   558
Compensation Packages Can Be Complicated   559
Compensation of Third Country Nationals   560
International Status   561
Perks   561
What's Important to You?   561

Summary   563
Key Words   563
Questions   563
Research Task globalEDGE™.msu.edu   564

MINICASE 20.1: CASEY MILLER: SHOULD SHE ACCEPT
AN INTERNATIONAL ASSIGNMENT?   564

CHAPTER 21

Financial Management
and Accounting   566

Chinese IPOs Abandon New York   567
Capital Structure of the Firm   568

MINI MNE
Microloans: Debt That Is Almost Always Paid in Full   570

Cash Flow Management   571
Multilateral Netting   571
Leading and Lagging   571

MINI MNE
An Integrated Approach to Risk   572

Foreign Exchange Risk Management   572
Transaction Exposure   572

Translation Exposure   574
Economic Exposure   574
Swaps and Derivatives   574

WORLDVIEW
U.S. Law Has Unintended Consequences for
Overseas Funding   575

Swaps   575
Hedges and Swaps as "Derivatives"   576

Building Your Global Résumé
Earn Your MBA with a Specialization in International
Business   577

Networking to Find Partners   578
Sales without Money   578
Countertrade   578
Industrial Cooperation   579
Taxation and Transfer Pricing   580
International Accounting   581
Accounting and Foreign Currency   581
Accounting and Culture   582
Convergence of Accounting Standards   583
Triple-Bottom-Line Accounting   583

WORLDVIEW
Sarbanes-Oxley Not a Good Export   585

International Finance Center   585

Summary   585
Key Words   586
Questions   587
Research Task globalEDGE™.msu.edu   587

MINICASE 21.1: DEALING WITH TRANSACTION RISK
IN A YUAN CONTRACT   587

VIDEO CASES

CHAPTER 1 VIDEO CASE: CIRQUE DU SOLEIL   588

CHAPTER 2 VIDEO CASE: CHINA SYNDROME, CHINA BRANDS   589

CHAPTER 3 VIDEO CASE: WAL-MART IN CHINA   590

CHAPTER 4 VIDEO CASE: U.S. FARMERS AND CAFTA   591

CHAPTER 5 VIDEO CASE: INTERNATIONAL MONETARY FUND: ECONOMIC
AID IN SOUTH KOREA AND UGANDA   592

CHAPTER 6 VIDEO CASE: THE PEACE CORPS   593

CHAPTER 7 VIDEO CASE: CLEARING THE AIR   594

CHAPTER 8 VIDEO CASE: THREE BILLION NEW CAPITALISTS   596

CHAPTER 9 VIDEO CASE: CONTROVERSY OVER U.S. PORT
SECURITY   597

CHAPTER 10 VIDEO CASE: THE CHALLENGE OF ILLEGAL
IMMIGRATION   598

CHAPTER 11 VIDEO CASE: CHINA: CHANGING THE
YUAN/DOLLAR   600

CHAPTER 12 VIDEO CASE: OUTSOURCING   601

CHAPTER 13 VIDEO CASE: GM GLOBAL RESEARCH NETWORK   602

CHAPTER **14** VIDEO CASE: DHL GLOBAL DELIVERY SERVICE   603

CHAPTER **17** VIDEO CASE: CRETORS & CO.   604

CHAPTER **18** VIDEO CASE: DOMINO'S PIZZA IN MEXICO   605

CHAPTER **19** VIDEO CASE: STARBUCKS: BUILDING RELATIONSHIPS WITH COFFEE GROWERS   606

CHAPTER **20** VIDEO CASE: JOHNSON & JOHNSON: CREATING A GLOBAL LEARNING ORGANIZATION   607

ENDNOTES   609

GLOSSARY   G-1

PHOTO CREDITS   P-1

NAME INDEX   I-1

COMPANY INDEX   I-4

SUBJECT INDEX   I-7

List of Maps

NATO Member Countries   110

ASEAN Members   111

The G8 Members   119

African Trade Agreements   123

Regional Trade Agreements in Central America and South America   124

European Union: Current Member-Nations and Candidate Nations   127

EU Constitution: State of the Debate   129

World Religious   170

Major Languages of the World   178

Austria and Her Neighbors   193

ASEAN Members   194

Afghanistan Mountains   195

Spain   196

The Cantons and Major Language Areas of Switzerland   197

Topographical and Language Maps of China   198

Colombia   199

Australia   200

Canadian Shied   201

World Population Map   202

Rhine Main Danube Canal   203

Amazon River   205

Paraná-Paraguay Rivers Trade Corridor   206

Bolivia's Export Corridor   207

25 Megacities 1970–2015 (millions)   248

Inflation Map   315

International Business
The Challenge of Global Competition

11e

The Nature of International Business

Section One describes the nature and scope of international business and introduces the three environments in which international business managers must operate. How well they perform in their undertakings will depend in great measure on their understanding of domestic, international, and foreign environments.

Chapter 1 presents the concepts of the three environments and their forces. From the history of international business, we learn that although the international firm existed before the Civil War, it differed markedly from the present-day global company, which is characterized by its explosive growth and closer central control of foreign operations.

In Chapter 2, information is presented to help you comprehend the dynamic growth and the magnitude of both international trade and foreign investment. We discuss why firms go abroad, and we examine the seven dimensions along which managers can globalize if they take their companies international.

An overview of the theories of international trade and investment is given in Chapter 3. A basic understanding of this material will help explain the actions already taken by managers and by government officials and provide insight into what they plan to do in the future.

1

The Rapid Change of International Business

In the past, complex international transactions were the domain of diplomats and international policy and business experts. Today a converging set of powerful economic, technological, demographic and geopolitical trends will demand that all citizens, not just the elite, have that kind of global fluency. Knowledge of the world is no longer a luxury, it is a necessity.

—*Nicholas Platt, president emeritus of the Asia Society*

Why You Need International Business Experience and How to Get It

Gary Ellis, a young assistant controller for Medtronic, a Fortune 500 manufacturer of pacemakers and other medical equipment, was thought to be on the fast track for a top management position. However, company executives felt he first needed broader experience, so they sent him to head their European headquarters in Belgium. In his new job Gary was responsible for many top-level duties and worked with an array of officials (labor, government, production, and marketing, as well as financial).

Two years later, when the corporate controller's job in the company's home office in Minneapolis became vacant, Ellis was given the job. Bill George, Medtronic's CEO, summed up the company philosophy regarding necessary experience: "Successful executives of the future will have all lived in another country for several years."[a]

Medtronic is not the only firm with this policy. At FMC Corp., a heavy machinery and chemicals producer, the vice president for human resources says that his company believes that "no one will be in a general management job by the end of the decade who didn't have international exposure and experience."[b] Evidently, the boards of directors of many other American corporations have the same policy. Companies such as McDonald's, Coke, Kellogg, Alcoa, Altria, and Schering-Plough have all appointed leaders who had extensive experience as the heads of international operations. William Sullivan, the CEO of Agilent Technologies, commented on his three years in Singapore as an operations manager by saying, "It was a real career changer. In today's environment, having that overseas experience is a big deal."[c] As Carlos Gutierrez, who was the CEO of Kellogg before becoming the U.S. secretary of commerce, said, "Having a foreign perspective gives you an advantage not only for doing business outside the U.S. but domestically, where we have the most diverse society in the world. There's a built-in understanding that differences exist and are good."[d]

Although many American managers want their top executives at company headquarters to have years of foreign experience, do CEOs of the major firms recognize the value of internationalized business education for all employees in management? Surveying the CEOs of *Forbes*'s "100 Largest Multinational Firms" and *Fortune*'s "America's 50 Biggest Exporters," we found that (1) 79 percent believed that all business majors should take an introduction to international business course; (2) about 70 percent felt that business graduates' expertise in foreign languages, international aspects of functional areas (e.g., marketing, finance), and business, human, or political relations outside the United States is an important consideration in making hiring decisions; and (3) a majority of the respondents believed that a number of courses in the international business curriculum (e.g., international marketing, international finance, export–import, international management) are relevant to their companies.

It appears from our study, then, that the CEOs of major American firms doing business overseas are convinced that the business graduates they hire should have some education in the international aspects of business. Most seem to agree with the executive vice president of Texas Instruments, who said, "Managers must become familiar with other markets, cultures, and customs. That is because we operate under the notion that it is (one world, one market) and we must be able to compete with—and sell to—the best companies around the world."

CONCEPT PREVIEWS

After reading this chapter, you should be able to:

appreciate the dramatic internationalization of markets

understand the various names given to firms that have substantial operations in more than one country

understand the five kinds of drivers, all based on change, that are leading international firms to the globalization of their operations

comprehend why international business differs from domestic business

describe the three environments—domestic, foreign, and international—in which an international company operates

Clearly, the top executives from some of the largest corporations in the world are saying that they prefer business graduates who know something about markets, customs, and cultures in other countries. Companies that do business overseas have always needed some people who could work and live successfully outside their own countries, but now it seems that managers wanting to advance in their firms must have some foreign experience as well.

Did you note the reason for this emphasis on foreign experience for managers? It is increased involvement of the firm in international business. The top executives of many corporations want their employees to have a global business perspective. What about companies that have no foreign operations of any kind? Do their managers need this global perspective? They do indeed, because it will help them not only to be alert for both sales and sourcing opportunities in foreign markets but also to be watchful for new foreign competitors preparing to invade their domestic market. In addition, according to recruiters, foreign experience reflects independence, resourcefulness, and entrepreneurship. People who work and support themselves overseas tend to be inquisitive, adaptive, and flexible—qualities that are valuable in today's work environment.

The realization that overseas experience is important for career advancement has heightened the competition for foreign assignments. For example, nearly 500 mid-level engineering and technical managers in GE's aircraft engine unit applied for the 14 positions in the company's global marketing training program. The global human resource manager at another GE unit, GE Medical Systems, claims, "We have far more candidates than we have jobs offshore."[e] Kellogg's Gutierrez commented, "When you're working at one small international unit, you get to meet more key people" than would middle managers posted at headquarters, because the company's executives come to visit the international operations.[f] In the face of such competition, what can you do to improve your chances to obtain an overseas post?

It can be valuable to take classes in the area of international business, perhaps leading to a degree in an international business–related field. In addition, even while you are in school or shortly after graduation, consider going abroad to study, to work (whether as a business intern, as a teacher, or even in such positions as bartender or child care provider), or to volunteer in community development activities. The experience of living and working in another culture can be important in personal development, as well as being a career booster. As Lauren DiCioccio said of her international experience as a cook and farmworker, "When I went, I was hesitant because people looked at me and were surprised that I would graduate with a degree from Colgate and take time off to work and backpack around Australia. So when I came back and had it on my résumé, I couldn't believe all of the interviews were about my time in Australia." Brandon Steiner, a 24-year-old teaching in Japan, said, "Having international experience under your belt—employers are enthusiastic. It looks good and is not a bad step out of college. It shows you already are open-minded."[g] Upon your return, this experience may help you to land a job that involves international business activities. Although most positions are based in a person's home country, they may involve some international travel to see clients or perform other job-related activities, thus providing an opportunity for you to further broaden your international skills and experience.

If you already have a job, you can enhance your opportunities for international experience by making your boss and the human resource management department personnel aware of your interest and the fact that you have studied international business. Look for opportunities to remind them that you continue to be interested (performance review is a good time). Try to meet people in the home office who work with the company's foreign subsidiaries as well as visitors from overseas. As evidence of your strong interest in foreign employment, take additional international business courses and study foreign languages. Make sure that people in your company know what you are doing.

Throughout this book you will find examples of ways to develop, apply, and promote your international skills and experience, through features such as "Building Your Global Résumé" and "Your Global Mentor." Hopefully, through effective application of these suggestions, you will build a successful foundation for your own international experiences! ∎

[a]"The Real Fast Track Is Overseas," *Fortune,* August 21, 1995, p. 129.

[b]"Path to Top Job Now Twists and Turns," *The Wall Street Journal,* March 15, 1993, p. B1.

[c]Erin White, "Future CEOs May Need to Have Broad Liberal-Arts Foundation," *The Wall Street Journal,* April 12, 2005, p. B4.

[d]Carol Hymowitz, "Why American Multinationals Have More Foreign-Born CEOs," *The Wall Street Journal Europe,* May 25, 2004, p. A10.

[e]"The Fast Track Leads Overseas," *BusinessWeek,* November 1993, pp. 64–68.

[f]Hymowitz, "Why American Multinationals Have More Foreign-Born CEOs."

[g]Hillary Chura, "A Year Abroad (or 3) as a Career Move," *New York Times,* February 25, 2006, www.nytimes.com/2006/02/25/business/worldbusiness/25abroad.html?ex=1298523600&en=6df6d07733a344ed&ei=5088&partner=rssnyt&emc=rss (July 5, 2006).

What about you? Are you involved in the global economy yet? Please read the nearby Worldview box, "Are You Really Buying American?" and then think back to how you began your own day. After you awoke, you may have looked at your Casio watch for the time, checked your Nokia cell phone for messages, and turned on your Samsung TV for the news and weather while you showered. After drying your hair with a Conair dryer, maybe you quickly swallowed some Dannon yogurt and a glass of Mott's apple juice, along with a cup of Taster's Choice coffee, brushed your teeth with Close-Up toothpaste, and drove off to class in your Honda with its Firestone tires and a tank full of Shell gasoline.

Meanwhile, on the other side of the world, a group of Japanese students dressed in Lacoste shirts, Levi's jeans, and Nike shoes may be turning off their Dell computers in the computer lab and debating whether they should stop for hamburgers and Cokes at McDonald's or coffee at Starbucks. They put on their Oakley sunglasses, get into their Ford Mustangs with Goodyear tires, and drive off.

What do you and the Japanese students have in common? You are all consuming products made by *foreign-owned companies*. This is international business.

All that you have read so far points to one salient fact: *All managers need to have a basic knowledge of international business to be able to meet the challenge of global competition.*

A Starbucks coffee store in Beijing China. Chairman Howard Schultz said China is the coffee chain's No.1 growth market.

International Business Terminology

Acquiring this knowledge consists, in part, of learning the special terminology of international business, an important function, as you already know, of every introductory course. To assist you in learning the international business "language," we've included a glossary at the end of the book and listed the most important terms at the end of each chapter. They also appear in bold print where they are first used in the text, with their definitions in the margin.

MULTINATIONAL, GLOBAL, INTERNATIONAL, AND TRANSNATIONAL COMPANIES

Because international business is a relatively new discipline and is extremely dynamic, you will find that the definitions of a number of terms vary among users. For example, some people use the words *world* and *global* interchangeably and *multinational* to describe a business with widespread international operations. (The nearby Worldview, "Global Company—By Whose Definition?" has additional discussion of this issue.) Others define a *global firm* as one that attempts to standardize operations in all functional areas but that responds to national market differences when necessary. In contrast, a *multinational company* has been defined by some as a kind of holding company with a number of overseas operations, each of which is left to adapt its products and marketing strategy to what local managers perceive to be unique aspects of their individual markets. Some academic writers suggest using terms such as *multidomestic* and *multilocal* as synonyms for this definition of *multinational*.

You will also find those who consider *multinational corporation* to be synonymous with *multinational enterprise* and *transnational corporation*.[1] However, the United Nations and the governments of many developing nations have been using *transnational* instead of *multinational* to describe any firm doing business in more than one country. The specialized agency, the United Nations Conference on Trade and Development (UNCTAD), for example,

Are You Really Buying American?

Consider the following scenario of a "typical" American family:

The Boltons, Mike and Barbara, live in New York City. Mike is a security consultant with the security services firm Wackenhut Corporation. Barbara is an advertising executive in the Global Head Office of J. Walter Thompson.

On her way home from work, Barbara listens to the new Dixie Chicks CD in her Chrysler van. She stops for gas at the Shell station, then drives to the grocery store. She fills her shopping cart with a variety of items, including Ortega taco shells and salsa, Hellmann's mayonnaise, ReaLemon lemon juice, Ragu spaghetti sauce, Carnation Instant Breakfast drink, a six-pack of Dr. Pepper, a quart of A&W Root Beer, a container of CoffeeMate nondairy coffee creamer, a can of Chicken-of-the-Sea tuna, Lipton tea, Mott's apple sauce, a half-dozen cans of Slim-Fast, frozen Bird's Eye vegetables, some Evian water, and several packages of Stouffer's Lean Cuisine frozen dinners. For a treat, she picks up a pint of Ben and Jerry's ice cream and a Baby Ruth candy bar. She also grabs several cans of Alpo for their dog, Sassy, and a box of Friskies and a bag of Tidy Cat cat litter for their cat, Millie. She selects a Philip Roth novel and a copy of *Elle* magazine, then goes down the toiletries aisle for some Dove soap and Jergen's moisturizing lotion. Before finishing, she calls Mike on her Samsung cellular phone from T-Mobile to see if there's anything else he needs. He asks her to pick up some PowerBars for him to take to the gym during his lunchtime workouts next week. On her way home, she stops at the bookstore and picks up a book—*The Da Vinci Code*.

After finishing up at work, Mike gets into his Jeep Cherokee and puts the new Ben Harper and the Innocent Criminals CD into the Clarion car stereo. He stops at the Amoco station to fill his gas tank and checks the air pressure in his Firestone tires. He makes a quick stop at Computerland to pick up the newest release of WordPerfect, signing the credit card slip with his Bic pen. Then he goes to the video store to pick up *The Pink Panther* on DVD, before heading to the package store for a bottle of Wild Turkey bourbon. He walks next door to the sporting goods store to pick up some Wilson racquetballs for his workouts next week and then heads home.

Barbara's favorite TV show, *Jeopardy!,* is just starting as Mike comes in the door, so she pours herself a glass of Beringer wine from Napa Valley and changes the Dish TV satellite channel on their Magnavox television so that she can watch her show. Before he prepares dinner, Mike opens a Miller beer and leafs through the day's mail, setting the most recent issue of *Road and Track* magazine aside to read later. Soon, dinner is ready and they sit down for their meal, while watching a show on the National Geographic Channel.

While this may sound like a very typical evening for many Americans, foreign-owned firms produced nearly every item that the Boltons purchased or consumed:

- Wackenhut is owned by Group 4 Falck of Denmark.
- J. Walter Thompson is owned by the WPP Group of the United Kingdom.
- Germany's DaimlerChrysler manufactures Chryslers and Jeeps.
- The British-Dutch company Royal Dutch Shell owns Shell.

employs the following definition: "A transnational corporation is generally regarded as an enterprise comprising entities in more than one country which operate under a system of decision-making that permits coherent policies and a common strategy. The entities are so linked, by ownership or otherwise, that one or more of them may be able to exercise a significant influence over the others and, in particular, to share knowledge, resources and responsibilities with the others."[2] More recently, some academic writers have employed the term *transnational* for a company that combines the characteristics of global and multinational firms: (1) trying to achieve economies of scale through global integration of its functional areas and, at the same time, (2) being highly responsive to different local environments (a newer name is *multicultural multinational*).[3] Managers, though, sometimes define a transnational as a company formed by a merger of two firms of approximately the same size that are from two different countries. Examples of such companies include Unilever (Dutch-English, food), TeliaSonera (Swedish-Finnish, telecommunications), Shell (Dutch-English, oil), and ABB (Swedish-Swiss, electrotechnical, power generating).

- Nestlé of Switzerland produces Alpo, Baby Ruth, Carnation Instant Breakfast, CoffeeMate, Friskies, Ortega, PowerBar, Stouffer's Lean Cuisine, and Tidy Cat.
- Unilever, a Dutch-based company, makes Slim-Fast, Dove bars, Hellmann's, Ragu, Lipton, Bird's Eye, and Ben & Jerry's.
- Cadbury Schweppes of the United Kingdom owns Mott's, Dr. Pepper, A&W Root Beer, and ReaLemon.
- Groupe Danone of France produces Evian water.
- Chicken-of-the-Sea is made by Thai Union International of Thailand.
- Japan's Kao owns Jergen's.
- Samsung cell phones are made by Korea's Samsung.
- T-Mobile is owned by Deutsche Telekom of Germany.
- Bertelsmann AG of Germany owns Random House and Doubleday (which published *The Da Vinci Code*).
- EMI of the United Kingdom owns Virgin Records, which releases Ben Harper and the Innocent Criminals CDs.
- *Road and Track* and *Elle* are published by Hachette Filipacchi Médias, a wholly owned subsidiary of France's Lagardére.
- Japan's Clarion Co. Ltd. Produces Clarion car stereos.
- Britain's BP owns Amoco.
- Japan's Bridgestone owns Firestone.
- Computerland is owned by Synnex Information Technologies, Inc., which is 56 percent owned by MiTac International Corporation of Taiwan.
- Corel Corporation of Canada owns WordPerfect.
- Bic of France produces Bic pens.
- Columbia Pictures, owned by Sony of Japan, released *The Pink Panther,* and Sony Pictures Television distributes *Jeopardy!* The Dixie Chicks CDs are produced by Sony BMG Music Entertainment (a 50-50 joint venture of Sony and Bertelsmann of Germany).
- Pernod Ricard of France produces Wild Turkey bourbon.
- Amer Group of Finland owns Wilson Sporting Goods.
- Beringer Winery of Napa, California, is owned by Australia's Foster's Group.
- News Corporation of Australia owns DirectTV and the National Geographic Channel.
- Magnavox is owned by Philips of the Netherlands.
- SABMiller of the United Kingdom makes Miller beer.

This simple example reflects the impact of extensive foreign investments in the United States, especially in recent years. Even some of the best-known "American" products and brands are now produced by foreign firms. "Why invest in the U.S.A.? It's simple. It's a great economy, and it produces great returns. Beyond that, the U.S. is so competitive that we know the things we learn operating there will help us in all of our other markets around the world," said Sir Ian Prosser, former chairman of the U.K.-based Six Continents hotel group.

Investments have also flowed outward from the United States. American companies such as Coca-Cola, Starbucks, McDonald's, the Gap, Microsoft, and Levi's are found in Japan, South Korea, Australia, Singapore, and nearly every European nation. American companies have also purchased a range of foreign companies and brands. Ford Motor Company owns the Jaguar, Land Rover, Aston Martin, and Volvo automobile brands; General Motors has purchased all or part of such companies as Daewoo, Opel, Suzuki, Vauxhall, and Saab.

With the exception of a rather small number of deals such as the potential takeover of Unocal by China's CNOOC, there has been almost no negative backlash among Americans to the flood of foreign investment into their country. Perhaps Americans realize that the buying and selling of companies around the world is just part of globalization, or perhaps Americans just do not realize how much their daily lives are impacted by foreign-owned companies. In fact, the livelihood of many Americans may depend on foreign investment, and approximately one in six U.S. jobs is tied to international trade and investment.

Source: From T. R. Reid, "Buying American? Maybe Not; Many U.S. Brands European-Owned," *Washington Post*, May 18, 2002; Nicholas Platt, "Make Global Skills a Top Priority," *Financial Times*, July 2, 2004, p. 13; and company Web sites (accessed July 3, 2006).

DEFINITIONS USED IN THIS TEXT

To avoid confusion due to the range of different definitions of terms in international business, in this text we will employ the definitions listed below, which are generally accepted by managers:

1. *International business* is business whose activities are carried out across national borders. This definition includes not only international trade and foreign manufacturing but also the growing service industry in areas such as transportation, tourism, advertising, construction, retailing, wholesaling, and mass communications.

2. *Foreign business* denotes the operations of a company outside its home or domestic market; many refer to this as business conducted within a foreign country. This term sometimes is used interchangeably with *international business* by some writers.

3. A **multidomestic company (MDC)** is an organization with multicountry affiliates, each of which formulates its own business strategy based on perceived market differences.

multidomestic company (MDC)
An organization with multicountry affiliates, each of which formulates its own business strategy based on perceived market differences

4. A **global company (GC)** is an organization that attempts to standardize and integrate operations worldwide in most or all functional areas.*

5. An **international company (IC)** is a global or multidomestic company.

Although we primarily use the terms *global, multidomestic,* and *international* firms or companies, at times we may use *multinational enterprise (MNE)* or *multinational company (MNC)* interchangeably with *international company (IC),* inasmuch as both terms are employed in the literature and in practice.

A Brief History of International Business

While international business as a discipline is relatively new, international business as a business practice is not. Well before the time of Christ, Phoenician and Greek merchants were sending representatives abroad to sell their goods. Subsequently, a vast expansion of agricultural and industrial production in China stimulated the emergence of an internationally integrated trading system. The saying that "all roads lead to China" had relevance within the international trade system of medieval times.

The impact of the emerging international trading system was extensive. Politics, the arts, agriculture, industry, and other sectors of human life were profoundly influenced by the goods and ideas that came with trade. Public health was also impacted. An interesting precursor to contemporary concerns about global health epidemics, such as severe acute respiratory syndrome (SARS) and avian flu, was international trade's association with the spread of the plague, one of the worst natural disasters in history. Believed to have originated in Asia, the plague moved west with traders and soldiers, carried by oriental rat fleas that lived on rodents that stowed away on ships and caravans. Called the Black Death in Europe and repeated in waves from the mid-1300s through the 1500s, the plague ravaged cities, caused widespread hysteria, and killed one-quarter of China's people and one-third of the population of Europe.[4]

The rise of the Ottoman Empire before 1300, ultimately spanning Europe, North Africa, and the Middle East, profoundly influenced the emerging trade routes for people, goods, money, animals, and microorganisms that spanned from England to China, across the Mediterranean and Northern Africa, and through Central Asia and the Indian Ocean region. The powerful central location of the Ottomans within this trading web had the effect of raising the cost of Asian trade for the Europeans. This spawned a search for sea routes to Asia, including expeditions that discovered the Americas.

In 1600, Great Britain's British East India Company, a newly formed trading firm, began to establish foreign branches throughout Asia, an action soon followed by many of the other European nations intent on exploiting trade opportunities for national advantage, including Portugal, the Netherlands, and France. In 1602, the Dutch East India Company was formed to carry out colonial activities in Asia and to open ocean trade routes to the East. The first company to issue stock, it is also frequently identified as the world's first multinational corporation.[5] By the end of the 1600s, ships commissioned by European trading companies regularly traveled to Asia via an interconnected Atlantic, Indian, and Pacific ocean system of government-protected trade routes. Their goal was to acquire goods for sale or resale within various Asian markets and ultimately to return to Europe with valuable cargoes of cloth, spices, and other goods that would yield significant profits for investors. The 17th and 18th centuries have frequently been termed the "age of mercantilism" because the power of nations depended directly on the sponsorship and control of merchant capital, which expanded under the direct subsidization and protection of national governments. The concept of mercantilism is discussed in Chapter 3.

Colonial traders in the Americas began operating in a similar fashion in the 1700s. Early examples of American foreign direct investment are the English plants set up by Colt Fire Arms and Ford[†] (vulcanized rubber), which were established before the Civil War. Both operations failed, however, after only a few years.

---

*Note that in this definition global ownership is not a requirement. However, you should be aware that some people do include this along with other criteria, such as the ratio of foreign to total employment or foreign to total assets.

[†]This Ford was no relation to Henry Ford.

Global Company—By Whose Definition?

After talking about having to be a multinational firm (a collection of national businesses) to gain a competitive advantage, consultants and managers turned to the buzzword *globalization* as a strategy to beat their competitors. Unfortunately, *globalization* and its root, *global*, are overused and misused in international business because of the prestige that managements believe these words bring to their companies. Here are elements of various definitions, which state that a global company is an organization that:

1. Searches the world for (*a*) market opportunities, (*b*) threats from competitors, (*c*) sources of products, raw materials, knowledge, innovation, and financing, and (*d*) personnel. In other words, it has global vision.

2. Maintains a presence in key markets around the world.

3. Looks for similarities, not differences, among markets.

4. Standardizes operations worldwide in one or more of the firm's functional areas.

5. Integrates its operations worldwide.

There are those who believe a global firm must possess all of these characteristics and have a worldwide locus of control and ownership. Critics of this definition claim there is no global firm by that definition. To see how firms define the term *global* to suit their purposes, compare the following two situations:

- Allen-Edmonds is a small, privately held shoe manufacturer in Port Washington, Wisconsin, whose sales rose from $9.5 million in 1978 to an estimated $70 million currently. The president explains that the firm accomplished this by "choosing a market niche—manufacturing high-quality dress shoes for men, and by viewing the whole globe as our marketplace. Today, although we produce all our shoes in [Wisconsin and Maine], Allen-Edmonds is a *global manufacturing company*."[a]

- Emerson's management describes its company this way: "Emerson is a *global company* that brings together technology and engineering to provide innovative solutions for our customers in a wide range of industrial, commercial, and consumer markets. . . . We have grown to become one of the world's leading manufacturing companies with operations around the globe. . . . Emerson has more than 60 divisions that operate approximately 275 manufacturing locations worldwide. . . . With a global presence spanning 150 countries, Emerson is advantageously positioned with the infrastructure, knowledge and experience to provide integrated product solutions around the world. . . . Over the past 100-plus years, Emerson has grown from a regional manufacturer into a global technology solutions powerhouse."[b]

Although the same term is used in both situations by both companies, the definitions are different. Allen-Edmonds' president claims the title *global* simply because his company exports to agents and distributors in 33 nations. Presumably, he calls his firm a global manufacturing company because Allen-Edmonds does its own manufacturing instead of subcontracting from China, Indonesia, and other Asian nations as Nike and Adidas do. For other firms, such as Emerson, attaining global company status requires meeting additional criteria, thereby reducing the number of companies able to reach that goal. Their definition is essentially based on marketing, production, supply chain, and technological globalization.

Recently, however, the definition of the term *global company* has taken on still more new criteria. A global company is now said to be more culturally diverse and to incorporate much more worldwide standardization in its marketing, technical, and production functions. To utilize its worldwide assets more efficiently against competitors, the new global company places production plants and other parts of its value chain in those places worldwide where the company can gain the benefits of lower-cost labor and better-educated workers. Improvements in communications technology such as electronic data interchange (EDI) data exchange (invoices, purchase orders) between computers of manufacturers and suppliers, international networking, and teleconferencing have made it possible for project teams around the world to meld ideas from different cultures for greater exploitation of geographically dispersed knowledge and to promote increased innovation.

Organizations are also removing the barriers within their companies to allow the free flow of people as well as ideas, suggesting a globalization in the corporate mind-set. Many firms are offering top management positions to citizens from countries other than the home country. Some are even calling this newly defined global company by a new name: *multicultural multinational.*

The aims of the "multicultural multinational" are (1) to be responsive to local markets, (2) to produce and market its products worldwide, and (3) to exploit its knowledge and technological capabilities on a global basis—elusive goals reached by few companies so far. Although it has become fashionable to speak of global corporations as being "stateless" or "borderless," measurement by any criterion shows that such firms don't exist. Each has a home government and tax authority and is owned by shareholders from primarily one nation, which essentially makes it a national firm with international operations.

[a]Allen Edmonds, "Corporate Fast Facts," www.allenedmonds.com/webapp/wcs/stores/servlet/AllenEdmonds/about/Allen-Edmonds_PressKit_2005_English.pdf (July 3, 2006).

[b]"Emerson's Global Reach," www.gotoemerson.com/global_reach/index.html (July 3, 2006); "About Emerson," www.gotoemerson.com/about_emerson/index.html (July 3, 2006); "Emerson Company History," www.gotoemerson.com/about_emerson/ae.ch.html (July 3, 2006).

Source: Vijay Govindarajan and Anil K. Gupta, *The Quest for Global Dominance* (San Francisco: Jossey-Bass, 2001); Yves Doz, Jose Santos, and Peter Williamson, *From Global to Metanational* (Boston, MA: Harvard Business School Press, 2001).

If you are interested in an international career but not sure how to find one, you can begin your search on the Internet. Numerous Web sites maintain listings for private industry and government jobs. Here are some good sites:

- The *Riley Guide* has hundreds of worldwide listings for companies and governments. The "Targeting and Research" section has information on business and employer research and living and working overseas. (www.rileyguide.com)

- *International Career Opportunities* (University of Montana) maintains a huge list of comprehensive sites for international jobs in a variety of fields and at a variety of international locations. (www.umt.edu/career/workabroad/international.htm)

- *"Go Global! The International Careers Web Site"* (University of Wisconsin) has links to numerous university Web sites that list employment opportunities from all over the world. Some will submit résumés to recruiters. (wiscinfo.doit.wisc.edu/globalstudies/goglobal/site-lists/external-centers.htm)

- *Internships Abroad* is an internship program offered through Ohio University for internships in the United Nations, in the U.S. Department of State, and in over 65 countries. (www.ohiou.edu/studyabroad/internships.htm)

- The *U.S. Department of Commerce* offers various intern programs. For example, Student Employment Opportunities covers a broad range of student employment and internship opportunities. (http://ohrm.os.doc.gov)

- The *U.S. Department of State* provides an extremely helpful description of student employment programs, with good information on how to apply for them. The Department of State holds oral prep sessions throughout the United States and Asia to assist candidates for the Foreign Service oral exam. (www.careers.state.gov/index.html)

- The *International Finance Corporation of the World Bank Group* hires recent graduates for a two-year period as investment analysts and then encourages them to get a graduate degree and become a member of the Global Transaction Team. (www.ifc.org)

- The *Organization of American States* runs a program designed for juniors, seniors, and graduate students at the university level that allows them to work within their fields of study. They must have at least a 3.0 GPA and command of two of the four official languages: English, Portuguese, Spanish, and French. The program has three sessions during the year: fall, winter-spring, and summer. (www.oas.org/EN/PINFO/HR/gen_information.htm)

- *Escape Artist* (www.escapeartist.com/jobs/overseas1.htm)
- *International Jobs Center* (www.internationaljobs.org)
- *Work Abroad* (http://workabroad.monster.com)
- *Jobs Abroad* (www.jobsabroad.com)

If you are a citizen of the United States, you will need a valid passport to travel internationally: http://travel.state.gov/passport/passport_1738.html.

A number of multinational companies existed in the late 1800s. One of the first to own foreign production facilities, have worldwide distribution networks, and market its products under global brands was Singer Sewing Machine. In 1868, it built a factory in Scotland, the first successful American venture into foreign production. By 1880, the company had become a global organization with an outstanding international sales organization and several overseas manufacturing plants. Other firms, such as J&P Coats (United Kingdom) and Ford, soon followed, and by 1914, at least 37 American companies had production facilities in two or more overseas locations.[6] Interestingly, and quite a contrast to today's situation, in the 1920s *all* cars sold in Japan were made in the United States by Ford and General Motors and sent to Japan in knocked-down kits to be assembled locally. European companies were also moving overseas. For example, Friedrich Bayer purchased an interest in a New York plant in 1865, two years after setting up his plant in Germany. Then, because of high import duties in his overseas markets, he proceeded to establish plants in Russia (1876), France (1882), and Belgium (1908).[7]

As you have just read, multinational firms existed well before World War I, and the level of intracompany trade of multinationals in 1930, as a percentage of overall world trade, may have exceeded the proportion at the end of the 20th century.[8] Yet only in recent years have multinationals become the object of much discussion and investigation, especially concerning the increasing globalization of their operations. What is globalization? What are the reasons for globalization?

Globalization—What Is It?

Although globalization is discussed everywhere—television shows, Internet chat rooms, political demonstrations, parliaments, management boardrooms, and labor union meetings—so far it has no widely accepted definition. In fact, its definition continues to broaden. Now, for example, social scientists discuss the political, social, environmental, historical, geographic, and even cultural implications of globalization.[9] Some also speak of technological globalization, political globalization, and the like.

However, the most common definition and the one used in international business is that of *economic globalization*—the tendency toward an international integration of goods, technology, information, labor, and capital, or the process of making this integration happen. The term *globalization* was first coined by Theodore Levitt in a *Harvard Business Review* article in which he maintained that new technologies had "proletarianized" communication, transport, and travel, creating worldwide markets for standardized consumer products at lower prices. He maintained that the future belonged to global corporations that did not cater to local differences in taste but, instead, adopted strategies that operated "as if the entire world (or major regions of it) were a single entity; [such an organization] sells the same things in the same way everywhere."[10]

Interestingly, at the 1999 World Economic Forum (WEF) annual meeting in Davos, Switzerland, a new word, *globality,* was introduced as the meeting's theme. Daniel Yergin, coauthor of *The Commanding Heights,* decided that since globalization is a process, a different word was needed for "the results of this process—a place, a condition, the situation that comes afterward," something that is unhampered by time zones or national boundaries. Professor Klaus Schwab, founder of the WEF, explained, "We wanted to look beyond the economic dimensions of what is happening. It is a globality." Bill Gates announced at the meeting that Microsoft would add *globality* to Microsoft's dictionary.[11] German sociologist Ulrich Beck stated, "Globality means that from now on nothing that happens on our planet is only a limited local event; all inventions, victories, and catastrophes affect the whole world."[12] Although globalization forces may affect all nations, not all of them have achieved the same extent of globalization. Table 1.1 provides two alternative efforts to assess the degree of globalization of different nations. As you can see, the ranking of different countries is strongly impacted by the dimensions of globalization being evaluated, highlighting the difficulties associated with measuring this complex concept.

GLOBALIZATION FORCES

Five major kinds of drivers, all based on change, are leading international firms to the globalization of their operations: (1) political, (2) technological, (3) market, (4) cost, and (5) competitive:

1. Political   There is a trend toward the unification and socialization of the global community. Preferential trading arrangements, such as the North American Free Trade Agreement and the European Union, that group several nations into a single market have presented firms with significant marketing opportunities. Many have moved swiftly to gain access to the combined markets of these trading partners, either through exporting or by producing in the area.

Two other aspects of this trend are contributing to the globalization of business operations: (a) the progressive reduction of barriers to trade and foreign investment by most governments, which is hastening the opening of new markets by international firms that are both exporting to them and building production facilities in them, and (b) the privatization of much of the industry in formerly communist nations and the opening of their economies to global competition.

2. Technological   Advances in computers and communications technology are permitting an increased flow of ideas and information across borders, enabling customers to learn about foreign goods. Cable and satellite TV systems in Europe and Asia, for example, allow an advertiser to reach numerous countries simultaneously, thus creating regional and sometimes global demand. Global communications networks enable manufacturing personnel to coordinate production and design functions worldwide so that plants in many parts of the world may be working on the same product.

The Internet and network computing enable small companies to compete globally because they make possible the rapid flow of information regardless of the physical location of

KOF 2006 Index of Globalization					A. T. Kearney/Foreign Policy 2005 Globalization Index					
Overall Globalization Rank	Nation	Economic Globalization Rank	Social Globalization Rank	Political Globalization Rank	Overall Globalization Index Rank	Nation	Economic Integration Ranking	Personal Contact Ranking	Technological Connectivity Ranking	Political Engagement Ranking
1	United States	28	1	1	1	Singapore	1	3	11	32
2	Sweden	12	4	5	2	Ireland	2	2	13	19
3	Canada	18	2	8	3	Switzerland	9	1	7	29
4	United Kingdom	27	12	2	4	United States	60	40	1	43
5	Luxembourg	1	14	102	5	Netherlands	5	11	8	4
6	Austria	10	13	12	6	Canada	27	8	2	10
7	France	17	22	3	7	Denmark	29	7	5	13
8	Australia	38	3	36	8	Sweden	12	10	9	16
9	Switzerland	7	9	33	9	Austria	10	5	14	2
10	Hong Kong, China	2	6	123	10	Finland	15	20	6	15
11	Ireland	3	23	24	11	New Zealand	36	16	3	21
12	Singapore	5	7	65	12	United Kingdom	32	12	10	5
13	New Zealand	13	5	59	13	Australia	37	34	4	25
14	Finland	8	11	34	14	Norway	35	15	12	17
15	Japan	44	8	27	15	Czech Republic	11	4	24	35
16	Belgium	6	32	7	16	Croatia	7	6	28	26
17	Netherlands	4	18	44	17	Israel	19	9	16	46
18	Denmark	30	15	15	18	France	24	17	21	3
19	Norway	20	10	30	19	Malaysia	4	19	27	49
20	Germany	35	20	10	20	Slovenia	17	13	20	23

Source: Axel Dreher, "Does Globalization Affect Growth? Evidence from a New Index of Globalization." *Applied Economics* 38, no. 10 (2006), pp. 1091–1110: "Measuring Globalization: The Global Top 20," *Foreign Policy*, May–June 2005, pp. 52–60.

the buyer and seller. Internet videoconferencing allows sellers to demonstrate their products to prospective buyers all over the world without the need to travel. It also permits international companies to hold corporate meetings between managers from headquarters and overseas subsidiaries without expensive, time-consuming travel. In addition, communicating by e-mail on the Internet is faster and more reliable than using postal mail and much less expensive than using a fax machine. Both Internet uses have given home office managers greater confidence in their ability to direct overseas operations.

The Internet and network computing enable small companies to compete globally because they make possible the rapid flow of information regardless of the physical location of the buyer and seller.

The ease of obtaining information and making transactions on the Internet has started to have a profound effect on many firms and especially on business-to-business commerce. Whereas companies formerly used faxes, telephones, or regular mail to complete their transactions, they now use the cheaper and faster Internet. The emergence of third-generation (3G) broadband wireless telecommunications technologies and associated applications promises to further accelerate this trend.

3. Market

As companies globalize, they also become global customers. For years, advertising agencies established offices in foreign markets when their major clients entered those markets to avoid having a competitor steal the accounts. Likewise, when an automaker, about to set up a foreign plant where there was no tire factory, asked a tire company if it was interested in setting up a plant in this new market, the response was, "When do you want us there?" It is also quite common for a global supplier to make global supply contracts with a global customer.

Finding the home market saturated also sends companies into foreign markets. According to a recent Dow Jones survey of the world's largest companies, 84 percent of the respondents expect that international markets will generate most of their growth in the next five years.[13] Indeed, since the United States has only about 5 percent of the world's population, the vast proportion of most companies' potential customers are located abroad.

4. Cost

Economies of scale to reduce unit costs are always a management goal. One means of achieving them is to globalize product lines to reduce development, production, and inventory costs. The company can also move production or other parts of the company's value chain to countries where the costs are lower. Dramatic reductions in the cost of generating and transmitting information due to innovations in computing and telecommunications, as well as the decline in transportation costs, have facilitated this trend toward relocating activities worldwide.

5. Competitive

Competition continues to increase in intensity. New firms, many from newly industrialized and developing countries, have entered world markets in automobiles, computers, and electronics, for example. Another competitive driving force for globalization is the fact that companies are defending their home markets from competitors by entering the competitors' home markets to distract them. Many firms that would not have entered a single country because it lacked sufficient market size have established plants in the comparatively larger trading groups (European Union, ASEAN, Mercosur). It is one thing to be shut out of Belgium, but it is another to be excluded from all Europe.

The result of this rush to globalization has been an explosive growth in international business.

EXPLOSIVE GROWTH

Both the size and the number of U.S. and foreign international concerns have been increasing very rapidly.

Foreign Direct Investment and Exporting

One variable commonly used to measure where and how fast internationalization is taking place is the increase in total foreign direct investment (FDI). **Foreign direct investment** refers to direct investments in equipment,

foreign direct investment
Direct investments in equipment, structures, and organizations in a foreign country at a level that is sufficient to obtain significant management control; does not include mere foreign investment in stock markets

>>A Little Guy Makes Global Business Easier for the Little Guys

DE Technologies, a tiny Virginia-based private company with only six employees and offices in the United States and Canada, has patented a technology for using the Internet/intranet to process sales globally. Intended for small and medium-size enterprises, development of the technology was stimulated by the frustrations that DE Technologies' founder encountered while attempting to arrange international trade deals in Russia for his own small company. Traditional systems for international trade, involving multiple, inefficient, and time-consuming layers of vertical service industries, can require 20 or more forms and 60 days to complete and cost 5 to 40 percent of the cost of the total transaction.

With DE's system, which is called the Electronic Commerce Backbone System (ECBS), small and medium-size firms can automatically export and import goods and services without previous international trade experience. The ECBS allows buyers and sellers to buy products in the currency of the destination country, view product descriptions in the language of the destination country, view digital still or motion video displays of the products for sale, and view the calculations and displays of prices for air, land, and sea transportation; it also ensures direct payment of goods via credit cards or documentary credit.

Procedures such as the preparation and filing of export–import documents, freight, insurance, titles, letters of credit, pro forma invoices, and bills of lading are done by the program. This eliminates the necessity of engaging foreign freight forwarders, export and import agents, and other international channels-of-distribution members. Thus, ECBS reduces the costs of ocean and air freight, banking, and human resources.

Small and medium-size enterprises (SMEs) can become members by paying a small membership fee, which gives them access to the ECBS. A transactional fee of 0.3 percent also is levied. According to the founder of DE Technologies, "the capability of the system will allow thousands of SMEs to compete effectively in the Import/Export business with 'The Big Guys' as the barriers to entry will be lowered tremendously."

The ECBS can be supplemented with the Borderless Order Entry System (BOES), a patented process for electronically managing international trade transactions in an integrated manner. It allows companies to create and file necessary electronic documents (in any currency or language), monitor and track steps in the transaction, calculate applicable freight costs as well as taxes and duties, and perform financial arrangements of a sophisticated nature. The result is a reduction of as much as 30 percent in the costs of conducting international trade transactions. SMEs can export and import products from any nation, using the Internet or Intranets, and thereby expand market share in international markets.

Source: "Cutting through a World of Red Tape," *Business Week Online*, www.businesswe . . . m/smallbiz/0006/te000628.htm?script Framed (June 30, 2000); "Electronic Commerce Backbone System (ECBS)," *DE Technologies Web site*, www.detechnologies.com/ecbs.htm (July 1, 2004); "Information Technology and International Trade Position Paper," *DE Technologies Web site*, www.detechnologies.com/ecbs.htm (July 3, 2006); and "Borderless Order Entry Systems," *DE Technologies Web site*, www.detechnologies.com/boes.htm (July 3, 2006).

structures, and organizations in a foreign country at a level that is sufficient to obtain significant management control. It does not include mere foreign investment in stock markets. In the United States, 10 percent ownership in a company is considered sufficient in order to be listed as FDI; in other countries, an investment is not considered FDI until a share of 20 or 25 percent is reached. The world stock of outward FDI was over $9.7 *trillion* in 2004, which was more than 17 times what it was 24 years earlier, in 1980 (see Table 1.2).

Note, in Table 1.2, that the total assets of multinational foreign affiliates were $26.5 trillion, generating $17.7 trillion in sales and 53.1 million jobs in 2002. The value of cross-border mergers and acquisitions (M&As) increased from $134 billion in 1995 to $1,144 billion in 2000, before declining to $594 billion in 2001 in response to economic recession in many nations and declining stock markets. The value of cross-border M&As then began increasing again, reaching an estimated $567 billion in 2006.

Of course, a substantial amount of international business involves exporting rather than FDI. **Exporting** is the transportation of any domestic good or service to a destination outside a country or region. It is the opposite of importing, which is the transportation of any good or service into a country or region, from a foreign origination point. Merchandise exports have grown faster than world output in nearly each of the past 55 years. Between 1980 and 2004, the level of world merchandise exports more than quadrupled, from $2,031 billion to $8,907

exporting

The transportation of any domestic good or service to a destination outside a country or region; the opposite of importing, which is the transportation of any good or service into a country or region, from a foreign origination point

FDI Data	Value ($ billions)				As % of Gross Domestic Product			
	1980	1990	2000	2004	1980	1990	2000	2004
Inflows	$ 55	$ 209	$1,393	$ 648				
Outflows	54	242	1,201	730				
Inward stock	699	1,954	6,147	8,895	6.1%	8.9%	20.0%	21.7%
Outward stock	564	1,763	5,992	9,732	5.4	8.4	19.6	24.0

	1990–1995 (annual average)	1996	1997	1998	1999	2000	2001	2002	2003	2004
Cross-border M&As	$118	$227	$305	$532	$766	$1,144	$594	$370	$297	$381

Foreign Affiliate Data	Value at Current Prices ($ billions)						
	1996	1997	2000	2002	1996–2000	2001	2002
Sales	$ 9,372	$ 9,728	$ 15,680	$ 17,685	10.9%	9.2%	7.4%
Total assets	11,246	12,211	21,102	26,543	19.2	4.5	8.3
Exports	1,841	2,035	3,572	2,613	9.6	−3.3	4.2
Employment (000s)	30,941	31,630	45,587	53,094	14.2	−1.5	5.7

Source: "Table 1. Selected Indicators of FDI and International Production, 1982–2000," *World Investment Report 2001*, UNCTAD; "Country Fact Sheet: United States," *World Investment Report 2005*, UNCTAD; "Foreign Direct Investment Flows," UNCTAD GlobStat database, http://globstat.unctad.org/html/index.html (July 4, 2004); and "Foreign Affiliates in Host Economies," UNCTAD GlobStat database, http://globstat.unctad.org/html/index.html (July 4, 2004).

billion. The level of service exports worldwide increased more than 5.5 times during the same period, growing from $385 billion to $2,125 billion.[14] Trends regarding FDI and exporting are discussed in Chapter 2, and theories for exporting and FDI are discussed in Chapter 3.

Number of International Companies   We also have estimates of the number of global and multidomestic firms in the world. UNCTAD, the United Nations agency in charge of all matters relating to FDI and international corporations, estimated that there were 70,000 companies in 2004, with a total of 690,000 foreign affiliates, that accounted for approximately 25 percent of global output. They accounted for two-thirds of world trade. Foreign affiliates' sales (almost $19 trillion in 2004) were far in excess of global trade ($11 trillion).[15] In 1995, UNCTAD estimated that there were only 45,000 parent companies with 280,000 foreign affiliates, with total sales of US$7 trillion.[16]

As a result of this expansion, the subsidiaries of foreign companies have become increasingly important in the industrial and economic life of many nations, developed and developing. This situation is in sharp contrast to the one that existed when the dominant economic interests were in the hands of local citizens. The expanding importance of foreign-owned firms in local economies came to be viewed by a number of governments as a threat to their autonomy. However, there has been a marked liberalization of government policies and attitudes toward foreign investment in both developed and developing nations since the early 1980s. Leaders of these governments know that local firms must obtain modern commercial technology in the form of direct investment, purchase of capital goods, and the right to use the international company's expertise if they are to be competitive in world markets.*

Despite this change in attitude, there are still critics of large global firms who cite such statistics as the following to "prove" that host governments are powerless before them:

1. In 2004, only 19 nations had gross national incomes (GNIs) greater than the total annual sales of Wal-Mart, the company with the world's greatest sales.

2. Also in 2004, the total amount of money spent in Wal-Marts worldwide was greater than the combined GNIs of the 112 smallest economies of the 208 listed in the World Bank's World Development Indicators database.

As Table 1.3 indicates, these statements are true. In fact, when nations and industrial firms are ranked by GNI and total sales, respectively, 50 of the first 100 on the list are industrial firms. However, a nation's GNI and a company's sales are not directly comparable because GNI is a measure of value added, not sales. If a nation's total sales were computed, the result would be far greater than its GNI because there would be triple and quadruple counting. For example, suppose a steel manufacturer sells steel wire to a tire company, which uses it to build tires. Then the tire company sells the tires to automakers, which mount them on their automobiles, which they in turn sell to the public. Sales of the wire would be counted three times. However, in calculating GNI, governments merely sum the values added in each transaction, which is the difference between the sales of the company and the costs of materials bought outside the company. If company sales were measured by value added, Wal-Mart's sales of $288 billion would have been $65 billion. While Wal-Mart's sales are twice as large as Iceland's GNI, when the economy is measured by the value added, Iceland's economy is more than twice the size of Wal-Mart.

A firm's size may at times give it bargaining power, as in the case of a government that wants a firm to set up a subsidiary because of the employment it will offer and the purchases it will make from other firms in that country. Yet, regardless of the parent firm's size, each subsidiary is a local company that must comply with the laws in the country where it is located. If it does not, it can be subject to legal action or even government seizure.

THE GLOBALIZATION DEBATE AND YOU

Recently the merits of globalization have been the subject of many heated debates. When the World Trade Organization met in Seattle in 1999, there were extensive public protests about globalization and the liberalization of international trade. Further antiglobalization protests occurred when the WTO met in Davos, Switzerland, in early 2001, and at other gatherings of international organizations and leaders since that time. The debate is, in many respects, waged by diametrically opposed groups with extremely different views regarding the consequences of globalization. Sifting through the propaganda and hyperbole spouted by both sides is a challenge. However, it is important to recognize the various perspectives on globalization, as their arguments can generate appeal (or rejection) both intellectually and emotionally. The contributions of free trade and globalization to dramatic reductions in worldwide poverty are contrasted with anecdotal stories of people losing their livelihoods under the growing power of multinationals. Likewise, increases in service sector employment are contrasted against losses in high-paying manufacturing jobs.

We believe that a book such as this should acquaint you with the arguments from both sides, because how this debate is resolved will have a great effect on the international business activities you will one day manage, deal with, or be affected by. The evolution of the debate will

Protesters carry a banner linking free trade practices and sea turtle survival during the WTO meeting in Seattle in 1999. All seven species of sea turtles are currently endangered.

---

*Granting the right to use a firm's expertise for a fee is called *licensing.* See Chapter 16 for more details about licensing and other forms of international market entry.

Ranking	Nation or Company	GNI or Total Sales for 2004 ($ billion)	Ranking	Nation or Company	GNI or Total Sales for 2004 ($ billion)
1	United States	$12,168	51	Malaysia	113
2	Japan	4,734	52	Volkswagen (G)	111
3	Germany	2,532	53	Citigroup (U.S.)	108
4	United Kingdom	2,013	54	ING Group (N)	106
5	China	1,938	55	Venezuela, RB	105
6	France	1,888	56	Singapore	105
7	Italy	1,513	57	United Arab Emirates	103
8	Spain	919	58	Nippon Telegraph & Telephone (J)	101
9	Canada	905	59	American Int'l Group (U.S.)	98
10	Mexico	705	60	IBM (U.S.)	96
11	India	673	61	Philippines	95
12	Korea, Rep.	673	62	Czech Republic	93
13	Brazil	552	63	Siemens (G)	91
14	Australia	544	64	Colombia	91
15	Netherlands	523	65	Pakistan	91
16	Russian Federation	489	66	Egypt, Arab Rep.	91
17	Switzerland	366	67	Carrefour (F)	90
18	Belgium	326	68	Hungary	85
19	Sweden	322	69	Chile	84
20	Wal-Mart Stores (U.S.)	288	70	Hitachi (J)	84
21	BP (U.K.)	285	71	Assicurazioni Generali (It)	83
22	Exxon Mobil (U.S.)	271	72	New Zealand	81
23	Turkey	269	73	Matsushita Electric Industrial (J)	81
24	Royal Dutch Shell (U.K.-N)	269	74	McKesson (U.S.)	81
25	Austria	264	75	Honda (J)	80
26	Indonesia	248	76	Hewlett-Packard (U.S.)	80
27	Saudi Arabia	243	77	Nissan (J)	80
28	Norway	238	78	Fortis (B-N)	76
29	Poland	233	79	Sinopec (PRC)	75
30	Denmark	220	80	Berkshire Hathaway (U.S.)	74
31	General Motors (U.S.)	194	81	ENI (It)	74
32	Greece	185	82	Algeria	73
33	Hong Kong, China	184	83	Home Depot (U.S.)	73
34	DaimlerChrysler (G)	177	84	Aviva (U.K.)	73
35	Toyota (J)	173	85	HSBC Holdings (U.K.)	73
36	Finland	172	86	Deutsche Telekom (G)	72
37	Ford (U.S.)	172	87	Verizon Communications (U.S.)	72
38	South Africa	165	88	Samsung Electronics (K)	72
39	Thailand	158	89	State Grid (PRC)	71
40	Iran, Islamic Rep.	155	90	Peugeot (F)	71
41	General Electric (U.S.)	153	91	Metro (G)	70
42	Total (F)	153	92	Nestlé (S)	70
43	Portugal	149	93	U.S. Postal Service (U.S.)	69
44	Chevron Texaco (U.S.)	148	94	BNP Paribas (F)	69
45	Ireland	140	95	China National Petroleum (PRC)	68
46	Argentina	137	96	Sony (J)	67
47	ConocoPhillips (U.S.)	122	97	Cardinal Health (U.S.)	65
48	AXA (F)	122	98	Peru	65
49	Allianz (G)	119	99	Royal Ahold (N)	65
50	Israel	118	100	Altria Group (U.S.)	64

Note: Belgium (B), China (PRC), France (F), Germany (G), Italy (It), Netherlands (N), Switzerland (S), United Kingdom (U.K.), and United States (U.S.).

Source: *World Development Indicators* database, http://devdata.worldbank.org/data-query/ (July 4, 2006); and Fortune 2005 Global 500, http://money.cnn.com/magazines/fortune/global500/2005 (July 4, 2006).

affect all our lives. The nearby Worldview box, "The Debate on Globalization of Trade and Investment," briefly summarizes some of the arguments for and against the globalization process and its outcomes. Many of the issues associated with globalization are highly complex, and it is not possible to deal with them fully within an introductory text such as this. As was shown in Table 1.1, there is no single measure of globalization or of integration within the world economy. Each element of global integration can have different effects. However, the material presented in the various chapters of this book can help you, the reader, become more informed about globalization and the relative merits of various positions being taken regarding this important subject.

If the debate about globalization has been rancorous and divisive, the outcome of this debate is likely to change substantially the various aspects of the economic environment—both within and between various countries—and it will strongly affect your future as a participant in international business or a teacher of it. As you read the Worldview synopsis of the issues and arguments of supporters and opponents of globalization, and throughout your reading of this book, we hope that you will consider carefully the goals and process of globalization. Through informed education, perhaps the public debate can move beyond a simplistic argument for or against globalization and toward how best to strengthen the working of the global economy and thereby contribute to the enhancement of the welfare of the world and its inhabitants.

Why Is International Business Different?

International business differs from domestic business in that a firm operating across borders must deal with the forces of three kinds of environments—domestic, foreign, and international. In contrast, a firm whose business activities are carried out within the borders of one country needs to be concerned essentially with only the domestic environment. However, no domestic firm is entirely free from foreign or international environmental forces because the possibility of having to face competition from foreign imports or from foreign competitors that set up operations in its own market is always present. Let us first examine these forces and then see how they operate in the three environments.

FORCES IN THE ENVIRONMENTS

environment
All the forces surrounding and influencing the life and development of the firm

uncontrollable forces
External forces over which management has no direct control, although it can exert an influence

The term **environment** as used here means all the forces influencing the life and development of the firm. The forces themselves can be classified as *external* or *internal*. The external forces are commonly called **uncontrollable forces.** Management has no direct control over them, although it can exert influences such as lobbying for a change in a law and heavily promoting a new product that requires a change in a cultural attitude. External forces consist of the following:

1. *Competitive:* kinds and numbers of competitors, their locations, and their activities.

2. *Distributive:* national and international agencies available for distributing goods and services.

3. *Economic:* variables (such as GNP, unit labor cost, and personal consumption expenditure) that influence a firm's ability to do business.

4. *Socioeconomic:* characteristics and distribution of the human population.

5. *Financial:* variables such as interest rates, inflation rates, and taxation.

6. *Legal:* the many foreign and domestic laws governing how international firms must operate.

7. *Physical:* elements of nature such as topography, climate, and natural resources.

8. *Political:* elements of nations' political climates such as nationalism, forms of government, and international organizations.

9. *Sociocultural:* elements of culture (such as attitudes, beliefs, and opinions) important to international managers.

The Debate on Globalization of Trade and Investment

In recent years, the rapid pace of globalization of trade and investment has been accompanied by corresponding debate regarding globalization's implications. This Worldview provides a brief overview of some of the issues and arguments associated with the globalization debate; we hope it will whet your appetite for examining many of these issues in more depth in the chapters that follow.

Arguments supporting globalization

Expanding trade by collectively reducing barriers is the most powerful tool that countries, working together, can deploy to reduce poverty and raise living standards.

—Horst Kohler and James Wolfensohn

That free trade is the best strategy for advancing the world's economic development is one of the few propositions on which almost all economists agree, not only because it is theoretically compelling but also because it has been demonstrated in practice. On a wide range of measures—poverty, education, health, and life expectancy—more people have become better off at a faster pace in the past 60 years than at any other time in history. Evidence is strong regarding the dramatic decline in both the proportion and the absolute number of destitute people. The latest World Development Indicators from the World Bank show that the number of people in extreme poverty fell from 1.5 billion in 1981 to 1.1 billion in 2001. Measured as a proportion of the population in developing countries, the decline was from 39.5 percent in 1981 to 21.3 percent in 2001. Between 1981 and 1999, the proportion of people in the East Asia and Pacific region living on less than $1 a day fell from 56 to 16 percent. In China, it plummeted from 61 to 17 percent. In South Asia, it fell from 52 to 31 percent. The proportion of people living in nations with daily food supplies under 2,200 calories per capita has declined from 56 percent in the mid-1960s to less than 10 percent. Life expectancy in the developing world has nearly doubled since World War II, and infant mortality has decreased in all of the developing regions of the world. The proportion of children in the labor force fell from 24 percent in 1960 to 10 percent in 2000. Global literacy grew from 52 percent in 1950 to 81 percent in 1999, and on average the more globally integrated countries spend more on public education, especially in developing countries. Citizens from more globally integrated countries have greater levels of civil liberties and political rights. Within a generation's time, there has been an enormous improvement in the human condition, and every one of the development success stories was based on export-led growth facilitated by the liberalization of trade.

Of course, countries can reject globalization, and some have, including Myanmar, the Democratic Republic of Congo, Sierra Leone, Rwanda, Madagascar, Guinea-Bissau, Algeria, the Republic of Congo, Burundi, Albania, Syria, and Ukraine. They are among the most impoverished countries in the world.

As an article in the *Financial Times* puts it, "They are victims of their refusal to globalize."

Expanded trade is also linked with the creation of more and better jobs. Over the past two decades—a period of immense technological change and growth in trade—around 40 million more jobs were created than were destroyed in the United States. It is true that when a country opens to trade, just as when new technologies are developed, some of its sectors may not be competitive. Companies may go out of business, and some jobs will be lost. But trade creates new jobs, and these tend to be better than the old ones. The key is not to block change but, instead, to manage the costs of trade adjustment and to support the transition of workers to more competitive employment.

Concerns with globalization

We're not against trade; we want trade rules that allow Americans to compete fairly in the marketplace. The record is clear: Current trade policy isn't working. It has led to tremendous job loss and human rights abuses. The [proposed] FTAA [Free Trade Area of the Americas] will leave plant closings, trashed environments and sweatshops in its wake.

—Richard Trumka, secretary-treasurer, AFL-CIO

Broadly publicized demonstrations—such as the so-called Battle of Seattle that wrecked the Seattle World Trade Organization trade talks in 1999, as well as subsequent disruptions at venues such as the International Monetary Fund/World Bank meetings in Washington, D.C., and Prague—brought widespread public attention to the antiglobalization movement. Those expressing concern with globalization have come from a range of sectors of society, and they express a correspondingly diverse set of concerns. Some fundamentally oppose the very process and outcomes of globalization on ideological grounds, while others may merely be concerned about finding ways to better manage globalization processes and the resulting outcomes. Some of the opponents' concerns may be viewed as naïve or clearly inconsistent with the preponderance of evidence. Other challenges to globalization may have theoretic merit or other supporting evidence and certainly may be worthy of discussion and the fostering of substantive change.

Although perspectives on the globalization debate may in many respects depend on one's values and ideology, thus further compounding efforts to reach a mutually agreed-on resolution, let us first ask this question: What are some of the primary concerns of the opponents of globalization? While many of the antiglobalizers concede that globalization "increases the size of the pie," they also claim that it has been accompanied by a broad array of injurious social implications. Among their concerns, let us briefly examine three primary ones here: (1) that globalization has produced uneven results across nations and people, (2) that globalization has had deleterious effects on labor and labor standards, and (3) that globalization has contributed to a decline in environmental and health conditions.

(continued)

1. *Globalization has produced uneven results across nations and people.* In stark contrast to the positive picture presented by supporters of globalization, opponents describe the painful impact of foreign investment and trade liberalization on the people of the world. Far from everyone has been a winner, they say. The promise of export-led growth has failed to materialize in several places. For example, Latin America has failed to replicate Asia's success despite efforts to liberalize, privatize, and deregulate its economies, with results ranging from disappointment in Mexico to catastrophe in Argentina. Similarly, efforts in sub-Saharan Africa have failed to yield benefits, and the share of the population living in extreme poverty there rose from 42 to 47 percent between 1981 and 2001. Open world markets, it seems, may offer the possibility of economic development—but the recipe is neither easy in its implementation nor universal in its outcomes.

   Many opponents of globalization have claimed that there is a huge gap between the world's rich and poor and that globalization has caused that gap to increase. That there is a gap between rich and poor is unquestionable, but the evidence is perhaps not so clear regarding the charge that globalization has increased this inequality. Although Martin Wolf's analysis shows that income inequality has not risen in most developing countries that have integrated with the world economy, it does show that inequality has increased in some places, most notably in China. Inequality has risen in some high-income countries as well, but he attributes that more to the nature of technological change than to globalization. When income data are adjusted to reflect relative purchasing power, the inequality in income between poor and rich nations diminishes. Wolf also notes that while globalization of trade and investment is an enabler to improved income and living standards, the results may vary if obstacles exist such as poor governance or excessive borrowing.

2. *Globalization has had deleterious effects on labor and labor standards.* The issue of the impact of globalization on labor standards has become an oft-mentioned concern of workers in the United States and other nations. With trade liberalization through the World Trade Organization and increased mobility of capital, measures to keep a country's industries within its borders have been reduced and companies have an easier time divesting their interests in one country and moving to another. Workers in developed countries frequently voice concerns that their jobs will migrate to developing nations where there are lower standards, and thus lower costs, leading to the infamous "race to the bottom," where developed nations with more rigorous labor standards become disadvantaged. Indeed, the Labor Secretariat for the North American Free Trade Agreement commissioned a report that found over half of firms surveyed used threats to close U.S. operations as a tool to fight union-organizing efforts. Since NAFTA's inception and the subsequent reduction in trade and investment barriers, these threats have become more plausible. As reported by Alan Tonelson, "In fact, more than 10 percent of employers studied . . . 'directly threatened to move to Mexico,' and 15 percent of firms, when forced to bargain with a union, actually closed part or all of a factory—triple the rate found in the late 1980s, before NAFTA."

   The concern can run both ways, however. Although labor standards in developing countries are usually lower than in industrialized countries, they are rising and evidence shows that multinationals investing in host nations pay higher wages, create new jobs at a faster rate, and spend more on R&D than do local firms. Developing countries may also view the imposition of more demanding labor standards within their borders as a barrier to free trade. They may feel that lower-cost labor constitutes their competitive advantage and that if they are forced to implement more stringent labor standards, then companies may no longer have an incentive to set up operations in their countries, damaging their prospects for improved economic development. As the authors of *Globaphobia* ask, "Is it humane for the United States to refuse to trade with these countries because their labor standards are not as high as we would prefer? The consequence of taking this position is that many third-world

10. *Labor:* composition, skills, and attitudes of labor.

11. *Technological:* the technical skills and equipment that affect how resources are converted to products.

controllable forces

Internal forces that management administers to adapt to changes in the uncontrollable forces

The elements over which management does have some control are the internal forces, such as the factors of production (capital, raw materials, and people) and the activities of the organization (personnel, finance, production, and marketing). These are the **controllable forces** management must administer in order to adapt to changes in the uncontrollable environmental variables. Look at how one change in the political forces—the expansion of the European Union in 2004—has affected all the controllable forces of firms worldwide that do business in or with the 25 member-nations. Suddenly these firms had to examine their business practices and change those affected by this new expansion. For example, some European concerns and foreign subsidiaries in the EU have relocated parts of their operations to other nations in the Union in order to exploit the lower wages there. Some American and Asian workers will have no jobs at all, or must take jobs that pay even lower wages and have even worse working conditions than those currently available in the export-oriented sector." A November 2003 study by the Carnegie Endowment for International Peace found that Mexico's agricultural sector, which provides most of the country's employment, had lost 1.3 million jobs since NAFTA was implemented in 1994. In addition, far from diminishing under NAFTA, the flow of impoverished Mexicans into the United States has risen dramatically, the study says.

3. *Globalization has contributed to a decline in environmental and health conditions.* Regarding concerns of antiglobalization forces that globalization contributes to declining environmental standards, former president Zedillo of Mexico stated, "Economic integration tends to favor, not worsen the environment. Since trade favors economic growth, it brings about at least part of the necessary means to preserve the environment. The better off people are, the more they demand a clean environment. Furthermore, it is not uncommon that employment opportunities in export activities encourage people to give up highly polluting marginal occupations." Yet a difficulty caused by the North American Free Trade Agreement and the maquiladora program that began before NAFTA has been the substantial increases in ground, water, and air pollution along the Mexico-U.S. border. Damage to the environment has been caused by the many new production facilities and the movement of thousands of Mexicans to that area to work in them. In addition, some health and environmental issues extend beyond the scope of trade agreements. Some of NAFTA's rules on trade in services may cause governments to weaken environmental standards for sometimes hazardous industries like logging, trucking, water supply, and real estate development. For example, to comply with NAFTA's rules on trade in services, the Bush administration recently waived U.S. clean air standards in order to allow trucks based in Mexico to haul freight on U.S. highways. Globalization opponents argue that this could increase air pollution and associated health concerns in border states, as the

aging Mexican truck fleet pollutes more than similar U.S. trucks and these vehicles do not use the cleaner fuels required in the United States. Protesters have also claimed that, under liberalized rules regarding the globalization of trade and investment, businesses have an incentive to move their highly polluting activities to nations that have the least rigorous environmental regulations or a lower risk of liability associated with operations that can create environmental or health-related problems. On the other hand, the economic growth fostered by globalization can help generate and distribute additional resources for protecting the environment, and improved trade and investment can enhance the exchange of more environmentally friendly technologies and best practices, particularly within developing nations.

Source: Gary Burtless, Robert Z. Lawrence, Robert E. Litan, and Robert J. Shapiro, *Globaphobia: Confronting Fears about Open Trade* (Washington, DC: Brookings Institution Press, 1998); Alan Tonelson, *The Race to the Bottom: Why a Worldwide Worker Surplus and Uncontrolled Free Trade Are Sinking American Living Standards* (Boulder, CO: Westview Press, 2002); "Globalization," http://en.wikipedia.org/wiki/Globalization (July 5, 2006); "United States Rises, Russia Plummets in Annual Ranking of World's Most Globalized Nations," www.atkearney.com/main.taf?p=1,5,1,157 (July 5, 2006); "ICC Brief on Globalization," www.iccwbo.org/home/commercial_practice/case_for_the_global_economy/globalization%20brief/globalization_brief.asp (July 5, 2006); Daniel Seligman, "On NAFTA's Tenth Anniversary, Americans Demand Safe, Clean and Fair Trade," Sierra Club, San Francisco, www.sierraclub.org/pressroom/releases/pr2003-12-23a.asp (March 6, 2004); John-Thor Dahlburg, "Protesters Tell a Different Tale of Free Trade," *Los Angeles Times*, November 20, 2003, p. A3; Paul Krugman, "The Good News," *New York Times*, November 28, 2003, p. A31; Horst Kohler and James Wolfensohn, "We Can Trade Up to a Better World," *Financial Times*, December 12, 2003, p. 19; Martin Wolf, *Why Globalization Works* (New Haven, CT: Yale University Press, 2004); *Human Development Report 2003*, United Nations Development Program, New York, http://hdr.undp.org/reports/global/2003/pdf/hdr03_HDI.pdf (July 15, 2004); *World Development Indicators 2004*, World Bank, http://www.worldbank.org/data/countrydata/countrydata.html (July 15, 2004); and John Audley, Sandra Polaski, Demetrios G. Papademetriou, and Scott Vaughan, *NAFTA's Promise and Reality: Lessons from Mexico for the Hemisphere*, (Washington, DC: Carnegie Endowment for International Peace, 2003).

companies have set up production in one of the member-countries to supply this giant free trade area. By doing this, they avoid paying import duties on products coming from their home countries.

THE DOMESTIC ENVIRONMENT

The **domestic environment** is all the uncontrollable forces originating in the home country that influence the life and development of the firm. Obviously, these are the forces with which managers are most familiar. Being domestic forces does not preclude their affecting foreign operations, however. For example, if the home country is suffering from a shortage of foreign currency, the government may place restrictions on overseas investment to reduce its outflow. As a result, managements of multinationals find that they cannot expand overseas facilities as they would like to do. In another instance from real life, a labor union striking the home-based plants learned that management was supplying parts from its foreign

domestic environment
All the uncontrollable forces originating in the home country that surround and influence the firm's life and development

subsidiaries. The strikers contacted the foreign unions, which pledged not to work overtime to supply what the struck plants could not. The impact of this domestic environmental force was felt overseas as well as at home.

THE FOREIGN ENVIRONMENT

foreign environment
All the uncontrollable forces originating outside the home country that surround and influence the firm

The forces in the **foreign environment** are the same as those in the domestic environment except that they occur in foreign nations.* However, they operate differently for several reasons, including those below.

Forces Have Different Values

Even though the kinds of forces in the two environments are identical, their values often differ widely, and at times they are completely opposed to each other. A classic example of diametrically opposed political-force values and the bewilderment they create for multinational managers was the case of Dresser Industries and the gas pipeline in the former Soviet Union. When President Reagan extended the American embargo against shipments of equipment for the pipeline to include foreign companies manufacturing equipment under license from U.S. firms, the Dresser home office instructed its French subsidiary to stop work on an order for compressors. Meanwhile, the French government ordered Dresser-France to defy the embargo and begin scheduled deliveries under penalty of both civil and criminal sanctions. As a Dresser's vice president put it, "The order put Dresser between a rock and a hard place."

A similar case occurred when, because of the American export embargo on shipments to Cuba, that country could not buy buses from the U.S. manufacturer with which it had done business for years. To circumvent the embargo, the government ordered the buses from the firm's Argentine subsidiary. When word came from the firm's American headquarters that the order should not be filled because of the American embargo, the Argentine government ordered the Argentine subsidiary to fill the order, saying that Argentine companies, of which the subsidiary was one, did not answer to the demands of a foreign government. The Argentine management of the subsidiary was in a quandary. Finally, headquarters relented and permitted its Argentine subsidiary to fill the order.

Forces Can Be Difficult to Assess

Another problem with foreign forces is that they are frequently difficult to assess. This is especially true of legal and political forces. A highly nationalistic law may be passed to appease a section of the local population. To all outward appearances, the government may appear to be against foreign investment; yet pragmatic leaders may actually encourage it. A good example is Mexico, which until 1988 had a law prohibiting foreigners from owning a majority interest in a Mexican company. However, a clause permitted exceptions "if the investment contributes to the welfare of the nation." IBM, Eaton, and others were successful in obtaining permission to establish a wholly owned subsidiary under this clause.

The Forces Are Interrelated

In the chapters that follow, it will be evident that the forces are often interrelated. This in itself is not a novelty, because the same situation confronts a domestic manager. On the foreign scene, however, the kinds of interaction that occur and the outcomes may differ. For instance, the combination of high-cost capital and an abundance of unskilled labor in many developing countries may lead to the use of a lower level of technology than would be employed in the more industrialized nations. In other words, given a choice between installing costly, specialized machinery needing few workers and installing less expensive, general-purpose machinery requiring a larger labor force,

---

Foreign has multiple definitions according to the *American Heritage Dictionary,* including (1) originating from the outside—external, (2) originating from a country other than one's own, and (3) conducted or involved with other nations or governments. *Extrinsic* is a synonym. Note that we are not using another possible definition—unfamiliar or strange. Some writers have this last definition in mind when they state that overseas markets in which the firm does business are not foreign because their managers know them well. However, according to any of the first three definitions, the degree of familiarity has no bearing.

management will frequently choose the latter when faced with high interest rates and a large pool of available workers. Another example is the interaction between physical and sociocultural forces. Barriers to the free movement of a nation's people, such as mountain ranges and deserts, help maintain pockets of distinct cultures within a country, and this has an effect on decision making.

THE INTERNATIONAL ENVIRONMENT

The **international environment** consists of the interactions (1) between the domestic environmental forces and the foreign environmental forces and (2) between the foreign environmental forces of two countries when an affiliate in one country does business with customers in another. This agrees with the definition of international business: business that involves the crossing of national borders.

international environment
Interaction between domestic and foreign environmental forces or between sets of foreign environmental forces

For example, personnel at the headquarters of a multidomestic or global company work in the international environment if they are involved in any way with another nation, whereas those in a foreign subsidiary do not unless they too are engaged in international business through exporting or the management of other affiliates. In other words, a sales manager of Nokia's China operations does not work in the international environment if he or she sells cellular phones only in China. If Nokia's China operations export cell phones to Thailand, then the sales manager is affected by forces of both the domestic environment of China and the foreign environment of Thailand and therefore is working in the international environment. International organizations whose actions affect the international environment are also properly part of it. These organizations include (1) worldwide bodies (e.g., World Bank), (2) regional economic groupings of nations (e.g., North American Free Trade Agreement, European Union), and (3) organizations bound by industry agreements (e.g., Organization of Petroleum Exporting Countries).

Decision Making Is More Complex   Those who work in the international environment find that decision making is more complex than it is in a purely domestic environment. Consider managers in a home office who must make decisions affecting subsidiaries in just 10 different countries (many internationals are in 20 or more countries). They not only must take into account the domestic forces but also must evaluate the influence of 10 foreign national environments. Instead of having to consider the effects of a single set of 10 forces, as do their domestic counterparts, they have to contend with 10 sets of 10 forces, *both individually and collectively,* because there may be some interaction.

For example, if management agrees to labor's demands at one foreign subsidiary, chances are it will have to offer a similar settlement at another subsidiary because of the tendency of unions to exchange information across borders. Furthermore, as we shall observe throughout this text, not only are there many sets of forces, but there are also extreme differences among them.

Another common cause of the added complexity of foreign environments is managers' unfamiliarity with other cultures. To make matters worse, some managers will ascribe to others their own preferences and reactions. Thus, the foreign production manager, facing a backlog of orders, may offer the workers extra pay for overtime. When they fail to show up, the manager is perplexed: "Back home they always want to earn more money." This manager has failed to understand that the workers prefer time off to more money. This unconscious reference to the manager's own cultural values, called the **self-reference criterion**, is probably the biggest cause of international business blunders. Successful managers are careful to examine a problem in terms of the local cultural traits as well as their own.

self-reference criterion
Unconscious reference to one's own cultural values when judging behaviors of others in a new and different environment

International Business Model

The relationships of the forces in the three environments we have been discussing form the basis of our international business environments model, shown in Figure 1.1. The external or uncontrollable forces in both the domestic and the foreign environments surround the internal forces controlled by management. The domestic environment of the international firm's home country is surrounded by as many sets of foreign environments as there are countries in which the company does business. Solid lines connecting the internal forces at the home office to the internal forces in the foreign affiliates indicate the lines of control. The orange areas indicate the international environment in which personnel in the headquarters of the international firm work. If, for example, the affiliate in foreign environment A exports to or manages the affiliate in foreign environment B, then its personnel are also working in the international environment, as shown by the orange section.

Organization of This Book

We shall be using the international business environments model throughout the book. After describing the nature of international business in Section One, we examine the international institutions and the international monetary system in Section Two. In Section Three, we analyze the uncontrollable forces that make up the foreign and domestic environments and

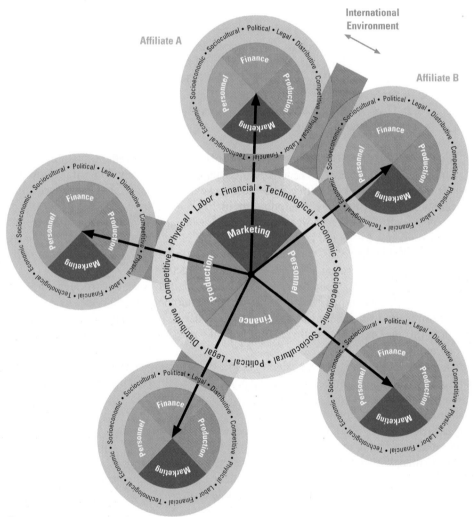

FIGURE 1.1

International
Business
Environments

● **International environment**

○ **Domestic environment**
(Includes socioeconomic, sociocultural, political, legal, distributive, competitive, physical, labor, financial, technological, and economic environments)

● **Foreign environment**
(Includes socioeconomic, sociocultural, political, legal, distributive, competitive, physical, labor, financial, technological, and economic environments)

illustrate their effect on management functions. Finally, we reverse the procedure in Section Four and deal with the management functions, demonstrating how they are influenced by the uncontrollable forces.

A solid understanding of the business concepts and techniques employed in the United States and other advanced industrial nations is a requisite for success in international business. However, because transactions take place across national borders, three environments—domestic, foreign, and international—may be involved instead of just one. Thus, in international business, the international manager has three choices in deciding what to do with a concept or a technique employed in domestic operations: (1) transfer it intact, (2) adapt it to local conditions, or (3) not use it overseas. International managers who have discovered that there are differences in the environmental forces are better prepared to decide which option to follow. To be sure, no one can be an expert on all these forces for all nations, but just knowing that differences may exist will cause people to "work with their antennas extended." In other words, when they enter international business, they will know they must look out for important variations in many of the forces that they take as given in the domestic environment. It is to the study of the three environments that this text is directed.

Summary

Appreciate the dramatic internationalization of markets.

Global competition is mounting. The huge increase in import penetration, plus the massive amounts of overseas investment, means that firms of all sizes face competitors from everywhere in the world. This increasing internationalization of business is requiring managers to have a global business perspective gained through experience, education, or both.

Understand the various names given to firms that have substantial operations in more than one country.

The following definitions are used in this text: A *global company* is an organization that attempts to standardize operations worldwide in all functional areas. A *multidomestic company*, by contrast, is an organization with multicountry affiliates, each of which formulates its own business strategy based on perceived market differences. The term *international company* is often used to refer to both global and multidomestic firms.

Understand the five kinds of drivers, all based on change, that are leading international firms to the globalization of their operations.

Following are the five change-based drivers that are leading international firms to globalize their operations, with an example for each kind: (1) *political*—preferential trading agreements, (2) *technological*—advances in communications technology, (3) *market*—global firms become global customers, (4) *cost*—globalization of product lines and production helps reduce costs by achieving economies of scale, and

(5) *competitive*—firms are defending their home markets from foreign competitors by entering the foreign competitors' markets.

Comprehend why international business differs from domestic business.

International business differs from its domestic counterpart in that it involves three environments—domestic, foreign, and international—instead of one. Although the kinds of forces are the same in the domestic and foreign environments, their values often differ, and changes in the values of foreign forces are at times more difficult to assess. The international environment is defined as the interactions (1) between the domestic environmental forces and the foreign environmental forces and (2) between the foreign environmental forces of two countries when an affiliate in one country does business with customers in another. An international business model helps explain this relationship.

Describe the three environments—domestic, foreign, and international—in which an international company operates.

The *domestic environment* is composed of all the uncontrollable forces originating in the home country that influence the firm's life and development. The *foreign environment* is composed of all the forces originating outside the home country that influence the firm. The *international environment* is the interaction between the domestic and foreign environment forces or between sets of foreign environmental forces.

Key Words

multidomestic company (MDC) (p. 9)
global company (GC) (p. 10)
international company (IC) (p. 10)
foreign direct investment (p. 15)

exporting (p. 16)
environment (p. 20)
uncontrollable forces (p. 20)
controllable forces (p. 22)

domestic environment (p. 23)
foreign environment (p. 24)
international environment (p. 25)
self-reference criterion (p. 25)

Questions

1. What are the differences between international, global, and multidomestic companies?

2. Give examples to show how an international business manager might manipulate one of the controllable forces in answer to a change in the uncontrollable forces.

3. "A nation whose GNI is smaller than the sales volume of a global firm is in no position to enforce its wishes on the local subsidiary of that firm." True or false? Explain.

4. Discuss the forces that are leading international firms to the globalization of their sourcing, production, and marketing.

5. Business is business, and every firm has to produce and market its goods. Why, then, might managers be unable to apply the techniques and concepts they have learned in their own country to other areas of the world?

6. What do you believe makes foreign business activities more complex than purely domestic ones?

7. Discuss some possible conflicts between host governments and foreign-owned companies.

8. Why, in your opinion, do the authors regard the use of the self-reference criterion as "probably the biggest cause of international business blunders"? Can you think of an example?

9. You have decided to take a job in your hometown after graduation. Why should you study international business?

10. Although forces in the foreign environment are the same as those in the domestic environment, they operate differently. Why is this so?

11. What examples of globalization can you identify within your community? How would you classify each of these examples (e.g., international investment, international trade)?

12. Why is there opposition to globalization of trade and integration of the world's economy? Please assess the major arguments for and against such globalization efforts.

Research Task

Use the globalEDGE site (http://globalEDGE.msu.edu/) to complete the following exercises:

1. Several classifications and rankings of multinational corporations (MNCs) are published to assess their relative size and success. One such set of rankings is the *Global 2000* published by Forbes. Which countries are represented in the top 25 of this list? You are required to analyze any industry patterns that may exist across the different countries represented in this list. Do you notice any differences in the industries represented? Is there a predominant industry that appears in the top

25 for the United States? What about the other countries represented in the top 25?

2. The WTO's *International Trade Statistics* is an annual report that provides comprehensive, comparable, and current statistics on trade in merchandise and commercial services. This report allows for an assessment of world trade flows by country and by main product or service categories. Using the most recent statistics available, identify the top five countries that lead in the export and import of merchandise, respectively.

Which of the following companies or brands are foreign-owned? Who are the owners and which country(ies) are the owners based in?

1. 7-Eleven Stores
2. Chesebrough-Pond (Vaseline)
3. Snapple
4. Coors beer
5. 7 Up
6. Baby Ruth (candy bar)
7. Holiday Inn
8. *Fast Company* magazine
9. TriStar Pictures
10. Arco (gasoline)
11. Scott Paper (Kleenex)
12. Elizabeth Arden
13. *Woman's Day* magazine
14. Ralston Purina
15. Motel 6
16. Pinkerton (security guards)
17. Ban deodorant
18. RCA Records
19. IBM Thinkpad (laptop computers)
20. Shaeffer pens

2

International Trade and Foreign Direct Investment

If you care about global poverty and, for that matter, about equality, your aim should be to raise the growth rates of poor countries. Successful countries have all exploited global market opportunities, predominantly international trade and, to a more variable extent, foreign direct investment, to accelerate their growth. Successful globalization has, in short, reduced both poverty and inequality.

—Martin Wolf, global business analyst

Large International Firms Invest Overseas, and They Also Export

Large American international firms, responding to such factors as (1) global competition, (2) liberalization by host governments in regard to foreign investment, and (3) advances in technology, were a major reason that American outward foreign direct investment (FDI) reached its highest level ever, $252 billion, in 2004. This represented nearly six times the U.S. average during the period from 1985 to 1995 and more than double the level of 2003.[a] Inasmuch as foreign direct investment generally is used to set up or acquire assets to produce goods and services abroad, have U.S. exports dropped as a result of the $1.26 trillion in U.S. FDI in the period 1996–2004?

Apparently not. Although some flows of goods and services from the United States to foreign markets have been replaced due to production from these investments abroad, the overall level of American exports of goods and services increased from $783 billion in 1995 to $1,272 billion in 2005, an increase of 62 percent in a decade.[b] Are small firms, large firms, or both kinds responsible for this growth? It is a common belief that small and medium-size companies, because they lack the financial and human resources, supply their foreign markets by exporting to them rather than producing in them and that large international companies do just the opposite. In fact, the U.S. Department of Commerce states that approximately two-thirds of U.S. exports of goods are by U.S.-owned multinational corporations, with over one-third of those exports being shipped by the U.S. parent to foreign affiliates.

We examined the largest multinationals in the 2006 Fortune Global 500 list of the largest multinationals. Among the companies examined, the ratio of foreign sales to total sales ranged from 86 percent for Daimler-Chrysler to 20 percent for Wal-Mart Stores, with an average of 50.0 percent (see Table 2.1). A similar examination of the world's 100 largest multinationals reported that foreign sales averaged 54 percent of these companies' total sales.[c] Many of the companies on these two lists sell to 100 countries or more. Even though large international companies such as these typically have numerous production facilities overseas, it is usually not feasible for them to have a factory in every market. The foreign investment would be too great for them to attempt to set up production facilities in each market. Also, many markets are too small to support local manufacturing; they must be served by exports.

To appreciate the importance of international trade and foreign investment for these companies, examine the last column in Table 2.1, which shows that the ratio of net income from foreign sales to total net income averaged 52 percent for these large multinationals. Overall, for the 500 members of the Standard & Poor's stock index, about 30 percent of their total worldwide profit came from overseas.[d] Without sales and profits generated from foreign operations, the competitiveness of many of these companies would be seriously damaged and some of them might be unable to remain in business. ■

[a]"Country Fact Sheet: United States," *World Investment Report 2005* (Geneva: UNCTAD, September 2005), and Finfacts Team, "US Foreign Direct Investment Outflow Hits Record; Ireland's Inflow Down in 20," www.finfacts.com/irelandbusinessnews/publish/article_10002361.shtml (July 14, 2006).

[b]*International Trade Statistics 2005* (Geneva: World Trade Organization, 2005), pp. 197 and 205, www.wto.org/english/res_e/statis_e/its2005_e/its2005_e.pdf (July 11, 2006), and "Table E.1, U.S. International Transactions in Goods and Services," *Survey of Current Business*, May 2006, p. D-58.

[c]"Table 1.4, Snapshot of the World's 100 Largest TNCs: Assets, Sales and Employment, 2002, 2003," *World Investment Report 2005* (Geneva: UNCTAD, 2005), p. 17.

[d]Based on figures for 2003, as presented in "Kerry Plan on Trade Irks Firms," *International Herald Tribune,* July 20, 2004, p. 17.

CONCEPT PREVIEWS

After reading this chapter, you should be able to:

appreciate the magnitude of international trade and how it has grown

identify the direction of trade, or who trades with whom

explain the size, growth, and direction of foreign direct investment, worldwide and in the United States

identify who invests and how much is invested in the United States

understand the reasons for entering foreign markets

comprehend that globalization of an international firm occurs over at least seven dimensions and that a company can be partially global in some dimensions and completely global in others

Rank in 2006 Fortune Global 500 list	Company	Total Sales ($ billions)	Total Net Income ($ billions)	Foreign Sales ($ billions)	Foreign Sales as % of Total Sales	Net Income from Foreign Operations ($ billions)	Income from Foreign Operations as % of Total Net Profit
1	ExxonMobil	$340	$36	—	—	$25	69%
2	Wal-Mart Stores	316	11	$ 63	20%	3	30
3	Royal Dutch/Shell	307	25	205	67	—	—
5	General Motors	193	−11	65	34	—	—
6	Chevron	190	14	112	59	9	66
7	DaimlerChrysler	186	4	160	86	–	—
8	Toyota Motor	186	12	99	57	3	26
9	Ford Motor	177	2	80	45	—	—
10	ConocoPhillips	167	14	49	29	6	42
11	General Electric	157	16	78	52	13	78
	Average				50		52

Note: Foreign sales refers to sales outside the home country of the company. All figures are based on 2005 fiscal year, as reported in 2006, except for Wal-Mart Stores, whose fiscal year ended January 31, 2006. This list excludes BP, which was ranked the 4th largest, because the company's annual report did not provide information on either foreign sales or net income from foreign operations.
— = information not provided in company annual report.

Source: Company annual reports, Fortune magazine's 2006 Global 500 listing of world's largest companies, http://money.cnn.com/magazines/fortune/global500/2006/full_list (July 14, 2006).

The opening section of this chapter illustrates the fact that both means of supplying overseas markets—*exporting* to and *production* in those markets—are essential to most major U.S. corporations. Moreover, these two international business activities are not confined to manufacturing concerns. Among the companies *Fortune* listed as the 500 largest multinationals, over 40 percent are classified as service companies with primary activities in banking, finance, insurance, business services, entertainment, computer software and services, transportation and travel, and retailing. However, smaller firms also have operations overseas. According to a division of the U.S. Department of Commerce, small and medium-size firms accounted for 97 percent of all U.S. exporters and over 27 percent of the value of American exports (see the nearby mini-MNE box).

In this chapter, we examine two topics directly related to exporting and production in foreign countries: (1) *international trade,* which includes exports and imports, and (2) *foreign direct investment,* which international companies must make to establish and expand their overseas operations.[1] Our focus in this chapter will be on trends and traits of international trade and investment across the globe. Chapter 3 will present an overview of theories that have been developed to explain the incidence and level of international trade and investment that we see in results presented in this chapter. Later, in the chapters on importing and global supply chain management (Chapters 17 and 19, respectively), we shall discuss the third activity of international business—**foreign sourcing**, the overseas procurement of raw materials, components, and products.

foreign sourcing

The overseas procurement of raw materials, components, and products

International Trade

The following discussion of international trade first examines the volume of trade, including which nations account for the largest volume of the world's exports and imports. We then discuss the direction of trade and the trend toward increased regionalization of international trade. We finish this section of the chapter by examining major trading partners and their relevance for managers.

>>How Important Are Small and Medium-Size Enterprises in Generating Export Sales?

The Exporter Data Base (a joint project of the International Trade Administration and the Census Bureau) provides some insight into the relative importance of small and medium-size enterprises (SMEs) in generating U.S. exports. If SMEs are categorized as companies with fewer than 500 employees, an analysis of the Exporter Data Base reveals the following:

- The total number of American companies exporting goods in 2003 was 225,190, nearly double the 112,854 companies that exported in 1992.[a] Of these exporters, 218,382 were SMEs (97 percent of all U.S. exporters). Nonmanufacturing companies, such as wholesalers, accounted for 68 percent of all SME exporters and 60 percent of the value of exports by SMEs.

- Very small companies, with fewer than 20 employees, accounted for 69 percent of all U.S. exporting firms. Firms with fewer than 100 employees generated 21 percent of the volume of U.S. merchandise exports.

- California has the largest number of SME exporters (53,700 companies), but 17 states have more than 5,000 SME exporters each.

- 61 percent of SME exporters sold goods to only one foreign market, and 5 percent sold to 10 or more countries.

- 93 percent of firms that exported advanced technology products were SMEs.

- 63 percent of all exports of wood products, 43 percent of textiles and fabric products, and 40 percent of apparel and accessories were made by SMEs.

- The proportion of U.S. merchandise exports generated by SMEs has been increasing, rising to over 27 percent of merchandise exports in 2003.

- The total export revenues of SMEs increased to $171.5 billion in 2003, a 67 percent increase in 11 years. Of all exports by SMEs, 28 percent ($48 billion) went to NAFTA countries (SMEs accounted for 95 percent of the American companies exporting to Canada, and 91 percent of those exporting to Mexico). The next-largest market in sales was Japan ($14 billion), followed by China and the United Kingdom ($9 billion each), South Korea ($7 billion), and Germany ($6 billion). The countries representing the largest growth in SME exports in the prior decade were China (increasing 416 percent), Malaysia (up 259 percent), Ireland (up 227 percent), and Brazil (increasing by 152 percent).

- California had the highest value of exports by SMEs, at $35.5 billion, followed by Texas ($19.5 billion), New York ($15.9 billion), Florida ($11.0 billion), and Illinois ($5.6 billion). SMEs accounted for 40 to 75 percent of all exports from nine states, including Alaska, California, Florida, Hawaii, Montana, New Hampshire, New York, Rhode Island, and Wyoming.

- In comparison to large companies, SMEs are highly dependent on initiatives undertaken by the U.S. government to open foreign markets to trade. Unlike large exporting companies, most SMEs lack offshore subsidiaries that can circumvent trade barriers and improve market access. Almost 90 percent of SME exporters operate from a single location in the United States, while only 11 percent of large exporting companies operate from a single location.

[a]The Exporter Data Base may slightly understate the total number of exporters. The database excludes exporters of services and includes only direct exporters. Only exporters with shipments exceeding $2,500 were included in the database.

Source: *Small and Medium-Sized Exporting Companies, Statistical Overview, 2003* (Washington, DC: International Trade Administration, Office of Trade and Economic Analysis, U.S. Department of Commerce), www.ita.doc.gov/td/industry/otea/ sme_handbook/SME_index.htm (July 11, 2006).

VOLUME OF TRADE

In 1990, a milestone was reached when the volume of international trade in goods and services measured in current dollars surpassed $4 trillion. Fourteen years later, despite a global economic slowdown that began in 2000, international trade in goods and services had nearly tripled, exceeding $11 trillion (see Figure 2.1). The dollar value of total world exports in 2004 was greater than the gross national product of every nation in the world except the United States. One-fourth of everything grown or made in the world is now exported, another measure of the significance of international trade.

Of the $11 trillion in international trade in goods and services in 2004, exports of merchandise were $8.9 trillion, about 4.5 times what they had been 24 years earlier. While smaller in absolute terms, worldwide trade in services, at more than $2.1 trillion in 2004, has grown faster since 1980 than has trade in merchandise. Inflation was responsible for part of

FIGURE 2.1 World Exports of Merchandise and Commercial Services, by Selected Region and Nation (FOB values; billions of current U.S. dollars)

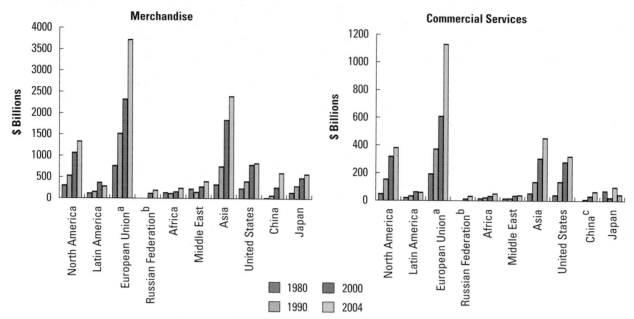

[a] Includes 15 members for 1980–2000, 25 members for 2004.

[b] Data not available for 1980 and 1990.

[c] Data not available for 1980.

Source: *Monthly Bulletin of Statistics* (New York: United Nations, June 1997), pp. 92–102 and 266–71; *Monthly Bulletin of Statistics* (New York: United Nations, August 2000), pp. 92–111 and 122; "World Merchandise Exports by Region and Selected Economy, 1980, 1985, 1990, 1995 and 1999–2001," World Trade Organization, Statistics Division, www.wto.org/english/res_e/statis_e/statis_e.htm (June 30, 2002); "World Exports of Commercial Services by Selected Region and Economy, 1980–2001," World Trade Organization, Statistics Division, www.wto.org/english/res_e/statis_e/statis_e.htm (June 5, 2002); "World Service Exports by Region and Selected Economy, 1992–02," *International Trade Statistics 2003* (Geneva: World Trade Organization, 2003), pp. 171–74, 179–81; and "Growth in the Value of World Merchandise Trade by Region, 2004," *International Trade Statistics 2005* (Geneva: World Trade Organization, 2005) pp. 20, 23.

this trade increase, but using a quantum index that eliminates the effects of inflation from the data shows that the volume of world trade in 2004 was approximately four times what it had been in 1970.

How even has this growth in trade been? Have some nations fared better than others? As Figure 2.1 shows, the proportion of world merchandise exports varied to some extent across regions during the time periods listed. Although the absolute value of their merchandise exports increased, the proportion of exports coming from the regions of Latin America, Africa, and the Middle East decreased between 1980 and 2004. For example, the level of exports from Africa grew by 92 percent from 1980 to 2004, yet the region's proportion of overall world merchandise exports declined by more than half. In contrast, the proportion of merchandise exports from Asia increased by about 70 percent between 1980 and 2004, with China accounting for just over half of that increase. The European Union and North America increased their proportion of world trade as well, although part of that increase is attributable to the expansion of the EU to 25 member-countries.

The results for services exports share some similarity with merchandise exports. The extensive growth in the level of overall worldwide trade in services means that all of the regions and essentially all of the primary nations have experienced an absolute increase in the dollar volume of services exports. The proportion of world exports of commercial services accounted for by Latin America, Africa, and the Middle East has evidenced an overall decline since 1980. However, the developed countries as a whole have been accounting for a large and rising proportion of services exports, particularly the United States. Asia has also been increasing its proportion of services exports, increasing from 13.7 to 21.2 percent between 1980 and 2004.

The rapid expansion of world exports since 1980 demonstrates that the opportunity to increase sales by exporting is a viable growth strategy. As you saw in Table 2.1, there are numerous large international firms that need these sales to survive. At the same time, however, the export growth of individual nations should be a warning to managers that they must be prepared to meet increased competition from exports to their own domestic markets. Figure 2.2 shows that the proportion of manufacturing value added that is located in developed countries has been roughly stable for the past 20 years, although Western Europe's share of this value-adding activity has slipped by over 20 percent since 1990. Developing countries' share of value added has been increasing during this time, although the location of value-adding activities has been changing substantially. For example, while Africa and Latin America have not added appreciably to their proportion of world-wide manufacturing value added, the proportion generated by the countries of Central and Eastern Europe declined dramatically in the years immediately before and after the demise of the Soviet Union. Further, South and East Asia's share of the world's manufacturing value added has nearly quadrupled since 1980. These trends have important implications for managers in terms of not merely where there may be new markets (e.g., for machine tools or other capital goods used by expanding manufacturing sectors) but also where competition in manufacturing may be intensifying or where new sources of export competition might emerge.

Which Nations Account for the Most Exports and Imports? Which nations are responsible for the large and growing levels of merchandise and services trade that we have seen worldwide? Table 2.2 presents the world's 20 largest nations in terms of exporters and importers of merchandise and of services. As you can see, the largest exporters and importers of merchandise are generally developed countries, although emerging economies such as China, Mexico, and Malaysia are also represented among the largest 20. These data also show that the largest exporters and importers account for a very high proportion of overall merchandise trade, approximately 75 percent of both exports and imports.

Trade in services evidences many similarities to trade in merchandise, in terms of the countries represented among the leaders. A notable difference is that the only emerging economies ranking among the leaders for both exports and imports of services are China and India. The concentration of worldwide services trade is approximately the same as that for merchandise trade, approximately 75 percent of both exports and imports.

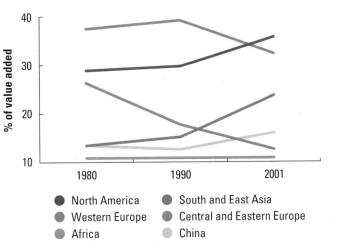

Source: "Foreign Direct Investment: Foreign Direct Investment Flows," United Nations Conference on Trade and Development, http://globstat.unctad.org/html/index.html (July 14, 2006).

FIGURE 2.2

Manufacturing Value-Added for Developed and Developing Regions (percentage of value added at current prices)

TABLE 2.2 20 Leading Exporters and Importers in World Merchandise and Service Trade (billions of dollars and percentage)

	Merchandise Exporters				Merchandise Importers				Service Exporters				Service Importers		
Rank	Nation	Value	Share	Rank	Nation	Value	Share	Rank	Nation	Value	Share	Rank	Nation	Value	Share
1	Germany	$912	10.0	1	United States	$1,526	16.1	1	United States	318	15.0	1	United States	260	12.4
2	United States	819	8.9	2	Germany	717	7.6	2	United Kingdom	172	8.1	2	Germany	193	9.2
3	China	593	6.5	3	China	561	5.9	3	Germany	134	6.3	3	United Kingdom	136	6.5
4	Japan	566	6.2	4	France	466	4.9	4	France	110	5.1	4	Japan	134	6.4
5	France	449	4.9	5	United Kingdom	464	4.9	5	Japan	95	4.5	5	France	96	4.6
6	Netherlands	358	3.9	6	Japan	455	4.8	6	Spain	85	4.0	6	Italy	81	3.8
7	Italy	349	3.8	7	Italy	351	3.7	7	Italy	82	3.9	7	Netherlands	72	3.5
8	United Kingdom	347	3.8	8	Netherlands	319	3.4	8	Netherlands	73	3.4	8	China	72	3.4
9	Canada	317	3.5	9	Belgium	286	3.0	9	China	62	2.9	9	Ireland	58	2.8
10	Belgium	307	3.3	10	Canada	280	2.9	10	Hong Kong	54	2.5	10	Canada	56	2.7
11	Hong Kong	266	2.9	11	Hong Kong	273	2.9	11	Belgium	49	2.3	11	Spain	54	2.6
12	S. Korea	254	2.7	12	Spain	249	2.6	12	Austria	48	2.3	12	S. Korea	50	2.4
13	Mexico	189	2.1	13	S. Korea	225	2.4	13	Ireland	47	2.2	13	Belgium	48	2.3
14	Russian Federation	184	2.0	14	Mexico	206	2.2	14	Canada	47	2.2	14	Austria	47	2.2
15	Taiwan, ROC	182	2.0	15	Taiwan, ROC	168	1.8	15	S. Korea	40	1.9	15	India	41	2.0
16	Singapore	180	2.0	16	Singapore	164	1.7	16	India	40	1.9	16	Singapore	36	1.7
17	Spain	179	2.0	17	Austria	118	1.2	17	Sweden	38	1.8	17	Denmark	33	1.6
18	Malaysia	127	1.4	18	Switzerland	112	1.2	18	Switzerland	37	1.7	18	Sweden	33	1.6
19	Saudi Arabia	126	1.4	19	Australia	109	1.2	19	Singapore	37	1.7	19	Russian Fed'n	33	1.6
20	Sweden	123	1.3	20	Malaysia	105	1.1	20	Denmark	36	1.7	20	Taiwan, ROC	30	1.4

Note: Rankings are based on trade data for 2004.

Source: World Trade Organization, *International Trade Statistics 2005* (Geneva: World Trade Organization, 2005), pp. 21, 23.

DIRECTION OF TRADE

What are the destinations of these merchandise exports? If you never have examined trade flows, you may think that international trade consists mainly of manufactured goods exported by the industrialized nations to the developing nations in return for raw materials. However, Table 2.3 shows that this is only partially correct. While more than half the exports from developing nations do go to developed countries, this proportion has been declining over the past 35 years, from 72 percent in 1970 to under 53 percent in 2004. Also, over 70 percent of exports from developed economies go to other industrialized nations, not to developing countries. As shown in the table, Japan and the United States are exceptions, with each sending a larger portion of its exports to developing nations than is the case for developed economies as a whole.

One reason Japan sells more to developing nations than most developed nations do is that it has had an extensive distribution system in those markets since the early 1900s. Because the country has no local sources for many raw materials, it has used general trading companies (*sogo shosha* in Japanese) to import many of the raw materials and components necessary for Japanese industry. The trading companies' offices in developing nations—where these raw materials and components are obtained—also market Japanese manufactured products to those nations (including components for industrial and consumer markets, such as electronic equipment and parts, as well as capital goods, such as machine tools). Many Japanese companies in consumer electronics, computers, and other areas have moved manufacturing operations to lower-cost nations such as China and various Southeast Asian countries, producing substantial "reverse imports" to Japan as these goods replace products traditionally manufactured in Japan. Overall, the percentage of Japanese imports coming from the "Asia-9" nations (China, Hong Kong, Indonesia, Korea, Malaysia, Philippines, Singapore, Taiwan, and Thailand) increased approximately 50 percent between 1990 and 2004. About 50 percent of Japan's imports come from developing countries in Asia, and about 50 percent of Japan's exports go to developing nations in Asia.[2]

The United States also exports a smaller proportion to other developed countries (DCs) and more to the developing nations than do developed countries generally, but for reasons somewhat different from those of Japan. American firms have significantly more subsidiaries in developing nations than Japanese companies do; these subsidiaries are captive customers for their American owners. In addition, some buyers in Southeast Asian countries, remembering that Japan was an aggressor nation in World War II and before, have preferred to buy from American firms. Notice also the high percentage of American exports that go to Latin America; this indicates the relative importance of this market to American firms. American exports to developing nations in the Americas were 21 percent of all American exports in 2004, and the dollar value of U.S. exports to that region is more than twice the value of these developing nations' exports to each other.

The Increasing Regionalization of Trade   The data in Table 2.3 illustrate how the direction of trade frequently changes over time among nations or regions of the world. The development of expanded regional trade agreements (discussed in Chapter 4), such as the Association of Southeast Asian Nations (ASEAN) and the EU, can substantially alter the level and proportion of trade flows within and across regions. For example, in Table 2.3, you see that most of Canada's exports go to the United States, mainly as a result, after 1989, of the U.S.-Canada Free Trade Agreement and the subsequent North American Free Trade Agreement. Over 20 percent of total American exports went to Canada in 2004, and their 2003 dollar value of $169 billion was more than double that in 1991. The $111 billion value of U.S. exports to Mexico in 2004 was over three times the level in 1991. The proportion of their total exports that Mexico, Canada, and the United States sent to one of their two partners in NAFTA increased from 46 percent in 1995 to over 55 percent in 2004. Overall, the share of world trade accounted for by members of regional trade agreements increased from 37 percent in 1980 to 60 percent in 1990 and to over 70 percent by 2005.

It appears that the American exporters have made major inroads in developing country markets, which in turn are selling more to the United States. This is due in part to their increasing ability to export manufactured goods and the growing intracompany trade among

TABLE 2.3

Direction of Trade for Selected Regions and Countries (percentage of region's or country's total merchandise exports to regions or countries in columns)

Exports from	Year	\<center>Exports to:\</center>								
		DE	U.S.	Can.	Jap.	EU	Dev.	DA	D. Am	East Eur.
Developed economies (DE)	1970	77	13	5	7	40	18	4	6	n.a.
	1980	71	19	4	10	43	25	5	6	3
	1990	71	20	5	8	46	20	2	4	2
	2000	72	16	5	3	44	23	2	6	3
	2004	70	14	4	3	48	23	2	5	2
United States (U.S.)	1970	70	—	21	11	27	29	2	15	n.a.
	1980	60	—	16	10	27	36	2	18	2
	1990	65	—	21	12	25	34	2	14	1
	2000	58	—	23	9	22	41	1	21	1
	2004	55	—	21	7	22	44	1	21	1
Canada (Can.)	1970	91	65	—	5	16	7	1	4	n.a.
	1980	85	63	—	6	13	12	1	5	3
	1990	91	75	—	6	8	8	1	2	1
	2000	95	87	—	2	5	5	<1	1	<1
	2004	93	85	—	2	6	6	<1	2	<1
Japan (Jap.)	1970	55	31	3	—	11	39	6	6	n.a.
	1980	48	25	2	—	14	50	5	7	3
	1990	59	32	2	—	19	40	1	3	1
	2000	51	30	2	—	16	48	1	4	1
	2004	46	25	1	—	16	53	1	3	<1
European Union (EU)	1970	81	8	1	1	51	14	5	4	n.a.
	1980	77	6	1	1	56	19	7	3	4
	1990	83	7	1	2	61	13	3	2	3
	2000	79	9	1	2	66	14	2	2	5
	2004	77	9	1	2	64	14	2	2	2
Developing economies (Dev.)	1970	72	18	2	11	34	20	3	7	n.a.
	1980	68	20	1	14	29	27	3	8	4
	1990	61	21	1	12	22	33	3	4	3
	2000	57	26	1	9	18	38	2	5	1
	2004	53	22	1	8	19	45	2	5	1
Developing Africa (DA)	1970	81	7	1	4	61	11	6	2	n.a.
	1980	83	26	<1	2	46	14	3	6	3
	1990	83	18	1	2	59	13	6	2	3
	2000	70	18	1	2	44	25	8	4	2
	2004	73	17	2	1	49	25	9	3	<1
Developing America (D. Am.)	1970	74	32	3	5	26	19	1	17	n.a.
	1980	64	32	3	4	22	28	2	21	7
	1990	63	33	1	5	21	21	1	14	3
	2000	74	56	2	2	12	24	1	18	1
	2004	71	52	2	2	14	27	1	18	1
Former USSR and Eastern Europe (East Eur.)	1980	28	1	<1	1	19	21	3	3	51
	1990	38	1	<1	2	28	23	2	5	40
	2000	46	4	<1	2	34	23	2	4	31
	2004	37	3	<1	1	33	23	2	2	19

Source: *Monthly Bulletin of Statistics* (New York: United Nations), July 2001, pp. 266–71, July 2000, pp. 258–61, June 1997, pp. 255–62, June 1993, pp. 266–71; *Statistical Yearbook* (New York: United Nations, 1969), pp. 376–83; and "International Trade—World Exports by Provenance and Destination," http://unstats.un.org/unsd/mbs/t41-July05-online.pdf (July 14, 2006).

international companies' affiliates. The fact that members of trade groups are increasingly selling more to each other is a development that will influence international companies' choices of locations for their plants and other operations. Note too that the United States and Japan, but not Europe, are fast approaching a 50-50 split in their exports to developing and developed nations.

MAJOR TRADING PARTNERS: THEIR RELEVANCE FOR MANAGERS

An analysis of the major trading partners of a firm's home country and those of the nations where it has affiliates that export can provide valuable insights to management.

Why Focus on Major Trading Partners?

There are a number of advantages to focusing attention on a nation that is already a sizable purchaser of goods coming from the would-be exporter's country:

1. The business climate in the importing nation is relatively favorable.

2. Export and import regulations are not insurmountable.

3. There should be no strong cultural objections to buying that nation's goods.

4. Satisfactory transportation facilities have already been established.

5. Import channel members (merchants, banks, and customs brokers) are experienced in handling import shipments from the exporter's area.

6. Foreign exchange to pay for the exports is available.

7. The government of a trading partner may be applying pressure on importers to buy from countries that are good customers for that nation's exports. We have seen the efforts of the Japanese, Korean, and Taiwanese governments to persuade their citizens to buy more American goods. They have also sent buying missions to the United States.

Major Trading Partners of the United States

Table 2.4 shows the major trading partners of the United States. The data indicate that the United States, an industrialized nation, generally follows the tendency we found in Table 2.3; that is, developed nations trade with one another. Mexico and Canada are major trading partners in great part because they share a common border with the United States. Freight charges are lower, delivery times are shorter, and contacts between buyers and sellers are easier and less expensive. Being joined with the United States in the North American Free Trade Agreement helps ensure that the three nations' mutual importance as trading partners will remain strong.

Note the changes in the rankings of America's trading partners in four decades. Of the top 15 nations, 8 have remained on the list over the years listed, including Canada, Mexico, Japan, Germany, the United Kingdom, France, Italy, and Brazil. However, each nation's ranking has changed over time, and some new nations have been added to replace other nations that have become relatively less important as trade partners. Nations from East and Southeast Asia, besides long-term trade partner Japan, have become increasingly important trade partners in recent years. China, South Korea, Taiwan, and Malaysia are supplying the United States with huge quantities of electronic products and components as well as a variety of largely labor-intensive manufactured goods, many of which are produced by affiliates of American international companies. Between 1991 and 2004, China rose from sixth to second place in exports to the United States (from $19 to $197 billion, a more than 900 percent increase in 13 years), and it also moved up to fifth place as an importer of U.S. goods in 2004 (although the $35 billion level of Chinese imports is less than 18 percent of the level of exports it sends to the United States).

Many of the same Asian countries appear as importers of American goods as well because (1) their rising standards of living enable their people to afford more imported products, and the countries' export earnings provide the foreign exchange to pay for them, (2) they

TABLE 2.4 Major Trading Partners of the United States, 1965, 1991, and 2004 ($ billions)

1965 Imports from	Amount	1991 Imports from	Amount	2004 Imports from	Amount
1. Canada	$4.8	1. Japan	$92	1. Canada	$256
2. Japan	2.4	2. Canada	91	2. China	197
3. United Kingdom	1.4	3. Mexico	31	3. Mexico	156
4. W. Germany	1.3	4. Germany	26	4. Japan	130
5. Venezuela	1.0	5. Taiwan	23	5. Germany	77
6. Mexico	0.6	6. China	19	6. United Kingdom	46
7. Italy	0.6	7. United Kingdom	18	7. S. Korea	46
8. France	0.6	8. S. Korea	17	8. Taiwan	35
9. Brazil	0.5	9. France	13	9. France	32
10. Belgium & Luxembourg	0.5	10. Italy	12	10. Malaysia	28
11. Philippines	0.4	11. Saudi Arabia	11	11. Italy	28
12. India	0.4	12. Singapore	10	12. Ireland	27
13. Hong Kong	0.3	13. Hong Kong	9	13. Venezuela	25
14. Netherlands Antilles	0.3	14. Venezuela	8	14. Brazil	21
15. Australia	0.3	15. Brazil	7	15. Saudi Arabia	21

1965 Exports to	Amount	1991 Exports to	Amount	2004 Exports to	Amount
1. Canada	$5.6	1. Canada	$85	1. Canada	$190
2. Japan	2.1	2. Japan	48	2. Mexico	111
3. W. Germany	1.7	3. Mexico	33	3. Japan	54
4. United Kingdom	1.6	4. United Kingdom	22	4. United Kingdom	36
5. Mexico	1.1	5. Germany	21	5. China	35
6. Netherlands	1.1	6. S. Korea	16	6. Germany	31
7. France	1.0	7. France	15	7. S. Korea	26
8. India	0.9	8. Netherlands	14	8. Netherlands	24
9. Italy	0.9	9. Taiwan	13	9. Taiwan	22
10. Australia	0.8	10. Belgium & Luxembourg	11	10. France	21
11. Belgium & Luxembourg	0.7	11. Singapore	9	11. Singapore	20
12. Venezuela	0.6	12. Italy	9	12. Belgium	17
13. Spain	0.5	13. Australia	8	13. Hong Kong	16
14. S. Africa	0.4	14. Hong Kong	8	14. Australia	14
15. Switzerland	0.4	15. Saudi Arabia	7	15. Brazil	14

Source: "U.S. Aggregate Foreign Trade Data, 1999 and Prior Years," *U.S. Foreign Trade Highlights,* tables 10 and 11, U.S. Department of Commerce International Trade Administration, www.ita.doc.gov/td/industry/otea/usfth/aggregate/H99t10.txt, www.ita.doc.gov/td/industry/otea/usfth/aggregate/H99t.11.txt; "Table 11: Top 50 Suppliers of U.S. Imports in 2004," U.S. Department of Commerce International Trade Administration, www.ita.doc.gov/td/industry/otea/usfth/tabcon.html (July 14, 2006); "Table 10: Top 50 Purchasers of U.S. Exports in 2004," U.S. Department of Commerce International Trade Administration, www.ita.doc.gov/td/industry/otea/usfth/tabcon.html (July 14, 2006).

are purchasing large amounts of capital goods to further their industrial expansion, (3) they are importing raw materials and components that will be assembled into subassemblies or finished goods that will subsequently be exported, often to the United States, and (4) their governments, pressured by the American government to lower their trade surpluses with the United States, have sent buying missions to this country to look for products to import.

The analysis of foreign trade that we have described would be helpful to anyone just starting to search outside the home market for new business opportunities. The preliminary steps of (1) studying the general growth and direction of trade (Table 2.3) and (2) analyzing major trading partners (Table 2.4) would provide an idea of where the trading activity is. What kinds of products do these countries import from the United States? The Department of Commerce's Office of Trade and Economic Analysis maintains a site on the Internet with downloadable files of trade statistics. One entry, "U.S. Foreign Trade Highlights," contains over 100 tables of goods and services, including one that reports on the top U.S. exports to and imports from its 80 largest trading partners. There are also tables from the Commerce Department's annual publication *U.S. Industry and Trade Outlook,* which replace the tables from *U.S. Industrial Outlook*. These tables compare the imports and exports of more than 100 industries for the last four years, providing an idea of their competitiveness in world markets.[3] Foreign trade reports are no longer available in hard copy. Trade data with much more information are available on CD-ROMs that are sent monthly to government depositories, such as many college and university libraries, or at online databases. The new reports have been expanded to contain additional data on units that permit analysts to make price comparisons by calculating average prices on exports and imports on a country basis.

The topic we have been examining—international trade—exists because firms export. As you know, however, exporting is only one aspect of international business. Another—overseas production—requires foreign investment, the topic of the next section.

Foreign Investment

Foreign investment can be divided into two components: **portfolio investment,** which is the purchase of stocks and bonds solely for the purpose of obtaining a return on the funds invested, and **direct investment,** by which the investors participate in the management of the firm in addition to receiving a return on their money. The distinction between these two components has begun to blur, particularly with the growing size and number of international mergers, acquisitions, and alliances in recent years. For example, investments by a foreign investor in the stock of a domestic company generally are treated as direct investment when the investor's equity participation ratio is 10 percent or more. In contrast, deals that do not result in the foreign investor's obtaining at least 10 percent of the shareholdings are classified as portfolio investments. With the increasing pace of business globalization, it is not uncommon for companies to form strategic relationships with firms from other nations in order to pool resources (such as manufacturing, marketing, and technology and other know-how) while still keeping their equity participation below 10 percent. Financing from foreign venture capitalists also tends to be treated as a portfolio investment, although these investors frequently become actively involved in the target company's business operations, with the goal of ultimately realizing substantial capital gains when the target company goes public.

PORTFOLIO INVESTMENT

Although portfolio investors are not directly concerned with the control of a firm, they invest immense amounts in stocks and bonds from other countries. For example, data from the Department of Commerce show that persons residing outside the United States owned American stocks and bonds other than U.S. Treasury securities with a value of $4,391 billion in 2005 (including $2,115 billion in corporate stocks).[4] This represents a 190 percent increase over 1997. The very substantial proportion of the increase in the valuation of American stock held by persons residing outside this country is associated with the large number and scale of acquisitions of U.S. companies by foreign companies.

portfolio investment
The purchase of stocks and bonds to obtain a return on the funds invested

direct investment
The purchase of sufficient stock in a firm to obtain significant management control

How Do Trade and Investment Impact Economic and Social Development?

All economies are increasingly open in today's economic environment of globalization. Trade plays a vital role in shaping economic and social performance and prospects of countries around the world, especially those of developing countries. No country has grown without trade. However, the contribution of trade to development depends a great deal on the context in which it works and the objectives it serves.

The above quote is the way the United Nations Conference on Trade and Development (UNCTAD) begins its groundbreaking report examining international trade and developing countries. International trade clearly has an important role in influencing nations' economic and social performance in a world of globalization. This role is even more fundamental in the case of developing countries. Yet the mere expansion of trade does not guarantee improvement for a country and its people. Rather, it is essential that trade performance be viewed in the context of its effects on employment levels, economic growth, development, and an improvement in the overall human condition.

To assist in efforts to ensure that trade plays a full and constructive role in enhancing growth and development, UNCTAD has launched an ambitious new initiative. Part of this initiative is the construction of the Trade and Development Index (TDI), a tool whose goal is to assist efforts "to systematically monitor the trade and development performance of developing countries with a view to facilitating national and international policies and strategies that would ensure that trade serves as a key instrument of development." By capturing the interactions among a range of factors underlying trade and development, the TDI attempts to provide a quantitative indication of a nation's trade and development performance. Although UNCTAD created the TDI primarily for assessing performance in developing nations, to facilitate comparisons and insight it also constructed the TDI for developed countries and for newly industrializing countries. Overall, 110 countries are evaluated. The 20 top- and bottom-ranked countries are listed in the accompanying table.

The average score for developed countries was 783, versus 408 for developing countries and 244 for the least developed countries. However, the top 10 performers from the developing countries had an average of 601, which was very close to the 637 average for the 10 nations that joined the European Union since May 2004, indicating that the gap in development can be shrunk—and has been in the case of several nations.

Results of the initial TDI evaluation reveal that the 30 highest-ranked nations are all developed countries, except for Singapore, South Korea, and Malaysia. This result is interpreted as evidence that few developing nations have been able to come close to the developed countries in terms of their trade and development performance. All of the bottom 10 nations are African, accentuating the severity of the trade and development problems confronting sub-Saharan Africa and least developed nations in general. The best regional performance among developing nations was that of the countries of the East Asia and Pacific region, followed by the Latin America and Caribbean region and the Middle East and North Africa region. The regions of South Asia and of sub-Saharan Africa significantly lagged behind the other three regional groups in terms of their TDI scores.

The most important factor contributing to high TDI scores is trade liberalization. The importance of this factor is highest for countries with lower TDI scores, and vice versa. This suggests that the extent of trade liberalization has much greater importance for developing countries, and especially the least developed countries, than for developed nations. In general, over the longer term and in the absence of externalities or market failures, trade liberalization is an effective policy promoting development. However, efforts to liberalize too rapidly can also result in short-term adjustment problems.

Both external and internal factors were found to influence a nation's export performance. External factors include market access conditions (e.g., transportation costs, geography, physical infrastructure, trade barriers, competition) and other factors that influence demand for imports. Internal factors include supply-side conditions within a nation (e.g., raw materials, labor and capital costs, access to technology, economic policy, institutional environment). A country's extent of market access is particularly important, since limitations on access for foreign markets is a major cause of poor export performance.

Americans, by contrast, owned $4,073 billion in foreign securities in 2005, of which $3,086 billion was in corporate stocks. This represents an increase of 145 percent over the corresponding level for 1997.[5] This increase reflects net U.S. purchases of foreign stocks, acquisitions of foreign companies by U.S. companies, and price appreciation in many foreign stocks. As you can see, foreign portfolio investment is sizable and will continue to grow as more international firms list their bonds and equities on foreign exchanges.

FOREIGN DIRECT INVESTMENT

The following discussion examines the volume, level, and direction of foreign direct investment, and the influence of international trade on foreign direct investment.

Top-Ranked Countries			Bottom-Ranked Countries		
Rank	Country	TDI Score	Rank	Country	TDI Score
1	Denmark	874	91	Madagascar	295
2	United States	854	92	Yemen	295
3	United Kingdom	825	93	Bangladesh	294
4	Sweden	811	94	Papua New Guinea	290
5	Norway	806	95	Pakistan	275
6	Japan	806	96	Malawi	272
7	Switzerland	805	97	Zambia	262
8	Germany	804	98	Nepal	255
9	Austria	791	99	Ivory Coast	254
10	Canada	790	100	Cameroon	248
11	France	774	101	Mozambique	238
12	Belgium-Luxembourg	773	102	Togo	230
13	Australia	772	103	Tanzania	229
14	New Zealand	770	104	Benin	225
15	Singapore	762	105	Sudan	206
16	Finland	761	106	Burkina Faso	195
17	Ireland	758	107	Ethiopia	186
18	Portugal	756	108	Nigeria	172
19	Spain	744	109	Mali	161
20	Italy	729	110	Niger	136

Foreign direct investment (FDI) was found to have a significant and positive impact on export performance across all of the nations studied and for every time period studied. FDI has a key role in influencing the composition of exports, including the technological content and the development of export supply capacity, and especially in knowledge-based industries. The impact of FDI is strongest for the two poorest-performing groups of exporters and at their early stages of export development.

UNCTAD emphasizes that merely improving trade factors, such as liberalizing the trade environment, will yield only marginal benefits for a nation unless these efforts are done in conjunction with a focus on other factors associated with development and poverty reduction. There is a strong need for integration and consistency between trade policy and other social, political, and economic undertakings. For example, nations must act simultaneously both on domestic capacity to supply goods and services and on access to foreign markets in order to produce strong performance. At early stages of development, important factors influencing domestic supply capacity include transportation infrastructure and macroeconomic stability.

Source: UNCTAD, *Developing Countries in International Trade 2005: Trade and Development Index*(New York: United Nations, 2005).

Volume   This section discusses the overall level of foreign direct investment, as well as annual outflows and inflows of FDI.

The Outstanding Stock of FDI   The *book value*—or the value of the total outstanding stock—of all foreign direct investment (FDI) worldwide was nearly $10 trillion at the end of 2004. Figure 2.3 shows how this total is divided among the largest investor nations. Individuals and corporations from the United States had over $2 billion invested abroad, which was 1.46 times the FDI of the next-largest investor, the United Kingdom, and 2.4 times that of the third-largest investor, Germany. The proportion of FDI accounted for by the United States declined by over 40 percent between 1985 and 2004, however, from 36 to 21 percent. During the same time period, the proportion of FDI accounted for by the European Union increased by over 25 percent, from 41 to 53 percent, although a portion of that increase was due to the inclusion of additional member-countries in the EU calculations. Japan's proportion of FDI declined from 12 percent in 1990 to 4 percent in 2004. Reflecting their continued economic development, developing countries have more than doubled their proportion of FDI, from 5 percent in 1985 to 11 percent in 2004.

Annual Outflows of FDI   Annual FDI outflows (the amount invested each year into other nations) hit a historical high in 2000—$1,201 billion, more than 250 percent of the level in 1997 (see Table 2.5). However, the slowdown that began to hit most of the world's economies in late 2000 resulted in a subsequent decline in the overall level of annual FDI flows. By 2002, the total was only $647 billion, only about 54 percent of the 2000 figure but still the fifth-highest annual level of FDI to that point in history. Outflows subsequently increased to $730 billion by 2004.

Although the United States had been the leading source of FDI outflows through most of the 1990s, in 2000 both the United Kingdom and France passed the United States. Indeed, the proportion of worldwide outward FDI accounted for by the United States declined from an average of 21 percent in 1985–1996 to 12 percent by 2000. However, the U.S. proportion rebounded, and the United States regained leadership on outward FDI from 2001 through 2004; American FDI outflows of $229 billion in 2004 exceeded by over 350 percent the outflows of the second-largest source of FDI, the United Kingdom (with $65 billion). The European Union's proportion of outward FDI grew from an average of around 47 percent in 1985–1997 to a peak of 75 percent by 2000, before subsequently declining to 61 percent of global outward FDI in 2002 and 38 percent in 2004. Japan declined from being the world's largest source of total global annual outflows of FDI in 1990, accounting for 22 percent of the total, to a position as the twelfth-largest in 2000, before rebounding by 2004 to being the sixth-largest source of outward FDI.

Although the overall volume of outward FDI from developing nations nearly quadrupled by 2004 compared to its average from 1985 to 1995, the proportion of worldwide outward FDI that comes from developing nations declined from 14 percent in 1997 to 11 percent by 2004. As a result, Table 2.5 shows that the vast proportion of outward FDI, over 87 percent, originates from the developed countries. The United States and the EU have been accounting for an increasing share, with their proportion of worldwide FDI increasing from an average of 68 percent in 1985–1995 to 87 percent by 2000, before falling back to 80 percent in 2002 and 70 percent in 2004. Much of this increase in outward FDI has been associated with mergers,

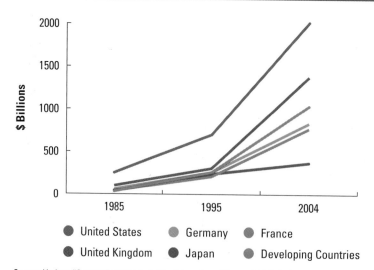

FIGURE 2.3

Stocks of Outward Foreign Direct Investment, Selected Countries, 1985, 1995, and 2004 ($ billions)

Source: Various "Country Fact Sheets," *World Investment Report 2001*, United Nations Conference on Trade and Development, Geneva, October 2001, and *World Investment Report 2005*, United Nations Conference on Trade and Development, Geneva, September 2005.

TABLE 2.5	Direction of Foreign Direct Investment (Annual Flows) for Selected Regions and Countries, 1985–2004 ($ billions)			
Where Funds Originate (net investment)	**1985–1995 (annual average)**	**1996**	**2000**	**2004**
World	$203	$391	$1,201	$730
Developed countries	182	332	1,098	637
Developing countries	22	58	99	83
North America	49	98	190	279
United States	43	84	143	229
Canada	6	13	47	48
Mexico	<1	<1	1	2
European Union	96	182	819	280
United Kingdom	26	34	250	65
Germany	18	51	57	−7
France	18	30	177	48
Italy	5	9	12	19
Russian Federation	<1	n.a.	3	10
Africa	1	<1	1	3
South, East, & Southeast Asia	17	50	81	67
India	<1	n.a.	<1	2
Japan	25	23	32	31
Hong Kong, China	8	27	59	40
China	2	2	1	2
Latin America & Caribbean	3	6	14	11
Where Funds Go (net investment)				
World	181	278	1,393	648
Developed countries	128	220	1,121	380
Developing countries	50	145	246	233
North America	54	103	396	119
United States	44	85	314	96
Canada	6	10	67	6
Mexico	4	9	16	17
European Union	66	109	684	216
United Kingdom	17	24	130	78
Germany	3	7	203	−39
France	12	22	43	24
Italy	3	4	13	17
Russian Federation	<1	n.a.	3	12
Africa	4	6	9	18
South, East, & Southeast Asia	30	88	139	126
India	<1	n.a.	2	5
Japan	1	<1	8	8
Hong Kong, China	4	11	62	34
China	12	40	41	61
Latin America & Caribbean	14	46	95	68

Note: Because of rounding, values may not equal 100%.

Source: Various "Country Fact Sheets," *World Investment Report 2001,* United Nations Conference on Trade and Development, Geneva, October 2001, and *World Investment Report 2005,* United Nations Conference on Trade and Development, Geneva, September 2005.

acquisitions, and other international investments made by companies in industries that are facing increased competition and consolidation globally. In fact, the developed countries accounted for 92 percent of the value of all cross-border purchases of foreign companies from 1995 to 2004, investing over $4.4 trillion into such acquisitions. Over 70 percent of the total amount of outward FDI by developed countries from 1997 to 2004 was used for the purchase of companies in other nations.

Annual Inflows of FDI   In which countries are investments being made, and where do the investments come from? Table 2.5 indicates that the industrialized nations invest primarily in one another, just as they trade more with one another. An average of over 70 percent of annual FDI investments have been going into developed countries. The United States and the EU accounted for an average of over 60 percent of all inward FDI from 1985 to 2004, exceeding 80 percent in 1999 and 2000. As noted above, much of this inward investment has gone to mergers and acquisitions made by companies whose businesses are confronting competition and consolidation globally. Japan has not been a significant recipient of inward FDI, averaging less than 1 percent of worldwide FDI from 1985 to 2004.

Worldwide, the developing countries as a whole obtained a 70 percent increase in the level of FDI between 1996 and 2000, before falling back by about one-third during the worldwide economic slowdown of the next two years. Although the overall dollar value of FDI going to developing countries increased, the proportion of FDI funds going to these nations declined from 15 percent in 1996 to 8 percent in 2000, before increasing again to over 11 percent by 2004. African nations participated relatively little in the growing flow of inward FDI, accounting for an average of less than 2 percent of all inflows from 1985 to 2004. The small nation of Singapore (population 3 million) received approximately as much foreign investment as the entire African continent did during this time. In Latin America, annual FDI inflows between 1997 and 2004 were 300 percent to more than 750 percent above the average of 1985–1995, although the annual flows fluctuated substantially. The proportion of worldwide inward FDI flows that have gone to Latin America declined from 15 percent in 1997 to 8.6 percent in 2002 before rising again to 10.5 percent in 2004. For Asia as a whole, total inflows to the region rose to a record $139 billion in 2000, more than 400 percent of the average inward investments during 1985 to 1995, yet the proportion of worldwide FDI inflows declined steadily from 1996 to 1999, at least partly due to the Asian financial crisis that hit in 1997. The proportion of investment going to Asia has increased since 1999, reaching over 19 percent by 2004. Asia as a whole moved up to being the second most popular region for inward FDI by 2004, behind the EU. Asia accounted for over one-third of all investments not directed to the United States and the European Union from 1985 to 2004. A particularly important trend is the proportion of Asian FDI that has been directed to China and its territories. Their combined proportion of Asian FDI grew from 52.4 percent during 1985–1995 to 75 percent in 2004, and it appears that some of the FDI previously directed toward other Asian nations might have been redirected toward these Chinese investments.

At a country level, the United States was the leader in terms of FDI inflows in 2000, which at $314 billion was the highest level of annual inward FDI ever recorded for a single nation. However, factors such as a declining stock market, slowed economy, and depreciating currency caused the level of inward FDI going to the United States to decline by over 90 percent in the next two years, to $30 billion in 2002, before subsequently rebounding. Still, from 2001 through 2004, the nation with the largest annual FDI inflows was China/Hong Kong, representing the first time that a developing economy has achieved such a distinction.

Level and Direction of FDI   Even though it is impossible to make an accurate determination of the present value of foreign investments, we can get an idea of the rate and amounts of such investments and of the places in which they are being made. This is the kind of information that interests managers and government leaders. It is analogous to what is sought in the analysis of international trade. If a nation is continuing to receive appreciable amounts of foreign investment, its investment climate must be favorable. This means that the political forces of the foreign environment are relatively attractive and that the opportunity to earn a profit is greater there than elsewhere. Other reasons for investing exist, to be sure; however, if the above factors are absent, foreign investment is not likely to occur.

Trade Leads to FDI Historically, foreign direct investment has followed foreign trade. One reason is that engaging in foreign trade is typically less costly and less risky than making a direct investment into foreign markets. Also, management can expand the business in small increments rather than through the considerably greater amounts of investment and market size that a foreign production facility requires. Typically, a firm would use domestic or foreign agents to export. As the export business increased, the firm would set up an export department and perhaps hire sales representatives to live in overseas markets. The firm might even establish its own sales company to import in its own name.

Meanwhile, managers would watch the total market size closely because they would know that their competitors were making similar studies. Generally, because the local market would not be large enough to support local production by all the firms exporting to it, the situation would become one of seeing who could begin manufacturing there first. Experienced managers know that governments often limit the number of local firms making a given product so that those that do set up local operations will be assured of having a profitable and continuing business. This is especially important to developing countries that are dependent on foreign investment to provide jobs and tax revenue.

Does Trade Lead FDI or Does FDI Lead Trade? The previous section described the linear path to market expansion that many international firms have taken and still take today. However, the new business environment of fewer government barriers to trade, increased competition from globalizing firms, and new production and communications technology is causing many international firms to disperse the activities of their production systems to locations close to available resources. They then integrate the entire production process either regionally or globally. As a result, the decision about where to locate may be either an FDI or a trade decision, illustrating just how closely FDI and trade are interlinked.

U.S. FOREIGN DIRECT INVESTMENT ABROAD

You saw in Figure 2.3 that the United States is by far the largest foreign investor (21 percent of the total outstanding stock of outward FDI stock in 2004), and American firms have invested much more in the developed nations (approximately 70 percent of the total, as of 2004) than they have in the developing nations. As Figure 2.4a indicates, during the two decades from 1985 to 2004, the proportion of total U.S. investment that went to Europe increased by nearly 14 percent (from 46 to 52 percent), while the proportion to Canada declined by approximately 50 percent. In 2004, the United Kingdom (15 percent) and the Netherlands (10 percent) represented the largest recipients of U.S. FDI among the European nations. Latin America's proportion of American FDI increased by over 30 percent, from 12 percent in 1985 to 16 percent in 2004. The proportion of American FDI in Asia and the Pacific increased over 25 percent during this time, from 15 to 19 percent. Although American firms had more FDI invested in Africa and the Middle East in 2004 than in 1985, the percentages of these two regions among total U.S. FDI abroad were less than half of what they had been in 1985.

Japan provides an interesting contrast to the United States in terms of recent FDI experience. During the early and middle 1990s, the focus of Japan's FDI outflows shifted from developed nations (down from 83 percent in 1989–1991 to 58 percent in 1994–1995) to Southeast Asia (up from 17 to 42 percent). However, the level of Japanese FDI going to Asian locations declined substantially at the end of the decade, falling from 22.6 percent in 1997 to 16 percent in 1998 and 12.2 percent in 2000. The proportion of Japanese FDI going to the United States and Europe was over 70 percent in 2003.[6]

FIGURE 2.4

U.S. Direct Investment Position Abroad and Foreign Direct Investment in the U.S., on a Historical-Cost Basis, 1985 and 2004 ($ billions)

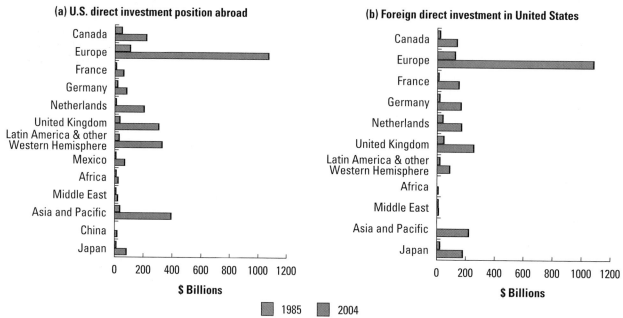

Source: Maria Borga and Daniel R. Yorgason, "Direct Investment Positions for 2001: Country and Industry Detail," *Survey of Current Business,* July 2002, pp. 32–35; Jennifer L. Konez and Daniel R. Yorgason, "Direct Investment Positions for 2004: Country and Industry Detail," Survey of Current Business, July 2005, pp.50–53; and *Survey of Current Business, June 1986, pp. 31, 34.*

FOREIGN DIRECT INVESTMENT IN THE UNITED STATES

Foreign direct investment in the United States rose rapidly from $185 billion in 1985 to $1,874 billion in 2005 (see Figure 2.4b). This is an average annual increase of nearly 13 percent. Observe how concentrated FDI is in the United States. Approximately 85 percent of the total stock was owned by firms or individuals from just eight nations: (1) United Kingdom (17 percent), (2) Japan (12 percent), (3) Germany (11 percent), (4) Netherlands (11 percent), (5) France (10 percent), (6) Canada (9 percent), (7) Switzerland (8 percent), and (8) Luxembourg (7 percent). The proportion of FDI in the United States owned by Europeans increased from 66 percent in 1985 to 71 percent in 2004. The proportion owned by Latin Americans declined from 9 percent in 1985 to 6 percent in 2004.

Comparing the level of U.S. FDI abroad with the level of FDI in the United States reveals an important trend. Figure 2.5 examines this trend annually from 1976 through 2005. As this figure shows, the level of U.S. investment abroad exceeded the amount of foreign investment in the United States until 1986. Since that time, there has been an almost continuous increase in the excess of the value of foreign investment in the United States versus the value of the level of American FDI abroad. By 2005, FDI in the United States was nearly $2.4 trillion more than U.S. FDI abroad, an amount approximately three times larger than six years earlier, in 1999. Implications of this imbalance in foreign direct investment, as well as the imbalance between American exports and imports of goods and services, will be discussed in later chapters, particularly in Sections Two and Three.

Acquire Going Companies or Build New Ones? As seen in Figure 2.5, foreign firms invested $1.5 trillion in the United States from 1999 to 2005. Approximately two-thirds of the value of their investments have been spent to acquire going companies rather than to establish new ones (similarly, the majority of American investments into foreign markets have gone to the acquisition of going companies). A number of reasons are responsible for this fact: (1) Corporate restructuring in the United States caused management to put on the market businesses or other assets that either did not meet management's profit standards or were considered to be unrelated to the company's main business; (2) foreign companies wanted to gain

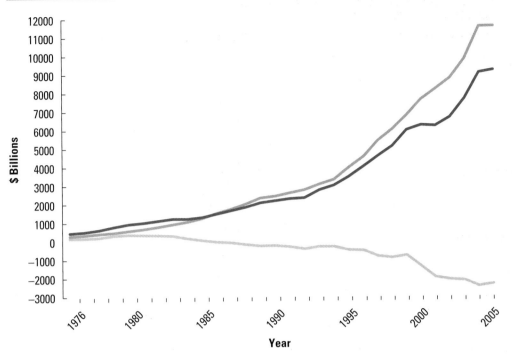

FIGURE 2.5

International Investment Position of the United States, 1976–2005 (billions of dollars)

● U.S.-owned assets abroad
● Foreign-owned assets in United States
● Net international investment position of the United States

Note: Figures are based on current cost.

Source: Elena L. Nguyen, "The International Investment Position of the United States at Year-End 2002," *Survey of Current Business,* July 2003, pp. 20–21;

rapid access in the United States to advanced technology, especially in computers and communications; (3) management of foreign firms felt that entrance into the large and prosperous American market could be more successful if they acquired known brand names rather than spending the time and money to promote new, unknown ones; and (4) increased international competitive pressures, including the pursuit of improved economies of scale, has led to restructuring and consolidation in many industries, and the acquisition of companies in major markets such as the United States has been a by-product of these industrial trends.

Why Enter Foreign Markets?

In the previous section, we mentioned briefly some of the reasons why foreign investors acquire companies more often than they establish them in the United States. Now let us examine the reasons why international firms enter foreign markets, which are all linked to the desire to increase profits and sales or protect them from being eroded by competitors.

INCREASE PROFITS AND SALES

Enter New Markets Managers are always under pressure to increase the sales and profits of their firms, and when they face a mature, saturated market at home, they begin to search for new markets outside the home country. They find that (1) markets with a rising GDP per capita and population growth appear to be viable candidates for their operations and (2) the economies of some nations where they are not doing business are growing at a considerably faster rate than is the economy of their own market.

New Market Creation As we will discuss in Chapter 15, there are many ways in which potential new markets can be identified and assessed. Sources of potential market size and overall market growth rate can be found in publications such as the annual *Human Development*

Why Doesn't More FDI Flow to Africa?

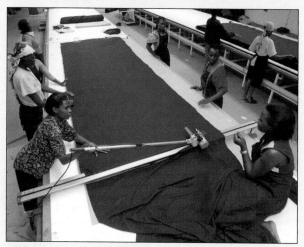

Factory workers cut material in July of 2003 at the Tristar clothing factory in Kampala, Uganda.

Despite the dramatic increases in international flows of foreign direct investment over the past two decades, the countries of sub-Saharan Africa have largely missed out on this trend. As a result, the problem of extensive and increasing levels of poverty among the populations of the sub-Saharan nations has been exacerbated. Taken as a whole, the 700 million residents of this region are experiencing declining per capita incomes, reduced life expectancy, increasing poverty, and social devastation resulting from epidemics such as HIV/AIDS and malaria.

Why hasn't more FDI flowed into the nations of Africa? Historically, many of these nations have suffered from glaring inadequacies of their regulatory and administrative practices with respect to the treatment of foreign investors and the protection of their investments, which sharply diminished the attractiveness of these nations for receiving incoming FDI. Combined with a range of additional social, political, economic, and other challenges on the continent, this has hindered Africa's ability to compete, when compared to investment opportunities within developed countries and in many of the other developing countries of the world.

There is some reason for hope, however, as the past decade has seen changes in attitudes toward FDI. The majority of African nations have introduced FDI liberalizing legislation as well as entered into trade agreements with other nations from Africa and other continents. State-owned enterprises are being privatized, often in conjunction with investment by foreign firms, although the pace of privatization lags behind that of other parts of the world. Regulatory conditions in many African nations are comparable with those in most other developing nations.

The introduction of sound standards for FDI is a positive step forward for attracting foreign investment. However, much work remains. According to the United Nations Conference on Trade and Development, the following problems still need to be addressed in order for sub-Saharan Africa to improve its attractiveness as a destination for foreign investment:

Report of the United Nations Development Program (www.sd.undp.org/HDR/HDR05e. pdf). Reviewing data in such reports will reveal great variety in growth rates among countries when ranked by variables such as GDP per capita.

Although nearly everyone looks to GDP per capita (or the counterpart statistic of GNI per capita) as a basis for making comparisons of nations' economies, extreme care must be exercised to avoid drawing unwarranted conclusions. First, because the statistical systems in many developing nations are deficient, the reliability of the data provided by such nations is questionable.

Second, to arrive at a common base of U.S. dollars, the World Bank and other international agencies convert local currencies to dollars. The Bank uses an average of the exchange rates for that year and the previous two years after adjusting for differences in relative inflation between the particular country and the United States.[7] World Bank economists admit that official exchange rates do not reflect the relative domestic purchasing powers of currencies. "However," they say, "exchange rates remain the only generally available means of converting GDP from national currencies to U.S. dollars."[8]

Third, you must remember that GDP per capita is merely an arithmetic mean obtained by dividing GDP by the total population. However, a nation with a lower GDP but more evenly distributed income may be a more desirable market than one with a higher GDP. On the other hand, as you will note in the chapter on economic forces (Chapter 8), a skewed distribution of income in a nation with a low GDP per capita may indicate that there is a viable market, especially for luxury goods.

1. Most countries have fiscal regimes that lack international competitiveness in terms of FDI for export-oriented activities. Many of the processes for providing investment incentives are slow, arbitrary, and lacking in integration.

2. Many countries lack good regulations with regard to the management of labor relations and dispute resolutions, an essential factor in a nation's attractiveness for investment in labor-intensive export manufacturing sectors.

3. Many countries lack updated systems for providing work and residence permits for expatriate personnel, who are often critical resources for the foreign investor during the early stages of an investment project due to the managerial and technical expertise they provide.

4. Potential investors frequently discount Africa as a destination for FDI because of a negative image of the continent as a whole, rather than understanding the diversity of economic performance among the various African countries and the existence of attractive investment opportunities in individual nations.

Despite these and other problems that continue to hinder FDI inflows, there are promising signs that political and economic changes currently under way may be able to be sustained. Economic performance of the region has substantially improved from the mid-1990s, exceeding a real growth rate of 5 percent per year in 2004 and 2005. There has been progress in unifying foreign exchange markets, achieving high levels of macroeconomic stability in many nations, and improving management of financial resources and public expenditures. Improved prices for oil and other nonfuel export commodities have contributed to growth in exports and GDP. Signs of momentum on economic and political reforms are evidenced by the 23 African nations that joined the African Peer Review Mechanism (APRM). The goal of the APRM is to encourage improved transparency and integrity in economic and political governance of the member-countries and thereby increase confidence of foreign investors in the sustainability of reform efforts in Africa.

Combined with the rich resource base found in many of the nations, these developments could provide a stronger foundation for future improvements in international investment and trade by African nations and improvements in the human condition on this vast continent. Recently, there have been increases in FDI into some of the African countries, which some observers have seen as a sign that Africa may be on the cusp of an "economic renaissance." Yet FDI can have costs as well as benefits for a host nation, and the receipt of FDI alone will not be sufficient to cure the ills of this region. Properly balanced and integrated with a range of other social, economic, and governance initiatives, however, FDI could indeed help to transform Africa and help its people to experience some of the prosperity that has characterized Asia and other developing regions in the past 30 years.

Source: United Nations Conference on Trade and Development, *World Investment Report 2003* (New York: United Nations, 2003), pp. 33–40; International Chamber of Commerce, "Business and UN Promote Foreign Investment in Africa," Press Release, Geneva, July 5, 1999, www.iccwbo.org/home/news_archives/1999/ business_and_un_for_african_fdi.asp (July 20, 2004); UNCTAD, "For Five African Least Developed Countries, 2002 a Bad Year for FDI," February 13, 2004, www.globalpolicy.org/socecon/ffd/fdi/2004/0213africa.htm (July 20, 2004); United Nations, *Foreign Direct Investment in Africa: Performance and Potential*, (New York: United Nations, 1999); UNCTAD, *Economic Development in Africa: Rethinking the Role of Foreign Direct Investment* (New York: United Nations, September 2005); and UNCTAD, *World Economic Situation and Prospects 2006* (New York: United Nations, 2006).

Data from sources such as the *Human Development Report* indicate that from a macro perspective, markets around the world are growing. However, this does not mean that equally good opportunities exist for all kinds of business. Perhaps surprisingly, economic growth in a nation causes markets for some products to be lost forever while, simultaneously, markets for other products are being created. Take the case of a country in the initial stage of development. With little local manufacturing, it is a good market for exporters of consumer goods. As economic development continues, however, managers see profit-making opportunities in (1) producing locally the kinds of consumer goods that require simple technology or (2) assembling from imported parts the products that demand a more advanced technology. Given the tendency of governments to protect local industry, the importation of goods being produced in that country will normally be prohibited or discouraged through taxes, tariffs, or other means once local production of those goods has been established. Thus, exporters of easy-to-manufacture consumer goods, such as paint, adhesives, toilet articles, clothing, and almost anything made of plastic, will begin to lose this market, which now becomes a new market for producers of the inputs to these "infant industries."

Preferential Trading Arrangements   The fact that most nations have experienced growth in population and GDP per capita does not necessarily mean they have attained sufficient size to warrant investment by an international firm in either (1) an organization for marketing exports from the home country or (2) a local manufacturing plant. For many products, a number of these nations still lack sufficient market potential. When such nations make some kind

preferential trading arrangement

An agreement by a small group of nations to establish free trade among themselves while maintaining trade restrictions with all other nations

of **preferential trading arrangement** (for example, the EU or the North American Free Trade Agreement), the resultant market is much larger. As a result, firms frequently bypass what is often the first step of exporting and make their initial market entry with local manufacturing facilities.

Faster-Growing Markets   Not only are new foreign markets appearing, but many of them are growing at a faster rate than is the home market. A firm looking for a market large enough to support the local production of appliances or machinery, for example, would be attracted by the wealth, growth, and population size of Japan and Spain. When you examine the low GDP per capita and negative growth rates of so many of the African nations, you realize why foreign direct investment in that entire continent is so low. Clearly, market analysts will investigate other factors, such as the legal and political situations (discussed in Chapters 9 and 10), but an examination of variables such as those contained in the *Human Development Report* mentioned above is a good place to start. Interestingly, 70 of the 177 countries in the World Bank database (40 percent) referenced in this report had average annual GDP per capita growth rates that were higher than or equal to the U.S. growth rate for the period 1990–2003.[9]

Faster growth in the markets of developing nations frequently occurs for another reason. When a firm that has supplied the market by exporting builds a factory for local production, the host government often prohibits imports or erects barriers that make it difficult for imports to be competitive. The firm, which may have had to share the market with 10 or 20 competitors during its exporting days, now might essentially have the local market all to itself or share it with only a small number of other local producers. That is a situation that allows for growth.

Improved Communications   This might be considered a supportive reason for opening up new markets overseas, because certainly the ability to communicate rapidly and less expensively with customers and subordinates by electronic mail, wireless and wired telephones, and videoconferencing, as we discussed in Chapter 1, has given managers confidence in their ability to control foreign operations. Advances in computer-based communications are allowing virtual integration, which permits firms to become more physically fragmented as their managements search the world for lower-cost inputs. For example, anyone in the home office or in a subsidiary anywhere in the world can instantly access databases and computer-generated drawings.

Good, relatively inexpensive international communication enables large insurance, banking, software, and other firms to "body shop," that is, transmit computer-oriented tasks worldwide to a cheap but skilled labor force. The clients of numerous Indian software companies are in the United States. A few years ago, software teams were required to fly back and forth between the two countries. Now, at the end of the day, customers in the United States e-mail their problems to India, and while they are sleeping, the Indians work on the solutions and have them back in the United States before the Americans have had breakfast. For their work, Indian software engineers receive only 15 to 20 percent as much as do their American counterparts. This "offshoring" of work has become increasingly common, as we will see in later chapters, including Chapters 3 and 20.

Obtain Greater Profits   As you know, greater profits may be obtained by either increasing total revenue or decreasing the cost of goods sold, and often conditions are such that a firm can do both.

Greater Revenue   Rarely will all of a firm's domestic competitors be in every foreign market in which it is located. Where there is less competition, the firm may be able to obtain a better price for its goods or services.

Increasingly, firms are obtaining greater revenue by simultaneously introducing products in foreign markets and in their domestic markets as they move toward greater globalization of their operations. This results in greater sales volume while lowering the cost of the goods sold.

Lower Cost of Goods Sold   Going abroad, whether by exporting or by producing overseas, can frequently lower the cost of goods sold. Increasing total sales by exporting not only will reduce research and development (R&D) costs per unit but also will make other economies of scale possible.

Another factor that can positively affect the cost of goods sold is the inducements that some governments offer to attract new investment. For example, Turkey offers a range of incentives for new investors, including the following: (1) exemptions from customs fees, taxes, and duties, as well as value-added taxes (VAT), for imported machinery and equipment, (2) investment allowances of 20 to 70 percent of total fixed investment, (3) subsidized investment for research and development projects and environment investments, (4) exemption from building and construction taxes, (5) allocation of public land for company operations in priority development regions and industrial belts, (6) exemption from corporate taxes, and (7) export incentives such as exemptions on VAT, export taxes and duties, and export credits.[10] Incentives such as these are designed to attract prospective investors but generally are not a sufficient motive for foreign investment. Nevertheless, they do have a positive influence on the cost of goods sold.

Higher Overseas Profits as an Investment Motive   There is no question that greater profits on overseas investments were a strong motive for going abroad in the early 1970s and 1980s. *Business International* reported that 90 percent of 140 Fortune 500 companies surveyed had achieved higher profitability on foreign than domestic assets in 1974, for example.[11] This trend continued into the 1990s. As an example, in 1993, only 18 of the 100 largest multinationals earned more than 50 percent of their revenue overseas, but 33 earned more than 50 percent of their profits from foreign operations.[12] Profits from foreign markets remain critical for U.S. multinationals. In 2004, for example, earnings from overseas operations accounted for 40 percent of the total profit growth achieved by U.S. companies, including those without international operations. The $315 billion in profits from overseas operations was up 26 percent from 2003 and 78 percent since 2000. The consulting firm McKinsey estimates that profits from overseas operations account for $2.7 trillion in stock market capitalization for American companies.[13]

Test Market
Occasionally, an international firm will test-market a product in a foreign location that is less important to the company than its home market and major overseas markets. This provides an opportunity to make changes, if necessary, to any part of the marketing mix (product, promotion, price, channels of distribution) or drop the entire venture if the test indicates that this should be done. Management's thinking is that any mistakes made in the test market should not adversely affect the firm in any of its major markets. Since companies usually monitor their competitors' actions in all markets, there is always the danger that a market test will give those competitors an early warning. We shall examine this point again in Chapter 15, "Assessing and Analyzing Markets." Let's now look at some reasons for going abroad that are more related to the protection of present markets, profits, and sales.

PROTECT MARKETS, PROFITS, AND SALES

Protect Domestic Market
Frequently, a firm will go abroad to protect its home market.

Follow Customers Overseas   Service companies (for example, accounting, advertising, marketing research, banking, law) will establish foreign operations in markets where their principal accounts are to prevent competitors from gaining access to those accounts. They know that once a competitor has been able to demonstrate to top management what it can do by servicing a foreign subsidiary, it may be able to take over the entire account. Similarly, suppliers to original equipment manufacturers (for example, battery manufacturers supplying automobile producers) often follow their large customers. These suppliers have an added advantage in that they are moving into new markets with a guaranteed customer base.

Attack in Competitor's Home Market
Occasionally, a firm will set up an operation in the home country of a major competitor with the idea of keeping the competitor so occupied defending that market that it will have less energy to compete in the firm's home country.

Using Foreign Production to Lower Costs   A company may also go abroad to protect its domestic market when it faces competition from lower-priced foreign imports. By moving part or all of its production facilities to the countries from which its competition is coming, it can enjoy such advantages as less costly labor, raw materials, and energy. Management may decide to produce certain components abroad and assemble them in the home country, or, if the final product requires considerable labor in the final assembly, it may send the components overseas for this operation. Many nations, especially developing countries, offer **export processing zones** in which firms, mostly foreign manufacturers, enjoy almost complete absence of taxation and regulation of materials brought into the zones for processing and subsequent re-export. This can also be accomplished by using in-bond plants.

In-Bond (Maquiladora) Plants.   **In-bond plants,** often called **maquiladoras,** came into existence because of an arrangement between Mexico and the United States. The Mexican government permitted duty-free importation of parts and materials from the United States for assembly, processing, and packaging within the in-bond plant, provided that the finished products were re-exported. The American government permitted the finished product containing the American-made parts and materials to be imported, with import duty paid only on the value added in Mexico.

Over 80 percent of Mexican trade with the United States, and more than 40 percent of all exports from Mexico, are from the maquiladora industry.[14] Maquiladoras employ nearly 1.2 million workers, or about one in five Mexican manufacturing jobs.[15] Their production, led by electronics, electronic machinery, transportation equipment, and textiles and apparel, was projected to exceed $115 billion in 2006. Although the number of in-bond plants has declined by 23 percent since 2001, partly due to the emergence of China as a competitor, there were over 2,800 in-bond plants in 2006.

The maquiladora sector is undergoing a major shift from so-called first-generation activities (those that are highly labor-intensive and entail limited technology) and toward higher-value-added work. This transformation is being hastened by rising Mexican wage rates, which increased more than 50 percent between 1998 and 2006, compounded by competition from China and other nations with labor cost advantages. China's labor costs are one-fourth the level of Mexico's, making the latter country uncompetitive in many low-skill, labor-intensive products. Minicase 2.1, on Jabil Circuit Inc., provides an example of one company that is attempting to navigate this changing competitive environment.

Protect Foreign Markets   Changing the method of going abroad from exporting to overseas production is often necessary to protect foreign markets. The management of a firm supplying a profitable overseas market by exporting may begin to note some ominous signs that this market is being threatened.

Lack of Foreign Exchange   One of the first signs is a delay in payment by the importers. The importers may have sufficient local currency but may be facing delays in buying foreign exchange (currency) from the government's central bank. The credit manager in the exporting firm, by checking with his or her bank and other exporters, learns that this condition is becoming endemic—a reliable sign that the country is facing a lack of foreign exchange. In examining the country's balance of payments, the financial manager may find that its export revenue has declined while the import volume remains high. Experienced exporters know that import and foreign exchange controls are in the offing and that there is a good chance of losing the market, especially if they sell consumer products. In times of foreign exchange scarcity, governments will invariably give priority to the importation of raw materials and capital goods.

If the advantages of making the investment outweigh the disadvantages, the company may decide to protect this market by producing locally. Managers know that once the company has a plant in the country, the government will do its utmost to provide foreign exchange for raw materials to keep the plant, a source of employment, in operation. Because imports of competing products are prohibited, the only competition, if any, will have to come from other local manufacturers.

Local Production by Competitors Lack of foreign exchange is not the only reason a company might change from exporting to manufacturing in a market. For instance, while a firm may enjoy a growing export business and prompt payments, it still may be forced to set up a plant in the market. It may be that its competitors have also noticed their export volumes will support local production.

Should a competing firm move to put up a factory in the market, management must decide rapidly whether to follow suit or risk losing the market forever. Managers know that many governments, especially those in developing nations, not only will prohibit further imports once the product is produced in the country but also will permit only two or three other companies to enter so as to maintain a sufficient market for these local firms. For example, many foreign companies from sectors such as banking, insurance, securities underwriting, telecommunications, legal, and distribution services tried for years to enter the People's Republic of China. The Chinese government, however, prohibited or sharply restricted the options available to foreign firms for entering these sectors and competing with local companies, most of which were owned by local governmental organizations. Only as a result of negotiations associated with China's entry into the World Trade Organization were regulations liberalized to allow substantially increased participation of foreign firms within the Chinese market for these services.[16] As a result of these changes, numerous foreign firms have established operations in China for serving the local market.

Downstream Markets A number of Organization of Petroleum Exporting Countries (OPEC) nations have invested in refining and marketing outlets, such as filling stations and heating-oil distributors, to guarantee a market for their crude oil at more favorable prices. Petróleos de Venezuela, owner of Citgo, is one of the largest foreign investors in the United States. Kuwait bought Gulf Oil's refining and marketing network in three European countries and also owns a substantial portion of BP Amoco, which has one of the largest foreign investments in the United States. Lukoil, Russia's largest oil company, bought the Getty Oil chain of gasoline retailers in the eastern United States. These are just three examples.

Protectionism When a government sees that local industry is threatened by imports, it may erect import barriers to stop or reduce them.* Even threats to do this can be sufficient to induce the exporter to invest in production facilities in the importing country. This and a strong yen, which makes it more difficult for Japanese exports to compete with American products, are important reasons for Japanese investment in the United States.

Guarantee Supply of Raw Materials

Few developed nations possess sufficient domestic supplies of raw materials. Japan and Europe are almost totally dependent on foreign sources for many important materials, and even the United States depends on imports for more than half of its aluminum, chromium, manganese, nickel, tin, and zinc. Furthermore, the Department of the Interior estimates that iron, lead, tungsten, copper, potassium, and sulfur will be added soon to the critical list.[†]

To ensure a continuous supply, manufacturers in the industrialized countries are being forced to invest primarily in the developing nations, where most new deposits are being discovered. Interestingly, although Japan does this as well, for years it has also looked to the United States as a source of raw materials. A Japanese deputy general consul once stated,

> *The United States offers an abundance of many raw materials. Because Japan has long depended on the United States for various materials, such as grain, coking coal, and lumber, it is entirely logical for Japanese firms to establish facilities close to the sources of these essential raw materials.*

*See Chapter 3 for a discussion of import barriers.
†See Chapter 7 for a discussion of scarce industrial minerals.

Some analysts claim that the Japanese-American trade flows approximate those between an industrialized country and a developing country: The industrialized nation sends manufactured goods to the developing nation in return for raw materials. This is somewhat exaggerated, but practically all of Japan's exports to the United States consist of manufactured goods and services, while approximately one-third of American exports to Japan consist of foodstuffs, raw materials, and mineral fuels.

Acquire Technology and Management Know-How A reason often cited by foreign firms for investing in the United States is the acquisition of technology and management know-how. Nippon Mining, for example, a Japanese copper mining company, came to Illinois and paid $1 billion for Gould Inc. to acquire technology leadership and market share in producing the copper foil used in printed circuit boards for electronics products.

Geographic Diversification Many companies have chosen geographic diversification as a means of maintaining stable sales and earnings when the domestic economy or their industry goes into a slump. Often, in other parts of the world, the industry or the other economies are at their peak. Remember that the firms in Table 2.1 obtained an average of 50 percent of their revenues overseas and that an even higher proportion of their profits came from abroad.

Satisfy Management's Desire for Expansion The faster growth mentioned previously helps fulfill management's desire for expansion. Stockholders and financial analysts also expect firms to continue to grow, and those companies operating only in the domestic market have found it increasingly difficult to sustain that expectation. As a result, many firms have expanded into foreign markets. This, of course, is what companies based in small countries, such as Nestlé (Switzerland), SKF Bearing (Sweden), and Nokia (Finland), discovered decades ago.

Another aspect of this reason sometimes motivates a company's top managers to begin searching for overseas markets. Being able to claim that the firm is a "multinational" creates the impression of importance, which can influence the firm's customers. Sun Microsystems, a manufacturer of computer workstations, opened a technical center in Germany and built a factory in Scotland. "To be a major player in the marketplace, you have to be internationally recognized," said the head of Sun's European operations.[17]

We also know of instances in which a company has examined and then entered a market because its president brought it to the attention of the market planners after enjoying a pleasant vacation there.

How to Enter Foreign Markets

Once a company has determined from an analysis such as the preceding that it needs or wants to enter into international markets, it must then address what means to use in order to enter these markets. As you learned in Chapter 1, all of the means for supplying foreign markets may be subsumed in just two activities: (1) exporting to a foreign market and (2) manufacturing in it. Chapter 16 provides a discussion of the various options available to a firm under each of these two activities.

Multidomestic or Global Strategy?

Many large global and multidomestic firms with numerous manufacturing subsidiaries all over the world began their foreign operations by exporting. Once they succeeded at this stage, they often established sales companies overseas to market their exports. Where sales companies were able to develop sufficiently large markets, their firms set up plants to assemble imported parts. Finally, complete products were produced locally. However, this sequence of foreign trade to foreign direct investment does not represent the only way firms have entered.

More than likely, your first job in international business will *not* come with a business class airline ticket to Tokyo, London, or Rio de Janeiro and a "sky's the limit" expense account. More realistically, it will come with a desk, phone, FAX machine, e-mail, and a computer. Many entry-level jobs in international business involve handling import–export documentation to move shipments across international boarders; tracking shipments by boat, plane, train, and truck; following sales to make sure orders and payments are received; and dealing with foreign customers by phone, FAX, and e-mail. Is this the glamour of international business? Probably not. But it is business, and it is international, and it does put your career track in the international arena, which is where you need to be to start your international business career. In addition to your willingness to take that all-important entry-level international job and work to be successful at it, here are several other suggestions:

- Let your boss and your company's human resource department know you are interested in a career in international business.

- Join several international business trade associations in your city, and regularly attend their meetings. For example:

  International Chamber of Commerce, www.iccwbo.org

  International Association of Business Communicators (IABC), www.iabc.com

  International Trade Association of the U.S. Department of Commerce (offers seminars and workshops), http://trade.gov/index.asp

  Federation of International Trade Associations (FITA) (offers a directory of international trade associations by specialty, with locations), www.fita.org

  Your state's Department of Commerce or Economic Development (offers workshops and seminars on international trade)

  By attending these meetings, you get to know the association's members, so they get to know you and learn about your interest in a career in international business.

- Read international business publications so that you are current with issues, trends, and practices in international trade. Here are several:

  World Trade (this is free), www.worldtrademag.com

  International Trade Update (published monthly by the International Trade Association of the U.S. Department of Commerce), http://trade.gov/press/publications/newsletters/ita_0506/index_0506.asp

  International Herald Tribune, www.iht.com

  Financial Times, www.ft.com

  The Economist, www.economist.com

- Find a mentor to teach, guide, and assist you in building your international business career.

- Be ready to travel internationally at a moment's notice—hold a valid passport.

- Not all international jobs are in business. Explore the possibilities.

World Fact: Brazil has the largest ethnic Japanese population outside Japan, approximately 1.5 million.

Culture Cue: In the United States, "business casual" dress and informality when addressing superiors and subordinates by their first name may be accepted, but in many parts of the world this behavior is considered rude, offensive, and disrespectful. Learn the business norms of the country you will be working in before you start. If you are not sure, it is safer to be conservative and formal in your dress and behavior.

World Wide Resource:

- www.transitionsabroad.com/listings/work/careers/keywebsitesprofessionspecific.shtml

THE WORLD ENVIRONMENT IS CHANGING

While this linear relationship still holds, changes in the world environment that affect trade and foreign investment are occurring: (1) Governments generally have liberalized the flows of capital, technology, people, and goods, and (2) improvements in information technology enable managers to direct company activities in diverse areas over long distances. As a result, global competition has increased, forcing companies to strive for better-quality and lower-cost products. To reduce costs, they have moved some production activities to lower-cost countries and, through acquisitions and mergers, have increased company size to achieve economies of scale. Increasing sales by opening up new markets also will provide more economies of scale for the manufacturing system, especially if the firm sells the same products in all markets.

The aforementioned increased global competition will drive companies to open up new markets either to take market share from their competitors or to go to markets where there is less competition. It is evident that numerous conditions are forcing companies to enter foreign markets. Which strategy will management follow—multidomestic or global? In other words, what can the company standardize worldwide?

SEVEN GLOBAL DIMENSIONS

There are at least seven dimensions along which management can globalize (standardize): (1) product, (2) markets, (3) promotion, (4) where value is added to the product, (5) competitive strategy, (6) use of non-home-country personnel, and (7) extent of global ownership in the firm. The possibilities range from zero standardization (multidomestic) to standardization along all seven dimensions (completely global). The challenge for company managers is to determine how far the firm should go with each one. Usually the amount of globalization will vary among the dimensions. For example, the promotion for washing machines might be standardized to a great extent: People use them to get their clothes clean, but for economic reasons, in poorer countries the machines must be simpler and less costly. Therefore, the product is not standardized worldwide. We shall return to this topic in various parts of the text, particularly in Chapter 13.

Summary

Appreciate the magnitude of international trade and how it has grown.

The volume of international trade in goods and services measured in current dollars exceeded $11 trillion in 2004. Merchandise exports, at $8.9 trillion, were about 4.5 times what they were in 1980. Services exports were only $2.1 trillion in 2004, but their rate of growth since 1980 has been faster than that of merchandise exports.

Identify the direction of trade, or who trades with whom.

Developed countries tend to trade with developed countries, with such trade accounting for more than 70 percent of their total trade, and they account for a majority of the exports worldwide. More than half of the exports from developed countries also go to developed countries, though this proportion has been declining for the past 35 years. The results for services exports are similar in many ways to those found for merchandise exports. The rise of regional trade agreements, as well as other factors, is transforming the volume and direction of world trade in merchandise and services. Over 70 percent of world trade now occurs between members of regional trade agreements.

Explain the size, growth, and direction of foreign direct investment, worldwide and in the United States.

The book value of foreign direct investment was nearly $10 trillion at the end of 2004. The United States is the largest source of this FDI, with a total value of outstanding investments 1.46 times that of the United Kingdom, the next-largest investor, and 2.4 times that of Germany, the third-largest investor. The proportion of global foreign direct investment accounted for by the United States has been declining, falling from 36 percent in 1985 to 21 percent in 2004, while the proportion accounted for by the European Union has risen to 53 percent. The proportion of FDI originating in the developing nations has also been increasing, reaching 11 percent in 2004. On an annual basis, the United States was the largest source of FDI flows in 2004, with $229 billion in outflows, over 350 percent of the level of the second-largest FDI source, the United Kingdom. Overall, over 70 percent of annual FDI investments flow into developed countries, with a majority of this investment occurring in the form of acquisitions of existing companies. The leader in FDI inflows at a national level was China for each of the years 2001 through 2004, the first time an emerging market has held such a distinction as the target for worldwide FDI investments. The direction of FDI follows the direction of foreign trade; that is, developed nations invest in each other just as they trade with each other. Note that because of the new business environment, many international firms are dispersing the activities of their manufacturing systems to locations closer to available resources. Deciding where to locate may be either an FDI or a trade decision.

Identify who invests and how much is invested in the United States.

Foreign direct investment in the United States rose from $185 billion in 1985 to $1,874 billion in 2005. Firms from just eight nations—United Kingdom, Japan, Germany, Netherlands, France, Canada, Switzerland, and Luxembourg—own about 85 percent of the total stock of foreign direct investment in the United States.

Understand the reasons for entering foreign markets.

Companies enter foreign markets (exporting to and manufacturing in) to increase sales and profits and to protect markets, sales, and profits. Foreign firms often buy American firms to acquire technology and marketing know-how. Foreign investment also enables a company to diversify geographically.

Comprehend that globalization of an international firm occurs over at least seven dimensions and that a company can be partially global in some dimensions and completely global in others.

A firm can have, and usually does have, an international strategy that is partially multidomestic in some dimensions and partially global in others. Management must decide the extent to which the firm should globalize along each dimension.

foreign sourcing (p. 32)

portfolio investment (p. 41)

direct investment (p. 41)

preferential trading arrangement (p. 52)

export processing zone (p. 54)

in-bond plants (maquiladoras) (p. 54)

1. How large and important a role do small and medium-size enterprises play in generating export sales?

2. How has trade in merchandise and services changed over the past decade? What have been the major trends? How might this information be of value to a manager?

3. "The greater part of international trade consists of an exchange of raw materials from developing nations for manufactured goods from developed nations." True or false? Explain.

4. "The volume of exports has increased, but the ranking of U.S. trading partners in order of importance remains the same year after year." True or false? Of what use is this information to a manager?

5. What is the value of analyzing foreign trade data? For example, what should the quadrupling in real terms of exports in less than 35 years indicate to managers?

6. Knowing that a nation is a major trading partner of another signifies what to a marketing analyst?

7. What are the different components of foreign investment? Why has the distinction between them begun to blur in recent years?

8. How has the level and direction of FDI changed over the past decade, both overall and in terms of annual outflows and inflows? Why would this information be of relevance to managers?

9. Why has FDI historically followed foreign trade? What is it about the new international business environment that is causing this path to market expansion to change?

10. Why has most foreign direct investment gone into acquiring existing companies rather than establishing new ones?

11. What are the main reasons that a firm might enter into foreign markets?

12. What are in-bond plants? Why might they be an attractive alternative for a manufacturing company?

13. How can a firm protect its domestic market by investing overseas?

14. What are the seven dimensions along which management can globalize? How is it possible for a firm to be multidomestic on one dimension of globalization and global on another?

globalEDGE globalEDGE.msu.edu

Use the globalEDGE site (http://globalEDGE.msu.edu/) to complete the following exercises:

1. An important element of understanding the nature of international trade is identifying the breadth of non-financial transnational corporations (TNCs). Using the *Largest Transnational Corporations*, a series of rankings published by UNCTAD, locate a ranking of the world's largest 100 non-financial TNCs by foreign assets. Then, identify the ten TNCs with the highest Transnationality Index (TNI). What are the home

economies and industries of these TNCs? Also, where do they rank in the overall survey?

2. The number of member-nations of the World Trade Organization (WTO) has increased recently. In addition to nations with full member status, some non–member countries have observer status that requires accession negotiations to begin within five years of attaining this preliminary position. Identify the current total number of WTO members. Also, prepare a list of observer countries.

Jabil Circuit Inc. is a St. Petersburg, Florida–based company involved in providing electronic manufacturing services for international electronics companies in the electronics and technology industries. Established in 1966, Jabil now has 55,000 employees in over 40 facilities located in 20 nations worldwide, and it generated $7.5 billion in revenues in 2005.

One of Jabil's facilities is a factory for electronics manufacturing located in Guadalajara, Mexico. It was set up to make electronics products for export to companies such as Dell Inc. and Nokia Corporation, taking advantage of lower wage costs and the proximity to the U.S. market.

The initial 150,000-square-foot facility was opened in November 1997, with subsequent expansions increasing it to 363,000 square feet. In announcing the expansion, Wesley "Butch" Edwards, senior vice president of operations, said, "We are seeing a strong demand for additional North American capacity, especially in areas that provide access to low-cost manufacturing. [Increasing] the size of our Mexico facility is an indication of the strength of both current and new business opportunities in Mexico." Edwards said the expansion of the Guadalajara plant would allow both current and new customers to take advantage of Mexico's lower production costs. The factory would continue to offer cost levels that would allow delivery of products to North American markets at globally competitive prices.

The electronics industry in Guadalajara had experienced great success after the North American Free Trade Agreement was signed in 1993. Between 1994 and 2000, Guadalajara's electronics exports increased from $2 billion to $10 billion. Jabil's Mexican facility shared in this success. Jabil's plant in Guadalajara was one of the electronics facilities being heralded as a model for the successful industrialization of Mexico. By August 2000, employment at the plant had expanded to 3,500 people, and in February 2001, the company was busy scaling up its business to the highest volume of production in its history. Its future looked bright.

Within three months, by May 2001, output at the Guadalajara facility had declined by 40 percent. Economic recession in the United States, a stronger peso, and a doubling of average wage rates helped to trigger a rapid movement of production activities out of Mexico as companies attempted to find and exploit lower costs in other nations. Much of this business ended up being transferred to low-cost suppliers in China. Within a year, almost every product being produced in the Guadalajara plant had been transferred to one of seven plants that the parent Jabil company had established in China. By the summer of 2002, Jabil's Guadalajara workforce had been cut in half, to 1,750 employees.

Jabil's experience was not unique. Between 2001 and 2004, an estimated 400,000 jobs were moved to China from Mexico as companies attempted to maintain their competitiveness by finding lower-cost production sites. China's rapid export growth catapulted it into the position of second-largest exporter to the United States—behind Canada but ahead of Mexico, the previous number-two exporter.

Struggling for survival, Jabil's managers had to decide how to proceed. One option was to try to compete against the Chinese, despite Mexican labor costs approximately four times higher than those in China. However, the futility of trying to compete in such a scenario was apparent. "We realized we couldn't compete with China's labor cost. We needed to compete as a North American factory. After all, that's where we are," said Ernesto Sanchez, the general director of the Guadalajara factory.

Its proximity to the U.S. marketplace gave the Guadalajara facility an opportunity to leverage logistical factors to its advantage. Product development and support activities between companies operating in the United States and China can be particularly challenging, requiring off-hour calls or lengthy and expensive travel, which was a factor in the Guadalajara site's advantage. Although workers in Mexican manufacturing plants earned an average of three to four times more than their counterparts in China, logistics costs for Mexican products tend to be a small fraction of the costs required to ship products from Asia. Many U.S. customers were trying to manage inventory costs, while simultaneously being able to respond quickly to market developments, and being located near the U.S. market meant that factories like Jabil's in Guadalajara could achieve delivery times that were several weeks quicker than shipping times from a plant in Asia. The supply chain between Mexico and the United States was also better understood and was supported by prompt and reliable truck and rail transport. As a result of such factors, Jabil's Mexican plant had the potential to create value that could not be achieved by its Chinese competitors, helping to negate the difference in labor costs. "The one advantage we have is our geographic position. We are close to one of the biggest markets in the world, plus our labor force is still less expensive than either the U.S. or Canada," said Sanchez.

One example of the benefits of location is the case of cell phones. One company discovered that a model of its cell phone cost 50 cents less to build in China, but the cost of transportation was 14 cents if shipped by sea and 71 cents if shipped by air versus only 5 cents if shipped from Mexico by truck. The added shipping time associated with sea transport from China—typically 21 to 23 days, as opposed to less than 8 hours from Mexico—as well as tightened customs procedures imposed on shipping from Asia to manage risks from terrorism, also required that the company carry a higher level of buffer inventory, another significant cost.

As a result of factors such as these, the managers in the Guadalajara plant decided to move away from their traditional low-end manufacturing orientation, where their competitiveness on labor costs had eroded quickly as opposed to the rapidly emerging Chinese market. Instead, they focused on the production of more complex and higher-value-added products, such as computer routers and handheld credit card machines used by restaurants. They particularly emphasized goods made by smaller U.S. manufacturers, against whom the Mexican facility still had a strong edge in labor costs.

In order to produce more complex products, many of which required a significant level of customization, the plant's managers had to make a number of changes. The production lines were reengineered to allow employees to quickly switch components, software, and engineering diagrams among different products or models of a product. The plant's inventory system was restructured to allow the effective management of the more extensive range of parts being used in the new product lines. Workers were trained to perform a broader range of tasks. High levels of absenteeism and turnover have been an endemic problem in many Mexican companies, so the company remodeled the cafeteria and broadened the range of food offerings in order to enhance worker satisfaction. Management also established quarterly meetings with line employees to listen to complaints and solicit suggestions. Despite these efforts, the transformation of the company and its production and inventory processes still encountered a range of problems, and it took months to identify and overcome the myriad difficulties that arose.

In the end, though, the plant achieved a remarkable turnaround. Many of the plant's initial new orders were taken from a Jabil factory in Boise, Idaho, a modern 500-employee facility that had opened in 2000. Within four months of the changeover, the Guadalajara facility had surpassed the performance of the Boise plant on such measures as quality, cost, and on-time delivery. The spare-parts tracking software that it developed ended up being adopted as the standard for the company's worldwide operations. Jabil's efforts in Mexico ultimately led to the closure of the Idaho plant. The Guadalajara plant has expanded to nearly 4,000 employees and produces over 600 different types of products for its customers, including communications switches, specialized handheld credit card processing machines, Internet firewalls, and electronic controls for washing machines.

Despite this success, Jabil's managers in Guadalajara cannot become complacent. As Ernesto Sanchez said, "Right now we're able to do more complex products than China, although you may be sure they are coming up very quickly."

Source: David Luhnow, "As Jobs Move East, Plants in Mexico Retool to Compete," *The Wall Street Journal,* March 5, 2004, pp. A1, A8; Joel Millman, "The Outlook," *The Wall Street Journal,* February 23, 2004, p. A2; Andrew MacLellan, "Mexico Hangs Tough as Alternative to China," *EBN,* September 15, 2003, p. 1; William Atkinson, "Mexico or China? Lower Costs Tip Scales toward Far East," *Purchasing,* April 17, 2003, pp. 15–16; "Jabil Announces Plans for Mexico Expansion," December 4, 1998, www.jabil.com/390_601.asp (July 21, 2004); Jabil Circuit Inc., 2005 Annual Report, http://jbl.client.shareholder.com/downloads/2005Annual.pdf (July 12, 2006); and "Company Profile," www.jabil.com/about.asp (July 12, 2006).

3

Theories of International Trade and Investment

Santiago, Chile, skyline at dusk.

If a foreign country can supply us with a commodity cheaper than we ourselves can make it, better buy it of them with some part of our own industry, employed in a way in which we have some advantage.

—*Adam Smith, The Wealth of Nations*

Free-Market Reforms Revive Chile's Economy

Business managers must have a good knowledge of economic theory to be able to understand a nation's economic development strategy, which depends greatly on the beliefs and education of the government's economic planners. By closely following the actions and speeches of government leaders, managers often can discover the economic theories on which those actions and speeches are based. If they know the underlying theories, they can anticipate changes in government strategy and use that knowledge to their advantage. As an example, look at what happened in Chile after the changeover from the Marxist regime of Salvador Allende.

The economy was in a shambles after Allende's regime. Inflation was running over 1,000 percent annually, and the nation's debt load was totally unmanageable. The Allende government had been following the policy of many developing nations at that time—heavy involvement in the economy. This included placing high duties on imports to protect local industry, levying high income taxes on the private sector to obtain funds for government-directed investment, and granting huge subsidies to selected industries.

Realizing that drastic changes had to be made, the post-Allende government appointed a group of conservative Chilean economists to design a new program. Known as the "Chicago Boys" for having graduated from the University of Chicago, they were followers of the free-market teachings of its economics professor and Nobel Prize winner Milton Friedman.

The contents of the Chicago Boys' program and its impact on Chilean business did not surprise anyone with knowledge of economic theory. In fact, much of what they proposed was based on the theory of comparative advantage. Managers who understood the significance of the proposals knew that Chile soon would have a free-market economy that would require a massive restructuring of Chilean manufacturing plants.

One of the most important reforms recommended by the economists and put into effect by the government was the reduction of import duties from a high of 1,000 percent to a basic level of 10 percent. Moreover, all other import barriers were removed so that virtually anyone was free to import anything. As a result, manufacturers and growers were forced to compete in world markets to stay in business. In addition, the lower import duties reduced the cost of imported capital equipment, which encouraged business investment. What was the reaction of the managers who were prepared to change to the new system?

The president of Chile's largest appliance maker, whose industry had been protected from foreign competition by a 1,000 percent import duty, gave his opinion of the new program: "We used to have 5,000 workers and an annual productivity of only $9,000 per worker. Now we have 1,860 workers and a productivity of $43,000 per worker, and we are finally showing a profit."

It was no surprise to those with knowledge of economics that there would be a contraction of local industry when companies lost their protection from imports. Although the leading appliance maker mentioned above was able to compete after losing its import protection, a number of other local appliance makers were forced to go out of business or contract their operations. "We're going to lose a large part of our appliance industry," conceded Alvaro Bardon, a 37-year-old Chicago Boy who was then the head of the central bank of Chile, "and also our electronics industry

CONCEPT PREVIEWS

After reading this chapter, you should be able to:

explain the theories that attempt to explain why certain goods are traded internationally

discuss the arguments for imposing trade restrictions

explain the two basic kinds of import restrictions: tariff and nontariff trade barriers

appreciate the relevance of the changing status of tariff and nontariff barriers to managers

explain some of the theories of foreign direct investment

and our automobile assembly plants." Bardon was hardly disappointed, however. "Those are products we should be importing," he said. "We have other things based on our farm products, our timberlands, our fisheries, and our mineral resources that we should be making because they give us a natural advantage over other countries."

How successful were these free-market policies adopted by Chile's government? Growth in real GDP averaged 8 percent during 1991–1997. Although tight monetary policies associated with a global financial crisis, accompanied by a severe drought, caused growth to decline in 1998 and 1999, Chile maintained its free-market policies and the confidence of the international markets. Recovery began by the end of 1999, and growth had accelerated to over 6 percent by 2006, while still maintaining a low inflation rate. Chile has subsequently signed free trade agreements with several nations or regions, including the European Union, Mercosur, the United States, Canada, Korea, Peru, Venezuela, Bolivia,

Columbia, Ecuador, China, and Mexico. The total stock of foreign direct investment in Chile exceeds $55 billion. The *Country Commercial Guide (CCG)* prepared by the combined efforts of various U.S. government agencies reported, "Chile is one of the Latin American region's most dynamic and promising markets. . . . Market-led reforms adopted close to 30 years ago and an increasingly diversified economy with strong ties to buyers and suppliers in the Americas, Europe, and Asia have given Chile a wide range of options for further growth. Prudent economic policy-making has secured long-term stability unknown elsewhere in Latin America." ■

Source: *World Development Indicators 2006* (Washington, DC: World Bank, 2006); *2006 CIA World Factbook*, www.cia.gov/cia/publications/factbook/geos/ci.html (July 7, 2006); UNCTAD, "Chile," *World Investment Report 2005*, www.unctad.org/templates/Page.asp?intItemID=2441&lang=1 (July 7, 2006); Dennis R. Appleyard, Alfred J. Field, Jr., and Steven L. Cobb, *International Economics*, 5th ed. (New York: McGraw-Hill Irwin, 2006); "Why Chile's Economy Roared While the World's Slumbered," *The Wall Street Journal*, January 22, 1993, p. A11; and *Doing Business in Chile—Country Commercial Guide* (Santiago, Chile: U.S. Commercial Service, 2004), www.buyusa.gov/chile/en/doing_business_in_chile.html (July 7, 2006).

The economic program that the Chilean economists put into effect is a practical application of the keystone of international trade theory—the law of comparative advantage. Note the education of the head of Chile's central bank. Economists are commonly found in governments as policy makers and advisers to government leaders worldwide. When they have a particularly strong influence in government affairs, they are frequently dubbed with such pejorative names as the "Chicago Boys" in Chile, "tecnicos" in Mexico, and the "Berkeley Mafia" (economists educated at the University of California–Berkeley) in Indonesia.

What is the significance for international managers? For one thing, since they frequently will be dealing with government officials trained in economics, managers must be prepared to speak their language. When presenting plans requiring governmental approval, managers must take care that the plans are economically sound, for they are almost certain to be studied by economists and will often need to be approved by them. Marketers proposing large projects to government planners must be aware that the key determinant now is economic efficiency rather than mere financial soundness.[1] Moreover, as you have seen in the case of Chile, knowledge of economic concepts, especially in the areas of (1) international trade, (2) economic development, and (3) foreign direct investment, frequently provide insights into future government action.

mercantilism

An economic philosophy based on the belief that (1) a nation's wealth depends on accumulated treasure, usually gold, and (2) to increase wealth, government policies should promote exports and discourage imports

International Trade Theory

Why do nations trade? This question and the equally important proposition of predicting the direction, composition, and volume of goods traded are what international trade theory attempts to address. Interestingly, as is the case with numerous economic writings, the first formulation of international trade theory was politically motivated. Adam Smith, incensed by government intervention and control over both domestic and foreign trade, published *An Inquiry into the Nature and Causes of the Wealth of Nations* (1776), in which he tried to destroy the mercantilist philosophy.

MERCANTILISM

Mercantilism, the economic philosophy Smith attacked, evolved in Europe between the 16th and 18th centuries. A complex political and economic arrangement, mercantilism traditionally has been interpreted as viewing the accumulation of precious metals as an activity essential to a nation's welfare. These metals were, in the mercantilists' view, the only source of wealth. Because England had no mines, the mercantilists looked to international trade to supply gold and silver. The government established economic policies that promoted exports and stifled imports, resulting in a trade surplus to be paid for in gold and silver. Import restrictions such as import duties reduced imports, while government subsidies to exporters increased exports. Those acts created a trade surplus, in addition to protecting jobs within the mercantilist nation. Of course, another outcome of mercantilism was the generation of benefits for certain economic groups, such as domestic merchants, artisans, and shippers, albeit at a cost to other groups such as consumers and emerging industrialists.

Although the mercantilist era ended in the late 1700s, its arguments live on. Many people still argue that exports are "good" for a person's country since they create jobs, while imports are "bad" because they transfer jobs from a person's country to other nations. This view essentially sees trade as a zero-sum activity, where one party must lose in order for another to gain. Similarly, a "favorable" trade balance still means that a nation exports more goods and services than it imports. In balance-of-payments accounting, an export that brings dollars to the country is called *positive*, but imports that cause dollar outflow are labeled *negative*.

In the United States, many managers believe that Japan, because of its protectionism, remains largely a nearly impenetrable market—a present-day "fortress of mercantilism." American managers are concerned that Japan's barriers to their imports are the result of Japanese insularity, traditional preoccupation with self-sufficiency, and "us against them" mentality. A U.S. secretary of commerce once said, "They tell us they have to protect their markets because of their culture. They haven't joined the world yet." Comments from the Japanese seem to confirm what some Americans are saying. "The public is not in favor of perfect markets," says a Japanese bank manager. "We would like to preserve the substance of our culture. If we move to free trade, we may lose Japanese virtue in the process."[2] One part of this mercantilist effort is Japan's continuing effort to maintain a cheap yen in order to capture attractive export markets while reducing the threat of imports. For example, the Bank of Japan spent 15 trillion yen in the first three months of 2004 to push the yen down against the U.S. dollar. As G. Richard Wagoner, Jr., chairman of General Motors, said, the Japanese "are keeping their currency artificially weak against the dollar and euro and really reducing the competitive position" of U.S. and European companies.[3] A similar neo-mercantilist argument has recently been made regarding China's approach to valuing their currency.

> *Despite impressive economic growth and burgeoning trade surpluses, Chinese authorities have resisted efforts to revalue their currency, instead continuing to hold their currency, the yuan, within a tight trading range relative to the U.S. dollar. By not allowing the yuan to appreciate in value relative to the dollar, the Chinese authorities were accused of engaging in mercantilist behavior because they were helping the international cost-competitiveness of Chinese companies relative to companies from the U.S. and other nations.*

THEORY OF ABSOLUTE ADVANTAGE

Adam Smith argued against mercantilism by claiming that market forces, not government controls, should determine the direction, volume, and composition of international trade. He argued that under free, unregulated trade, each nation should specialize in producing those goods it could produce most efficiently (for which it had an **absolute advantage,** either natural or acquired). Some of these goods would be exported to pay for imports of goods that could be produced more efficiently elsewhere. Smith showed by his example of absolute advantage that both nations would gain from trade.

An Example   Assume that a world of two countries and two products has perfect competition and no transportation costs. Suppose that in the United States and China (1) one unit of input (combination of land, labor, and capital) can produce the quantities of soybeans and cloth listed below, (2) each nation has two input units it can use to produce either soybeans or cloth, and (3) each country uses one unit of input to produce each product. If

absolute advantage
Theory that a nation has absolute advantage when it can produce a larger amount of a good or service for the same amount of inputs as can another country or when it can produce the same amount of a good or service using fewer inputs than could another country

Successful international business professionals look beyond their home country borders and continually explore and learn more about the world in which they live and work. Can you answer these questions?

- Where is East Timor?
- What do you do with souvlaki and tzaziki? Where do they come from?
- How many time zones are in the world?
- On the globe, where does East become West?
- What is the International Date Line? Where is it?
- What is the largest country in the world? The smallest country?

To become a successful international business professional, you must become a "citizen of the world." To be a citizen of the world requires that you know about the world. The international business professional knows world facts and data and keeps current with world events that will impact his or her ability to successfully engage in global business transactions.

World Fact: The U.S. State Department recognizes 192 independent nations in the world. If Taiwan were recognized, the number would be 193. However, numerous territories and colonies under the governmental control of other countries are thought to be independent countries. Some of these are Bermuda, Greenland, Puerto Rico, and Western Sahara. England, Scotland, Wales, and Northern Ireland are part of the United Kingdom.

Culture Cue: In dealing with your foreign counterparts, listen as much as you speak. Feel free to talk about your home country, but also ask the people you are meeting to tell you about their country, their customs, and their way of life. This type of conversation helps you to learn more about their part of the world and it builds rapport. In many parts of the world, rapport and friendship must first be established before business will ever be discussed. This is a critical first step to doing business in much of Latin America, the Middle East, and Asia, for example.

World Wide Resources:

www.cia.gov/cia/publications/factbook

A link to English language newspapers from around the world listed by country:

www.unc.edu/world/Global%20Updates%202006/May_June/May06.htm

---

neither country imports or exports, the quantities shown in the table are also those that are available for local consumption. The total output of both nations is 4 tons of soybeans and 6 bolts of cloth.

Commodity	United States	China	Total
Tons of soybeans	3	1	4
Bolts of cloth	2	4	6

In the United States, 3 tons of soybeans or 2 bolts of cloth can be produced with one unit of output. Therefore, 3 tons of soybeans should have the same price as 2 bolts of cloth. In China, however, since only 1 ton of soybeans can be produced with the input unit that can produce 4 bolts of cloth, 1 ton of soybeans should cost as much as 4 bolts of cloth.

The United States has an absolute advantage in soybean production (3 to 1). China's absolute advantage is in cloth making (4 to 2). Will anyone anywhere give the Chinese cloth maker more than 1 ton of soybeans for 4 bolts of cloth? According to the example, all American soybean producers should because they can get only 2 bolts of cloth for 3 tons of soybeans at home. Similarly, Chinese cloth makers, once they learn that they can obtain more than 1 ton of soybeans for every 4 bolts of cloth in the United States, will be eager to trade Chinese cloth for American soybeans.

Each Country Specializes

Suppose each nation decides to use its resources to produce only the product at which it is more efficient. The following table shows each nation's output. Note that with the same quantity of input units, the total output is now greater.

Commodity	United States	China	Total
Tons of soybeans	6	0	6
Bolts of cloth	0	8	8

Terms of Trade (Ratio of International Prices)   With specialization, now the total production of both goods is greater, but to consume both products, the two countries must trade some of their surplus. What are the limits within which both countries are willing to trade? Clearly, the Chinese cloth makers will trade some of their cloth for soybeans if they can get more than the 1 ton of soybeans that they get for 4 bolts of cloth in China. Likewise, the American soybean growers will trade their soybeans for Chinese cloth if they get a bolt of cloth for less than the 1.5 tons of soybeans it costs them in the United States.

If the two nations take the midpoint of the two trading limits so that each shares equally in the benefits of trade, they will agree to swap 1.33 bolts of cloth for 1 ton of soybeans. Both will gain from specialization because each now has the following quantities:

Commodity	United States	China	Total
Tons of soybeans	3	3	6
Bolts of cloth	4	4	8

Gains from Specialization and Trade   Because each nation specialized in producing the product at which it was more efficient and then traded its surplus for goods that it could not produce as efficiently, both gained the following:

Commodity	United States	China
Tons of soybeans		2
Bolts of cloth	2	

Certainly, both nations have gained by trading.

Although Adam Smith's logic helped to convince many governments to dismantle trade barriers and encourage increased international trade, it failed to calm concerns of those whose countries lacked any absolute advantage. What if one country has an absolute advantage in the production of both soybeans and cloth? Will there still be a basis for trade?

THEORY OF COMPARATIVE ADVANTAGE

David Ricardo demonstrated in 1817 that even though one nation held an absolute advantage over another in the production of each of two different goods, international trade could still create benefit for each country (thus representing a positive-sum game, or one in which both countries "win" from engaging in trade). The only limitation to such benefit-creating trade is that the less efficient nation cannot be *equally* less efficient in the production of both goods.[4] To illustrate how this can occur, let us slightly change our first example so that now China has an absolute advantage in producing *both* soybeans and cloth. Note that compared to China, the United States is less inefficient in producing soybeans than in manufacturing cloth. Therefore, it has a relative advantage, or **comparative advantage,** according to Ricardo, in producing soybeans.

comparative advantage
Theory that a nation having absolute disadvantages in the production of two goods with respect to another nation has a comparative or relative advantage in the production of the good in which its absolute disadvantage is less

Commodity	United States	China	Total
Tons of soybeans	4	5	9
Bolts of cloth	2	5	7

Each Country Specializes   If each country specializes in what it does best, its output will be as follows:

Commodity	United States	China	Total
Tons of soybeans	8	0	8
Bolts of cloth	0	10	10

Terms of Trade   In this case, the terms of trade will be somewhere between the 1 ton of soybeans for 1 bolt of cloth that Chinese soybean growers must pay in China and the $\frac{1}{2}$ bolt of cloth that American cloth makers must pay for 1 ton of American soybeans. Although the theory of comparative advantage did not address the ratios of exchange, it did state that the range of advantageous trade for both parties lies between the pre-trade price ratios.

Let us assume that the traders agree on an exchange rate of $\frac{3}{4}$ bolt of cloth for 1 ton of soybeans. Both will gain from this exchange and specialization, as the following table shows:

Commodity	United States	China
Tons of soybeans	4	4
Bolts of cloth	3	7

Note that this trade left China with 2 surplus bolts of cloth and 1 less ton of soybeans than it had before. America has the same quantity of soybeans and 1 more bolt of cloth. However, the Chinese cloth manufacturers should be able to trade 1 bolt of surplus cloth for at least 1 ton of soybeans elsewhere. Then the final result will be as follows:

Commodity	United States	China
Tons of soybeans	4	5
Bolts of cloth	3	6

Gains from Specialization and Trade   Gains from specialization and trade in this case are the following:

Commodity	United States	China
Tons of soybeans		
Bolts of cloth	1	1

Production Possibility Frontiers   We can also illustrate the gains from trade graphically, using production possibility frontiers. Figure 3.1 graphs the Chinese and U.S. production possibility frontiers using constant costs for simplicity. These curves, in the absence of trade, also illustrate the possible combinations of goods for consumption. Before trade, China might be producing and consuming 5 tons of soybeans and 5 bolts of cloth (point A), while the United States is producing and consuming 4 tons of soybeans and 2 bolts of cloth (point A).

FIGURE 3.1

Production and Consumption Possibility Frontiers before and after Trade

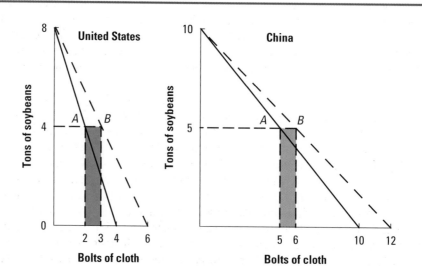

With each nation specializing in the production of the goods in which it has a comparative advantage and trading its surplus with the other, both nations are able to consume at point *B*. The shaded areas under each curve indicate the gains from trade.

This simple concept of comparative advantage serves as a basis for international trade, even when one nation has an advantage over another in the production of each of the goods being traded.

Note that in our examples we mentioned a unit of input. This is a more modern version of the examples of Ricardo and Smith, who used only labor input. They did so because at that time only labor was considered important in calculating production costs.[5] Also, no consideration was given to the possibility of producing the same goods with different combinations of factors, and no explanation was given as to why production costs differed. Not until 1933 did Bertil Ohlin, a Swedish economist building on work presented in 1919 by his Swedish economics professor, Eli Heckscher, develop the theory of factor endowment.[6]

HECKSCHER-OHLIN THEORY OF FACTOR ENDOWMENT

The Heckscher-Ohlin theory of **factor endowment** states that international and interregional differences in production costs occur because of differences in the supply of production factors. The goods that require a large amount of a nation's abundant—thus less costly—factor will have lower production costs, enabling those goods to be sold for less in international markets. For example, India, relatively well endowed with labor compared to Germany, ought to concentrate on producing labor-intensive goods; Germany, with relatively more capital than labor, should specialize in capital-intensive products. When these countries trade, each will obtain at a lower price those goods that require large amounts of the production factor that is relatively scarce in their own country, and both will benefit from the transaction.

How useful is this theory for explaining present-day trading patterns? In general, trade patterns correspond fairly well with the Heckscher-Ohlin theory. Countries with relatively large amounts of land (such as Australia) do export land-intensive products (such as grain and cattle), whereas countries with relatively large populations (such as Indonesia and Bangladesh) export labor-intensive goods.[7] There are exceptions, however, due in part to Ohlin's assumptions. One assumption was that the prices of the factors depend only on the factor endowment. We know this is untrue. Factor prices are not set in a perfect market. For example, legislated minimum wages and benefits can force the cost of labor to rise to a point greater than the value of the product that many workers can produce. Investment tax credits can reduce the cost of capital below market cost, and so forth. As a result, factor prices do not fully reflect factor supply.

Ohlin also assumed that a given technology is universally available, but this is not so. There is always a lag between the introduction of a new production method and its application worldwide. As a result, superior technology often permits a nation to produce goods at a cost lower than that of a country better endowed with the required factor. A closely related assumption was that a given product is either labor- or capital-intensive. Yet observation of construction methods in, for example, a less developed nation would show that wet concrete can be poured either by a gang of laborers with buckets or by a crane and its operator.

factor endowment
Heckscher-Ohlin theory that countries export products requiring large amounts of their abundant production factors and import products requiring large amounts of their scarce production factors

Leontief Paradox   A study made in 1953 by the economist Wassily Leontief disputed the usefulness of the Heckscher-Ohlin theory as a predictor of the direction of trade. The study, known as the *Leontief paradox*, found that the United States, one of the most capital-intensive countries in the world, was exporting relatively labor-intensive products in exchange for relatively capital-intensive products. Economists have speculated that this occurred because the United States exports technology-intensive products produced by highly skilled labor requiring a large capital investment to educate and train and at the same time imports goods made with mature technology requiring capital-intensive mass-production processes operated by unskilled labor. A study by the Harvard economists Sachs and Shatz did in fact show that the United States has increased its exports of skill-intensive goods to developing nations while reducing its production of unskilled goods.[8] Another possible explanation

Comparative Advantage and Offshoring of Service Jobs to India

Wipro employees in Bangalore, India, undergo training in the use of specialized software to provide services to overseas clients.

India, a nation with approximately 1 billion people, has relatively few other resources compared to developed nations. Therefore, it should have a comparative advantage in production of goods or services that require large amounts of labor and relatively little capital. However, India has an additional comparative advantage since many of its citizens speak English (which is taught in many Indian schools and universities rather than using one of the other 18 major languages and 844 dialects spoken in the country). Thus labor has a relatively low price due to the large Indian work force (about 450 million, with nearly 10 million additional people entering the work force each year) and high levels of unemployment or underemployment (officially an unemployment rate of 8 percent, but a poverty rate that exceeds 20 percent). As Internet and cellular telephone communications continue to become less expensive, India increasingly is using its English-speaking pool of labor to export services—such as software engineering, customer service, telemarketing, reviews of credit or mortgage applications, analysis of blood tests and other medical services, and claims processing—to foreign companies and their customers, a process known as *offshoring*.

In 2005, the Indian IT industry generated revenues of $36 billion, nearly 5 percent of India's GDP, and exports of $60 billion are projected by 2010. Fortune 500 companies such as Amazon.com, International Business Machines, and American Express, as well as a range of more moderate-size firms, have already offshored millions of jobs. Gartner, the IT consultancy, estimated that up to 25 percent of traditional IT jobs will be offshored to developing countries by 2010. By 2015, it has been estimated that 3.4 million U.S. jobs, representing $136 billion in wages, will have been offshored, and India is well positioned to capture much of this business. According to Noshir Kaka of the consulting firm McKinsey, "This industry can do for India what automobiles did for Japan and oil for Saudi Arabia."

For example, over 250,000 U.S. individual and corporate tax returns were prepared in India in 2005, an increase from only about 20,000 in 2002, and these numbers are predicted to surge dramatically in subsequent years. Documents obtained from taxpayers are scanned and shipped electronically to India, where forms are completed and sent back to the United States to be examined, approved, and signed by an American accountant. While a U.S. tax preparer might cost $3,000 per month during the peak tax season, a comparable Indian worker might cost less than $300. There is no requirement that the taxpayer be informed that the tax work is done abroad, and most accounting firms charge the same fees as those charged if the job is done by accountants in the United States, thus helping to boost profitability.

Companies in financial services and insurance have also been actively pursuing offshoring. Over 80 percent of global financial services companies have an offshore facility. The international insurance giant Aviva, for example, expects to have 7,800 of its 59,000-person work force offshored by late 2007, primarily to India, and the range of services being

for this apparent paradox in trade patterns is that many products may be produced by either capital- or labor-intensive processes, as was noted in the previous paragraph. The international structure of barriers to trade could also partially explain Leontief's result. An important outcome of Leontief's work was recognizing the potential for differences in, for example, the kinds of labor (e.g., some labor is skilled, other labor is largely unskilled, and the potential productivity of these two groups can be quite different), as well as differences in natural and capital resources, and these factors can help to explain the level and direction of trade.[9]

offshored is rapidly being broadened, including IT, accounting, and claims processing. "Offshoring has released a new competitive dynamic. Larger firms are driving change across the financial services industry and using offshoring to open up a competitive advantage over their smaller rivals," said Chris Gentle of the professional services firm Deloitte. "Offshoring is fundamentally changing the way financial institutions do business, creating a global division of labor that demands new operating models, new structures and new management skills."

"This is a global industry in the throes of flux. It is a sector where [Indian companies] are rewriting the rules of the game. That is the difference that has become apparent and increasingly accepted," says Nandan Nilekani, CEO of the rapidly expanding Indian company Infosys Technologies. The basis for this change, he says, is the "global delivery model" being pioneered in India and replicated in other low-cost nations. In the IT sector, for example, a plentiful supply of Indian software engineers can work on projects "offshore," delivering the finished product to clients "on-site" in the United States. "Our business innovation is forcing rivals to redesign the way they do things."

This disruptive change is threatening to transform the business models in operation across a broad range of industries. Although many people think of low-skill jobs like telemarketing and call centers when they think of outsourcing to India, the sophistication and skill levels associated with processes being outsourced are rising rapidly. A big driver for this trend is the wealth of qualified personnel in India. A NASSCOM-McKinsey study found that India has 28 percent of the overall supply of skilled services personnel in low-cost nations, and these potential employees remain amazingly inexpensive. According to the Boston Consulting Group, an Indian IT engineer earns a typical annual salary of $5,000 and one with a master's degree in business earns $7,500—about one-tenth the level of their American counterparts.

Services represent 60 percent of the U.S. economy and employ about two-thirds of American workers, so it is not surprising that the offshoring of service jobs has generated concerns across a broad spectrum of society. John Steadman, president of the Institute of Electrical and Electronics Engineers, cautioned, "If we continue to offshore high-skilled professional jobs, the U.S. risks surrendering its leading role in innovation." Andrew Grove, CEO of Intel Corp., warned that "it's a very valid question" whether the United States could lose its dominance in information technology as a result of this trend, as it did in electronics manufacturing. Responding to the outsourcing to an Indian firm of calls from New Jersey welfare recipients about their benefits, state senator Shirley Turner said, "I was outraged. Here we are in New Jersey, as we are in every state, requiring welfare recipients to go to work. And yet, we were

sending these jobs overseas ... so that corporations can make more money." She noted that unemployed people do not pay taxes, and the loss of these tax revenues exacerbates budget deficits. Ironically, widespread publicity regarding concerns about offshoring may have hastened the trend by making more companies aware of the possible cost savings from such undertakings.

On the other hand, some have argued that offshoring will help to strengthen American industry and the economy as a whole. Outsourcing is not necessarily a zero-sum game, where one Indian worker substitutes for one American worker. When American firms hire lower-cost labor abroad, they often must hire other workers to complement the increased level of foreign labor. Overseas expansion can also cause companies to modify the scope of activities undertaken in the United States, placing increasing emphasis on higher-value-added activities rather than the lower-skill positions that have been offshored. Shifting work to lower-cost locations abroad has the potential to lower prices in the United States, thus raising the purchasing power of American consumers, enhancing consumer spending and economic activity, and thereby creating more jobs. As *The Wall Street Journal* editorialized, "The world economy is a dynamic enterprise. Jobs created overseas generate jobs at home. Not just more jobs for Americans, but higher-skilled and better paying ones. At the same time, trade offers consumers a greater quantity and variety of goods and services for lower prices. David Ricardo lives."

By companies' exploiting India's comparative advantage in providing English-speaking personnel for labor-intensive service activities, you may increasingly discover that you are discussing your charge card billing statement or online purchase with, or receiving assistance to fix your malfunctioning computer from, a service person who is located in India, not your own country.

Sources: Meg Fletcher, "Moving Services Offshore," *Business Insurance*, June 2006, pp. 16–17; Joanna Slater, "In India, a Job Paradox," *The Wall Street Journal*, May 5, 2004, p. A12; Julie Gallagher, "Redefining the Business Case for Offshore Outsourcing," *Insurance & Technology*, April 2002, pp. A5, A8–A9; Khozem Merchant, "The Future on India's Shores," *Financial Times*, April 21, 2004, p. 8; "Outsourcing 101," *The Wall Street Journal*, May 27, 2004, p. A20; Rebecca Paley, "Fighting for the Down and Out(sourced)," *Mother Jones*, May/June 2004, pp. 20–21; Paul Taylor, "Outsourcing of IT Jobs Predicted to Continue," *Financial Times*, March 17, 2004, p. 6; Manjeet Kripalani and Pete Engardio, "The Rise of India," *BusinessWeek*, December 8, 2003, pp. 66–76; Robert Orr, "Offshoring Opens Gap in Financial Services Race," *Financial Times*, June 29, 2004, p. 9; and Richard D. Brody, Mary J. Miller, and Michael J. Rolleri, "Outsourcing Income Tax Returns to India: Legal, Ethical, and Professional Issues," *CPA Journal*, www.nysscpa.org/cpajournal/2004/1204/perspectives/p12.htm (July 10, 2006).

Differences in Taste   Heckscher-Ohlin also ignored transportation costs, but there are goods for which freight charges are so high that the landed cost (export sales price plus transportation charges) is greater than the cost of a locally made product. In that case, there will be little trade. Why not say there will be no trade? It is because of a demand-side construct that is always difficult to deal with in economic theory and that we have so far neglected—*differences in taste*. Managers, however, cannot neglect this difference, which enables trade to flow in a direction completely contrary to that predicted by the theory of comparative advantage—from high- to low-cost nations. France sells wine, cosmetics, clothing, and even drinking water to the United States, all of which are produced in America and generally sold at lower prices. Germany and Italy send Porsches and Maseratis to America, even though the United States is one of the largest automobile producers in the world. Americans buy these goods not only on the basis of price, the implied independent variable in the trade theory we have been examining, but also because of taste preferences. Differences in cultures, climates, income levels, and population structures can produce diversity in preferences, and thus influence trade patterns.

We have presented the theory of comparative advantage without mentioning money; however, a nation's comparative advantage can be affected by differences between the costs of production factors in that country's currency and their costs in other currencies. As we shall see in the next section, money can change the direction of trade.

HOW MONEY CAN CHANGE THE DIRECTION OF TRADE

Suppose the total cost of land, labor, and capital to produce the daily output of soybeans or cloth in the example on absolute advantage is $10,000 in the United States and 80,000 yuan in China. The cost per unit is as follows:

Commodity	Price per Unit	
	United States	China
Ton of soybeans	$10,000/3 = $3,333/ton	80,000 yuan/1 = 80,000 yuan/ton
Bolt of cloth	$10,000/2 = $5,000/bolt	80,000 yuan/4 = 20,000 yuan/bolt

To determine whether it is more advantageous to buy locally or to import, the traders need to know the prices in their own currencies. To convert from foreign to domestic currency, they use the *exchange rate*.

exchange rate
The price of one currency stated in terms of another currency

Exchange Rate The **exchange rate** is the price of one currency stated in terms of the other. If the prevailing rate is $1 = 8 yuan, then 1 yuan must be worth 0.125 dollar.* Using the exchange rate of $1 = 8 yuan, the prices in the preceding example appear to the U.S. trader as follows:

Commodity	Price per Unit (dollars)	
	United States	China
Ton of soybeans	$3,333	$10,000
Bolt of cloth	$5,000	$2,500

The American soybean producers can earn $6,667 more per ton by exporting soybeans to China than they can by selling locally,† but can the Chinese cloth makers gain by exporting to the United States? To find out, they must convert the American prices to Chinese yuan.

Commodity	Price per Unit (yuan)	
	United States	China
Ton of soybeans	26,664 yuan	80,000 yuan
Bolt of cloth	40,000 yuan	20,000 yuan

*If $1 = 8 yuan, to find the value of 1 yuan in dollars, divide both sides of the equation by 8. Then 1 yuan = 1/8 = $0.125.
†For example, to calculate this figure, you would multiply the American price of $3,333 per ton of soybeans times 8 yuan per dollar, yielding a price of 26,664 yuan per ton.

It is apparent that the Chinese cloth makers will export cloth to the United States because they can sell at the higher price of 40,000 yuan per bolt. The American cloth makers, however, will need some very strong sales arguments to sell in the United States if they are to overcome the $2,500 price differential. Ricardo did not consider this possibility; in his time, products were considered homogeneous and therefore were sold primarily on the basis of price.

Influence of Exchange Rate   Soybeans to China and cloth to the United States will be the direction of trade as long as the exchange rate remains around $1 = 8 yuan. But if the dollar strengthens to $1 = 24 yuan, American soybeans will cost as much in yuan as do Chinese soybeans, and importation will cease. On the other hand, should the dollar weaken to $1 = 4 yuan, then 1 bolt of Chinese cloth will cost $5,000 to American traders, and they will have little reason to import.

On December 4, 2005, the euro traded at a rate of 1.1720 per U.S. dollar. By June 6, 2006, the euro had decreased in value by more than 10 percent, reaching a rate of 1.2923 per dollar. American companies were pressured to decrease the dollar prices of their exports to Europe in order to maintain their market share. The following example demonstrates the impact of the euro's depreciation on the euro prices of American imports into Europe.

Suppose Boeing wanted $150 million for one of its 787 Dreamliner jet aircraft in December 2006. At an exchange rate of 1.1720 euros = $1, the company would have had to charge 175.8 million euros for its aircraft. To get $150 million for the aircraft in June 2006, with the exchange rate of 1.2923 euros = $1, Boeing would have had to charge over 193.8 million euros, or an additional 18 million euros. This change could place Boeing at some disadvantage versus a Europe-based competitor such as Airbus when trying to sell aircraft to price-sensitive airline companies in Europe.

Another way a nation can attempt to regain competitiveness in world markets is through **currency devaluation** (lowering its price in terms of other currencies). Note that in many but by no means all cases, this action can leave domestic prices largely unchanged.

currency devaluation
The lowering of a currency's price in terms of other currencies

To fight rampant inflation, the government of Argentina decided to set a fixed exchange rate of 1 peso to 1 U.S. dollar. Although the dollar peg succeeded in bringing financial stability to the country, it also made Argentina one of the world's most expensive economies for doing business. Many also blamed the peg for a recession that had dragged on since 1998 and had resulted in high unemployment. Although average wages were $600 per month, many prices were similar to those in Europe. Popular unrest led to widespread rioting, and the Argentine president resigned from office. In January 2002, three days after taking office, Argentina's interim government abandoned the decade-old fixed exchange rate policy. Almost immediately, the peso experienced a dramatic and sudden devaluation, declining from $1 to only 27 cents within five months. Imports became expensive, and exporting became attractive. Within a year of devaluation, exports had grown from 2 to 7 percent of national output. Increased domestic investment and production replaced imports. Unemployment was cut in half, to 13 percent. Gross domestic product increased 38 percent in three years.

SOME NEWER EXPLANATIONS FOR THE DIRECTION OF TRADE

The international trade theory we have been discussing was essentially the only theoretical explanation of trade available to us until the second half of the 20th century. Since that time, however, several other possible explanations for international trade have been developed.

The Linder Theory of Overlapping Demand   Another Swedish economist, Stefan Linder, recognized that the supply-oriented Heckscher-Ohlin theory, which depended on factor endowments, was adequate to explain international trade in primary products. However, he believed that another explanation was needed for trade in manufactured goods. In its purest form, the Heckscher-Ohlin theory would expect developed countries to be more likely to trade with developing countries, which have very different factor endowments, rather than with other developed countries that would have similar factor endowments. In contrast,

Linder's demand-oriented theory stated that customers' tastes are strongly affected by income levels, and therefore a nation's income per capita level determines the kinds of goods they will demand. Because an entrepreneur will produce goods to meet this demand, the kinds of products manufactured reflect the country's level of income per capita. Goods produced for domestic consumption will eventually be exported, due to similarity of income levels and therefore demand in other countries.

The Linder theory thus deduces that international trade in manufactured goods will be greater between nations with similar levels of per capita income than between those with dissimilar levels of per capita income, the very situation observed in Chapter 2 during our review of trade data. Even though two developed countries may have similar factor endowments, which under the Heckscher-Ohlin theory would result in limited trade between them, these nations still can have a large volume of trade with each other. The goods that will be traded are those for which there is an *overlapping demand* (consumers in both countries are demanding the same good).[10] For example, if a Finnish company such as Nokia invents a sophisticated cell phone with advanced features for its home market, the best export opportunities for this phone will be in other advanced nations such as the United States, Japan, and Western European countries, even if these countries have their own domestic producers of cell phones. Note that the Linder model differs from the model of comparative advantage in that it does not specify in which direction a given good will go. In fact, Linder specified that a good may go in either direction. You recognize, of course, that this intraindustry trade occurs because of *product differentiation*; for example, Motorola exports its cell phones to Sweden and Japan and Sony-Ericsson exports its cell phones to the United States, because consumers in both countries perceive a difference in the brands.

International Product Life Cycle   The hypothesis of an *international product life cycle* was formulated by Raymond Vernon in the 1960s.[11] This concept, which concerns the role of innovation in trade patterns, views a product as going through a full life cycle from the internationalization stage to standardization. The initial innovation stage of the cycle borrows from the Linder theory in terms of the motivations and response of entrepreneurs to perceived market opportunities. The subsequent three stages through which a product is said to pass are illustrated in Figure 3.2 and described below. This concept can be applied to new product introduction by firms in any of the industrialized nations, but because more new products have been successfully introduced on a commercial scale in the United States, let us examine the **international product life cycle (IPLC)** as it applies to this country.

international product life cycle (IPLC)

A theory explaining why a product that begins as a nation's export eventually becomes its import

---

FIGURE 3.2

International Product Life Cycle

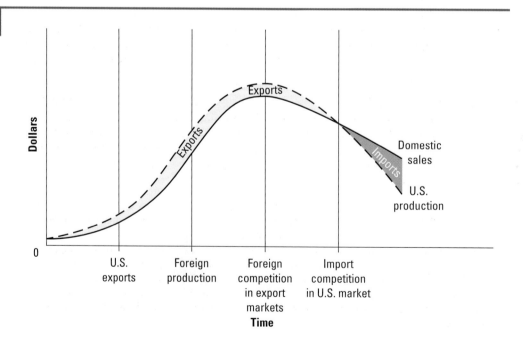

1. *U.S. exports:* Because the United States possesses the largest population of high-income consumers of any country in the world, competition for their patronage is intense. Manufacturers are therefore forced to search constantly for better ways to satisfy their customers' needs. To provide new products, companies maintain large research and development laboratories, which must be in constant contact with suppliers of the materials they need for product development. The fact that their suppliers are also in this country facilitates the contact.[12] In the early stages of the product life cycle, the design and the production methods are changing. By being close to the market, management can react quickly to customer feedback and more easily provide local repair services. These factors combine to make the United States a leader in new product introduction. For a while, American firms will be the only manufacturers of the product; overseas customers, as they learn of the product, will therefore have to buy from American firms. The export market develops.

2. *Foreign production begins:* Overseas consumers, especially those in developed nations, have similar needs and the ability to purchase the product. Export volume grows and becomes large enough to support local production. The technology for producing the good has become fairly stable, and if the innovator is a multinational firm, it will be sending its subsidiaries new product information with complete details on how to produce it. Where there are no affiliates, foreign managers, as they learn of the product, will obtain licenses for its production. Foreign production will begin, which also provides advantages of reduced costs for transportation and local communication. The American firm will still be exporting to those markets where there is no production, but its export growth will diminish as licensing and foreign direct investment substitutes for exports as a source of supply to various international markets.

3. *Foreign competition in export markets:* Later, as early foreign manufacturers gain experience in marketing and production, their costs will fall. Saturation of their local markets will cause them to look for buyers elsewhere. They may even be able to undersell the American producers if they enjoy an advantage such as lower labor or raw material costs. In this stage, foreign firms are competing in export markets, and as a result, American export sales will continue to decline. By this stage, the innovating American firms may have developed newer versions of the product and begun scaling back production of the original product in order to begin focusing instead on the newer innovations.

4. *Import competition in the United States:* If domestic and export sales enable foreign producers to attain the economies of scale enjoyed by the American firm, they may reach a point where they can compete in quality and undersell American firms in the American market. From that point on, the U.S. market will be served exclusively (or nearly so) by imports. Televisions, footwear, and DRAM (dynamic random access memory) semiconductor chips are examples of such products.

Authors discussing the IPLC concept have claimed that this cycle may be repeated as the less developed countries (LDCs) with still lower labor costs obtain the technology and thus acquire a cost advantage over the more industrialized nations. Although little research has been done to substantiate the IPLC concept, a World Bank study seems to provide a plausible reason for these changes in production locations, as suggested in the following excerpt:

> *With countries progressing on the comparative advantage scale, their exports can supplement the exports of countries that graduate to a higher level. . . . A case in point is Japan, whose comparative advantage has shifted towards highly capital-intensive exports. In turn, developing countries with a relatively high human capital endowment . . . can take Japan's place in exporting relatively human capital–intensive products, and countries with a relatively high physical capital endowment, such as Brazil and Mexico, can take Japan's place in exporting relatively physical capital–intensive products. Finally, countries at lower levels of development can supplant the middle-level countries in exporting unskilled labor–intensive commodities.*[13]

Technology Life Cycle It is useful to distinguish between new products and new technologies used in the production of products (such as improved casting processes in steel-making or robotic painting equipment in automobile manufacturing). While the IPLC concept discussed above focuses primarily on final goods for consumption, there seems to be a closely related phenomenon regarding production technology, which might be termed the *international technology life cycle*. Production techniques and equipment seem to have a cycle from initial development and use in industrially advanced countries to eventual adoption in developing nations. This cycle is important because production technologies and equipment can be important exports from industrialized countries.

The concept of a technology life cycle emanates from the tendency of industrialized countries to have high incomes—and high wages. There is an incentive to invest in new, labor-reducing technology in order to reduce the costs associated with high-cost labor. Industrialized countries therefore tend to be innovators in developing new production technology that increases labor productivity. Increased productivity tends to produce further increases in wages, contributing to continued efforts to develop new technology.

The result of these developments can be a technology cycle that resembles the IPLC. The initial stage involves the development of new technology (e.g., a machine for automating the welding of panels on an automobile) in an industrialized country. This technology is used in the innovating country and subsequently exported to other developed countries with high-cost labor. This technology would not be as quickly exported to developing nations, because the existence of abundant low-cost labor in such countries would make the use of the new technology too capital-intensive. Over time, the increasing cost of labor in the industrialized country reaches a point where it is no longer profitable to use the technology in that nation. At the same time, labor costs in some developing nations rise to the stage where the technology can be profitably employed. The technology becomes an export from the industrialized nation to the developing nation. Later in the cycle, the technology (e.g., a machine) might be produced abroad for domestic consumption in that developing nation or even for export to other international markets.

Of course, the industrialized nations have an incentive to continuously develop improved technology in order to maintain high incomes and economic prosperity. This pressure is particularly acute in situations where the developing countries are rapidly advancing up a technology "ladder," from production of simpler, more standardized goods to innovation of technologies and products. This process appears to be well under way in countries such as Korea, Taiwan, and Singapore, while nations such as China, Thailand, and India are at an earlier stage of advancement but have aspirations to also move quickly toward technological competence on an international scale. The quickening of this technology cycle, through developments such as improved capability and lower costs of telecommunications, greater freedom in the movement of capital and goods across borders, and increasing internationalization of markets and competition, is exacerbating the challenge for wealthy nations to maintain their positions as technological leaders.

Technology evolution need not always follow the cycle suggested above. Initial application of the technical innovation could even begin in a foreign, developing country market, as the following example suggests.

> *Automakers have recently begun applying a new technological approach called "modularity" within their manufacturing operations. Rather than supplying individual parts, suppliers instead provide modules of assembled parts to the automaker, such as complete suspension systems or dashboards. American labor unions have resisted modularization, viewing it as a form of outsourcing that would reduce the number of jobs in the automaker's operations. Consequently, Chrysler initiated the modularization concept within its Brazilian operations. As a result, for example, a local supplier is responsible for just-in-time delivery of the entire frame for the Chrysler Dakota pickup truck. It is expected that this production process innovation could reduce per-vehicle manufacturing costs by thousands of dollars.[14]*

Economies of Scale and the Experience Curve In the 1920s, economists began to consider the fact that most industries benefit from economies of scale; that is, as a plant gets larger and output increases, the average cost of producing each unit of output decreases.

This occurs because larger and more efficient equipment can be employed, companies can obtain volume discounts on their larger-volume purchases, and fixed costs such as those of research and design and administrative overheads can be allocated over a larger quantity of output. Most manufacturing is subject to economies of scale, and mining and transportation industries also tend to benefit from increasing returns to scale. Production costs also drop because of the *learning curve*. As firms produce more products, they learn ways to improve production efficiency, causing production costs to decline by a predictable amount.[15]

Economies of scale and the experience curve affect international trade because they can permit a nation's industries to become low-cost producers without requiring that the nation have an abundance of a certain class of production factors. Then, just as in the case of comparative advantage, nations specialize in the production of a few products and trade with others to supply the rest of their needs. International trade is promoted because a nation's companies may not be able to fully achieve the potential scale economies through serving only the domestic market, even within countries as large as the United States. Examples include semiconductors, computers, and commercial aircraft. American consumers can benefit from higher quality and lower prices for these products because companies like Intel, Hewlett-Packard, and Boeing can spread very high fixed costs over sales within foreign as well as home markets.

Imperfect Competition
By combining the concept of economies of scale with the existence of differentiated products, Paul Krugman developed a model that helps to explain the observed levels of intraindustry (within-industry) trade between nations.[16] Krugman reasoned that production of goods is concentrated geographically, due to economies of scale. He also reasoned that factors associated with resource constraints and imperfect competition cause companies in otherwise identical nations to produce some unique varieties of products in order to avoid direct competition. The existence of this *product differentiation*—the creation of a separate identity for a product, through actual (styling) or perceived (image) differences that are typically supported with advertising in order to encourage brand loyalty—is an important element in Krugman's model. Because products are differentiated, each company may act like a monopolist with respect to its own unique product, and more firms and more variety of goods will be present in the market. Because firms from different nations each produce unique varieties, but consumers in each nation buy some volume of each variety (as predicted by Linder), we see intraindustry trade between similar or even otherwise-identical nations. The existence of international trade can create a larger market, which allows for better utilization of internal (company-specific) economies of scale by the trading firms. Empirical support for Krugman's model has been shown in many studies, including such industries as automobiles, specialty chemicals, and wine, and this model helps to explain the high proportion (roughly one-quarter) of intraindustry trade in overall international trade.

First-Mover Theory
As suggested in the preceding section, countries typically specialize when there are increasing returns to scale and experience. However, the observed pattern of trade in goods subject to scale economies may be determined by historical factors, such as which country entered an industry first. Some management theorists argue that firms that enter the market first (first movers) will be able to gain large market share, permitting them to obtain the benefits of reduced costs and improved technical expertise early. This can discourage foreign entrants that might have to enter at a higher cost, at least initially. One study across a broad range of industries revealed that first movers held a 30 percent market share compared to just 13 percent for late entries. Another found that 70 percent of the leaders in present-day markets were first movers.

New research, however, indicates that previous studies were flawed because they were based on surveys of surviving firms and did not include a large number of the true pioneers. As an example, it was an American firm, Ampex, that made the first VCRs, but because it charged so much ($50,000), it sold only a few. Sony and Matsushita saw the market potential and worked for 20 years to make a VCR they could sell for $500. They reached that goal and cornered the market. The researchers argue that the early success has gone to the companies that entered the market on average 13 years after the "first movers."[17]

National competitiveness involves a nation's ability to design, produce, distribute, or service products within an international trading context while earning increasing returns on its resources. A nation's ability to achieve sustained international success within a particular industry may be explained by variables other than the factors of production on which the theories of comparative advantage and Heckscher-Ohlin are based. For example, Alfred Marshall's seminal work on economic theory helped to explain why, in many industries, firms tend to cluster together on a geographic basis.[18] He suggested that geographic clusters appeared for three reasons: (1) advantages associated with pooling of a common labor force so that staffing requirements can be met quickly, even with unexpected fluctuations in demand; (2) gains from the development of specialized local suppliers whose operations and skills can be coordinated with the needs of the buyers; and (3) benefits that result within the geographic region from the sharing of technological information and corresponding enhancement of the rate of innovation.

Michael Porter, an economics professor at Harvard, extended the work of Marshall.[19] His Diamond Model of national advantage claims that four kinds of variables will have an impact on the ability of the local firms in a country to utilize the country's resources to gain a competitive advantage:

1. *Demand conditions:* the nature, rather than merely the size, of the domestic demand. If a firm's customers are sophisticated and demanding, it will strive to produce high-quality and innovative products and, in doing so, will obtain a global competitive advantage over companies located where domestic pressure is less. This might have been the case in the past, when international firms introduced their new products in home markets first (a condition of the international product life cycle theory), but as more firms introduce new products globally, this variable will lose importance.

2. *Factor conditions:* level and composition of factors of production. Porter distinguishes between the basic factors (Heckscher-Ohlin theory) and the advanced factors (a nation's infrastructure, such as telecommunications and transportation systems, or university research institutes). He also distinguishes between created factors (e.g., from investments made by individuals, companies, or governments) and inherited factors (e.g., natural resources, location). Lack of natural endowments has caused nations to invest in the creation of the advanced factors, such as education of its work force, free ports, and advanced communications systems, to enable their industries to be competitive globally. Various Caribbean nations have upgraded their communications systems to attract banking and other service companies that have little dependence on the basic factors of production.

3. *Related and supporting industries:* suppliers and industry support services. For decades, firms in an industry with their suppliers, the suppliers' suppliers, and so forth, have tended to form a cluster in a given location, often without any apparent initial reason. Yet these related and supporting industries serve as an important foundation for competitive success by providing a network of suppliers, subcontractors, and a commercial infrastructure. For example, the San Francisco Bay Area has a range of related and supporting industries for the personal computer industry. These include research, design, production, or service operations of such suppliers as semiconductor designers, semiconductor manufacturers, technologically savvy venture capitalists, and intellectual property rights lawyers, as well as related industries such as scientific equipment, electronics (e.g., MP3 players, personal digital assistants), telecommunications equipment, software developers, and a wide range of Internet-related companies.[20]

4. *Firm strategy, structure, and rivalry:* the extent of domestic competition, the existence of barriers to entry, and the firms' management style and organization. Porter states that companies subject to heavy competition in their domestic markets are constantly striving to improve their efficiency and innovativeness, which makes them more competitive internationally. For decades, firms in oligopolistic industries have carefully watched their competitors' every move and have even entered foreign markets because their competitors had gone there. For example, Japanese automakers such as Toyota,

national competitiveness
A nation's relative ability to design, produce, distribute, or service products within an international trading context while earning increasing returns on its resources

Honda, Nissan, and Mitsubishi, have competed vigorously with each other for decades in their domestic marketplace, constantly pressuring each other to improve the quality and performance of their products or else risk the loss of market share. This vigorous competition has enabled these firms to develop world-leading capabilities in auto design and manufacturing. As soon as one of these companies ventures forth into a new international market such as the United States, Europe, or Southeast Asia for the sale or manufacturing of autos, the competitors tend to be close behind in order to avoid a decline in their relative international competitiveness.

Porter argues that these four factors are fundamentally interrelated, creating a "virtuous circle" of resource generation and application, as well as responsiveness in meeting the demands of customers, as depicted in Figure 3.3.

Porter's work complements the theories of Ricardo and Heckscher-Ohlin. However, as the noted economist John Dunning stated, there is nothing new in Porter's analysis, but Porter does set out a model in which the determinants of national competitiveness may be identified.[21] Another problem is that Porter's evidence is anecdotal, rather than based on rigorous empirical research.[22] Furthermore, competitiveness generally applies to companies, rather than nations, although nation-specific factors can provide a critical foundation for creating and enhancing the competitiveness of a company, or industry, on an international level.

SUMMARY OF INTERNATIONAL TRADE THEORY

International trade occurs primarily because of relative price differences among nations. These differences stem from differences in production costs, which result from:

1. Differences in the endowments of the factors of production.

2. Differences in the levels of technology that determine the factor intensities used.

3. Differences in the efficiencies with which these factor intensities are utilized.

4. Foreign exchange rates.

However, taste differences, a demand variable, can reverse the direction of trade predicted by the theory.

International trade theory shows that nations will attain a higher level of living by specializing in goods for which they possess a comparative advantage and importing those for which they have a comparative disadvantage. Generally, trade restrictions that stop this free flow of goods will harm a nation's welfare. If this is true, why is every nation in the world surrounded by trade restrictions?

FIGURE 3.3

Variables Impacting Competitive Advantage: Porter's Diamond

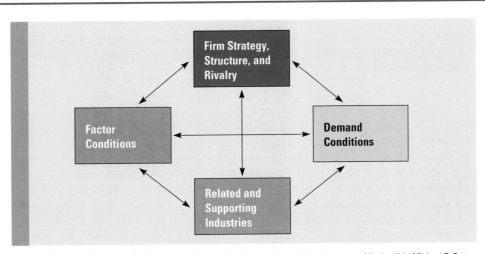

Trade Restrictions

This apparent contradiction occurs because the government officials who make decisions about import restrictions are particularly sensitive to the interest groups that will be hurt by the international competition. These groups consist of a small, easily identified body of people or organizations—as contrasted to the large, widespread number of consumers who typically benefit from free trade. In political debates over a proposed import restriction, the protectionist group will usually be united in exerting pressure on government officials, whereas pro-trade consumers rarely mount an organized effort. For example, for the past couple of decades, steel companies and steelworker unions have repeatedly initiated vehement protests to Congress and various government officials about the threat posed by lower-priced imported steel, yet consumer organizations have largely been silent about the potential negative impact of trade barriers on consumers' welfare. In other words, if you are employed by a chemical manufacturer or a hospital, you probably are not going to fight for unrestricted steel imports even though you may believe they contribute to a lower price for your automobile. As you read through the next section, note the importance of special-interest groups.

ARGUMENTS FOR TRADE RESTRICTIONS AND THEIR REBUTTAL

A number of arguments have traditionally been presented in support of efforts to restrict trade. In this section, we will address several of the most common such arguments, as well as associated rebuttal arguments.

National Defense

The argument supporting trade restrictions due to national defense factors suggests that certain industries need protection from imports because they are vital to the defense or security of a nation and must be kept operating even though they are at a comparative disadvantage with respect to foreign competitors. If competition from foreign firms drives these companies out of business and leaves the country dependent on imports, those imports may not be available in a time of war or some other threat to national security.

One problem with this argument is that the armed forces require hundreds of products, ranging from panty hose to bombs, and it is difficult to argue that any particular product is more critical to national security than another.

> The U.S. shoe industry, after failing to obtain relief from imports with arguments about loss of jobs, requested Congress to impose restrictions based on the fact that growing reliance on imported footwear was "jeopardizing the national security of the United States." Speaking to the Armed Services Committee of the U.S. Congress, the president of the Footwear Industry of America stated: "In the event of war or other national emergency, it is unlikely that the domestic footwear industry could provide sufficient footwear for the military and civilian population. . . . We won't be able to wait for ships to deliver shoes from Taiwan, or Korea or Brazil or Eastern Europe. . . . Improper footwear can lead to needless casualties and turn sure victory into possible defeat." A Defense Department spokesman said he knew of no plan to investigate the prospects of a wartime shoe crisis. Furthermore, federal law already requires the armed forces to buy U.S.-made footwear exclusively.[23]

Critics of the defense argument claim it would be far more efficient for the government to subsidize a number of firms to maintain sufficient capacity for wartime use only. The output of these companies could be varied according to the calculated defense needs. Moreover, a subsidy would clearly indicate to taxpayers the cost of maintaining these companies in the name of national security—something, however, that some interests do not want known. Currently, most American ocean shipping companies receive government subsidies without which they could not remain in business because of the competition from foreign firms with lower operating costs. In this way, we have a merchant marine ready in case of hostility, and we know what this state of readiness costs us.

Similar arguments have been offered in support of bans on the export of advanced technologies. Such bans, proponents argue, prevent valuable technologies from being used to strengthen competitors, especially militarily. However, these bans can reduce export revenues for the country's manufacturers by closing off potential markets. The bans can also impede efforts to sustain international market share and fund continued innovation, enabling competitors from other nations to improve their competitiveness.

Sanctions to Punish Offending Nations   A related argument for imposing trade restrictions is to inflict economic damage on other nations in order to punish them or otherwise encourage them to modify behavior. A common approach is to pass legislation that prohibits trade with the "offending" nation. A 2002 study found that the United States, for example, had some form of sanctions against over 75 countries.[24] Targeted nations have included Cuba, Iraq, Libya, North Korea, Iran, Syria, Sudan, and Myanmar.

What is typically ignored when imposing sanctions is that not only do they seldom achieve their goal of forcing change in the targeted country but they also tend to produce collateral economic damage in the nations applying them.[25] It was estimated that economic sanctions during the 1990s cost the United States approximately $15 billion to $23 billion annually in exports, in addition to losses resulting from restrictions on foreign direct investment, capital flows, tourism, and other sources of income or output.[26] During the time that the United States was imposing sanctions on Iraq that prohibited American firms from doing business there, it was reported that companies from France, Russia, and other nations were generating billions of dollars from business contracts that American firms were excluded from bidding for. It was also reported that the Iraqi trade sanctions unintentionally imposed substantial economic damage on Turkey, Jordan, and Greece, nations that had historically engaged in extensive trade with Iraq. In addition, limitations on exporting Iraqi oil resulted in substantial economic gains by Libya and Iran, nations whose behavior had also subjected them to U.S. trade sanctions.[27] Prior to the 2003 invasion and overthrow of Saddam Hussein's government, sanctions on Iraq tended to fall disproportionately on the poor and on Kurds and Shiite Muslims, rather than on the Sunni Muslim–dominated ruling Baath Party.

Protect Infant (or Dying) Industry   Advocates for the protection of an infant industry may claim that in the long run the industry will have a comparative advantage but that its firms need protection from imports until the required investment capital is obtained, the labor force is trained, production techniques are mastered, and economies of scale are achieved. When these objectives are met, import protection will no longer be necessary. Without the protection, advocates argue, a firm will not be able to survive because lower-cost imports from more mature foreign competitors will underprice it in its local market. Although the logic that a government will be able to predict future comparative advantage is questionable, international managers will find that the infant-industry argument is readily accepted by the governments of most developing nations. "There is a respectable historical case for tariff protection for industries that are not yet profitable, especially in developing countries," asserted Ha Joon Chang, writing for the South Centre, an intergovernmental forum for developing countries. "In the same way that we protect our children until they grow up and are able to compete with adults in the labor market, developing country governments need to protect their newly emerging industries until they go through a period of learning and become able to compete with the producers from more advanced countries."[28]

> *China's 10th five-year plan calls for an increase in semiconductor production from $2 billion in 2000 to $24 billion in 2010, and the country has encouraged the development of a domestic semiconductor manufacturing industry. In March 2004, the United States initiated proceedings for a World Trade Organization complaint, charging that China's policies offered its semiconductor industry unfair protection by refunding 82 percent of the 17 percent value-added tax imposed on semiconductors. Foreign companies argued that this tax break, which was not available for imported semiconductors unless designed in China, was part of a concerted effort to force foreign companies to establish joint venture production activities in China and to transfer their technology. "The rebate is to protect our infant industry," commented Li Ke of the China Semiconductor Industry Association. "You cannot say this is a discriminatory tax policy." After negotiations, the offending tax policy was changed and the WTO complaint resolved in July 2004.[29]*

Efforts to protect emerging industries are not limited to developing nations, of course. For example, in early 2006, Representative Ken Salazar of Colorado argued for the maintenance of a protective 54-cents-a-gallon import duty on foreign-produced ethanol, including imports from low-cost producer Brazil, in order to give "our infant industries a greater chance to grow." The United States produced more gallons of ethanol in 2005 than any other nation, although the cost of subsidizing the American ethanol industry is estimated at $1 billion to $4 billion annually.[30]

Protection is meant to be temporary for the emerging industry, but realistically a protected firm will rarely admit it has matured and no longer needs this assistance. Protected from foreign competition by high import duties, the company's managers have little reason to improve efficiency or product quality.

A related argument concerns the protection of a "dying" industry, one threatened by a rapid onslaught of imports that endangers the survival of domestic companies and the jobs they provide. Under this argument, it takes time to make the necessary adjustments to move labor and capital out of the industry and into other sectors. Protecting the industry from imports can therefore facilitate a smoother transition. This sort of logic has been used in justifying protection for such sectors as textiles and footwear in the United States and Europe, in response to the rapid expansion of imports from China after the end of the Multifiber Agreement in 2005. Other assistance, such as subsidies for relocating to different geographic or industrial areas and for providing assistance to displaced workers, may also be part of the proposed solution.

Current international trade rules of the World Trade Organization prohibit import protection or government subsidies whose intent is primarily to help domestic industry to compete and gain international market share.

Protect Domestic Jobs from Cheap Foreign Labor

Protectionists who use this argument usually compare lower foreign hourly wage rates to those paid in their home country. They conclude that foreign exporters can flood the home country's market with low-priced goods, and thus simultaneously eliminate jobs of home country workers. The first fallacy of this argument is that wage costs are neither all of the production costs nor all of the labor costs, so a comparison merely based on relative hourly wages would be misleading. As discussed in Chapter 12, "Labor Forces," in many LDCs, legislated fringe benefits are a much higher percentage of direct wages than they are in industrialized countries.

Furthermore, the productivity per worker is frequently much greater in developed countries because of more capital per worker, superior management, and advanced technology. As a result, the labor cost component of the goods being produced is lower even though wages are higher.

The second fallacy results from failure to consider the costs of the other factors of production. Where wage rates are low, the capital costs are usually high, and thus production costs may actually be higher in a low-wage nation. Ironically, one of the arguments for protection used by manufacturers in developing nations is that they cannot compete against the low-cost, highly productive firms in the industrialized countries.

Those who might be persuaded by this argument to stop imports to save domestic jobs should remember that exports create jobs. For example, every $1 billion in American exports creates an average of 25,000 new jobs in the United States. If a nation imposes barriers on imports from a second country, that second country's government may retaliate with greater import duties on exports from the first nation. The result could be a net loss of jobs rather than the gain that was anticipated.

Scientific Tariff or Fair Competition

Supporters of this argument say they believe in fair competition. They simply want an import duty that will bring the cost of the imported goods up to the cost of the domestically produced article. This will eliminate any "unfair" advantage that a foreign competitor might have because of superior technology, lower raw material costs, lower taxes, or lower labor costs. It is not their intent to ban exports; they wish only to equalize the process for "fair" competition. If this were law, no doubt the rate of duty would be set to protect the least efficient American producer, thereby enabling the more efficient domestic manufacturers to earn large profits. The efficient foreign producers would be penalized, and, of course, their comparative advantage would be nullified. The impact on consumers might also be viewed as unfair, since the import duty would most assuredly result in an increase in the prices that they pay.

Retaliation   Representatives of an industry whose exports have had import restrictions placed on them by another country may ask their government to retaliate with similar restrictions. An example of how retaliation begins is the ban by the European Union (EU) on imports of hormone-treated beef from the United States.

> *Because the use of hormones in animal production is considered a health hazard in the EU, the European Union closed its market to $100 million worth of beef (12 percent of total U.S. meat exports) in 1988. American beef producers complained that no scientific evidence supported the claim, and the United States promptly retaliated by putting import duties on about $100 million worth of EU products, including boneless beef and pork, fruit juices, wine coolers, tomatoes, French cheese, and instant coffee. The EU then threatened to ban U.S. shipments of honey, canned soybeans, walnuts, and dried fruit worth $140 million. In reply, the United States announced that it would follow the EU ban with a ban on all European meat. If that had happened, about $500 million in U.S.-EU trade would have been affected.*
>
> *Generally, disputes like these go to the World Trade Organization (WTO). After having its beef banned by the EU for eight years, the United States launched a formal dispute settlement procedure with the WTO in May 1996, challenging the ban. When the WTO Appellate Body announced that the EU ban had been imposed without reason, the EU declared in March 1998 that it would implement the Appellate Body ruling, but it did not comply by May 1999, the date set by the WTO. When the United States asked the WTO for permission to retaliate, the EU requested arbitration to settle the amount. On July 26, 1999, the WTO authorized the United States to retaliate, resulting in the imposition of a 100 percent import duty on a list of EU products with an annual trade value of $116.8 million. In September 2003, the EU announced a new directive that it asserted was in compliance with the WTO's ruling, although it still banned most American and Canadian beef. The United States claimed that the new EU guidelines still violated WTO requirements. As of 2006, about 18 years after the imposition of EU barriers on hormone-treated beef from the United States, the full import duty penalty valued at $116.8 million was being applied to designated imports from the EU.*[31]

Dumping   Retaliation also occurs for **dumping.** According to WTO guidelines, dumping is the selling of a product abroad for less than (1) the average cost of production in the exporting nation, (2) the market price in the exporting nation, or (3) the price to third countries. A manufacturer may engage in dumping as a means of selling excess production without disrupting prices in its domestic market or as a response to cyclical or seasonal factors (e.g., during an economic downturn or at the end of a fashion season). A manufacturer may also lower its export price to force the importing nation's domestic producers out of business, expecting to raise prices once that objective is accomplished. This is called *predatory dumping.*

The United States became the first country to prohibit dumping of foreign goods into its own market, in 1916 (there is no U.S. law prohibiting American firms from dumping their goods abroad, though). Dumping is now within the domain of the WTO, which is the recipient of many related complaints through appeals by countries opposing the imposition of antidumping protections against their companies. In the United States, when a manufacturer believes a foreign producer is dumping a product, it can ask the Office of Investigation in the Department of Commerce to make a preliminary investigation. If Commerce finds that products have been dumped, the case goes to the International Trade Commission to determine whether the imports are injuring U.S. producers.* If the commission finds that they are, then the case is referred to the U.S. president, who decides whether antidumping tariffs should be assessed. Unlike most trade restrictions, which are applied to all exporters of a product, antidumping measures are applied to specific producers in selected nations.

Most governments retaliate when dumping is perceived to be harming local industry. For example:

dumping
Selling a product abroad for less than the cost of production, the price in the home market, or the price to third countries

---

* The International Trade Commission is a government agency that provides technical assistance and advice to the president and Congress on matters of international trade and tariffs.

In 2005, the average price of shoes imported into the European Union from China fell by about one-quarter, and the volume of imported shoes rose by nearly 700 percent in the first seven months after quotas were abolished. This resulted in complaints from European shoemakers that they were being harmed by dumping from Chinese and Vietnamese shoe manufacturers. Critics warned that unfair foreign competition in shoes and textiles was undermining national labor and social standards and causing job losses. Stating that there was "compelling evidence" that imported leather shoes were being illegally sold below cost and fearing that domestic EU footwear manufacturers could be forced out of business, in July 2006 the European Commission's trade department proposed antidumping tariffs on shoe imports from those two countries. The proposal would allow importation—without any "dumping duty"—of 140 million pairs of leather shoes from China and 95 million pairs from Vietnam. These volumes were about half the level of imports in 2005. Chinese imports above those quotas would face a 23 percent duty, while excess shoes from Vietnam would face a 29.5 percent duty. A spokesperson for EU trade commissioner Peter Mandelson said, "This is a fair and balanced system. While correcting the effects of unfair trade, the proposed allowance before dumping duties apply will allow substantial trade." Wang Shichun, director-general of the Bureau of Fair Trade of China's Commerce Ministry, said, "The European Union's accusations lack basis. European products did not suffer actual harm." Said the general manager of one Chinese manufacturer, "It's no good limiting [the export of] Chinese goods. Nobody benefits—neither retailers nor consumers."[32]

New Types of Dumping   There are at least five new kinds of dumping for which fair-trade lobbies consider sanctions to be justified in order to level the playing field for international trade. In reality, these special-interest groups calling for level playing fields are seeking to raise the production costs of their overseas competitors to protect their local high-cost manufacturers. The classes of dumping include:

1. *Social dumping:* unfair competition caused by firms, usually from developing nations that have lower labor costs and poorer working conditions, which undermines social support systems, including worker benefits.

2. *Environmental dumping:* unfair competition caused by a country's lax environmental standards. It has been argued that globalization provides incentives to national governments to set weak environmental policies, particularly regarding industries whose plants can be relocated internationally.

   The United States' refusal to commit to standards of the Kyoto treaty was criticized because American exporters would not bear the same costs as firms in signatory countries. A statement issued by Friends of the Earth (Europe) said, "The U.S. rejection of the Kyoto Protocol is unfair and puts European business at a disadvantage. With Bush's increasing rejection of international agreements that are essential to protect the environment, Europe should have the right to penalize U.S. goods for the pollution they cause."[33]

3. *Financial services dumping:* unfair competition caused by a nation's low requirements for bank capital-asset ratios.

4. *Cultural dumping:* unfair competition caused by cultural barriers aiding local firms.

5. *Tax dumping:* unfair competition caused by differences in corporate tax rates or related special breaks.

   In 2006 Slovakia was accused of tax dumping because its low (19 percent) corporate tax rate and generous incentive policies were perceived to give it an advantage over other European nations in attracting investment from multinationals.[34]

subsidies

Financial contributions, provided directly or indirectly by a government, which confer a benefit; include grants, preferential tax treatment, and government assumption of normal business expenses

Subsidies   Another cause of retaliation may be **subsidies** that a government makes to a domestic firm either to encourage exports or to help protect it from imports. Some examples are cash payments, government participation in ownership, low-cost loans to foreign buyers and exporters, and preferential tax treatment.

As shown in Figure 3.4, OECD nations provide $280 billion per year in subsidies to their farmers, including $133 billion in the EU, $49 billion in Japan, and $47 billion in the United

FIGURE 3.4   Value of OECD Member Farm Subsidies

Percent of value of production

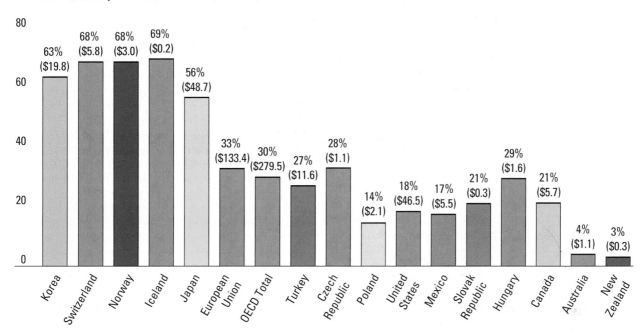

Source: "Agriculture: Support Estimates, 2004," *OECD in Figures: Statistics on the Member Countries.* Accessed 7/2005. Link: http://dx.doi.org/10.1787/758034618756.

States.[35] In the case of rice, Japan imposes a tariff of nearly 500 percent in an effort to protect its farmers from international competition, while the maximum tariff on dairy products in the EU is over 200 percent. Perhaps the greatest damage caused by this assistance is its effect on the millions of farmers in the world's poorest nations. High customs duties restrict access to wealthy countries' markets, while subsidized overproduction in developed countries artificially depresses prices in world markets, harming the income of farmers in poorer nations. Most of the agricultural subsidies in developed countries go to a small percentage of recipients, usually large enterprises. For example, 72 percent of U.S. farm subsidies from 1995 to 2003 were distributed among only 10 percent of U.S. farmers, and the top 15 percent of French farmers received 60 percent of that country's direct subsidies.[36] Substantial reduction in agricultural subsidies has been a major focus of the Doha Round of world trade negotiations and reportedly a major factor leading to breakdown in negotiations.

Competitors in importing nations frequently ask their governments to impose **countervailing duties** to offset the effects of a subsidy. In the United States, when the Department of Commerce receives a petition from an American firm claiming that imports from a particular country are subsidized, it first determines whether a subsidy actually was given. If the findings are positive, Commerce proceeds to impose countervailing duties equal to the subsidy's amount. In most cases involving members of the WTO, another independent government agency, the U.S. International Trade Commission, must determine whether the firm has been injured by the subsidy before Commerce assesses the duty.

countervailing duties

Additional import taxes levied on imports that have benefited from export subsidies

Other Arguments   The arguments we have examined are probably the ones most frequently given in support of trade restrictions. Others include the use of protection from imports to (1) permit diversification of the domestic economy or (2) improve the balance of trade. You should have gathered from this discussion that protection from imports generally serves the narrow interests of a special-interest group at the expense of many. Although the application of trade restrictions can sometimes buy time for the protected industry to modernize and become more competitive in the world market, a real danger exists that a nation's

Sugar Subsidies: Sweet for Producers, Not for Consumers

Nicaraguan Jackson Riveras carries a load of freshly cut sugarcane on a plantation near Turrucares of Alajuela, Costa Rica. Like many Nicaraguan immigrants, Ramirez came to Costa Rica to work the harvest season in order to earn higher wages and send money back to his family.

Although they lack comparative advantage in sugar production, the United States, Japan, and the EU, among others, have maintained strong protection for their domestic sugar industries. A World Bank report called sugar the "most policy-distorted of all commodities." Protectionism by developed countries harms foreign sugar producers, many of which are poor farmers in developing countries, by reducing demand and prices for their product. Brazil loses $500 million per year due to American sugar subsidies, and Oxfam estimated in 2004 that EU sugar supports had cost Ethiopia, Mozambique, and Malawi $238 million since 2001. Malawi's losses exceeded its total budget for primary health care. Before being forced by the WTO into making changes in November 2005, the EU maintained domestic sugar prices that were triple world market prices, and the EU spent 3.30 in subsidies for every 1 of the 5 million tons of sugar that it exported. Even after reducing its guaranteed prices by 36 percent over the subsequent four years, the EU still sharply restricted imports from least developed countries, delaying full access until as late as 2020.

In the United States, sugar tariffs have been in place since 1789. Imports are allocated through tariff-rate quotas among 41 nations and limited to about 15 percent of the U.S. market, except in years when there is a shortfall in the U.S. domestic supply, as in 2005 after Hurricane Katrina. High price supports have resulted in overproduction of sugar domestically. As a result, the price of raw sugar in the United States has averaged more than double the world price during the past decade, costing American consumers an estimated $2 billion annually. Excess sugar production also contributes to environmental problems. In Florida, for example, pollution and disruption of water flows from sugar production have been cited as a major contributor to environmental degradation of the Everglades.

Although sugar protection costs each American an average of only an additional $8 per year, the benefits are highly concen-

trading partners will retaliate with restrictions of their own, causing injury to industries that have received no protection. Let's examine these restrictions.

TARIFF BARRIERS

tariffs

Taxes on imported goods for the purpose of raising their price to reduce competition for local producers or stimulate local production

Tariffs, or import duties, are taxes levied on imported goods primarily for the purpose of raising their selling price in the importing nation's market to reduce competition for domestic producers. A few smaller nations also use them to raise revenue on both imports and exports. Exports of commodities such as coffee and copper are commonly taxed in developing nations. However, imposition of tariffs can result in retaliation that is harmful rather than helpful for a country and its well-being.

In the late 1920s, declining economic fortunes caused American farmers to lobby Congress for tariff protection on agricultural products. There were few supporters for this proposal, and only the Republican party publicly supported the protectionist effort. Over time, more domestic producers joined with agricultural interests, seeking their own protection from foreign competitors. The resulting legislative proposal increased tariffs for more than 20,000 items across a broad range of industries. The broad industrial support for the legislation

trated among a small number of companies. One family that owns a leading Florida sugar company is estimated to gain an extra $65 million in annual profits due to protectionist U.S. sugar policies.

Mechanization has eliminated the labor intensity of producing sugar from sugar beets or sugarcane in the United States. Only about 60,000 people now work in the production or refining of sugar, about 0.04 percent of the American labor force. Movement to free trade in sugar is estimated to eliminate less than 2,300 workers in the sugar industry, meaning that the cost for each protected job is over $825,000. In addition, protection of the U.S. sugar industry has cost thousands of jobs in other sectors, such as food and beverage manufacturing. For example, sugar accounts for 32.7 percent of the total costs in the production of breakfast cereals. A 2006 study by the U.S. Department of Commerce estimated that high sugar prices led to the loss of over 10,000 jobs at sugar-consuming companies between 1997 and 2002. High sugar prices were also a major factor in companies' decisions to relocate operations to non-U.S. sites, contributing to an increase in imports of sugar-containing products from $10.2 billion in 1997 to $18.7 billion in 2004. Undersecretary for Trade Franklin Lavin said, "We are seeing U.S. jobs move to countries that don't have the competitive disadvantage of high sugar prices that we face in the United States."

Despite this situation, efforts to reform protection of the sugar industry have made minimal progress in recent decades, at least partly due to the strength of the sugar lobby. Sugar accounts for less than 1 percent of U.S. agricultural sales, but 17 percent of all agricultural political contributions since 1990. "It's a very effective lobby," commented Claude Barfield of the American Enterprise Institute, a conservative think tank. "They've traditionally given a lot of money to both parties." Sugar lobbying helped disrupt the trade liberalization agenda of President George W. Bush, causing the administration to succumb to pressure and exclude sugar completely from the U.S.-Australia free trade agreement. This was the first bilateral trade treaty in which the United States required that a product be entirely excluded, "a dangerous precedent" according to Republican senator Charles Grassley. The Australian prime minister, John Howard, considered terminating the entire trade deal with the United States because of American insistence on excluding sugar from the agreement, saying that Australian sugar producers were "the victims of a corrupted world trading system."

However, perhaps change may yet occur. In 2006, the United States and Mexico finally ended their decade-long battle over access to the U.S. sugar market under NAFTA, and in 2008 all barriers to the trade in sugar are to be removed between the two countries.

Source: U.S. Department of Commerce, *Employment Changes in U.S. Food Manufacturing: The Impact of Sugar Prices*, February 2006, http://ita.doc.gov/media/Publications/pdf/sugar06.pdf (July 9, 2006); "Who Is to Blame for Loss of Candy Production Industry?" *Manufacturing & Technology News*, February 17, 2006, www.allbusiness.com/periodicals/article/869916-1.html (July 9, 2006); Foodproductiondaily-USA.com, "US Confectionery Jobs Threatened by High Sugar Prices," www.foodproductiondaily-usa.com/news/printNewsBis.asp?id=65871 (July 9, 2006); Edward Alden and Neil Buckley, "Sweet Deals: 'Big Sugar' Fights Threats from Free Trade and a Global Drive to Limit Consumption," *Financial Times*, February 27, 2004, p. 11; Michael Schroeder, "Sugar Growers Hold Up Push for Free Trade," *The Wall Street Journal*, February 3, 2004, p. A13; "The Fruits of Free Trade: Protection's Price," *2002 Annual Report—Federal Reserve Bank of Dallas* (Dallas: Federal Reserve Bank of Dallas, 2002); Oxfam International, "Dumping on the World: How EU Sugar Policies Hurt Poor Countries," March 2004, www.oxfam.org.uk/what_we_do/issues/trade/bp61_sugar_dumping.htm (July 9, 2006); and "Trade Scene: An Unsweet Debate on Sugar," *Journal of Commerce*, March 29, 2004, p. 1.

caused the Democratic and Progressive political parties to join the Republicans on October 28, 1929, in supporting the Smoot-Hawley Tariff Act to establish some of the highest levels of tariffs ever imposed by what was already a protectionist United States. That day the stock market crashed, falling 12 percent. In the following months, 34 foreign governments filed protests against Smoot-Hawley, and over 1,000 economists urged President Herbert Hoover not to sign the bill. Nevertheless, on June 17, 1930, Hoover signed the bill. The result was a retaliatory trade war, characterized by tit-for-tat tariffs and protectionism between trading nations, which soon engulfed most of the world's economies. The outcome was predictable: world trade plummeted from $5.7 billion in 1929 to $1.9 billion in 1932, industrial efficiency and the effects of comparative advantage were sharply reduced, unemployment increased dramatically, and the world was pushed into a decade-long economic depression.[37]

Ad Valorem, Specific, and Compound Duties

Import duties are (1) *ad valorem*, (2) *specific*, or (3) a combination of the two called *compound*. An **ad valorem duty** is stated as a percentage of the invoice value of the product. For example, the U.S. tariff schedule states that flavoring extracts and fruit flavors not containing alcohol are subject to a 6 percent ad valorem duty. Therefore, when a shipment of flavoring extract invoiced at $10,000 arrives in the United States, the importer is required to pay $600 to U.S. Customs before

ad valorem duty
An import duty levied as a percentage of the invoice value of imported goods

specific duty
A fixed sum levied on a physical unit of an imported good

taking possession of the goods. A **specific duty** is a fixed sum of money charged for a specified physical unit of the product. A company importing dynamite in cartridges or sticks suitable for blasting would have to pay $0.37 per pound irrespective of the invoice value. When the flavoring extracts and fruit flavors mentioned above contain over 50 percent alcohol by weight, they are subject to a specific duty of $0.12 per pound plus a 3 percent ad valorem.

compound duty
A combination of specific and ad valorem duties

Thus, on a $10,000 shipment weighing 5,000 pounds, the importer would have to pay a **compound duty** of $900 [($0.12 × 5,000 pounds) + (0.03 × $10,000) = $600 + $300]. Note that in an inflationary period, a specific duty soon loses its importance unless changed frequently, whereas the amount collected from an ad valorem duty increases as the invoice price rises. Sometimes, however, an exporter may charge prices so much lower than domestic prices that the ad valorem duty fails to close the gap. Some governments set *official prices* or use *variable levies* to correct this deficiency.

Official Prices

Official prices are included in the customs tariff of some nations and are the basis for ad valorem duty calculations whenever the actual invoice price is lower. The official price guarantees that a certain minimum import duty will be paid irrespective of the actual invoice price. It thwarts a fairly common arrangement that numerous importers living in high-duty nations have with their foreign suppliers whereby a false low invoice price is issued to reduce the amount of duty to be paid. The importer sends the difference between the false invoice price and the true price separately.

variable levy
An import duty set at the difference between world market prices and local government-supported prices

Variable Levy

One form of **variable levy,** which guarantees that the market price of the import will be the same as that of domestically produced goods, has been used by the EU for imported grains. Calculated daily, the duty level is set at the difference between world market prices and the support price for domestic producers.

Lower Duty for More Local Input

Import duties are set by many nations in such a way that they encourage local input. For example, the finished product ready for sale to the consumer may have a 70 percent ad valorem duty. However, if the product is imported in bulk so that it must be packaged in the importing nation, the duty level may be 30 percent. To encourage some local production, the government may charge only a 10 percent duty on the semifinished inputs. These situations can provide opportunities for foreign manufacturers of low-technology products, such as paint articles and toiletries, to get behind a high-tariff wall with very modest investments.

When tariffs are assessed at very low rates, they are sometimes referred to as *nuisance tariffs*. That is because importers are still required to go through the frequently lengthy process of paying these tariffs, even though their low levels may no longer serve their original intention, such as protecting domestic producers.

NONTARIFF BARRIERS

nontariff barriers (NTBs)
All forms of discrimination against imports other than import duties

Nontariff barriers (NTBs) are all forms of discrimination against imports other than the import duties we have been examining. As nations progressively reduced import duties, nontariff barriers assumed greater relative importance and their use has been increasing rapidly, according to the United Nations.[38] For example, government-required testing and certification requirements increased 600 percent between 1994 and 2004. NTBs can take many forms, including the quantitative and nonquantitative ones discussed below, and the additional costs they impose on producers and exporters help to discourage trade.

quotas
Numerical limits placed on specific classes of imports

Quantitative

One type of quantitative barrier is **quotas,** which are numerical limits for a specific kind of good that a country will permit to be imported without restriction during a specified period. If the quota is *absolute*, once the specified amount has been imported, further importation for the rest of the period (usually a year) is prohibited. Quotas are generally *global*; that is, a total amount is fixed without regard to source. They may also be *allocated*, in which case the government of the importing nation assigns quantities to specific countries. The United States allocates quotas for specific tonnages of sugar to 41 nations. Because of their nature, allocated quotas are sometimes called *discriminatory quotas,* as exemplified by the example below on EU banana imports.

Some producers have used transshipping to fraudulently evade allocated quotas. In such cases, the finished goods are first shipped to a country with an unfilled quota, where the goods are labeled as products of that country, and then shipped to the quota-imposing nation. Prior to the ending of the Multi-Fiber Agreement in 2004 that limited textile imports from other nations, this deceptive labeling scheme was estimated to have brought $2 billion in illegal clothing imports from China into the United States annually. Gitano, for example, pled guilty to charges of fraud for importing Chinese blouses labeled "Made in the Maldives Islands."

Some goods are subject to *tariff-rate quotas*, which permit a stipulated amount to enter duty-free or at a low rate, but when that amount is reached, a much higher duty is charged for subsequent importations. For example, as of January 2006, the EU allows tariff-free importation of 775,000 tons of bananas annually from Caribbean and African countries. Imports beyond that level from Caribbean and African nations, as well as all imports from Central and South American producers, are subject to a tariff of 176 per ton. In effect, European consumers are subsidizing African and Caribbean banana producers (many of which are former colonies of European nations) to the detriment of Central and South American producers.[39]

For many years there has been an agreement among nations against imposing quotas unilaterally on goods (except agricultural products). Therefore, governments have negotiated **voluntary export restraints (VERs)** with other countries (e.g., the Japanese government established a VER to restrict the number of automobiles that its manufacturers could export to the United States annually, and the Canadian government agreed to a VER to limit the amount of Canadian lumber to be exported to the United States). Although *VER* is a generic term for all bilaterally agreed measures to restrict exports, it has a stricter legal definition in the United States: "an action unilaterally taken to restrict the volume or number of items to be exported during a given period and administered by the exporting country. It is 'voluntary' in the sense that the country has a formal right to eliminate or modify it." It is also voluntary in that the exporting nation may prefer its consequences to any trade barriers the importing nation might impose.

voluntary export restraints (VERs)
Export quotas imposed by the exporting nation

Orderly Marketing Arrangements

Orderly marketing arrangements are VERs consisting of formal agreements between the governments of exporting and importing countries to restrict international competition and preserve some of the national market for local producers. Usually, they stipulate the size of the export or import quotas that each nation will have for a particular good. The largest and oldest such arrangement was the Multi-Fiber Arrangement (MFA), which began in 1973 and regulated about 80 percent of the world's textile and clothing exports to the industrialized nations.

Most nontariff barriers such as quotas, VERs, and orderly marketing arrangements are scheduled to be eliminated as a result of the 1994 GATT negotiations (Uruguay Round). For example, textile quotas under the MFA were phased out as of January 1, 2005.[40]

orderly marketing arrangements
Formal agreements between exporting and importing countries that stipulate the import or export quotas each nation will have for a good

Nonquantitative Nontariff Barriers

Many international trade specialists claim that the most significant nontariff barriers are the nonquantitative type. Governments have tended to establish nontariff barriers to obtain the protection formerly afforded by import duties. A study of nonquantitative barriers revealed over 800 distinct forms, which may be classified under three major headings: (1) direct government participation in trade, (2) customs and other administrative procedures, and (3) standards.

1. *Direct government participation in trade:* The most common form of direct government participation is the subsidy. Besides protecting industries through subsidies, as was mentioned earlier, nearly all governments subsidize agriculture (see, for example, the earlier Worldview, "Sugar Subsidies: Sweet for Producers, Not for Consumers"). Agricultural support programs are often promoted as being targeted toward protecting smaller farms and traditional rural economies. However, the largest 25 percent of farms receive 90 percent of the total level of agricultural support in the United States, 75 percent in Canada, 70 percent in the EU, and 68 percent in Japan.[41]

Government procurement policies also are trade barriers because they usually favor domestic producers and severely restrict purchases of imported goods by government agencies. Policies may also require that products purchased by government agencies have a stipulated minimum *local content.* Since the WTO Government Procurement Agreement went into effect, most nations have opened their government business to foreign bidders to comply with its requirements. However, as noted by the EU, the American government still has policies in place that may substantially interfere with international trade. For example, similar to practices in Canada and elsewhere in the world, the Buy America Act has a range of measures that either prohibit public sector organizations from purchasing from foreign suppliers of goods or services or hinder such purchases through mechanisms such as requirements for local content or the provision of advantageous pricing terms for American suppliers. The Department of Defense, which is the U.S. government's largest public procurement agency, excludes foreign suppliers from many contracts, including but not restricted to "national security" issues that were discussed earlier in this chapter. During the reconstruction efforts in Iraq after the 2003 invasion, for example, many of the major contracts were permitted to be granted only to American firms.[42] The 1920 Jones Act requires that cargo being moved between U.S. ports travel only on ships built, owned, and crewed by Americans. The United States is one of only five nations that require ships for domestic use to be built in domestic shipyards.

2. *Customs and other administrative procedures:* These barriers cover a large variety of government policies and procedures that either discriminate against imports or favor exports. For example, in China, a product being imported may be subject to different rates of duty, depending on the port of entry and an arbitrary determination of the customs value. Because of this flexibility, customs charges often depend on negotiations between Chinese customs officials and managers. It is alleged that corruption is often involved.[43]

    Governments have also found ways to discriminate against the exportation of services. When serving international markets, airlines face a number of situations in which the national airline receives preferential treatment, such as in the provision of airport services, airport counter locations, and number of landing slots. Other examples of discrimination are the Canadian government's giving tax deductions to local businesses that advertise on Canadian TV, but not doing so when they use American stations across the border, and Australia's requiring that television commercials be shot in Australia.

3. *Standards:* Both governmental and private standards to protect the health and safety of a nation's citizens certainly are desirable, but for years exporting firms have been plagued by many standards that are complex and discriminatory. For example, Canadian regulations treat products such as calcium-enriched orange juice as drugs and thus subject to special production and marketing requirements.[44] Japan prohibits the importation of creamy mustard, light mayonnaise, or figs containing potassium sorbate, a food additive approved by numerous international food bodies and allowed by the Japanese in 36 other foods, primarily traditional Japanese products that are typically made only in Japan.[45] Kellogg Company must make four different versions of corn flakes at its European plants, because different nations have different standards regarding the vitamins that can be added to the cereal. Caterpillar discovered that requirements for the size and location of yield signs and license plate holders on the backs of vehicles differ, sometimes only by centimeters, from nation to nation.[46]

    The European Parliament passed biotech food labeling requirements that impose mandatory traceability of genetically modified (GM) organisms and stringent labeling of foods that contain GM ingredients. The rationale was ostensibly to protect consumers from potential harm associated with consumption of GMs, although the United States and other countries have protested that no scientific evidence exists of such harm. The requirements include labels stating "This product is produced from GM organisms" and strict limits on mixing GM and non-GM ingredients in food exported to the EU. The United States is one of the world's leading producers and exporters of GM crops, with 75 percent of soybeans, 71 percent of cotton, and 34 percent of corn being GM. "The new law will further restrict access for U.S. soybeans and soybean products while negatively impacting consumers in the EU," stated Ron Heck of the American Soybean Association. "Because there is a strong likelihood that the new labeling and traceability regime will simply serve as a 'replacement' nontariff barrier to trade with the EU, we are not particularly hopeful that the market will be open any time soon," stated Barbara Isman of the Canola Council of Canada. In response to U.S. threats to file a WTO complaint against the EU, the environmental group Friends of the Earth issued a press release that stated, "It is clear that this U.S. Administration, backed by some of the richest and most powerful lobbyists in U.S. politics, is determined to use the secretive, biased and undemocratic procedures of the WTO to bulldoze through attempts by other states to set minimum environmental, social and health standards. If this attempt succeeds, the U.S. will force GM foods onto European markets regardless of the wishes of consumers."[47]

These few examples give an idea of the complexity involved in trying to eliminate nontariff barriers. As a consequence of the Uruguay Round,* considerable progress has been made, but there is still much more work to be done before nontariff barriers and their trade-distorting effects are eliminated.

Exporting companies need to be informed about the changing status of tariff and nontariff barriers in the countries where they are doing business or would like to do business. Those that have stayed away from markets with extremely high import duties or nontariff barriers, such as product standards or customs procedures designed to keep out foreign products, may find these barriers no longer exist.

FROM MULTINATIONAL TO GLOBALLY INTEGRATED MANUFACTURING SYSTEMS

The lowering of import duties and the elimination or weakening of nontariff barriers are making it easier and less costly for companies to locate their production activities in lower-cost countries. Paying lower import duties on components manufactured elsewhere reduces their landed cost, and not having to overcome nontariff barriers makes the international dispersion of production activities possible and more economical. Also, a multidomestic company with numerous manufacturing plants, each of which has a complete manufacturing system to supply the country where it is located, may find that with lower barriers to importation, it has two possibilities for improving operational efficiency:

1. Close the least efficient plants, and supply their markets with imports from other subsidiaries.

2. Change the multidomestic manufacturing system to a globally integrated system in which each plant performs the activities at which it is most efficient.

COSTS OF BARRIERS TO TRADE

Trade restraints in the United States and other countries cost consumers tens of billions of dollars per year, while benefiting a relatively small number of companies in the protected sectors of the economy. The sugar industry provides an interesting example of this situation, as discussed in the earlier Worldview, "Sugar Subsidies: Sweet for Producers, Not for Consumers."

Sugar is not an isolated example of the costs associated with trade barriers. A recent study of just 20 product groups in protected industries showed that the average consumer cost per job saved was $231,289 per year. This means that consumers paid over seven times the average annual compensation of manufacturing workers to preserve jobs through import constraints. Many of these sectors have been shielded from imports for 45 years or more. Studies done in other countries show similar results.[48]

---

*The Uruguay Round is discussed in Chapter 4.

If you sell in one EU member-country, you can sell in them all, right? Wrong. EU rules allow member-countries to prohibit imports that threaten public safety, and there is no agreement on what constitutes such a threat. Dermont Manufacturing Co., a small firm ($25 million in sales), makes hoses that connect gas appliances to gas outlets. It had been selling them throughout Europe when, suddenly, one day a U.S. manufacturer of deep-fat fryers who was supplying McDonald's told Dermont's president, Evan Seagal, that McDonald's could no longer use his hoses in its British restaurants. Similar situations began occurring elsewhere: French health inspectors ordered Euro Disney to replace Dermont hoses. The reason for the different national standards was that the gas hoses were considered essential to the safe operation of the gas appliances and therefore fell under product safety rules, thus permitting each nation to establish its own standards.

Seagal studied the various rules and realized that his product could not meet them. As is often the case, the rules were written by committees composed of a nation's experts. Who were they? The producers of the hoses who were Dermont's competitors. Designs varied from country to country, and all were different from Dermont's

hose. Seagal argues that there were no reasons for the differences in design except to keep his product out of the local market. They had no bearing on either safety or performance. The president of the American National Standards Institute, the U.S. standards organization, claimed that the Dermont case is "clearly a case of European standards being used as a barrier to trade."

Meanwhile, Dermont has begun obtaining product approval from individual EU countries. The U.S. government has been urging the European Committee for Standardization to begin developing a harmonized European standard for gas connector hoses for years. The initial draft of such a harmonized European standard impedes access to the EU by Dermont due to its design specifications, and the company has experienced extensive difficulties in gaining access to the process for standard setting. Both the U.S. government and U.S. industry have continued to argue in favor of performance-based standards as well as increased transparency in the standard-setting process.

Sources: "Europe's 'Unity' Undoes a U.S. Exporter," *The Wall Street Journal*, April 1, 1996, p. B1; Office of the Foreign Trade Representative, "The 2000 Estimate Report on Foreign Trade Barriers," www.ustr.gov/reports/nte/2000//contents.html (August 28, 2000); and Office of the Foreign Trade Representative, *2006 National Trade Estimate Report on Foreign Trade Barriers* (Washington, DC: United States Trade Representative, 2006), pp. 236–37.

The International Monetary Fund estimated that removal of tariff and subsidy supports for agriculture would increase global economic welfare by $128 billion per year, with nearly one-quarter of that benefit going to developing countries, including food-exporting nations in sub-Saharan Africa that have many of the world's poorest people.[49] The secretary-general of the United Nations, Kofi Annan, commented on the effects of barriers to trade by saying:

> *Rich countries' average tariffs on manufactured products imported from developing countries are now four times higher than those they levy on products which come mainly from other industrialized countries. Quotas and "antidumping" penalties are also used to keep Third World imports out of First World markets, especially in sectors where poorer countries have a competitive edge, such as agriculture, textiles and clothing.*[50]

International Investment Theories

Contemporary international investment theory has been expanded considerably from the classical theory, which postulated that differences in interest rates for investments of equal risk were the reason international capital moved from one nation to another. For this to happen, there had to be perfect competition, but as Kindleberger, a noted economist, stated, "Under perfect competition, foreign direct investment would not occur, nor would it be likely to occur in a world wherein the conditions were even approximately competitive."[51] This section focuses specifically on theories of foreign direct investment, which comprises both ownership and control of international investments involving real or physical assets such as plants and other facilities, rather than theories regarding other types of international investment such as portfolios of stocks, bonds, or other forms of debt. Foreign direct investment involves the establishment of production or other facilities abroad, either through greenfield investment (the establishment of new facilities from the ground up) or cross-border acquisition (the purchase of an existing business in another nation). It is usually assumed that strategic motives will be the driving force for decisions to invest abroad, driven by desire to find new markets, access raw materials, achieve production efficiencies, gain access to new technologies or managerial expertise, enhance political safety of the firm's operations, or respond to competitive or other pressures in the external environment.[52]

MONOPOLISTIC ADVANTAGE THEORY

The modern **monopolistic advantage theory** stems from Stephen Hymer's dissertation in the 1960s, in which he demonstrated that foreign direct investment occurs largely in oligopolistic industries rather than in industries operating under near-perfect competition. This means that the firms in these industries must possess advantages not available to local firms in order to overcome liabilities associated with being a foreigner—such as lack of knowledge about local market conditions, increased costs of operating at a distance, or differences in culture, language, laws and regulations, or institutions—that cause a foreign company to be at a disadvantage against local firms. Hymer reasoned that the advantages must be economies of scale, superior technology, or superior knowledge in marketing, management, or finance. Foreign direct investment takes place because of these product and factor market imperfections, which enable the multinational enterprise to operate more profitably in foreign markets than can local competitors.[53]

monopolistic advantage theory
Theory that foreign direct investment is made by firms in oligopolistic industries possessing technical and other advantages over indigenous firms

PRODUCT AND FACTOR MARKET IMPERFECTIONS

Caves, a Harvard economist, expanded Hymer's work to show that superior knowledge permitted the investing firm to produce differentiated products that consumers would prefer to similar locally made goods and this would give the firm some control over the selling price and an advantage over indigenous firms. To support these contentions, he noted that companies investing overseas were in industries that typically engaged in heavy product research and marketing efforts.[54]

FINANCIAL FACTORS

Other theories relate to financial factors. Aliber believes that the imperfections in the foreign exchange markets may be responsible for foreign investment. Companies in nations with overvalued currencies are attracted to invest in countries whose currencies are undervalued.[55] Another financially based theory, portfolio theory, suggests that international operations allow for a diversification of risk and therefore tend to maximize the expected return on investment.[56]

INTERNATIONAL PRODUCT LIFE CYCLE

We have already examined this theory to help explain international trade flows, but as we said, there is a close relationship between international trade and international investment. As you saw, the IPLC concept also explains that foreign direct investment is a natural stage in the life of a product. To avoid losing a market that it serves by exporting, a company is often forced to invest in overseas production facilities when other companies begin to offer similar products. This move overseas will be heightened during the third and fourth stages as the company that introduced the product strives to remain competitive, first in its export markets (stage 3) and later in its home market (stage 4), by locating in countries where the factors of production are less expensive.

FOLLOW THE LEADER

Another theory was developed by Knickerbocker, who noted that when one firm, especially the leader in an oligopolistic industry, entered a market, other firms in the industry followed. The follow-the-leader theory is considered defensive because competitors invest to avoid losing the markets served by exports when the initial investor begins local production. They may also fear that the initiator will achieve some advantage of risk diversification that they will not have unless they also enter the market.[57] In addition, suspecting that the initiator knows something they do not, they may feel it is better to be safe than sorry.

CROSS INVESTMENT

Graham noted a tendency for **cross investment** by European and American firms in certain oligopolistic industries; that is, European firms tended to invest in the United States when American companies had gone to Europe. He postulated that such investments would permit the American subsidiaries of European firms to retaliate in the home market of U.S. companies if the European subsidiaries of these companies initiated some aggressive tactic, such as price cutting, in the European market.[58] Of course, as we noted in Chapter 2, there are a number of other reasons investment by multinationals takes place in a foreign country, such as *following the customer* (Japanese parts manufacturers following Japanese auto manufacturers into the United States, Canada, or Europe), *seeking knowledge* (Japanese and European investment in Silicon Valley), and *benefiting from political and economic stability of the host country.*

INTERNALIZATION THEORY

The **internalization theory** is an extension of the market imperfection theory. A firm has superior knowledge, but due to inefficiency in external markets, the firm may obtain a higher price for that knowledge by using the knowledge itself rather than by selling it in the open market. By investing in foreign subsidiaries for activities such as supply, production, or distribution, rather than licensing, the company is able to send the knowledge across borders while maintaining it within the firm. The expected result is the firm's ability to realize a superior return on the investment made to produce this knowledge, particularly as the knowledge is embodied in various products or services that are sold to customers.[59]

DYNAMIC CAPABILITIES

The **dynamic capability** perspective, which is linked to resource-based views of the firm, argues that ownership of specific knowledge or resources is necessary, but not sufficient, for achieving success in international FDI. The firm must also be able to effectively create and exploit dynamic capabilities for quality and/or quantity-based deployment, and these capabilities must be transferable to international environments in order to produce competitive advantage. Companies typically develop centers of excellence in order to develop distinctive competencies that will be subsequently applied to their investments within the host countries.

DUNNING'S ECLECTIC THEORY OF INTERNATIONAL PRODUCTION

The eclectic theory, which combines elements of some of those we have discussed, is the most widely cited and accepted theory of FDI currently. Developed by Dunning, the **eclectic theory of international production** attempts to provide an overall framework for explaining why firms choose to engage in FDI rather than serve foreign markets through alternatives such as exporting, licensing, management contracts, joint ventures, or strategic alliances. This theory maintains that if a firm is going to invest in production facilities overseas, it must have three kinds of advantages:

1. *Ownership-specific:* This is the extent to which a firm has or can develop a firm-specific advantage through ownership of tangible and intangible assets that are not available to other firms and can be transferred abroad. The three basic types of ownership-specific advantages include knowledge or technology, economies of scale or scope, and monopolistic advantages associated with unique access to critical inputs or outputs. The advantage generates lower costs and/or higher revenues that will offset the added costs of operating at a distance within a foreign location.

2. *Location-specific:* A foreign market must have specific characteristics, of an economic, social, or political nature, that will permit the firm to profitably exploit its firm-specific advantages by locating to that market.

3. *Internalization:* Firms have various alternatives for entering foreign markets, ranging from arm's-length market transactions to the use of hierarchy via a wholly owned subsidiary, as we will discuss in Chapter 16. It is in the firm's best interests to exploit its ownership-specific advantages through internalization in those situations where either the market does not exist or it functions inefficiently, causing the transaction costs of using market-based (arm's-length) options to be too high.

Because of the names of these three types of advantages that a firm must have, the eclectic theory of international production is sometimes referred to as the *OLI model*. This theory provides an explanation for an international firm's choice of its overseas production facilities. The firm must have both location and ownership advantages to invest in a foreign plant. It will invest where it is most profitable to internalize its monopolistic advantage.[60] These investments can be proactive, being strategically anticipated and controlled in advance by the firm's management team, or reactive, in response to the discovery of market imperfections.

There is one commonality to nearly all of these theories that is supported by empirical tests—the major part of direct foreign investment is made by large, research-intensive firms in oligopolistic industries. Also, all these theories offer reasons companies find it *profitable* to invest overseas. However, as we stated in Chapter 2, all motives can be linked in some way to the desire to increase or protect not only profits but also *sales* and *markets*.

Summary

Explain the theories that attempt to explain why certain goods are traded internationally.

Why do nations trade? Mercantilists did so to build up storehouses of gold. Later, Adam Smith showed that a nation will export goods that it can produce with less labor than can other nations. Ricardo then proved that even though a country is less efficient than other nations, that country can still profit by exporting goods if it holds a comparative advantage in the production of those goods.

The idea that a nation tends to export products requiring a large amount of a relatively abundant factor was offered by Heckscher and Ohlin in their theory of factor endowment. In the 1920s, economists realized that economies of scale affect international trade because they permit the industries of a nation to become low-cost producers without having an abundance of a class of production factors. As in the case of comparative advantage, nations specialize in the production of a few products and trade to supply the rest. The Linder theory of overlapping demand states that because customers' tastes are strongly affected by income levels, a nation's income level per capita determines the kind of goods they will demand. The kinds of goods produced to meet this demand reflect the country's income per capita level. International trade in manufactured goods will be greater between nations with similar levels of per capita income.

The international product life cycle theory states that many products first produced in the United States or other developed countries are eventually produced in less developed nations and become imports to the very countries in which their production began. Krugman showed how economies of scale and imperfect competition can explain high levels of intraindustry trade. Marshall and Porter helped to explain how nations can achieve competitive advantage through the emergence of regional clusters, with Porter claiming that four classes of variables are critical in this regard: demand conditions, factor conditions, related and supporting industries, and firm strategy, structure, and rivalry.

Discuss the arguments for imposing trade restrictions.

Special-interest groups demand protection for defense industries so that their country will have these industries' output in wartime and will not depend on imports, which might not be available. Critics say that it would be far more efficient to subsidize some firms, that is, pay them to be ready. New industries in developing nations frequently request barriers to imports of competing products from developed countries. The argument is that the infant industry must have time to gain experience before having to confront world competition. Protectionists argue for protection from cheap imports by claiming that other countries with lower hourly labor rates than those in the protectionist's nation can flood the protectionist's nation with low-priced goods and take away domestic jobs. However, hourly labor rates are just a small part of production costs for many industries. There may be legislated fringe benefits that are a much higher percentage of the direct wages than is the case in developed nations. Productivity per worker may be considerably lower in developing nations, so less is produced for a given hourly rate. Commonly, also, the costs of the other factors of production that must be included in the cost of production often are higher in developing nations. Others want "fair" competition, that is, an import duty to raise the cost of the imported good to the price of the imported article to eliminate any "unfair" advantage that the foreign competitor may have. This, of course, nullifies the comparative advantage. Companies will also demand that their government retaliate against dumping and subsidies offered by their competitors in other countries.

Explain the two basic kinds of import restrictions: tariff and nontariff trade barriers.

In response to demands for protection, governments impose import duties (tariff barriers); nontariff barriers, such as quotas, voluntary export restraints, and orderly marketing arrangements; and nonquantitative nontariff barriers, such as direct government participation in trade, customs, and other administrative procedures and standards for health, safety, and product quality.

Appreciate the relevance of the changing status of tariff and nontariff barriers to managers.

Exporting firms may find that because tariff and nontariff barriers have been eliminated or lowered, they can now enter markets that were previously closed to them. It also is easier for firms to locate production activities in lower-cost nations to improve the efficiency of their manufacturing systems. Multidomestic firms may be able to close less efficient plants and supply those markets by exporting from more efficient ones.

Explain some of the theories of foreign direct investment.

International investment theory attempts to explain why foreign direct investment (FDI) takes place. Product and factor market imperfections provide firms, primarily in oligopolistic industries, with advantages not open to indigenous companies. The international product life cycle theory explains international investment as well as international trade. Some firms follow the industry leader, and the tendency of European firms to invest in the United States and vice versa seems to indicate that cross investment is done for defensive reasons. There are two financially based explanations of foreign direct investment. One holds that foreign exchange market imperfections attract firms from nations with overvalued currencies to invest in nations with undervalued currencies. The second theory postulates that FDI is made to diversify risk. Empirical tests reveal that most FDI is made by large, research-intensive firms in oligopolistic industries. The internalization theory states that firms will seek to invest in foreign subsidiaries, rather than license their superior knowledge, to receive a better return on the investment used to develop that knowledge. The dynamic capabilities perspective suggests that firms must have not only ownership of specific knowledge or resources but also the ability to dynamically create and exploit capabilities in order to achieve success in international FDI. The eclectic theory of international production explains an international firm's choice of its overseas production facilities. The firm must have location and ownership advantages to invest in a foreign plant. It will invest where it is most profitable to internalize its monopolistic advantage.

Key Words

mercantilism (p. 64)

absolute advantage (p. 65)

comparative advantage (p. 67)

factor endowment (p. 69)

exchange rate (p. 72)

currency devaluation (p. 73)

international product life cycle (IPLC) (p. 74)

national competitiveness (p. 78)

dumping (p. 83)

subsidies (p. 84)

countervailing duties (p. 85)

tariffs (p. 86)

ad valorem duty (p. 87)

specific duty (p. 88)

compound duty (p. 88)

variable levy (p. 88)

nontariff barriers (NTBs) (p. 88)

quotas (p. 88)

voluntary export restraints (VERs) (p. 89)

orderly marketing arrangements (p. 89)

monopolistic advantage theory (p. 93)

cross investment (p. 94)

internalization theory (p. 94)

dynamic capability (p. 94)

eclectic theory of international production (p. 94)

1. Describe mercantilism, and explain why mercantilism has been argued to be a poor approach to use in order to promote economic development and prosperity.

2. a. Explain Adam Smith's theory of absolute advantage.
   b. How does Ricardo's theory of comparative advantage differ from the theory of absolute advantage?
   c. Using the example from the chapter, explain why no gains from specialization exist (and thus why two countries could not trade in a manner that benefits each) if there is no pattern of comparative advantage (if the ratios of soybeans to cloth production are the same in the two countries).

3. Consider the case in which a country does not have a comparative advantage in the production of a product, such as apples, because its soils or climate are not appropriate. Explain who would be likely to favor free trade, and who would be likely to oppose free trade, in this product.

4. What is the relationship between the Heckscher-Ohlin factor endowment theory and the theories in question 2?

5. Why were Leontief's empirical results considered to be paradoxical?

6. Why does most of the world's international trade take place between economies that are similar in their level of economic development?

7. Name some products that you believe have passed through the four stages of the international product life cycle.

8. What factors increase the cost of trading goods and services across borders? Can these costs be reduced? How?

9. It seems that free, unrestricted international trade, in which each nation produces and exports products for which it has a comparative advantage, will enable everyone to have a higher level of living. Why, then, does every country have import duty restrictions?

10. "We certainly need defense industries, and we must protect them from import competition by placing restrictions on competitive imports." True or false? Is there an alternative to trade restrictions that might make more economic sense?

11. Suppose that a country negotiates an agreement with its trade partners to restrict its imports through voluntary export restrictions (VERs). What impacts might be expected from implementing such VERs?

12. "Workers are paid $20 an hour in the United States but only $4 in Taiwan. Of course we can't compete. We need to protect our jobs from cheap foreign labor." What are some possible problems with this statement?

13. There are two general classifications of import duties: tariff and nontariff barriers.
    a. Describe the various types of tariff barriers.
    b. What are some of the nontariff barriers?

14. "A firm entering the market first will soon dominate it, and the large market share it acquires will enable it to obtain the benefits of economies of scale." True or false? Remember that there are at least two studies showing that first movers held large market shares.

15. According to theories presented in this chapter, why do companies engage in foreign direct investment?

Use the globalEDGE site (http://globalEDGE.msu.edu/) to complete the following exercises:

1. Just as the worldwide export of manufactured products and commercial services varies across regions of the world, so does the difference between nonfinancial and financial transnational corporations (TNCs). The *World Investment Report* provides electronic access to comprehensive statistics on the top financial TNCs worldwide. So you can compare the top 10 nonfinancial TNCs from the previous chapter with the current exercise, locate the list of the 50 largest financial TNCs. Which countries are represented in the top 10 on each list (nonfinancial and financial TNCs)? Is there any difference in the countries represented in the two rankings? Which three TNCs score highest on this survey's Internationalization Index (II)? How does this compare to the top three nonfinancial institutions? What is the difference between this survey's II and the previous chapter's ranking based on the TNI? Why would the United Nations use two different methods to measure internationalization?

2. Your company is considering opening a new factory in Latin America. As such, the strategic management division is in the process of evaluating the specific locations for such an operation. The pool of candidate countries has been narrowed to Argentina, Mexico, and Brazil. By using the *country fact sheets* available through a resource provided by the United Nations at the globalEDGE Web site, prepare a short report comparing the foreign direct investment (*FDI*) environment and other relevant regulations in these three countries.

Minicase 3.1 Is Your Chocolate the Result of Unfair Exploitation of Child Labor?

When you last savored a bar of rich chocolate, a cup of hot cocoa, or a piece of chocolate cake or scoop of chocolate ice cream, did you know that you may have unwittingly been consuming a product made with child slaves?

Chocolate, made from the fruit (cocoa bean) of the Theobroma cacao tree, is one of the most-traded agricultural products in the world. The top 10 chocolate-consuming nations are all developed countries in Europe or the United States. In the United States, two-thirds of the $13 billion chocolate industry is dominated by two firms: M&M Mars and Hershey.

About 70 percent of the world's cocoa is produced in West Africa. In practice, beans from different nations are usually mixed together during their exportation and transport to processing plants in the importing nations. So Hershey bars, Snickers, M&Ms, KitKats, Nestlé chocolates, fudge, hot chocolate—essentially all of these delicacies that are regularly enjoyed by hundreds of millions of consumers—will include cocoa from West Africa, especially the Côte d'Ivoire (Ivory Coast). With about 43 percent of the world's total cocoa production, Côte d'Ivoire produces more than three times the level of the second-largest cocoa producer.

Results of a survey on child labor in West Africa, released in 2002, found that 284,000 children were working in hazardous conditions on West African cocoa farms, with the majority (200,000) working in Côte d'Ivoire. Nearly two-thirds of the child laborers were under the age of 14. Working conditions were described as slavelike, with 29 percent of the surveyed child workers in the Côte d'Ivoire indicating that "they were not free to leave their place of employment should they so wish." Many of these children had been brought into the cocoa-growing areas from distant regions of the Côte d'Ivoire or from poverty stricken countries such as Burkina Faso, Mali, and Togo, often after being kidnapped. Some of the child laborers had been sold by their parents in the expectation that the child's earnings would be sent home. Although paid less than 60 percent of the rate of adult workers, children frequently worked for over 12 hours per day, 6 days a week, and were regularly beaten. Over half of the children applied pesticides without protective gear. Only 34 percent of the children working on cocoa farms went to school, which was about half the level for children who were not working on cocoa farms. The rate of school enrollment was even lower for girls.

These child laborers seemed to be trapped in a vicious cycle: They were forced into work due to kidnapping or economic circumstances faced by themselves and/or their families, they earned subsistence wages, and because most had not been to school and had minimal skills, their prospects for seeking other employment options were limited.

In the late 1990s, exploitation of child labor in the cocoa industry began to receive publicity, primarily by nongovernmental organizations. Efforts to raise awareness of the situation faced great challenges, and even today a majority of consumers seem unaware of the circumstances behind the production of their favorite chocolate treats. Yet the atrocious nature of the child labor situation in the cocoa industry compelled the media, public interest groups, and others to continue their efforts. Hard-hitting news stories began to appear on television and radio and in magazines and newspapers across North America and Europe. Pressure grew for intervention, such as international trade sanctions. The Harkin-Engel bill, passed by the U.S. House of Representatives, proposed a federal system of certification and labeling requirements that would state whether a cocoa-based product had been made in a "slave-free" manner.

Fearing the implications of boycotts, trade sanctions, or certification and labeling requirements in key markets such as the United States and Europe, representatives from the chocolate industry attempted to develop a strategy for dealing with the problem. After the Chocolate Manufacturers Association hired former senators George Mitchell and Bob Dole to lobby against the Harkin-Engel bill and prevent its passage in the U.S. Senate, the industry agreed to self-regulate and attempt to change the child labor practices. A protocol for the industry was developed that established a timetable for eliminating child labor and forced labor in the production of cocoa. A self-imposed deadline was set for establishing a viable monitoring and certification system: July 1, 2005.

Industry representatives have complained that progress toward eliminating child labor in cocoa production has been hindered by traditional culture in the agriculturally based producing nations, compounded by civil war and other complications. Yet the important cocoa-producing nations of Nigeria and Ghana, with the assistance of the International Labor Organization and the International Programme on the Elimination of Child Labour (IPEC), have subsequently established national programs to eliminate child labor in their countries. So far, the Côte d'Ivoire has made only limited effort to initiate such programs.

In February 2005, several U.S. congressmen held a news conference in which they declared that they would not be buying chocolate for their wives for Valentine's Day, because the candy had probably been made from cocoa produced in the Côte d'Ivoire with child slaves. Subsequently, after charging that the industry had failed to meet its self-imposed July 2005 deadline, the International Labor Rights Fund filed a lawsuit in federal court in Los Angeles against several international manufacturers of chocolate. The suit claimed that the manufacturers had ignored repeated, well-documented warnings about the exploitative use of child labor on cocoa farms in the Côte d'Ivoire.

In the absence of prompt and effective action by the chocolate and cocoa industry, a number of companies have begun producing fair-trade-certified chocolate. Through observing a strict set of guidelines associated with fair-trade certification, these companies guarantee that a consumer of one of their chocolate products is "not an unwitting participant in this very inhumane situation." Fairtrade Labeling Organizations International, a consortium of fair-trade organizations from Canada, the United States, Japan, and 17 European nations, establishes certification standards. In the United States, Transfair USA is the sole independent, third-party body for certifying fair-trade practices (www.transfairusa.org).

Fair-trade practices essentially involve international subsidies to farmers in developing countries, ensuring that farmers who are certified as engaging in fair-trade practices will receive a price for their produce that will at least cover their costs of production. By providing a price floor, fair-trade practices protect Third World farmers from the ruinous fluctuations in commodity prices that result from free trade practices. At the same time, fair-trade certification requires that farmers engage in appropriate social, labor, and environmental practices, such as paying livable wages and not using child or slave labor. In addition the cocoa program, fair-trade certification programs have been implemented for a range of other products, such as coffee, bananas, and crafts.

Although still a nascent movement, sales of fair-trade-certified products are growing. For example, Dunkin' Donuts sells only fair-trade coffee in its stores. Will there be a similar result for chocolate? Already, about two dozen companies make fair-trade chocolate in the United States, including Clif-Bar, Cloud Nine, Newman's Own Organics, Kailua Candy Company, and Sweet Earth Organic Chocolates.

Discussion Questions

1. Should labor practices in another country be a relevant consideration in international trade? Why or why not?

2. With regard to trade in products such as cocoa, what options are available to governments, businesses, and consumers for dealing with practices such as child labor or slave labor in other countries? What are the implications associated with each of these options?

3. How would international trade theorists view the fair-trade movement?

Source: "Child Labor in the Cocoa Sector of West Africa," International Institute of Tropical Agriculture, August 2002, www.iita.org/news/cocoa.pdf (August 2, 2006); "Combating Child Labour in Cocoa Growing," International Programme on the Elimination of Child Labour, Geneva, February 2005; "Cal Poly Professor Heading to Africa to Investigate Chocolate–Slave Labor Ties," www.calstate.edu/newsline/2005/n20050819slo1.shtml (August 2, 2006); Sweet Earth Organic Chocolates, "Our Philosophy," www.sweetearthchocolates.com/level.itml/icOid/68 (August 2, 2006); Tom Neuhaus, "A Luscious Exploration of 3 Fair-Trade-Certified Cocoa Cooperatives," *HopeDance Magazine*, www.hopedance.org/new/issues/47/article6.html (August 2, 2006); "Fair Trade Q&A," www.globalexchange.org/campaigns/fairtrade/fairtradeqa.html (August 2, 2006); and Samlanchith Chanthavong, "Chocolate and Slavery: Child Labor in Côte d'Ivoire," www.american.edu/TED/chocolate-slave.htm (August 2, 2006).

Cooperation among Nations

The world we share is becoming increasingly interconnected in complex and interesting ways. This complexity calls on international institutions and national governments to increase their cooperation to help ensure peace and lead to conditions that support international trade. Business students and business executives need to be aware of the significantly increasing role of intergovernmental and nongovernmental cooperation.

This section includes chapters on international institutions and the international monetary system. These institutions are important to the business student and business executive; they are becoming increasingly important in the daily news, as well, because our awareness of their impact and its potential is increasing. Years ago, a meeting of the IMF or the G8 (G4, G6 or G7) would draw little media attention, being of interest mainly to policy makers and academics. Today, such meetings draw huge numbers of people, many of whom appear to disagree with their objectives.

International institutions can be both a help and a hindrance to businesses. The UN, the World Bank, the IMF, the EU, and the Organization for Economic Cooperation and Development provide forums for coordination and are excellent sources of information for business executives and students. In addition, the World Bank and the regional development banks provide large amounts of financing for projects. On the other hand, businesses may be required to contact such organizations to secure licensing, merger approval, and a host of other items that national governments once provided.

The international institutions and agreements discussed in Chapter 4 are organizations of governments, along with some private organizations, whose main purpose is political, economic, or a combination of the two. Some of these organizations have large amounts of power (such as the EU), and others have less power, but all are important to business. The EU, for example, is especially important in its relationship to the U.S. Now the EU speaks for its 25 European member-countries in matters such as trade policy, antitrust issues, and monetary policy.

The international monetary system, discussed in Chapter 5, is developing and changing constantly, and the international business student and business executive do well to know the past in order to understand the system under which we operate today. Much like international institutions, the international monetary system is based on cooperation among governments, on multilateral cooperation. Chapter 5 reviews the history of our monetary system, moving from the gold standard to a fixed rate system, and on to the floating rate system that allows for today's huge growth in international trade. It concludes with a review of the balance of payments system.

101

4

International Institutions from an International Business Perspective

I believe that globalization—the removal of barriers to free trade and the closer integration of national economies—can be a force for good and that it has the potential to enrich everyone in the world, particularly the poor. But I also believe that if this is to be the case, the way globalization has been managed, including the international trade agreements that have played such a large role in removing those barriers and the policies that have been imposed on the developing countries in the process of globalization, need to be radically rethought.

—*Joseph E. Stiglitz, former Chief Economist of the World Bank*

In a world of interconnected threats and challenges, it is in each country's self-interest that all of them are addressed effectively. Hence, the cause of larger freedom can only be advanced by broad, deep and sustained global cooperation among States. Such cooperation is possible if every country's policies take into account not only the needs of its own citizens but also the needs of others. This kind of cooperation not only advances everyone's interests but also recognizes our common humanity.

—*Kofi A. Annan, former Secretary-General, United Nations,* In Larger Freedom, *2005*

The United Nations Millennium Goals: A Call for Change

Six billion human beings. Rapid globalization. Intractable conflicts. Genocide and ethnic cleansing. Promoting development. Combating poverty and AIDS. Controlling climate change. As humanity reflects on the challenges we face at this millennial milestone, it is a chance also to reflect on the only global organization to which we can turn: the United Nations.

—We the Peoples, the Millennium Assembly of the United Nations

These are facts about how others live on our shared globe: More than 1 billion people in the world live on less than one dollar a day. In total, 2.7 billion struggle to survive on less than two dollars per day. In some deeply impoverished nations less than half of the children are in primary school and under 20 percent go to secondary school. Around the world, a total of 114 million children do not get even a basic education, and 584 million women are illiterate. Overall illiteracy is 18 percent, 13 percent among males, and 23 percent among females.[a] To change these facts, at the beginning of the 21st century, at the largest meeting of world leaders in history, the United Nations established eight ambitious Millennium Development Goals, with a target date of 2015. These goals are to eradicate poverty and hunger, to achieve universal primary education, to promote gender equality and empower women, to reduce child mortality, to improve maternal health, to combat HIV/AIDS, malaria, and other diseases, to ensure environmental sustainability, and to develop a global partnership for development. The role of business organizations in these efforts is great, just as the achievement of these efforts is important to business. In addition to indicating the basic humanitarian obligation recognized by many businesses, these statistics represent potential markets and potential workers. The efforts themselves help to build a more stable world in which business can prosper.

The 2005 Millennium Development Goals Report indicates solid progress in some areas, with much greater work to be done in others. The progress chart on page 109 summarizes where the world stood as of September 2005 on the first seven goals. ■

[a]UNESCO Institute for Statistics, 2004 literacy assessment, http://portal.unesco.org/education/en/ev.php-URL_ID=35964&URL_DO=DO_TOPIC&URL_SECTION=201.html (accessed May 22, 2006).

CONCEPT PREVIEWS

After reading this chapter, you should be able to:

describe the influence the mainly political international institutions have on international businesses and their relevance to international business

identify the major organs of the United Nations, their general purpose, and their significance to international business

discuss the World Trade Organization and its predecessor, GATT

appreciate the resources of the Organisation for Economic Cooperation and Development

describe the major purpose and effectiveness of OPEC

identify economic integration agreements and the effectiveness of the major ones

explain the North American Free Trade Agreement and its impact on business

discuss the impact of the EU and its future challenges

Gli Affari Internazionali

cionales

onales Geschäft Παγοσμιο Business

Negócios Internacionais   Los Negócios Internacionais

Within any given country, the national government takes responsibility for providing the economic, political, legal, and monetary stability that businesses in that country require in order to prosper. For example, in the United States, the federal government seeks to ensure that the financial and money markets are orderly and that inflation is constrained. The federal government also provides an orderly, predictable legal and political environment so that business decision makers can assess the risks their activities might face and then develop ways to control these risks as part of their long-term investment plans. When business activities cross national borders, they need the same sort of stability and predictability. To meet this need, a variety of international political, legal, military, and economic institutions have been developed through cooperative agreements among nations. Knowledge of these institutions is important for several reasons. First, they exist to foster peace and stability among nations—conditions that matter greatly to the conduct of international business. Second, they often are valuable resources for commercial data and important information about market conditions, demographics, and trade relationships. Third, they also may have regulatory functions.

To illustrate the importance of strong international institutions, think about the roles of the United States as the sole superpower on the global stage and of China as an upcoming nation preparing for a major global role. Martin Wolfe, chief economist at the *Financial Times*, notes in a recent article that both nations are fated to cooperate.[1] Yet look at their differences: As Wolfe points out, one is a democracy, the other an autocracy; one is "a child of the enlightenment," the other an agrarian empire. Although working together will not be easy for either, international institutions facilitate such endeavors by developing multilateral solutions, in which all nations cooperate. For individual nations, agreeing to a mutually negotiated UN resolution or a World Trade Organization rule is easier than agreeing to a bilateral negotiation, where there is a winner and a loser and where power and prestige are at stake. There is no humiliation at stake with a negotiated UN resolution that applies to all nations' behavior.

Note, too, that these institutions provide opportunities for interesting careers. The United Nations and the Organisation for Economic Cooperation and Development routinely have career positions to fill in such fields as economics, languages, law, project management, and information technology. For more information, contact the specific organization through its Web site (e.g., the UN's main portal is www.un.org; the Organisation for Economic Cooperation and Development is www.oecd.org; and the World Trade Organization's is www.wto.org).

In this chapter, we examine a number of these institutions. Some of them are worldwide, while others operate in specific regions of the world. Some have memberships composed of many countries, while others have relatively few member-nations. Most are groupings of governments, but a few are private. Our review of them is organized according to the institution's primary purpose—political or economic. *Political* means related to administration and governance, while *economic* suggests a focus on money, trade, and commerce. Institutions are dynamic; they continuously evolve, and as they do, their purposes tend to shift because the world itself is changing. Complex international institutions, such as those discussed in this chapter, frequently have purposes that are neither all political nor all economic. The European Union (EU), for example, illustrates well the growing overlap of the political and the economic arenas. The EU began with a primarily economic purpose and has grown to have a strong political purpose as well. Figure 4.1 illustrates international institutions based on their primary organizational purpose: political, economic, or both.

Our review begins with a look at the political institutions: the United Nations; two smaller, cooperative military alliances; and the Association of Southeast Asian Nations. Next, we explore the economic institutions: the World Trade Organization (WTO); the Organisation for Economic Cooperation and Development (OECD); and two smaller economic alliances, the Organization for Petroleum Exporting Countries (OPEC) and the Group of 8. We then examine agreements for economic integration, from low levels of integration, such as free trade areas, to progressively higher levels, such as customs unions and common markets. Finally, we explore an institution that has accomplished both extensive economic and extensive political integration, the European Union.

FIGURE 4.1

International
Institutions by
Purpose

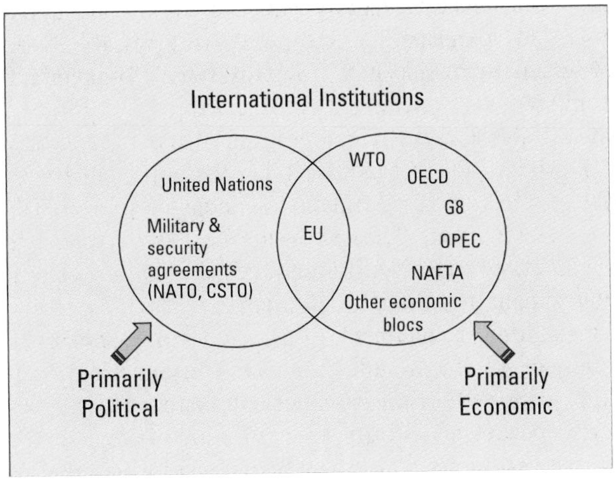

International Institutions

International Political Institutions

THE UNITED NATIONS

UN Background In 1944, representatives of China, the Soviet Union, the United Kingdom, and the United States, meeting at Dumbarton Oaks, in Washington, D.C., drew up draft proposals for an international political organization. On the basis of their plans, and in the optimism and hope that came with the close of World War II, representatives of 50 countries met in San Francisco in 1945 to develop the United Nations charter. The charter was signed by delegates of all 50 countries and later of Poland, for a total of 51 original member-states. Today the **United Nations (UN)** is probably the best-known worldwide organization. (For detailed information about the UN, including its organizational structure, see www.un.org.)

The UN has been responsible for many international agreements and much of the body of international law since 1945. For example, the Universal Declaration of Human Rights, which the General Assembly adopted in 1948, seeks to ensure basic human rights for all people worldwide. As a stabilizing force in the world economy, the UN contributes greatly to the conditions under which international business is conducted. Here are some general ways in which the UN plays a significant role:

- Provides the "soft infrastructure" for the global economy by setting technical standards and norms.

- Prepares the ground for investment in emerging economies (health, governance, political stability, etc.).

- Addresses the downside of globalization (crime, drugs, and arms traffic).

- Seeks solutions to global environmental problems.

- Addresses education and health issues that require global-level solutions.

- Promotes social justice and human and labor rights.

- Builds the cornerstones of an interdependent world: trust and shared values.[2]

UN Organization The work of the United Nations is carried out through five main bodies or organs: the General Assembly, the Security Council, the Economic and Social Council, the International Court of Justice, and the Secretariat. The UN conducts its work throughout the world and has offices in most major capitals. The International Court of Justice is located

United Nations (UN)

International organization of 191 member-nations dedicated to the promotion of peace and global stability; has many functions related to business

in The Hague, Netherlands. The other main bodies are at the United Nations headquarters in New York City. The six official languages of the United Nations are Arabic, Chinese, English, French, Russian, and Spanish.

The number of UN members has grown rapidly since 1945, and additional nations continue to join, including newly created nations that have just become eligible and established nations that have just decided to participate. The most recent members are East Timor and Switzerland, both of which joined in 2002. Today there are 191 members. Although there have been proposals to allow nongovernmental agencies to join the UN, at the current time only recognized nations may join. Thus, Taiwan, the Holy See, the European Union, and Palestine are not members of the UN, although they do maintain missions or offices at UN headquarters and participate in some UN activities.

General Assembly
Deliberative body of the UN made up of all member-nations, each with one vote regardless of size, wealth, or power

All UN member-nations are members of the **General Assembly,** in which each nation has one vote regardless of its size, wealth, or power. The General Assembly acts by adopting resolutions that express the will of the member-nations. Decisions on important questions, such as those involving peace and security, the admission of new member-nations, and budgetary matters, require a two-thirds majority, while decisions on other matters require a simple majority. Although these decisions have no legally binding force for governments or citizens in the member-nations, they carry the heavy weight of world opinion.

Security Council
Main policy-setting body of the UN, composed of 15 members including 5 permanent members

The second major organ of the UN is the **Security Council,** whose goal is to maintain international peace and security. It is composed of 15 members—5 permanent members and 10 nonpermanent members. Each of the permanent members—China, France, Russia, the United Kingdom, and the United States—has the power to veto any measure. The 10 nonpermanent members are chosen by the General Assembly for two-year terms. Five of the nonpermanent members always come from Africa and Asia, one from Eastern Europe, two from Latin America, and the remaining two from Western Europe and other areas. The Security Council's peacekeeping functions are probably what the UN is best known for. UN peacekeeping efforts have taken place in many areas throughout the world. Presently, UN peacekeeping forces are in Africa (Sudan, Burundi, Cote d'Ivoire, Liberia, Democratic Republic of the Congo, Ethiopia and Eritrea, and the Western Sahara); the Americas (Haiti); Asia (on the Pakistani and Indian border in the state of Jammu and Kashmir); Europe (Cyprus, Kosovo, and Georgia); and the Middle East (Golan and Lebanon).

Economic and Social Council (ECOSOC)
UN body concerned with economic and social issues such as trade, development, education, and human rights

The **Economic and Social Council (ECOSOC)**, the third UN organ, is concerned with economic issues, such as trade, transport, industrialization, and economic development, and social issues, including population growth, children, housing, women's rights, racial discrimination, illegal drugs, crime, social welfare, youth, the human environment, and food.

Members of the UN Security Council in session.

Given the complexities that face international business transactions, which are due to conducting business across national borders at geographic and cultural distances from the managers' home environment, global rules of the road are quite helpful. The UN provides such "soft infrastructure" (as former Secretary-General Kofi Annan called it) to facilitate the international exchange of goods, services, money, and information. Here are some examples of the UN's contributions to international business:

- The rules that protect freely sailing ships are legitimized in UN conferences.
- The International Civil Aviation Organization, part of the UN, negotiates the web of agreements that allow commercial airlines to fly across borders and land in case of emergencies.
- The World Health Organization sets standards for pharmaceutical quality and standardizes the names of drugs.

- Protocols of the universal Postal Union prevent losses and allow the mail to move across borders.
- The International Telecommunication Union allots airwave frequencies.
- The International Labor Organization promotes labor rights, work safety conditions, and training.
- The World Meteorological Organization collects and distributes data used in weather forecasting.
- The UN Sales Convention and the UN Convention on the Carriage of Goods by Sea contribute to establishing rights and obligations for buyers and sellers in international transactions.

Within the UN there are 28 major organizations, and each one contributes to commercial order and openness. The UN Commission on International Trade Law and the UN's International Labour Organization are noteworthy bodies from an international business perspective because they set conditions and protocols for international transactions and for labor standards.

Source: www.un.org/partners/business/index.asp (accessed May 19, 2006).

ECOSOC makes recommendations on how to improve education and health conditions and promotes respect for and observation of the human rights and freedom of people everywhere.

The **International Court of Justice (ICJ),** also known as the *World Court*, renders legal decisions involving disputes between national governments. Since only nations litigate before the court, governments often intervene on behalf of corporations and individuals in their countries. Even though the court has worldwide jurisdiction to hear disputes between governments, it hears relatively few cases, usually less than 10 a year. The ICJ has 15 judges, who must come from 15 different countries and serve nine-year terms. Majorities of the General Assembly and the Security Council must agree on the appointment of judges to the ICJ. The activities of the ICJ are explored more fully in Chapter 10.

The **Secretariat,** headed by the secretary-general of the United Nations, is the staff of the UN. It carries out administrative functions and administers the UN's programs and policies. The secretary-general, who is appointed by the General Assembly on the recommendation of the Security Council for a five-year renewable term, supervises the Secretariat. The seventh secretary-general, Kofi A. Annan of Ghana, was the first to be elected from the ranks of United Nations staff. In December 2001, Kofi Annan and the United Nations received the Nobel Peace Prize for their efforts in bringing nations together to work for peace. In this recognition, the Nobel Committee said that it wished "to proclaim that the only negotiable road to global peace and cooperation goes by way of the United Nations."[3]

About 8,600 people from 170 countries make up the UN Secretariat staff. As international civil servants, they and the secretary-general take an oath not to seek or receive instructions from any governmental or outside authority. Worldwide, over 52,000 people work for the UN and its related organizations.

The United Nations has been responsible for the development of many international efforts that facilitate business transactions around the world. One example is the International Telecommunication Union (ITU), a UN agency headquartered in Geneva, Switzerland, that assists governments and the private sector in coordination of global telecommunication

International Court of Justice (ICJ)
UN body that renders legal decisions involving disputes between national governments

Secretariat
The staff of the UN, headed by the secretary-general

networks and services. Another example is the International Trade Center of the UN, which provides trade information to assist developing countries in their business efforts. A third example is the International Civil Aviation Organization (ICAO), which is headquartered in Montreal, Canada, and works with civil aviation agencies throughout the world.

The Future of the UN As it becomes evident that many of today's problems require a global or regional solution, the UN faces formidable challenges: AIDS/HIV, terrorism and related issues of ethnicity that have led to genocide, environmental issues, humanitarian crises, military conflicts, and drug and human trafficking, to name but a few. Yet, for the first time in history, large groups of people throughout the world are connected in new ways. Much of the world's population reads and speaks English, so many people in diverse nations share a means of communication. Through technological advances, we can communicate almost everywhere, directly and immediately. We are also more informed than we were in the past, based on education levels, travel, and access to media, and we have access to the best minds in the world.[4] As we make efforts to meet many of the challenges that face our world, the UN is positioned to make a difference in leadership and coordination. There is no other body that brings together the world's citizens and addresses global needs. As mentioned at the start of the chapter, the UN's Millennium Development Goals aim to eliminate or reduce major social and environmental world problems. Figure 4.2 summarizes the progress made as of September 2005 on seven of the eight goals.

COOPERATIVE MILITARY AND SECURITY AGREEMENTS

Initially you might wonder why we include military and security alliances in our review of institutions whose goals are mainly political, since they are quite different from governance and trade alliances. Yet military alliances have a significant impact on international business because, when successful, they stabilize international conditions, and thus cross-border economic environments, just by their existence and not necessarily by their use. For example, the first NATO invocation of its Article 5 (any attack on one member is an attack on all members) did not occur until 42 years after its establishment, in 2001, just after 9/11. Military and security ties also complement and promote trade among partners. In considering the relationship between military alliances and international trade, Michael D. Kennedy, professor of sociology at the University of Michigan, argues that military alliances are a critical aspect of energy security.[5]

We briefly review below two current major military agreements, the North Atlantic Treaty Organization (NATO) and the Collective Security Treaty Organization (CSTO). This section concludes with a look at the Association of Southeast Asian Nations (ASEAN), an institution that began as a security agreement and has moved toward economic cooperation.

North Atlantic Treaty Organization (NATO)
Security alliance of 26 North American and European nations

North Atlantic Treaty Organization The **North Atlantic Treaty Organization (NATO)** is a security alliance of 26 North American and European nations governed by the North Atlantic Treaty of 1949. (See Figure 4.3.) The main provision of the treaty is the agreement "that an armed attack against one or more of them in Europe or North America shall be considered an attack against them all."[6] NATO was established after World War II in response to a perceived growing threat from the Soviet Union. The first NATO secretary-general, Lord Ismay, gave a more colloquial appraisal of the NATO purpose when he claimed it was for "keeping the Russians out, the Germans down, and the Americans in." The only time NATO has invoked the collective response that is at its core was after the September 11, 2001, terrorist attacks in the United States. Among NATO's members today are several former Soviet bloc countries, Estonia, Latvia, Lithuania, Bulgaria, Slovakia, and Slovenia, which became members in 2004. NATO also has a partnership agreement with Russia that gives Russia a voice in certain NATO decisions.[7]

Collective Security Treaty Organization (CSTO)
Security alliance of six members of the Commonwealth of Independent States (former Union of Soviet Socialist Republics)

Collective Security Treaty Organization The Commonwealth of Independent States (CIS), formerly the Union of Soviet Socialist Republics (U.S.S.R.), formed a security alliance under the Collective Security Treaty (CST) in 1992. This original group of nine member-nations was reduced to six, which formed the present **Collective Security Treaty Organization (CSTO)** in 2002. Current members are Russia, Belarus, Kazakhstan, Kyrgyzstan, Tajikistan, and Armenia. The nations that left are Azerbaijan, Georgia and Uzbekistan.

FIGURE 4.2 Millennium Development Goals Chart of Progress

Goals and Targets	Africa		Asia				Oceanla	Latin America & Caribbean	Commonwealth of Independent States	
	Northern	Sub-Saharan	Eastern	Sub-Eastern	Southern	Western			Europe	Asia

GOAL 1 | Eradicate extreme poverty and hunger

Reduce extreme poverty by half	low poverty	very high poverty	moderate poverty	moderate poverty	high poverty	low poverty	–	moderate poverty	low poverty	low poverty
Reduce hunger by half	very low hunger	very high hunger	moderate hunger	moderate hunger	high hunger	moderate hunger	moderate hunger	moderate hunger	very low hunger	high hunger

GOAL 2 | Achieve universal primary education

Universal primary schooling	high enrolment	low enrolment	high enrolment	high enrolment	moderate enrolment	moderate enrolment	moderate enrolment	high enrolment	moderate enrolment	high enrolment

GOAL 3 | Promote gender equality and empower women

Equal girls' enrolment in primary school	close to parity	far from parity	parity	parity	far from parity	nearly close to parity	close to parity	parity	parity	parity
Women's share of paid employment	low share	medium share	high share	medium share	low share	low share	medium share	high share	high share	high share
Women's equal representation in national parliaments	low representation	low representation	moderate representation	low representation	low representation	very low representation	very low representation	moderate representation	low representation	low representation

GOAL 4 | Reduce child mortality

Reduce mortality of under-five-year-olds by two thirds	moderate mortality	very high mortality	moderate mortality	moderate mortality	high mortality	moderate mortality	high mortality	moderate mortality	low mortality	high mortality
Measles immunization	high coverage	very low coverage	moderate coverage	moderate coverage	low coverage	moderate coverage	very low coverage	high coverage	high coverage	high coverage

GOAL 5 | Improve maternal health

Reduce maternal mortality by three quarters*	moderate mortality	very high mortality	low mortality	high mortality	very high mortality	moderate mortality	high mortality	moderate mortality	low mortality	low mortality

GOAL 6 | Combat HIV/AIDS, malaria and other diseases

Halt and reverse spread of HIV/AIDS	–	very high prevalence	low prevalence	moderate prevalence	moderate prevalence	–	moderate prevalence	moderate prevalence	high prevalence	low prevalence
Halt and reverse spread of malaria*	low risk	high risk	moderate risk	moderate risk	moderate risk	low risk	low risk	moderate risk	low risk	low risk
Halt and reverse spread of tuberculosis	low mortality	high mortality	moderate mortality	moderate mortality	moderate mortality	low mortality	moderate mortality	low mortality	moderate mortality	moderate mortality

GOAL 7 | Ensure environmental sustainability

Reverse loss of forests	small area	medium area	medium area	large area	medium area	small area	large area	large area	large area	small area
Halve proportion without improved drinking water	high coverage	low coverage	moderate coverage	moderate coverage	high coverage	high coverage	low coverage	high coverage	high coverage	moderate coverage
Halve proportion without sanitation	high coverage	very low coverage	low coverage	moderate coverage	very low coverage	high coverage	moderate coverage	high coverage	high coverage	moderate coverage
Improve the lives of slum-dwellers	moderate proportion of slum-dwellers	very high proportion of slum-dwellers	high proportion of slum-dwellers	moderate proportion of slum-dwellers	very high proportion of slum-dwellers	high proportion of slum-dwellers	–	high proportion of slum-dwellers	low proportion of slum-dwellers	moderate proportion of slum-dwellers

Country experiences in each region may differ significantly from the regional average.
For the regional groupings and country data, see http://millennummindicators.un.org.

Sources: United Nations, based on data and estimates provided by: Food and Agriculture Organization; Inter-Parliamentary Union; International Labour Organization; UNESCO; UNICEF, World Health Organization; UNAIDS; UN-Habitat, World Bank—based on statistics available September 2005. Compiled by: Statistics Division, UN DESA

The progress chart operates on two levels. The words in each box tell what the current rate of compliance with each target is.
The colours show the trend, toward meeting the target by 2015 or not. See legend below:

- ▣ Target already met or very close to being met.
- ▢ Target is expected to be met by 2015 if prevailing trends persist, or the problem that this target is designed to address is not a serious concern in the region.
- ▢ Target is not expected to be met by 2015, if prevailing trends persist.
- ▣ No progress, or a deterioration or reversal.
- ▢ Insufficient data.

*The available data for maternal mortality and malaria do not allow a trend analysis. Progress in the chart has been assessed by the responsible agencies on the basis of proxy indicators.

FIGURE 4.3   NATO Member Countries

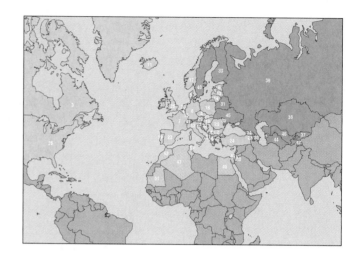

NATO Countries

☐ **Member countries**

1. Belgium
2. Bulgaria
3. Canada
4. Czech Republic
5. Denmark
6. Estonia
7. France
8. Germany
9. Greece
10. Hungary
11. Iceland
12. Italy
13. Latvia
14. Lithuania
15. Luxembourg
16. Netherlands
17. Norway
18. Poland
19. Portugal

20. Romania
21. Slovakia
22. Slovenia
23. Spain
24. Turkey
25. United Kingdom
26. United States

☐ **Partner countries**

27. Albania
28. Armenia
29. Austria
30. Azerbaijan
31. Belarus
32. Croatia
33. Finland
34. Georgia
35. Ireland
36. Kazakhstan
37. Kyrghyz Republic

38. Moldova
39. Russia
40. Sweden
41. Switzerland
42. Tajikistan
43. the former Yugoslav Republic of Macedonia*
44. Turkmenistan
45. Ukraine
46. Uzbekistan

☐ **Mediterranean Dialogue countries**

47. Algeria
48. Egypt
49. Israel
50. Jordan
51. Mauritania
52. Morroco
53. Tunisia

Source: www.nato.int/education/maps.htm.

Association of Southeast Asian Nations (ASEAN)

Ten-member body formed to promote peace and cooperation in the Southeast Asian region

Association of Southeast Asian Nations   Created in 1967, the **Association of Southeast Asian Nations (ASEAN)** was formed for political reasons, to foster peaceful relations among members and offer mutual protection against the growth of communism in their region. Political cooperation has led to some economic cooperation. The fundamental principles of ASEAN are:[8]

- Mutual respect for the independence, sovereignty, equality, territorial integrity, and national identity of all nations.

- The right of every state to lead its national existence free from external interference, subversion, or coercion.

- Noninterference by members in the internal affairs of one another.

- Settlement of differences or disputes in a peaceful manner.

- Renunciation of the threat or use of force.

- Effective cooperation among members.

Now that we are beyond the 1997 financial crisis, Southeast Asia is one of the most dynamic and fastest-developing economic regions in the world. Taken together, its members—Brunei, Cambodia, Indonesia, Laos, Malaysia, Myanmar (formerly Burma), the Philippines, Singapore, Thailand, and Vietnam—are major trading partners of the United States. Papua New Guinea has observer status. Figure 4.4 presents a map of ASEAN members. An ancillary institution, ASEAN +3, has recently been created to include China, Japan, and South Korea in some of the ASEAN discussions.

International Economic Institutions

The international institutions that result from economic agreements among countries are our focus in this section. They include the World Trade Organization (WTO), the Organisation for Economic Cooperation and Development (OECD), and economic agreements such as OPEC and the G8. Because of their unique nature, we devote a separate section, after this one, to institutions that are established by economic integration agreements among nations. The final section reviews the European Union (EU), an organization that began with an economic purpose and has evolved to include a political purpose as well.

WORLD TRADE ORGANIZATION

World Trade Organization (WTO)

A multinational body of 149 members that deals with rules of trade between nations

The **World Trade Organization (WTO)** is a multinational organization designed to establish and help implement rules of trade between nations. It currently has 149 members, including China (2001), Cambodia (2004), and Nepal (2004), and is headquartered in Geneva,

FIGURE 4.4

ASEAN Members

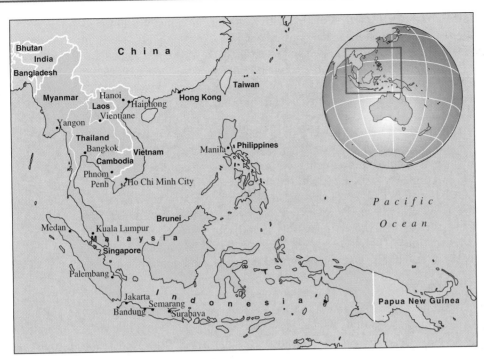

Members of Association of Southeast Asian Nations (ASEAN).

Source: Association of Southeast Asian Nations.

Switzerland. The WTO functions according to its core agreements, which have been negotiated, signed, and ratified by all of its members. Because it is a rules-based, member-driven organization, all WTO decisions are made by the member governments, and the rules are the outcome of negotiations among members. The WTO's goal is to reduce or eliminate trade barriers and restrictions worldwide. Such reductions help producers of goods and services, exporters, and importers conduct their business by reducing costs. The history of the WTO helps to explain its present contributions to trade liberalization.

The WTO Trade Negotiation Committee meets in Geneva. Note the interesting seating arrangements in which the negotiators face each other in a series of face-to-face rows, fronted by a dais where the administrative leaders sit.

The Early Years of Global Trade Cooperation After World War II, Western leaders shared a desire for an international trade organization that would function for commerce much as the UN functions in the political and peacekeeping areas. The allies drew up a charter for the International Trade Organization (ITO), but ITO never came into existence because the U.S. government did not ratify its charter. In 1947 President Truman did not even submit the ITO charter treaty to the Senate for ratification because he knew it would not have the votes to pass. After the war, U.S. politicians and some business interests feared that ceding any control or authority to outside interests would mean a loss of government sovereignty.

In preparation for an ITO, U.S. negotiators presented a draft of a general agreement on tariffs and trade to their ITO colleagues from 55 other nations at a meeting in Havana. The participants accepted this agreement as an interim measure pending ITO ratification. Thus the **General Agreement on Tariffs and Trade (GATT)** was born in 1947 with an initial membership of 23 nations.[9] The basic GATT principle was that member nations would treat all GATT members equally. So if two nations agreed to reduce a tariff, that tariff reduction was extended to all GATT members. This antidiscrimination agreement is known as the **most favored nation (MFN) clause.** GATT was extremely successful in the area of tariff reduction, as well as in the reduction of subsidies, quotas, and nontariff barriers.

GATT, 1947–1995

To reduce tariffs and other trade obstacles, GATT negotiations were conducted in eight extended conferences, called *rounds,* from the first in 1947 through the last, the **Uruguay Round,** which was launched in 1986 (see Table 4.1). The first seven rounds were very successful. Tariffs among developed countries were reduced from an average of 40 percent to 5 percent. In addition, 9 out of 10 disputes among trading nations brought to GATT were settled satisfactorily, discreetly, and without publicity. From 1947 through 2001, the volume of trade in manufactured goods multiplied 20-fold. Trade growth in manufactured goods grew at an average rate of 8 percent through the 1950s and 1960s, and throughout the GATT years trade growth consistently exceeded production growth.[10]

The Uruguay Round was a hugely ambitious undertaking. The seven preceding rounds had significantly reduced industrial product tariffs, and the Uruguay negotiators succeeded in lowering them by more than their target of an additional one-third. Uruguay also broke new GATT ground by writing international rules for trade in services and agriculture and for the protection of intellectual properties. Agreement was reached to phase out the multifiber arrangement, an agreement that covered textiles and clothing and was perhaps the oldest managed-trade system. Procedures to speed settlements of trade disputes were agreed on, as were means to reduce trade subsidies.

General Agreement on Tariffs and Trade (GATT)
International agreement that functioned to encourage trade liberalization from 1947 to 1995

most favored nation (MFN) clause
Agreement that GATT member-nations would treat all members equally in trade matters

Uruguay Round
The last extended conference of GATT negotiations

TABLE 4.1	GATT Rounds		
Year	**Place/Name**	**Subjects Covered**	**Countries**
1947	Geneva	Tariffs	23
1949	Annecy	Tariffs	13
1951	Torquay	Tariffs	38
1956	Geneva	Tariffs	26
1960–1961	Geneva, Dillon Round	Tariffs	26
1964–1967	Geneva, Kennedy Round	Tariffs and antidumping measures	62
1973–1979	Geneva, Tokyo Round	Tariffs, nontariff measures, framework agreements	102
1986–1994	Geneva, Uruguay Round	Tariffs, nontariff measures, rules, services, intellectual property, dispute settlement, textiles, agriculture, creation of WTO	123

Source: *OPEC Annual Statistical Bulletin, 2004.* Table 22. See http://www.ilo.org/public/english/fairglobalization/index.htm

Trade Benefits Uneven

The opening of borders, new trade agreements, and the World Trade Organization have not, so far, resulted in what trade theory (Chapter 3) suggests would be benefits for poorer nations. Instead, according to "A Fair Globalization," a UN study, the uneven benefits of globalization are building a growing divide between rich and poor countries, as well as within countries.* Globalization, it suggests, "is at a turning point and international institutions need to address social inequities as well as other consequences of open borders."†

The authors of the study, including the 2001 Nobel economist Joseph Stiglitz, were asked to describe the aspects of globalization that have given rise to growing protests about trade, the WTO, the World Bank, and other international institutions and agreements. The cochairs of the study, Tarja Halonen, president of Finland, and Benjamin William Mkapa, president of Tanzania, observe: "Currently, globalization is a divisive subject. It verges on a dialogue of the deaf, both nationally and internationally. Yet the future of our countries, and the destiny of our globe, demands that we all rethink globalization."

According to the report, 188 million people are unemployed worldwide, or 6.2 percent of the global labor force. Countries representing 14 percent of the world's population (largely the OECD countries) account for half the world's trade and foreign investment. The report also suggests that women's traditional livelihoods as small agricultural producers have been undermined by agricultural subsidies in the developed nations. In addition, when these women seek alternative occupations, they face discrimination. Two bright spots in the report are China and India, which together account for one-third of the global population. In both of these countries absolute poverty has declined. The future growth of world trade and the economic health of developed nations depend on getting globalization right so that all participants benefit from trade, just as a rising tide lifts all boats. New markets, an educated work force, economic growth, and political stability in emerging nations are all important for international business.

*The report can be found at www.ilo.org/public/english/fairglobalization/index.htm.

†Elizabeth Becker, "U.N. Study Finds Global Trade Benefits Are Uneven," *New York Times*, February 24, 2004, p. C5.

Many regarded a successful conclusion of the Uruguay Round as overambitious, but the negotiators met a GATT-imposed deadline by initialing a working agreement late on the last day of the deadline. There was disappointment with the final Uruguay Round agreement, though. Antidumping laws were not limited, and the United States entertainment industry wanted greater access to the European markets than the agreement allowed.[11] The Uruguay Round negotiators also recognized some of the weaknesses of GATT, and they created the World Trade Organization to take its place.

Creation of the World Trade Organization   At the start of the Uruguay Round, the economic environment was not positive, despite GATT's success at reducing tariffs. A series of economic recessions in the 1970s and 1980s led to initiatives by governments to create non-tariff barriers to trade for sectors in their economies facing increased foreign competition. High levels of unemployment and increased subsidies, especially in the agricultural sector, led trade negotiators to seek a more solid platform for trade liberalization than GATT had provided. GATT had been, as commentators had suggested, a slender reed on which to hang an entire world trade system. Its dispute mechanisms were convoluted; there were many loopholes in agriculture, textiles, and clothing; and services were not covered at all by GATT. The world trading system had evolved since 1947, and the slender reed no longer could provide a sufficient framework to support the evolving world trade system. The Uruguay Round GATT negotiations established the World Trade Organization, and as of January 1, 1995, this new organization began to administer international trade agreements with a broader mandate than had GATT. For example, a trade policy review mechanism raises issues for discussion on a regular agenda, replacing the previous GATT practice of periodic rounds of negotiation. The WTO established a permanent process for revising the trade rules. The final GATT round, the Uruguay Round, included 123 participants. As of August 2006, the WTO had 149 members.

WTO Principles   In WTO negotiations, members have established five basic principles on which the global trade system can rest. These principles are the foundations of the multilateral trading system whose individual agreements are lengthy legal documents that address trade activities in areas as varied as agriculture, textiles and clothing, banking, telecommunications, government purchases, industrial standards and product safety, food sanitation regulations, and intellectual property. The WTO principles of the trading system are:

1. *Trade will be without discrimination.* This is the most favored nation (MFN) principle, and it requires that nations treat all WTO members equally. If one nation grants another nation a special trade deal, that deal has to be extended to all WTO members. Another aspect of nondiscrimination is that foreigners and locals should be treated equally. This means that imported goods, once they are in the market, should not face discrimination.

2. *Trade should be freer, with trade barriers negotiated downward.* Lower trade barriers, both visible ones such as import tariffs and less visible ones such as red tape, encourage trade growth.

3. *Trade should be predictable.* Predictability helps businesses know what the real costs will be. The WTO operates with tariff "bindings," or agreements to not raise a specific tariff over a given time. Such promises are as good as lowering a tariff because they give businesspeople realistic data. Transparency, making trade rules as clear and accessible as possible, also helps businesspeople anticipate a stable future.

4. *Trade should be more competitive.* Although many describe the WTO as a "free trade" organization, and it certainly does work toward trade liberalization, the WTO also realizes that trade relationships among nations can be exceedingly complex. Many WTO agreements support fair competition in agriculture, services, and intellectual property, discouraging subsidies and the dumping of products at prices below the cost of their manufacture. These agreements connect directly to the fifth principle.

5. *Trade should be more beneficial for less developed countries, encouraging development and economic reform.* Three-quarters of the WTO's members are developing economies and those transitioning to market economies. These economies were quite active in the Uruguay Round and have been active in the WTO's current **Doha Development Agenda,** informally called the *Doha Round.* A ministerial decision adopted at the end of the Uruguay Round suggests that developed nations should give market access to goods from the very least developed countries and increase technical assistance for them. Developed countries have started to allow duty-free and quota-free imports for almost all products from the least developed countries. The current Doha Development Agenda includes developing countries' concerns about the difficulties they face in implementing the Uruguay Round agreements. The importance of this issue for the WTO, for developing countries, and for poverty reduction cannot be overstated.

Doha Development Agenda

WTO extended conference on trade; also called *Doha Round*

The WTO and Developing Nations

The WTO's present director general is Pascal Lamy, the former EU trade commissioner, who began his four-year term in 2005. He succeeded the first WTO director general to come from a developing nation, Dr. Supachai Panitchipakdi, of Thailand, who pushed an agenda for the present Doha Round that is especially important for developing countries. In an address in Sao Paulo, Brazil, on June 14, 2004, he recognized that if developing nations lose faith in the Doha Development agreements presently being negotiated, many of which address special needs of developing countries, "the world's poorest and most vulnerable countries would be the biggest losers from a focus on other deals at the expense of multilateralism."[12]

The Doha Agenda has seen discord on many issues connected to the trading needs of developing nations, and when agreement on how to proceed on these issues was not reached by the original deadline of January 2005, the Doha Agenda was extended. Earlier talks that were part of the Doha Round held in Cancun, Mexico, in September 2003 had collapsed when delegates from developing nations in Africa, the Caribbean, and Asia walked out because they felt that many of the developed nations were unwilling to compromise on agricultural issues. That was the first time that developing nations had established themselves as a force in the talks, challenging the leadership of the United States and the EU. Twenty-one nations banded together to make the case that the agricultural subsidies wealthy nations pay to their own farmers undermine the poor farmers around the world. In particular, African farmers asked that the subsidies given to U.S. and EU cotton farmers be reduced and that they be paid $300 million in compensation for the losses they suffered because of this unfair competition. In response, the United States and the EU proposed that the question be studied and that the Africans grow other crops.[13] In June 2004, the WTO delegates once again agreed to debate a proposal from the developing nations calling for the reduction and elimination of agricultural tariffs. In the ensuing year, Brazil successfully sued the United States in the WTO over cotton subsidies. Brazil, India, and South Africa are leading the group of developing countries. The United States and the EU have each agreed to reduce subsidies if the other does. After the disappointment in Cancun in 2003, there is some hope, albeit slim, that the WTO can reach agreement on agricultural subsidies and tariffs soon and go on to address industrial tariffs and issues of services. Industrialized countries have a way to go in reducing agricultural subsidies. WTO Director General Lamy, who is French, says he doesn't understand his own country's position on agricultural subsidies. "As an efficient farm producer, the strategy should be to reduce subsidies and prices, because others won't be able to compete with you," he remarked to a *Wall Street Journal* reporter.[14]

In Spring 2006, Lamy advised WTO members that "genuine and important progress has been made but not fast enough." The WTO did not meet the April 30, 2006, deadline, set at the Doha Agenda's Hong Kong Ministerial Conference in December 2005, for agreement on a framework for tariff and subsidy cuts in agriculture and for nonagricultural market access. The discussions are ongoing, and their progress can be monitored at the WTO site at www.wto.org.[15]

WTO Challenges

Trade negotiations are complex, especially among 149 countries—with differently developed economies, different cultures, and different priorities—that have committed to attempting consensus decisions. The progress of the GATT and the WTO has been impressive, with global trade up 14-fold and world gross product up sixfold.[16] As a result of the Uruguay Round and the early meetings on the Doha Agenda (Seattle, Cancun), developing nations have become more integrated into the WTO. Many of the current challenges relate to their increased role and their commitment to free trade. Economics professor Jagdish Bhagwati says that we should expect trade talks to be like a roller-coaster ride,[17] and so far the Doha Round has not disappointed. The Seattle meetings collapsed with violent demonstrations in 1999, so the round was re-launched in Doha in 2001 and continued in Cancun two years later and in Hong Kong, two years later still, in 2005. Protests, the core of which addressed the WTO's insensitivity toward environmental issues, human rights, working conditions, and labor protection, have died down since 9/11. The hurdles still facing the Doha Round include agricultural subsidies of the rich nations and manufactures subsidies of developing nations.

Regional trade agreements such as the European Union (EU) and the North American Free Trade Agreement (NAFTA) may weaken the WTO because such agreements could disrupt trade at the expense of countries that are not party to the agreements.[18] Since most of these trade agreements are among developed nations, the impact on developing nations could be substantial.

Another problem for the WTO is the question of whether its member-nations will abide by its decisions. For example, during the banana wars between the United States and the EU over the EU's failure to open its markets to U.S. banana imports, the WTO had twice ruled that the EU's policy was illegal.[19] Agreeing with Washington that the EU's preferential banana import rules were discriminatory, the WTO allowed the United States to impose $191.4 million in trade sanctions against EU goods. A cease-fire in the "banana war" has been reached. However, although initial EU lack of compliance with the ruling has changed, the underlying issue remains: The WTO relies on the goodwill of its members to implement its decisions. Recently both the EU and the United States have agreed to reduce agricultural subsidies as a result of WTO rulings.

Among the areas of negotiation at the WTO, one of the most difficult is **trade-related intellectual property rights (TRIPS).** The WTO agreement is that countries grant patents for 20-year periods and copyrights for 50 years. Intellectual property rights violations are endemic in several industries, such as music, software, and pharmaceuticals. These violations tend to occur in a small group of developing countries, with music and software piracy rampant in China and pharmaceutical patent violation legendary in India, China, and Brazil. The pharmaceutical patent infringement issue, however, also involves the ability of developing countries to provide health care. For example, Indian pharmaceutical companies can produce generic equivalents of

trade-related intellectual property rights (TRIPS)

the acronym TRIPS refers to the WTO agreement that protects copyrights, trademarks, trade secrets, and other intellectual property matters.

Lin (Jimmy) Chiang is the international marketing manager at the Photonics Division of Universal Microelectronics Co. (UMEC), Ltd., headquartered in Taichung, Taiwan, R.O.C. UMEC is an ISO-9001/140001-, QS-9000-certified company and one of the world's leading manufacturers of Photonics Products, including fiber-optic active and passive components, CATV integrated systems, magnetic components, power supplies, telecommunication products, and OEM assemblies. Over 80 percent of UMEC's production is exported to world markets. UMEC has branch offices in Taiwan, China, Hong Kong, the United States, Germany, and Italy. UMEC factories are located in Taichung, Taiwan, and in ShenZeng and Ningbo, China. Professionally, Lin travels to Japan, China, Thailand, Sweden, Denmark, Holland, Germany, Italy, France, the United Kingdom, and 23 U.S. cities.

Lin (Jimmy) Chiang.

Here's Lin's advice on how to get a job in international business:

- It is not difficult to get a job in international business. You only have to get a degree in international business or a related degree or related knowledge. (Lin holds undergraduate degrees in accounting, statistics, and business administration from colleges in Taiwan and an American MBA in international business.)

- Have language skills. English is the most popular language and Chinese is getting important. If you can understand both English and Chinese you can communicate with almost ⅔ of the people in the world.

- Be willing to work hard. Sometimes you have to work at night because your night is your customer's morning on the other side of the world.

- Be logical. Logic is a universal language. It can help you communicate and understand other parts of the world.

Here's Lin's advice on succeeding in international business:

- Develop good sales and marketing skills . . . international business is about selling your product globally.

- Do a Culture Analysis of your market—understand their culture before you do anything. You have to think and act locally. You even need to dress locally.

- Know about sports, music, and art. Doing business is not always talking business. If you can find out about your customer's hobbies and interests when you first meet, you increase the chance of business success.

- Show confidence. It will let your customer trust you are the best in the field.

- Have a humble attitude. This works in Asia, especially Taiwan, China, and Japan. Our ancestors always taught us that the more you know the more humble you act, so Asian people believe that humble people are the best.

- Give your customers quick responses and explanations. Cultures might be different, but the customer always thinks their own business is the most important, so prompt response is always necessary.

- On drinking: In all of Asia and some parts of South America, business is often settled at the dinner table, so it is quite important to reach your goal before you have too much to drink.

Source: www.umec-web.com.

---

drugs that are patent-protected in the West and sell these drugs in markets in developing countries at levels those countries can afford. The Doha meetings in 2001 stated that intellectual property should not take precedence over public health. Any country that adopts TRIPS will have the right to copy drugs patented before 1995. The WTO has also established a system of compulsory licensing which mandates that copyright holders license producers in developing countries.

The WTO has taken the GATT achievements, added a more stable framework to them, and continued progress in the development of a fair trading system for the world. How far forward the WTO can go remains to be seen, but it certainly is off to a good start in its efforts to stabilize the trading environment in which international business grows.

Organisation for Economic Cooperation and Development (OECD)
Group of developed countries dedicated to promoting economic expansion in its member-nations

ORGANISATION FOR ECONOMIC COOPERATION AND DEVELOPMENT

Headquartered in Paris, the **Organisation for Economic Cooperation and Development (OECD)** is often called the "rich man's club" because today it is composed of 30 of the wealthiest nations in the world (see Table 4.2).* Membership, though, is open to all nations committed to a market economy and a pluralistic democracy.

*Note that OECD uses the British spelling of *organisation* in its name.

TABLE 4.2	OECD Member Countries		
Country	**Date Joined**	**Country**	**Date Joined**
Australia	June 7, 1971	Korea	December 12, 1996
Austria	September 29, 1961	Luxembourg	December 7, 1961
Belgium	September 13, 1961	Mexico	May 18, 1994
Canada	April 10, 1961	Netherlands	November 13, 1961
Czech Republic	December 21, 1995	New Zealand	May 29, 1973
Denmark	May 30, 1961	Norway	July 4, 1961
Finland	January 28, 1969	Poland	November 22, 1996
France	August 7, 1961	Portugal	August 4, 1961
Germany	September 27, 1961	Slovak Republic	December 14, 2000
Greece	September 27, 1961	Spain	August 3, 1961
Hungary	May 7, 1996	Sweden	September 28, 1961
Iceland	June 5, 1961	Switzerland	September 28, 1961
Ireland	August 17, 1961	Turkey	August 2, 1961
Italy	March 29, 1962	United Kingdom	May 2, 1961
Japan	April 28, 1964	United States	April 12, 1961

The OECD developed from an earlier collaboration, the Organisation for European Economic Cooperation (OEEC), that was established to administer the Marshall Plan aid distribution in Europe after World War II and to begin to build economic cooperation within Europe. The OECD provides information on economic and other activities within its member-nations and gives them a setting in which to discuss economic and social policy. It publishes extensive research on a wide variety of international business and economic subjects, including highly regarded individual country surveys (see www.oecd.org). These publications and resource materials are valuable to researchers and businesspeople. Member-nations of OECD seek answers to common problems and work to coordinate domestic and international policies.

The OECD has been instrumental in many areas, including encouraging member-nations to eliminate bribery, to establish a code of conduct for multinational companies, and to propose the adoption of specific legislation. The Business and Industry Advisory Committee (BIAC) of OECD, created in 1962 to represent business and industry, works in various areas that concern business, such as trade liberalization, sustainable development, e-commerce, taxation, and biotechnology. Information about the BIAC can be found at www.biac.org.

OTHER ECONOMIC INSTITUTIONS

There are many other international institutions whose basic purpose is an economic one. Here we look at two of them that have considerable influence on international business, the Organization of Petroleum Exporting Countries (OPEC) and the Group of Eight (G8).

Organization of Petroleum Exporting Countries

Realizing that if the oil-exporting countries were united they could bargain more effectively with the large oil companies, Iran and Venezuela in 1959 joined the existing Arab Petroleum Congress at a meeting in Cairo. Discussions and secret agreements at that meeting became the seeds for OPEC.[20]

Early in 1960, the Venezuelan minister of mines and hydrocarbons and the Saudi oil minister wrote to the oil companies operating in Venezuela and the Middle East, requesting that they consult with the host governments before making any price changes. In August 1960, the oil companies reduced oil prices, and the host governments reported that they learned of this price reduction only when they read about it in the newspapers. That they had not been consulted angered them and increased their anxiety about their control and conservation of their country's natural resources. In that atmosphere, they called a meeting in Baghdad. Attending the meeting were representatives of Iran, Iraq, Kuwait, Saudi Arabia, and Venezuela. The

Organization of Petroleum Exporting Countries (OPEC) was formed, and the OPEC members took charge of pricing in order to control their valuable domestic natural resource.

Of the 11 OPEC member-nations today, all are developing economies. Most are in the Middle East (Iran, Iraq, Kuwait, Qatar, Saudi Arabia, and United Arab Emirates), but three are in Africa (Algeria, Libya, and Nigeria) and two are elsewhere in the world (Indonesia and Venezuela). There are other large oil-exporting countries (such as Mexico, Norway, Russia, and the United Kingdom) that are not members of OPEC.

OPEC's economic strength became evident to the oil-importing world in late 1973 and early 1974 through an oil embargo by its Arab members against the Netherlands and the United States, accompanied by very large price increases to all customers. Its strength stemmed from the comparative cohesiveness of the members and from its control of 68 percent of the world's known petroleum reserves.[21] OPEC supplied 84 percent of Europe's oil needs and over 90 percent of Japan's.[22]

Using its strength, OPEC drove up petroleum prices from about $3 a barrel (42 gallons) in 1973 to close to $35 in 1980. Such a drastic increase in energy prices caused recession and unemployment in oil-importing countries. It also sparked conservation measures and increased oil exploration in non-OPEC countries, along with research into alternative energy sources. Thanks to those initiatives, OPEC's market weakened, but its members refused to cut their production and an oversupply developed. OPEC had control of pricing in the mid-1970s, but by the early 1980s the free markets were setting prices, with major markets in Rotterdam, New York, and Chicago.[23] OPEC's control of the market has been diluted by the huge oil and gas projects being developed in Kazakhstan, Azerbaijan, and Russia.

The OPEC share of the world supply of oil in 2004 was 40 percent, compared with just over 20 percent in 1984. In addition, sustained low oil prices through the first half of 2005 weakened conservation efforts and made exploration, investment, and extraction less attractive. Oil sold at $42.32 a barrel in June 2004, but by August 2005 the price had jumped to over $60 a barrel, and in April 2006 it hit $75.35. Contributing to these high prices are the political instability in the Middle East, including the war in Iraq; Iran's nuclear crisis; hurricane disruptions to refining capability and oil platforms; Venezuelan political instability; political crises in West Africa; and increasing demand in developing countries such as China, India, and Indonesia.[24] At the same time, terrorism being exported from some of the oil-producing nations adds to the general instability. There is also the possibility that prices are reflecting a peak in the supply of this nonrenewable fossil fuel. Table 4.3 shows refined petroleum product consumption by region or country from 1960 through 2004. Consumption in developing countries continues to increase.

The Group of Eight (G8) The **Group of Eight (G8)** developed from a small group of industrial countries whose economies were profoundly affected by the 1973 oil crisis and the recession to which it led. Financial officials from the United States, Europe, and Japan

TABLE 4.3	World Refined Petroleum Products Consumption by Region, 1960–2004 (1000 b/d)					
	1960	**1970**	**1980**	**1990**	**2000**	**2004**
North America	10,035.0	15,204.2	18,839.4	18,369.0	21,407.9	22,857.8
Latin America	1,424.7	2,699.8	4,267.2	4,944.6	6,435.0	6,452.4
Eastern Europe	2,167.4	6,028.5	10,350.2	9,739.4	4,862.9	4,932.3
Western Europe	3,690.9	11,695.4	13,435.4	12,632.9	13,865.9	14,189.8
Middle East	231.5	510.7	1,694.5	2,582.4	3,873.3	4,603.6
Africa	323.3	631.0	1,339.0	1,778.3	2,219.8	2,506.1
Asia and Pacific	1,453.1	6,623.0	10,000.0	12,935.9	19,667.8	22,400.0
Total World	**19,775.9**	**43,392.6**	**59,925.6**	**62,982.5**	**72,332.5**	**77,942.1**
OPEC	317.7	651.6	2,480.4	3,808.3	5,102.4	6,000.2
OPEC percentage	1.6	1.5	4.1	6.0	7.1	7.7

met to discuss global financial issues. The French then proposed a regular meeting of such a group, forming the G6—France, West Germany, the United Kingdom, Italy, Japan, and the United States—in 1975. Canada joined these meetings the following year, forming the G7. After the end of the cold war, Russia joined the meetings, first provisionally (G7+1) and then as a regular member (G8). An extension to the G8 includes discussions held after the G8 meetings by finance ministers of the G8+5 (South Africa, Brazil, China, Mexico, and India). In addition, a G8 summit is held annually for heads of state. There are some meetings in which Russia does not participate, though, due to its economic and democratic instability. At these meetings, the group consists of finance ministers and is still known as the G7.[25] Neither the G7 nor the G8 has a permanent staff or budget. The government of the country that is hosting the summit in a given year also provides facilities for other G7 and G8 meetings during that year.

Discussion areas in the G8 meetings have also expanded. They now include topics of global concern and involve government officials concerned with health, the environment, safety, law enforcement, development, and other areas that present issues of mutual concern. For example, in June 2005, the G8 interior and justice ministers agreed at a meeting to create an international database on pedophiles. Cooperation on terrorism is also a focus area for various ministers of the G8 countries.

The G8 meetings have been the focus of substantial antiglobalization protest, especially those in Genoa, Italy, in 2001. One of the main points of criticism is the impact that trade among G8 nations has on developing nations. The United Nations Development Program's *Human Development Report 2005* illustrates that the OECD countries, a larger group closely aligned with the G8, represent over two-thirds of the total world economy.[26] Because the OECD nations tend to trade with each other, developing nations lose potential development opportunities. Seen from a developing nation perspective, the G8 can appear to be a relatively closed trade alliance among the wealthy countries. Other points of criticism concern carbon emissions and global warming, poverty, and the developed nations' lack of adequate response to the AIDS crisis.[27] The G8 is responsive to the underlying issues of global poverty, trade, health, and environmental issues but not responsive enough to satisfy its critics, who may have grouped reasonable criticisms with more general—and emotional—criticisms of globalization.

As with international political institutions, the activities of international institutions whose purpose is primarily economic have significant impacts on international business. In the next section, we examine another type of institution whose activities influence the conduct of international business. Basically economic in nature, it is formed by nations that agree to move toward unified economic integration.

FIGURE 4.5

The G8 Members (www.undp.org)

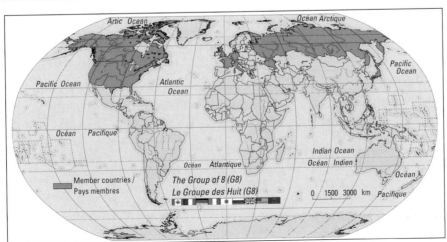

Source: Original map data provided by The Atlas of Canada. Produced under licence from Her Majesty the Queen in Right of Canada, with permission of Natural Resources Canada. http://atlas.nrcan.gc.ca/site/english/maps/reference/international/g8/map.jpg.

Economic Integration

Since the end of World War II, cooperation among nations has increased substantially. Often, the cooperation begins with a free trade area, develops into a customs union, and then evolves into a common market, and eventually the group may move toward complete economic integration. Such trading blocs are important for international businesspeople because they can greatly reduce costs to those inside the integrated area— through reduced tariffs, quotas, and other trade barriers—and increase costs to those outside it. Figure 4.6 compares the relative sizes of the major trading blocs and trading nations.

In a **free trade area (FTA)** tariffs are abolished among the members of the FTA, but each member-nation maintains its own external tariffs, those to countries in the rest of the world. So members have free trade among themselves but have their own trade restrictions with non-member nations. Within the FTA, restrictions generally remain on the movement of services (such as accounting, insurance, and legal services), people (labor), and capital. The North American Free Trade Agreement (NAFTA) and the European Free Trade Association (EFTA) are examples of FTAs.

A **customs union** adds common external tariffs to the FTA. This is a logical extension of the FTA: There are no tariffs between countries in the customs union, and the tariffs charged by member-nations to the rest of the world are consistent among the member-nations. Examples are the South African Customs Union (South Africa, Lesotho, Namibia, Swaziland, and Botswana); Mercosur, the Common Market of the South (Argentina, Brazil, Paraguay, and Uruguay); and the Andean Community (Peru, Venezuela, Equador, Bolivia, and Colombia).

A **common market** is a customs union that has no restrictions on the mobility of services, people, and capital among the member-nations. Mercosur hopes to develop in this direction. The EU has developed beyond a common market and is moving toward **complete economic integration.** Such integration involves a high degree of political integration as well, as member-nations surrender certain important elements of their sovereignty. A central bureaucracy at the EU is responsible for coordinating and harmonizing tax rates, labor systems, education systems, and other social and legal systems for all EU members, while monetary policy is developed by the European Central Bank. A single currency, the euro, has been established to replace member-nations' currencies. Let's take a closer look at some of these efforts toward economic integration.

NORTH AMERICAN FREE TRADE AGREEMENT

The **North American Free Trade Agreement (NAFTA)** created a free trade area among Canada, Mexico, and the United States that came into existence on January 1, 1994. NAFTA is intended to provide a framework to promote free trade among the three North American

---

free trade area (FTA)
Area in which tariffs among members have been eliminated, but members keep their external tariffs

customs Union
Collaboration that adds common external tariffs to an FTA

common Market
Customs union that includes mobility of services, people, and capital within the union

complete economic integration
Integration on both economic and political levels

FIGURE 4.6

Regional Trading Blocs and Major Trading Nations

Regional bloc	Area (sq km)	Population	GDP (US$)	GDP per capita	Members
EU	3,976,372	456,953,258	12.18 trillion	28,100	25
NAFTA	21,609,740	438,992,672	14.56 trillion	33,166	3
China	9,596,960	1,313,973,713	8.18 trillion	6,300	—
India	3,287,590	1,095,351,995	3.7 trillion	3,400	—
Russia	17,075,200	142,893,540	1.54 trillion	10,700	—
Canada	9,984,670	33,098,932	1.08 trillion	32,900	—
Mexico	1,972,550	107,449,525	1.07 trillion	10,100	—
ASEAN	4,400,000	553,900,000	2.172 trillion	4,044	10
United States	9,631,420	298,444,215	12.41 trillion	42,000	—
World	510.072 million	6,525,107,264	59.6 trillion GWP	9,300	

Source: CIA Factbook, www.cia.gov/cia/publications/factbook/, 2006.

signatories. Unlike the UN, the EU, and the WTO, NAFTA operates as part of the national law of each member-country.

The original 1988 debate in Canada over whether that country should join the United States in a bilateral agreement to promote trade was contentious. Proponents, including Prime Minister Brian Mulroney, argued that the agreement would be good for Canada and that free trade would open up large markets to the south to Canadian businesses. Opponents argued that Canadians would lose jobs and Canada would lose its national identity by approving the agreement. Some feared that the agreement would lead to the elimination of the border between Canada and the United States. Prime Minister Mulroney's party won the election, and the Canadian Parliament approved the agreement. The United States–Canada Free Trade Agreement proved so successful that both nations wanted to expand it to include Mexico and possibly other nations at a later date. Many also believed that opening markets in Mexico to U.S. interests would raise the standard of living and the wage rate of the citizens of Mexico. An improvement in the economy would increase Mexico's ability to retain valuable members of the work force who otherwise would be attracted by a higher wage rate in the United States. Discussions among the three nations were successful, and the agreement was presented to the elected officials in each country for approval. Despite fierce opposition from organized labor and some politicians, the negotiations succeeded and the national legislatures of Canada, Mexico, and the United States approved the NAFTA treaty. NAFTA was the first major trade agreement to include labor and environmental side agreements, topics that are now routinely included in trade deals.

Over the past 12 years, NAFTA has paved the way for strong economic growth and prosperity based on liberalized trade among the three nations. The U.S. trade representative, who participates on the NAFTA Trade Commission along with the Mexican secretary of the economy and the Canadian minister of international Trade, claims that NAFTA has delivered important benefits to consumers, businesses, workers, and farmers throughout North America.[28] Through NAFTA, the three countries have created the world's largest free trade zone—one of the most powerful productive forces in the global economy. NAFTA is expected to enourage continued growth in trade and investment flows, which lead to increased competitiveness and prosperity. In 2008, tariff liberalization is scheduled to be completed, and trade in North America will be virtually tariff-free.

The U.S. Department of Commerce reports substantial evidence across the United States, Canada, and Mexico that NAFTA has allowed firms to maximize efficiencies, remain globally competitive, and, as a result, increase sales and exports:[29]

- From 1993 to 2005, trade among NAFTA nations climbed 173 percent, from $297 billion to $810 billion. That's $2.2 billion in trilateral trade every day.

- U.S. merchandise exports to NAFTA grew at 133 percent, compared to growth in exports to the rest of the world, at 77 percent.

- Canada and Mexico are the largest export markets for the United States, totaling 36 percent of the U.S. export growth.

- In agriculture, Canada and Mexico account for 55 percent of the U.S. export growth since 1993.

- In real GDP, NAFTA nations have moved forward briskly, with growth from 1993 to 2005 for the United States at 48 percent, for Mexico at 40 percent, and for Canada at 49 percent.

Despite such positive results, the three nations have had serious and long-term trade disputes within NAFTA. One of the longest-standing ones is between the United States and Canada. The softwood lumber dispute actually predates NAFTA, but Canada brought its charge against the United States to a bi-national NAFTA review panel, a mechanism established for dispute settlement, in 2005 and again, to another panel, in 2006, as well as to the World Trade Organization. In May 2002 the United States had imposed tariffs of 27 percent on Canadian softwood exports to the United States, claiming that the Canadian lumber producers were unfairly subsidized by their government. The allegation was that

North American Free Trade Agreement (NAFTA) Agreement creating a free trade area among Canada, Mexico, and the United States

While NAFTA has had some positive results, controversy among member nations has continued. One of the longest debates was the softwood lumber dispute between the United States and Canada. After the United States imposed 27 percent tariffs on Canadian softwood lumber exports, Canada brought its complaint to both NAFTA and the WTO. When both panels ruled in favor of Canada, in 2006 the United States finally agreed to return most of the duties it had collected.

the fee Canadian producers pay the government to log public land, called a *stumpage fee*, was low and amounted to a subsidy when compared to what logging public land costs U.S. producers. In the United States, logging rights are auctioned at market values. In 2005 and again in 2006, NAFTA panels and the WTO ruled in favor of Canada, concluding that the figures supporting the U.S. claim were based on U.S. market realities, not Canadian. Finally, in 2006, the United States agreed to return to Canada 80 percent of the $5 billion in duties that U.S. Customs had collected.[30]

There are some serious noneconomic concerns about NAFTA, but many of them have abated as, over the past 12 years, the agreement's economic benefits have become clearer. One concern is that Mexico meet the NAFTA mandate to raise environmental standards to the level of those in the United States. To address these issues, two side agreements to NAFTA established the North American Commission for Environmental Cooperation and the North American Development Bank. They work together to develop and fund projects to support Mexican environmental protection and the development of infrastructure.[31]

Another area of concern is the increase in illegal immigration from Mexico to the United States since the implementation of NAFTA. Commercial farming in Mexico has been successful under NAFTA, and this development has forced up to 2.5 million peasant farmers off the land they were farming. In a sense, NAFTA actually may mean the end of peasant agriculture in Mexico, which was organized as subsistence collectives.[32] Many of the illegal immigrants are peasants who are economic exiles to the United States. The noneconomic cost of such land redistribution splits families and creates severe pressures for traditional rural agriculture.

Many in the United States, the Caribbean, and throughout Latin America want to extend NAFTA to include other countries in the free trade area. Chile was mentioned as a possible candidate for initial expansion and the parties started discussions, but enthusiasm for these efforts has faded. Presently Colombia is taking the initiative for consultations among 34 nations of the Americas that have expressed interest in the Free Trade Agreement of the Americas (FTAA). The many areas in which to build agreements among the potential members include market access, government agricultural policy, competition policy, intellectual property rights, investment policy, trade in services, subsidies, and antidumping policies. There also needs to be agreement on how to monitor compliance and how to adjudicate noncompliance.

EUROPEAN FREE TRADE AGREEMENT

European Free Trade Agreement (EFTA)
Four-nation non-EU FTA in Europe

The **European Free Trade Agreement (EFTA)** was founded in 1960 by seven European countries: Austria, Denmark, Norway, Portugal, Sweden, Switzerland, and the United Kingdom. Finland joined in 1961, Iceland in 1970, and Liechtenstein in 1991. In 1973, the UK and Denmark moved to the European Community, an earlier version of the European Union. They were followed by Portugal, Austria, Finland, and Sweden. The four EFTA members today are Iceland, Lichtenstein, Norway, and Switzerland. Their free trade agreement focuses on goods rather than services or labor. EFTA has also negotiated a series of trade agreements with other countries and trading blocs, including Eastern European and Mediterranean countries and Mexico, Chile, and Singapore, and has established bilateral trade agreements with the EU. In that sense, it is evolving toward a customs union, with common external trade policies. Increasingly, though, EFTA's internal agreements have addressed services, the movement of persons, transportation, and technical barriers to trade.

AFRICAN TRADE AGREEMENTS

To promote economic growth throughout the continent, African countries have formed regional trade groups. Many of them are in the negotiation stages. Most African countries, though, have their main trade relationships with developed countries, in many cases with former colonial powers. Except for South Africa, African economies are small and underdeveloped, and governments face daunting challenges: infrastructure development; public health needs connected to HIV/AIDS, tuberculosis, and malaria; corruption; and insurgencies and civil wars. The unstable environment is not conducive to economic growth, yet the collaborations persevere. Three of these groups are the *Economic Community of West African States (ECOWAS)*, the *Common Market for Eastern and Southern Africa (COMESA)*, and the *Southern African Development Community (SADC)*. Figure 4.7 includes their locations and member-nations. A new group has recently formed that may be able to build an institution that would provide solid trade benefits to its members. The *African Union (AU)* was established in 1999 to replace the Organization of African Unity (OAU), whose goals had focused on moving forward from colonization and apartheid. AU has 53 members and is modeled on the European Union. Its long-term goals, outlined on its Web site (www.au.org), include social and political initiatives as well as economic integration.

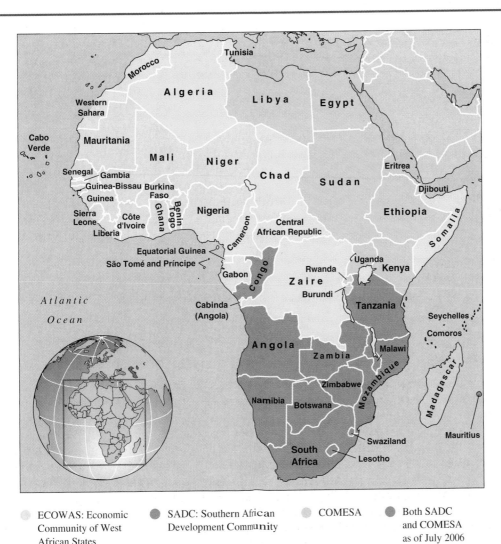

FIGURE 4.7

African Trade Agreements

- ECOWAS: Economic Community of West African States
- SADC: Southern African Development Community
- COMESA
- Both SADC and COMESA as of July 2006

MERCOSUR (MERCOSUL)

Mercosur (Mercosul)

Economic free trade area in South America modeled on the EU

Mercosur (Spanish) or *Mercosul* (Portuguese) is an acronym for Mercado Commun del Sur, or Common Market of the South. **Mercosur** was created in 1991 by the Treaty of Asunción, which united Argentina, Brazil, Paraguay, and Uruguay in an effort to create a common market. Venezuela has been accepted as a new member, to take effect in late 2006, and Bolivia has been invited to join. (See Figure 4.8.) Mercosur's purpose is to develop a common market; the alliance has made progress, and it is growing. Most trade within Mercosur is tariff-free. A common external tariff has been adopted on most products, but Mercosur has not yet become a customs union.

Since its inception, trade within Mercosur has grown rapidly, at an average of 27 percent a year, while trade with the rest of the world has expanded at an annual rate of 7.5 percent. Yet there is poor infrastructure (e.g., inadequate roads and bridges) in the member-nations, and the case has been made that by setting high external tariffs and thus insulating themselves from external markets, Mercosur members are allowing inefficiencies that make their production costly, especially for export outside Mercosur. At one point fairly recently, both Brazil and Argentina were believed to be able to lead Latin America out of its economic problems, but both major countries have undergone several years of severe economic challenges.

FIGURE 4.8

Regional Trade Agreements in Central America and South America

Andean Community   Central American Free Trade Zone   Mercosur   None

These problems will hinder Mercosur's future. In addition, Argentina and Uruguay have a serious border dispute. At issue is the construction of two cellulose factories, one Spanish and the other Finnish, on the river that forms their border. Argentina closed bridge access to Uruguay so that delivery of construction materials was hampered.[33] Late in the spring of 2006, Bolivia's socialist president nationalized the oil and gas industry in his country, encouraged by Venezuela's leader, Hugo Chavez. Brazil, as the largest consumer of Bolivian gas, is the main victim of Bolivia's decision to nationalize. Brazilians may pay up to 60 percent more for gas.[34] Relationships among the nations of Mercosur appear to be in considerable disarray.

CENTRAL AMERICAN FREE TRADE AGREEMENT

The United States and Guatemala, Honduras, Nicaragua, and El Salvador concluded an agreement in late 2003 establishing the **Central American Free Trade Agreement (CAFTA)**, which Costa Rica and the Dominican Republic later joined. (See Figure 4.8.) CAFTA opens all public services to private investment, grants guarantees to foreign investment, and opens government procurement to transnational bids. It also provides market access as a result of government pledges to reduce and eventually eliminate tariffs and other measures, including protectionist barriers in all sectors, that protect domestic products. CAFTA has agreed to duty-free imports and elimination of subsidies on agricultural products, the protection of intellectual property rights, antidumping rules, and the right of transnationals to sue countries in private international courts.

CAFTA has created the second-largest U.S. export market in Latin America. In 2004, the United States exported more to these six countries ($16 billion) than to Russia, India, and Indonesia combined.[35] U.S. export growth to the CAFTA region has outperformed overall U.S. exports. From 2000 to 2004, export shipments to CAFTA destinations grew by almost 16 percent, compared with less than 5 percent for overall U.S. exports.

Central American Free Trade Agreement (CAFTA)
FTA among the United States and several Central American nations

OTHER CENTRAL AND SOUTH AMERICAN TRADE AGREEMENTS

The **Andean Community (CAN)**, whose members are Colombia, Peru, Ecuador, Bolivia, and Venezuela (see Figure 4.8), is presently in a crisis over Venezuela's decision to withdraw from the community. Venezuela's President, Hugo Chavez, announced his country's withdrawal in the spring of 2006 because other Andean Community members, Colombia and Peru, had signed trade deals with the United States and are, in his view, "overly aligned with the U.S."[36]

The *Organization of American States (OAS)*, headquartered in Washington, D.C., is an organization of countries in the Western Hemisphere dedicated to promoting democracy and cooperation in the region. The OAS was formed in 1948 with the United States as one of the original 21 countries, but its origins date back to 1890, when the First International Conference of American States, held in Washington, D.C., established the International Union of American Republics. Today all 35 independent countries of the Americas have ratified the charter and are members of OAS. Even though Cuba is a member of the OAS, in 1962 the organization excluded the Cuban government from participation in its activities. The OAS focus has been on fostering democracy, protecting human rights, strengthening security, fostering free trade, combating illegal drugs, and fighting corruption.[37]

Andean Community (CAN)
South American five-nation trading bloc

ASIA-PACIFIC ECONOMIC COOPERATION

In response to the growing importance of the economies of the Pacific Rim countries, the *Asia-Pacific Economic Cooperation (APEC)* was established in 1989 to serve as a regional vehicle for promoting open trade and practical economic cooperation. The United States is one of the 21 current members. APEC is a nontreaty organization whose decisions are reached by consensus and are nonbinding. Information about APEC can be found at its Web site, www.apec.org.

The European Union, our next focus, has developed from an institution with an economic purpose, a common market, to one with an added political purpose.

The European Union

The **European Union** is an institution of 25 independent countries that have committed to develop close economic and political cooperation. The EU began as a customs union; developed into a common market, known as the European Community (EC) or European Economic Community (EEC); and now is substantially integrated economically and is well on the way to political integration. The EU's movement toward monetary integration is a huge step forward for both economic and political cooperation. So far 12 EU members use the EU currency, the euro (€), forming the euro zone. Slovenia was granted entry into the euro zone in 2007. Of the 15 EU countries that were members at the time the euro was introduced, only the United Kingdom, Denmark, and Sweden have not joined the euro zone.

EU BACKGROUND

World War II left Europe in shambles, with damage not only to physical structures from direct fighting but also to the economic, political, and social infrastructure from the necessity of devoting almost all resources and investments to the war effort. The war devastated people's lives along with buildings, railroads, highways, and businesses. Europeans found themselves with the enormous task of rebuilding European society—economically, politically, and culturally—and as they began, there was concern throughout the continent that the previous economic and political systems had failed. Out of this concern slowly developed a willingness to relinquish certain aspects of national sovereignty for the greater economic and political good.

While most Europeans understood the need to establish national democracies and free-market economies, many argued for greater continentwide cooperation as the way to peace. Much of the support for European unity came from resistance movements formed during the war. Resistance fighters had put aside their devotion to a political ideology to join others fighting for a common objective. One of the most ardent proponents of a united Europe was the Italian resistance fighter Altiero Spinelli. In 1944, Spinelli argued for "a federal Europe with a written constitution, a supranational government directly responsible to the people of Europe and not national governments, along with an army under its control, with no other military forces being permitted."[38] The end of the war, though, brought many changes in Europe, and with those changes, support for a "United States of Europe" waned. Exiled or imprisoned political leaders reemerged in their respective countries. Ideological and traditional divisions between socialists, communists, and conservatives that had been put aside during the resistance movement resurfaced. The emergence of the cold war and the resulting division of Europe helped blur the vision of a united Europe. Many of the proponents of greater European unity, including Britain's Winston Churchill, lost political power in their own nations. In addition to these factors, as a practical matter, many Europeans were concerned not with debates about politics and economics but with basic problems such as food supplies, fuel, shelter, and physical reconstruction. Thinking in terms of grand European unification was difficult when there was little food.

In 1950, Robert Schuman, the French foreign minister, proposed a united Europe, beginning with the integration of the coal and steel industries. The European Coal and Steel Community (ECSC) initially had six members—Belgium, West Germany, France, Italy, Luxembourg, and the Netherlands—held together by the Treaty of Paris. Continued integration led to the Treaty of Rome in 1957, which established a common market among the six members. By 1967, this core group had established the European Community (EC), with a European Parliament, a European Commission, and a Council of Ministers.

Early EU history shows that European integration was largely a continental European movement. Even though Winston Churchill in 1945 called for the building of a kind of United States of Europe, the United Kingdom did not join the European integration process until 1973. The United Kingdom had delayed because of its concerns about associating with its longtime adversary, France, and about losing its status as a world power by becoming an equal with other European nations.

FIGURE 4.9   European Union: Current Member-Nations and Candidate Nations

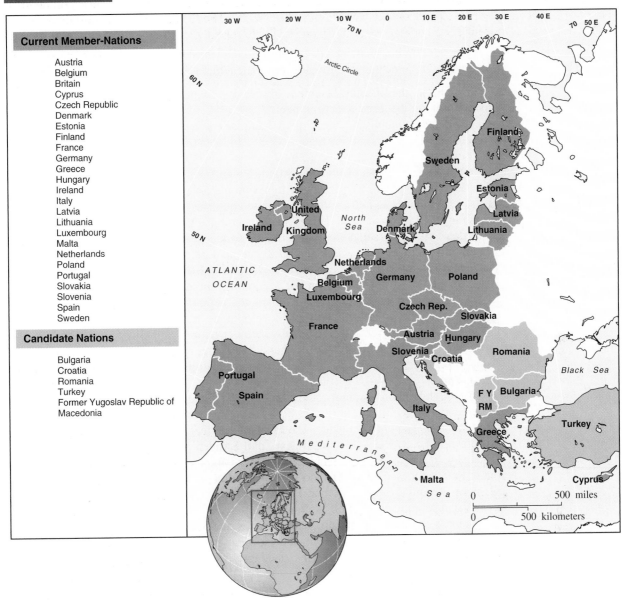

Current Member-Nations

Austria
Belgium
Britain
Cyprus
Czech Republic
Denmark
Estonia
Finland
France
Germany
Greece
Hungary
Ireland
Italy
Latvia
Lithuania
Luxembourg
Malta
Netherlands
Poland
Portugal
Slovakia
Slovenia
Spain
Sweden

Candidate Nations

Bulgaria
Croatia
Romania
Turkey
Former Yugoslav Republic of Macedonia

Source: European Union, http://europa.eu.int/abc/maps/print_index_en.htm, August 2, 2004 © European Communities, 1995–2004.

EU GROWTH

The EU has grown in size, with successive waves of accessions, to 25 member-countries, creating one body that includes most of the economic, industrial, and population strengths of Europe. Its highly educated population is presently 457 million people, far larger than the United States' population of 298.5 million, and it accounts for 42 percent of world merchandise trade.[39]

Any European country may apply for EU membership if it respects the principles of liberty, democracy, respect for human rights and fundamental freedoms, and the rule of law, principles that are common to the member-states. Accession, however, can follow only if the given country fulfills all the required criteria . Specifically, the country must:

- Have stable political institutions guaranteeing democracy, the rule of law, human rights, and respect for protection of minorities.

- Have a functioning market economy and the capacity to cope with competition and market forces in the EU.

- Have the capacity to take on the obligations of membership, including adherence to the objectives of political, economic, and monetary union.

- Agree to adoption of the *acquis communautaire* (the entire European legislation) and its effective implementation through appropriate administrative and judicial structures.

In addition, the EU must be able to absorb new members, so it reserves the right to decide when it will be ready to accept them.[40]

Denmark, Ireland, and the United Kingdom joined the EU in 1973, followed by Greece in 1981, Spain and Portugal in 1986, and Austria, Finland, and Sweden in 1995. The European Union welcomed 10 new countries in 2004: Cyprus, the Czech Republic, Estonia, Hungary, Latvia, Lithuania, Malta, Poland, Slovakia, and Slovenia. In 2006, the EU was debating when to bring in its next two members, Bulgaria and Romania, whose initial target date was 2007. Other candidate countries are Croatia, the former Yugoslav Republic of Macedonia, and Turkey, which have been approved for accession with an entry date still to be set. Some EU citizens wonder how far the EU should extend and whether a Muslim country will be culturally compatible with the EU. Albania, Bosnia and Herzegovina, and Serbia and Montenegro, including Kosovo, are potential candidates for EU membership. In the 2004 round of accessions, the new members, except Cyprus and Malta, were recent converts from socialism and centrally planned economies. The EU's enlargement process has guided their development into market economies with democratic governments. Actually, the 10 new member-nations add only 5 percent to the EU's gross domestic product. On the other hand, they offer low wages, low taxes, and undervalued exchange rates, which make them good locations for manufacturing and service operations.[41]

Although EU borders are theoretically open to the movement of labor, the EU accession agreements for the 10 new, mostly Eastern European, members included provisions to hold off on labor movement for a while. The EU members that have opened their borders fully to Eastern European labor—Britain, Ireland, and Sweden—have benefited greatly from enlargement, as has the EU as a whole.[42] A French campaign to keep Eastern European labor out of France focused on the dangers of Polish plumbers taking French jobs, making Polish plumbers a symbol of cheap labor. Poland's tourist board countered with a playful visit-Poland campaign featuring Polish plumbers who plan to stay in Poland.

Notable are the Western European countries that have rejected membership in the EU, Switzerland and Norway, both of which decided not to join on the basis of national elections. Norway's economy is based on North Sea oil reserves, and Switzerland has valued its role as a neutral country for a long time.

EVOLVING PURPOSE OF THE EU

The EU is a supranational body in that its governance transcends (*supra*) the national level; it is a regional government. In order to join the EU, member-nations cede some of their sovereignty to this larger body. The supranational status of the EU makes the EU different from other international organizations, such as the United Nations, and from treaties, such as the North American Free Trade Agreement (NAFTA). Because of its supranational status, the EU has certain powers that the UN and NAFTA lack. For example, it can tax member-nations directly and implement legislation directly in each of the member-nations, much as in the United States, where Congress has the power to enact legislation that has a direct effect in each of the states. The EU also has a court, the European Court of Justice, with the power to impose fines and other sanctions on individuals, companies, and even member-nations that violate the Treaty of Rome.

As originally established in the 1950s, European integration was limited to economic issues. In the 1957 Treaty of Rome, which still serves as the fundamental law of the EU, members sought to achieve four fundamental freedoms: movement of goods, services, capital, and people across national borders. Today, goods, services, capital, and people are able to move freely among most member-nations of the EU, with few negotiated limitations. For example, a citizen of the United Kingdom has the right to work in Greece without any additional approval from the Greek government. A dentist in Madrid can move to Berlin without any additional licensing or exams. This freedom of movement is in sharp contrast to the same situation under NAFTA: a citizen of Mexico must obtain the proper visa in order to work legally in the United States.

As the EU developed, it began to include monetary and political integration as well as economic. The development of a common foreign policy, security policy, approach to justice, and monetary union was initiated by the Maastricht Treaty of 1992. This treaty calls for the EU "to assert its identity on the international scene, in particular through the implementation of a common foreign and security policy including the eventual framing of a common defense policy, which might in time lead to a common defense." A common agricultural policy has developed to support food production and protection of the environment throughout the EU. Passport and customs checks have been abolished at most EU country internal borders.[43] The euro currency has been adopted in 12 of the original 15 EU member-countries, with the 10 new accession nations trying hard to meet the economic criteria to join this currency union. The Maastricht Treaty also established the European Central Bank to develop and implement monetary policy for the euro area.

Another step forward in political integration for the EU is a proposed EU constitution that establishes the EU as subsidiary to the member-states and describes the division of responsibilities, the decision-making process, the foreign and defense policy, the reform process, and a charter of individual rights. This constitution, designed to strengthen the institutional basis of the EU, was agreed to by the European Commission in 2004 but must be ratified by all EU members. (See Figure 4.10.) Spain, Luxembourg, Estonia, Latvia and Lithuania, Slovakia, Slovenia, Hungary, Austria, Italy, Greece, Malta, and Cyprus have ratified it. France and the Netherlands rejected the constitution in 2005. Presently it is on hold while the 25 EU members engage in a period of reflection, but European Commission president Jose Manuel Barroso of Spain describes the situation with some optimism: "We are going into extra time. We are not yet at the stage of penalty shoot-outs."[44]

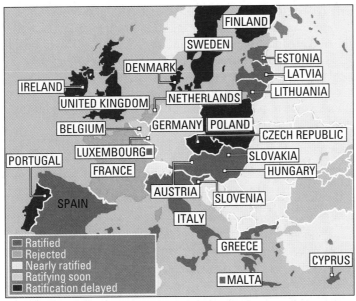

FIGURE 4.10

EU Constitution: State of the Debate

Source: EU Constitution: Where Member States Stand, http://news.bbe.co.uk/1/hi/world/europe/3954327.stm. Posted 9 May 2006. Accessed 13 May 2006.

Flag of the European Union.

INSTITUTIONS OF THE EU

There are nine main institutions of the EU that perform functions similar to those performed by a national government:[45] the European Parliament, the Council of the European Union, the European Commission, the Court of Justice, the Court of Auditors, the European Economic and Social Committee, the Committee of the Regions, the European Central Banks, and the European Investment Bank. Here we will examine the first four bodies in detail, because they are the most critical, and then briefly describe the roles of the remaining five.

European Parliament
EU legislative body whose members are popularly elected from member-nations

European Parliament

The **European Parliament** was first elected in 1979 and is now elected by popular vote throughout Europe every five years. The present EU Parliament was elected in June 2004 and has 732 members from all 25 EU countries. Parliament members are seated by political party affiliation rather than by their country. This party identification underscores the nature of the EU as a European rather than a national institution. Seven parties are presently represented, the largest representation going to the center-right European People's Party (Christian Democrats), followed by the Socialist Party, the Liberal Party, and the Green Party. The European Parliament holds its sessions in Strasbourg, France. The main function of the Parliament is to pass European laws, and it is widely seen as the voice of the European people in the EU. Parliamentary sessions are available live at www.europarl.europa.eu.

Council of the European Union
Group that is the EU's primary policy-setting institution

Council of the European Union

The **Council of the European Union** is the primary policy-setting institution of the EU and is the voice of the member-states. This is where important decisions are made on common foreign policy and security issues. The ministers who make up the Council are members of their respective national governments. Generally, when the Council meets, the minister who represents the area being discussed serves as the representative of that country. When financial matters are discussed, for example, the finance ministers of all countries are present. When agricultural matters are discussed, agricultural ministers are present. The presidency of the Council rotates among the member-nations, with each one holding the presidency for six months. So when the United Kingdom holds the presidency, the United Kingdom's prime minister is effectively the head of government of the EU. Each country has votes based on population, although the weighting favors the smaller countries. Sensitive issues before the Council such as immigration policy, security and defense policy, and foreign policy require unanimous votes to pass, and most other issues require majority vote. Here is the vote distribution:[46]

Germany, France, Italy, United Kingdom	29
Spain, Poland	27
Netherlands	13
Belgium, Czech Republic, Greece, Hungary, Portugal	12
Austria, Sweden	10
Denmark, Ireland, Lithuania, Slovakia, Finland	7
Cyprus, Estonia, Latvia, Luxembourg, Slovenia	4
Malta	3
Total	321

The Council presidency rotates among members in a predetermined sequence, with each holding the position for a six-month term. From 2007 through 2011, the rotation is Germany, Portugal, Slovenia, France, Czech Republic, Sweden, Spain, Belgium, Hungary, and Poland.

The president sets the agenda and the location of any meetings, so holding the presidency is quite important and the president has great power to influence EU policy decisions.

The Council's decisions are set forth in regulations and directives. Recent directives deal with foreign policy issues (support for elections in the Congo, declarations on Darfur, relations with other trading blocs such as Mercosur), issues of health and safety (bird flu precautions, disaster planning, workplace safety equipment, computer use rules, and environmental safety for workers), and issues related to terrorism. The Council has come under some criticism for its power relative to the other EU institutions and even to the national parliaments.[47] One frequently voiced concern is that the Council's decisions are not reviewed or evaluated through any democratic process.

European Commission

The **European Commission** is the executive institution and represents the interests of Europe as a whole. It administers the daily operations of the EU and ensures implementation of the provisions of the Treaty of Rome. In addition, the European Commission drafts laws that it presents to the European Parliament and the Council. The Commission consists of 25 commissioners, one from each member-nation. Commission members are nominated by their countries, appointed by the Commission president-elect, and then approved by a vote of the European Parliament. The present commissioners serve with Commission president Jose Manuel Barroso from 2004 to 2009, when his term expires.

European Commission
Institution that runs the EU's day-to-day operations

European Court of Justice

The **European Court of Justice (ECJ)** decides cases arising under the Treaty of Rome. On EU matters, its authority supersedes that of the member-nations' national courts. The influence of the ECJ is growing steadily as it is deciding an increasing number of cases. In addition, many decisions in the EU are now made by the EU Court of First Instance in the various member-nations, which has more limited jurisdiction than the ECJ. The responsibilities of the Court of First Instance include claims made in several areas of interest to businesspeople: competition, commercial policy, regional policy, social policy, institutional law, trademark law, and transport.

European Court of Justice (ECJ)
Court that rules on issues related to EU policies

Other EU Institutions

The remaining five EU institutions focus on financial and social issues. The *Court of Auditors* is the financial conscience of the EU. It reviews the spending of EU funds to make sure they are spent legally and for the intended purpose. EU funding is tax-based and includes the value-added tax (VAT), customs duties, and other fees paid by member-states. The 2005 EU budget amounted to $0.64 per day per citizen of the EU.[48] The *European Economic and Social Committee (EESC)* is an advisory and consultative body of specialists in areas of occupational and social interest groups. The 317 members are divided by member population size and represent employers, employees, and other social interests. Members are nominated by national governments to serve four-year terms. The *Committee of the Regions (CoR)* is a consultative group that represents local viewpoints on issues such as transportation, education, and health. Its 317 members are often local government leaders. The CoR ensures that the EU continues its commitment to four levels of participation: local, regional, national, and European. The **European Central Bank (ECB)** manages the euro to ensure the price stability of European markets. Its primary concern is to manage inflation, and it makes decisions independent of member governments. The *European Investment Bank (EIB)* supports lending programs for projects of interest to the EU, both internal and external. Activities of the EIB include developing infrastructure, such as transportation systems and buildings, especially in less developed regions; supporting small businesses; and lending to member governments.

European Central Bank (ECB)
Institution that sets and implements EU monetary policy

The term "Fortress Europe" has been used by outsiders, including Americans, Japanese, and others, to express their fear that the EU would deny its privileges to them, their companies, and their products.[49] Although such fears persist, with the recent accession of eight former Soviet bloc countries that had centrally planned economies, they are not as compelling.

THE EU GOING FORWARD

EU members cannot agree at present on whether they want to have a centralized federal system with most of the power held by the EU institutions (that is, the Parliament, Council, and Commission). Several members have shown reluctance to surrender their national currencies, central banks, and other powers to a distant authority, particularly an unelected one. Such decisions, represented in a constitution, will take time. After all, there are 25 sovereign nations in the EU—and more want to join—with long, proud histories and national loyalties, cultures, and languages. There have been bitter, bloody wars among them.

But one subject about which there is unhappy agreement is the concern about fraud that plagued the EU through 2004, especially in the area of the agriculture budget, the largest item in the EU budget. The Commission's public image was tarnished by revelation of fraudulently claimed agricultural subsidies by many EU members. The EU response has been impressive. It quickly established the Fraud Prevention Expert Group to investigate and deter fraudulent practices and function as a control group. As a result, the Court of Auditors, which reviews all expenditures, has been able to approve an increased number of payments in farm subsidies and regional development categories, the two largest spending areas. The Court of Auditors approved one-third of all payments in 2005, which is a huge step forward from 2004, when only 6 percent of the spending was approved.[50] The trend toward timely and effective monitoring appears to be in the right direction.

In the June 2004 EU elections, record low voter turnout was recorded across Europe, even in the newly acceded nations. The overall turnout was 44.2 percent, with 20 percent in Slovakia, 21 percent in Poland, and 27 percent in Estonia. (Even so, the election marked the largest democratic election in history, with almost 350 million voters.)[51] This poor voter turnout suggests that the EU is struggling to maintain credibility with its electorate; yet, at the same time, the EU has increased its own power.

EU ACHIEVEMENTS

The countries in the EU have made great strides toward union, and the EU is now a major world political and economic force. EU directives have superseded 25 sets of national rules. They have harmonized 100,000 national standards, labeling laws, testing procedures, and consumer protection measures covering everything from toys to food, stock brokering to teaching. The 25 nations have scrapped as many as 60 million customs and tax formalities at their shared borders. These successes are impressive, and many, Europeans and others, expect even more progress with continued European integration.

European Monetary Union (EMU)

Group that established use of euro (€) in the 12-country euro zone

The **European Monetary Union (EMU)** is one of the most significant agreements to come out of the EU. The euro, in both notes and coins, went into general usage in 12 of the original 15 EU countries on January 1, 2002, with Denmark, Sweden, and the United Kingdom standing outside the EMU. This single currency reduces the cost of doing business across EMU country borders, both because there are no currency exchange costs and because there is now no risk of currency exchange fluctuations among these 12 countries. The Web site for the European Central Bank, which sets monetary policy for the EMU, contains a discussion of the history of the EMU and the adoption of the euro. See www.ecb.int.

THE EU'S IMPACT

The EU increasingly is making its presence known in the world business community. It accounts for roughly 20 percent of world exports and imports and 30 percent of the world's foreign direct investment (FDI). It is the world's largest trading economy and the world's prime source of FDI outflows.

A significant number of EU regulations have an impact in the United States, Japan, China, and elsewhere because of the size of the EU and the importance of the EU as a trading partner. EU rules forced changes by Microsoft in its contracts with software makers and even forced McDonald's to stop serving soft-plastic toys with its Happy Meals. "Twenty years ago, if you designed something to U.S. standards you could pretty much sell it all over the world. Now the shoe's on the other foot," said Maja Wessels, a Brussels-based lobbyist for United Technologies Corporation.[52] For example, in an effort to prevent electrical and electronic equipment waste, the EU requires recycling of at least 50 percent of all such equipment, including cell phones, computers, household appliances, and televisions. It requires 80 percent recovery by weight for larger appliances, 75 percent for IT and telecommunications equipment, and 70 percent for small appliances.[53] In addition, the manufacturers are required to provide collection for the waste that is not from private households.

In fact, today the EU has built the economic force necessary to make many of the rules that influence world trade. Most notably, in 2001 the European Commission voted to veto a proposed merger between two U.S. companies, General Electric and Honeywell, that had been approved by the U.S. Justice Department. "The merger between GE and Honeywell, as it was notified, would have severely reduced competition in the aerospace industry and resulted ultimately in higher prices for customers, particularly airlines," observed EU Competition Commissioner Mario Monti. If the merger had taken place, the $42 billion giant would not have been able to operate in the EU, the largest single market in the world.

Microsoft's practices have also been influenced by the EU. In 2004, the European Commission ordered the company to pay €497 million, share its software code with competitors, and offer an unbundled version of the Windows operating system. Microsoft complied. Then, in 2005, the EU ruled that Microsoft would be fined $2.37 million per day if the software code it provided competitors didn't have better documentation. The point is clear: If foreign companies want access to the EU market, they must conduct business by the European Union's rules.

The three most important trading relationships the EU has, based on the value of trade flows, are those with China, Japan, and the United States. EU trade relations with China have changed dramatically over the last 20 years, going from a sizable trade surplus in the 1980s to a widening deficit with China in the 2000s (around €78.5 billion in 2004); this is the EU's biggest bilateral trade deficit. Overall, China is now the EU's second-largest trading partner after the United States, and the EU became China's largest trading partner in 2004. In recent years, EU companies have invested considerably in China, with total EU FDI at over $35 billion.

The EU trade deficit with China reflects, at least in part, the effect of trade barriers or market access obstacles in China. The EU list of trade barriers its merchants have encountered in China includes barriers in the pharmaceutical, automotive, agricultural and fisheries, chemical, and electronic sectors. EU policy in this area aims at the liberalization of markets, as does the policy of the World Trade Organization. Key objectives include the removal of barriers to imports of specific goods (price controls, discriminatory registration requirements, arbitrary sanitary standards); the removal of obstacles to investment (geographic restrictions, joint venture requirements, discriminatory licensing procedures, outright closure of certain sectors to foreigners, restrictive foreign exchange regulations); and the improvement of the business environment (protection of intellectual property rights).[54]

The EU trade relationship with Japan is one of the central trade relationships in the world. Along with the United States, the EU and Japan are the main pillars of the world economy.[55] Japan and the EU are responsible for 40 percent of world trade, with Japan accounting for 14 percent of that total. The Japanese economy is the largest economy in Asia and the EU's fifth-largest export market and import source. Europe is also an important export market for Japan. What is unusual about Japan is its high savings rate and large foreign currency reserves. Japanese savings total 250 percent of GDP, the highest rate in the world.

The United States and Europe have always enjoyed a well-established commercial relationship, and the increase in European prosperity as a result of the EU's success has made this relationship even stronger. The European Union and the United States are the world's largest economies and each other's largest trading partner. Their combined GDP accounts for approximately 57 percent of world GDP and 40 percent of world trade. In addition, these two economies greatly influence world trade patterns, since either the European Union or the United States is the largest trading partner for most other economies. Many businesses in the United States are realizing the EU's vast potential for trade opportunities. The cross-Atlantic trade flows are running at over €1.7 billion per day. Total foreign direct investment is over €1.5 trillion per year, with the EU being the largest source of FDI for the United States. This is not to say that no disputes occur. They do, but they affect only about 2 percent of the EU-U.S. trade.[56] The trade disputes have been over products as diverse as bananas, beef, and steel.

The EU Web site has a wealth of information in the 11 EU official languages (Danish, Dutch, English, Finnish, French, German, Greek, Italian, Portuguese, Spanish, and Swedish). See www.europa.eu. The EU has a special Web site that focuses on matters of interest concerning EU-U.S. relations and includes information about the EU's trade activities with individual states. See www.eurunion.org.

Summary

Describe the influence the mainly political international institutions have on international businesses and their relevance to international business.

International organizations such as the United Nations, military alliances, and ASEAN can have profound influence on international businesses. By providing a forum for governments to talk to each other, they contribute toward peace and stability, conditions that stimulate international business. Such dialogue also results in collaborative efforts that support multilateral cooperation in areas of immediate concern to business, such as maritime agreements, communication accords, and other rules and standards. In addition, many of these institutions support development projects, which stimulate business directly, through their contracts, and also through their support of the development of markets.

Identify the major organs of the United Nations, their general purpose, and their significance to international business.

The work of the United Nations is carried out through five main bodies or organs: the General Assembly, the Security Council, the Economic and Social Council, the International Court of Justice, and the Secretariat. The General Assembly is a forum where every nation has one vote; the Security Council focuses on peace and security and has permanent members and elected members; the Economic and Social Council addresses issues related to trade, education, health, and other economic and social issues; the International Court of Justice hears cases between nations; and the Secretariat, headed by the secretary-general,

is the administrative arm of the UN. The UN has a variety of agencies throughout the world that work to promote peace and stability and to facilitate trade and economic activity.

Discuss the World Trade Organization and its predecessor, GATT.

The WTO attempts to remove trade barriers worldwide. Its membership is composed of the major trading countries in the world, so it has the potential to significantly influence world trade. The WTO routinely issues decisions on trade disputes between countries. GATT, the predecessor of the WTO, greatly contributed to the growth of trade through trade liberalization.

Appreciate the resources of the Organisation for Economic Cooperation and Development.

OECD conducts extensive research on a wide variety of international business and economic subjects, and it produces highly regarded individual country surveys. These resource materials are valuable to researchers and businesspeople as they develop an understanding of markets.

Describe the major purpose and effectiveness of OPEC.

The major purpose of OPEC is to allow developing nations to increase their price control over the oil they are selling on international markets. OPEC has had periods of marked effectiveness. Today, despite unrest in the Middle East and the ability of OPEC to influence oil prices in the short term, the number of non-OPEC nations that produce or soon will be producing oil has increased significantly. Adding to the OPEC dilemma is the possibility that price gouging will lead to the development of fuel alternatives and increased conservation and, eventually, to a reduction in demand. Admittedly, the popularity of SUVs in the U.S. market suggests that the price of oil would have to escalate considerably to trigger this possibility.

Identify economic integration agreements and the effectiveness of the major ones.

The four major forms of economic integration are the free trade area (tariffs abolished among members), the customs union (a free trade agreement plus a common external tariff), the common market (a customs union plus mobility of services, people, and capital), and complete economic integration (a common market plus a common currency). NAFTA has been quite effective, while Mercosur, whose goal is a common market, has faced difficulties recently, as has the Andean Community. The EU has been markedly successful.

Explain the North American Free Trade Agreement and its impact on business.

NAFTA was ratified by Canada, Mexico, and the United States. Its purpose is to facilitate trade among the three countries. NAFTA lowers tariffs on goods moving from one NAFTA country to another and makes it easier for businesses to sell goods and operate in other NAFTA countries.

Discuss the impact of the EU and its future challenges.

The EU is a supranational entity with 25 European membernations. Its purpose is to integrate the economies of its membernations, creating a trading region where goods, services, people, and capital move freely. In recent years, the EU has made major steps toward political union as well. The EU is a regional government and as such has regulatory power over social and environmental matters, including mergers and business operations, in Europe. The EU adopted a common currency, the euro, which is being used in 12 EU countries. The EU's success at monetary integration reduces the risk for businesses within the EMU. The EU can be seen as one large market with fewer restrictions than existed among the 25 nations before integration.

Key Words

United Nations (UN) (p. 105)

General Assembly (p. 106)

Security Council (p. 106)

Economic and Social Council (ECOSOC) (p. 106)

International Court of Justice (ICJ) (p. 107)

Secretariat (p. 107)

North Atlantic Treaty Organization (NATO) (p. 108)

Collective Security Treaty Organization (CSTO) (p. 108)

Association of Southeast Asian Nations (ASEAN) (p. 110)

World Trade Organization (WTO) (p. 110)

General Agreement on Tariffs and Trade (GATT) (p. 112)

most favored nation (MFN) clause (p. 112)

Uruguay Round (p. 112)

Doha Development Agenda (p. 114)

trade-related intellectual property rights (TRIPS) (p. 115)

Organisation for Economic Cooperation and Development (OECD) (p. 116)

Organization of Petroleum Exporting Countries (p. 118)

Group of 8 (G8) (p. 118)

free trade area (FTA) (p. 120)

customs union (p. 120)

common market (p. 120)

complete economic integration (p. 120)

North American Free Trade Agreement (NAFTA) (p. 121)

European Free Trade Agreement (EFTA) (p. 122)

Mercosur (Mercosul) (p. 124)

Central American Free Trade Agreement (CAFTA) (p. 125)

Andean Community (CAN) (p. 125)

European Union (EU) (p. 126)

European Parliament (p. 130)

Council of the European Union (p. 130)

European Commission (p. 131)

European Court of Justice (ECJ) (p. 131)

European Central Bank (ECB) (p. 131)

European Monetary Union (EMU) (p. 132)

Questions

1. What are some reasons that businesspeople should be aware of important international institutions?

2. Even though the UN is best known for peacekeeping missions, it has many agencies involved in activities affecting businesses. In your judgment, do these activities justify support for the UN? Would it be better if the activities of these agencies were done by private entities such as trade groups?

3. How did the WTO come into existence? What purpose does it serve? Would bilateral trading agreements work better than the multilateral WTO approach?

4. What are the four main organs of the EU, and what is the purpose of each?

5. What is the impact of the EU on business?

6. The U.S. Congress approved the North American Free Trade Agreement despite strong opposition from organized labor. Why would labor have opposed NAFTA?

7. What is the importance of the OECD for business?

8. Mercosur's major trading partner is the EU rather than the United States. Why might this be the case?

9. How might a small businessperson in Des Moines, Iowa, who is exporting agricultural products find useful the international institutions and agreements that this chapter describes?

Research Task

globalEDGE.msu.edu

Use the globalEDGE site (http://globalEDGE.msu.edu/) to complete the following exercises:

1. You are currently making a decision concerning which landlocked and lesser developed country you will visit for your next overseas trip so you can better understand the dynamics of international institutions among developing countries. To assist in this process, *InfoNation* is an easy-to-use, two-step database that allows one to view and compare the most current statistical data for United Nations member states. Select the following six countries to facilitate your decision: Afghanistan, Bhutan, Chad, Lao People's Democratic Republic, Lesotho, and Rwanda. Then, to gain additional insight into the conditions in each country, select data for the following categories: Population-Population in 2003; Population-Largest Urban Agglomeration; Economy-Tourist Arrivals; Technology-Telephone Lines; Technology-

Television Receivers; and Environment-Water Resources per Capita. Which countries rank highest and lowest in each category? Which country would you choose for your next trip? Given the international regional organizations discussed in the text, which regional grouping of nations will you be visiting? What are your reasons for choosing this country? Were there other factors that influenced your decision? If so, what were they?

2. The *World Development Indicators* (WDI) is the World Bank's premier data compilation on development. Utilize the WDI for the Czech Republic to gather information on this country. Considering that your company currently produces an emerging video game system technology and is planning to enter this country soon, prepare a short report on the infrastructure of this country as it applies to your company's product.

You are an international business consultant in the United States. Your specialty is exporting to and investing, licensing, or franchising in developing countries.

One of your clients is a hotel company that wants to build, operate, and 100 percent own a hotel in a Latin American country.

To which organizations discussed in this chapter might you look for assistance in developing a list of country-selection criteria and then a list of possible sites for the investment?

5 Understanding the International Monetary System

The function of money is not to make money but to move goods. Money is only one part of our transportation system. It moves goods from man to man. A dollar bill is like a postage stamp: it is no good unless it will move commodities between persons. If a postage stamp will not carry a letter, or money will not move goods, it is just the same as an engine that will not run. Someone will have to get out and fix it.

—*widely attributed to Henry Ford in a speech at the Ford Motor Company*

All truth passes through three phases: First, it is ridiculed. Second, it is violently opposed, and Third, it is accepted as self-evident.

—*Schopenhauer*

Money Laundering, Terrorism, and International Monetary Institutions

One of the critical requirements for international terrorism is funding. Much of international terrorism's funding involves an ability to launder money, that is, disguise its sources, and move it unmonitored across international borders. If the money flow can be stopped, the terrorism will stop.

In the effort to combat money laundering connected to terrorist financing, international monetary institutions have taken a lead role, through the international Financial Action Task Force on Money Laundering (FATF). Established by the G7 countries (now G8), FATF develops and promotes policies, both national and international, that make money laundering more difficult and more risky. FATF works closely with the IMF, the World Bank, the United Nations, FATF-style regional bodies (FSRBs), and national bodies such as the U.S. Department of the Treasury.

FATF monitors what countries do to control the financing of terrorism and regularly publishes a list of countries that are not cooperating with international standards established to prevent money laundering. As of June 2006, the noncooperative countries and territories on the list are Myanmar and Nigeria. The list is markedly reduced from 2005, when it included the Cook Islands, Indonesia, Myanmar, Nauru, Nigeria, and the Philippines. Appearance on this list means that the international financial monitors sent in by FATF found serious problems: loopholes in financial regulations that allowed for money laundering, other domestic obstacles such as no requirements to register businesses, systemic obstacles to international cooperation, and/or inadequate resources for preventing and detecting money laundering activities.[1] Appearing on this list is *not* a goal of governments. It means that other governments have been notified to advise their banks and other financial institutions to give special attention to any transactions in the listed countries by exercising appropriate due diligence and caution. The financial world is watching you closely if you are on this list.

What suggestions does FATF offer to help safeguard against terrorism, from the finance side? Its recommendations include criminalizing the financing of terrorism, freezing and confiscating terrorist assets, reporting suspicious transactions related to terrorism, tracking parallel or alternative remittance systems, such as hawala (which avoids the banking system and relies on trust and family or religious connections),[2] and monitoring wire transfers, nonprofit organizations, and cash couriers. In the United States, the Department of the Treasury lists assets of suspected terrorist organizations and individuals that have been frozen by the government. You can see this list, which is updated regularly, at www.treasury.gov/offices/enforcement/key-issues/freezing. ■

CONCEPT PREVIEWS

After reading this chapter, you should be able to:

explain the functioning of the gold standard

describe the purposes of the IMF

appreciate the accomplishments of the Bretton Woods system and the developments shaping the world monetary system from the end of World War II to the present

describe the purpose of the World Bank

discuss the purpose of the Bank for International Settlements

discuss the floating exchange rate system

describe the development of the common currency area for the euro

explain the role of the balance of payments (BOP)

discuss the major BOP accounts

explain the uses of special drawing rights (SDRs)

Gli Affari Internazionali

onales Geschäft Παγοσμιο Business

Negócios Internacionais   Los Negócios Internacionais

internacionales   Affaires Internationales   国際商務   Παγοσμιο Business

The international monetary system consists of institutions, agreements, rules, and processes that allow for the payments, currency exchange, and movements of capital required by international transactions.[3] To gain a sense of where we are now in the arrangements of the international monetary system, it's useful to look first at where we've been with these arrangements. This will build an understanding of how the institutions and arrangements that facilitate payments across national borders have evolved. Thus we begin this chapter with a review of the gold standard and the Bretton Woods system. Next, we examine the institutions established at Bretton Woods—the International Monetary Fund (IMF) and the World Bank—and take a brief look at another institution that plays a central role in the international monetary system, the Bank for International Settlements. Then we consider the emergence of the floating exchange rate system and current exchange rate arrangements, including the newest currency development, the euro. Moving from the institutions that participate in the international monetary process to how the process is recorded, we conclude the chapter with an overview of the balance-of-payments accounts and special drawing rights (SDR).

This chapter addresses the cooperation among nations that makes possible and supports our international monetary system. How the foreign exchange market works is covered in Chapter 11, "Financial Forces."

The Gold Standard: A Brief History

Since ancient times, based on its scarcity and easily assessed level of purity, gold has been trusted as a way for people to store value, exchange value, and measure value. Actually, from about A.D. 1200 to the present, the price of gold has generally been going up.[4] In ancient trading, international traders used used both gold and silver coins until 1875. However, as trade grew, carrying large amounts of gold became impractical. Gold is heavy, has transportation and storage costs, and does not earn interest, plus its bulk made it an obvious target for thieves. These drawbacks led to the evolution of paper script that was backed by governments with a pledge to exchange the script for gold at a fixed rate.

In 1717, Sir Isaac Newton, the great mathematician who held a sinecure as master of the English mint, established the price of gold at 3 pounds, 17 shillings, 10.5 pence per ounce, putting England de facto on the gold standard. Except during the Napoleonic Wars, England stood willing to convert gold to currency, or vice versa, until World War I. During those two centuries, London was the dominant center of international finance. Estimates hold that more than 90 percent of world trade was financed in London.[5]

gold standard
The use of gold at an established number of units per currency

Most trading or industrial countries followed England's move and adopted the **gold standard.** Each country set a certain number of units of its currency per ounce of gold, and the ratios of their gold equivalence established the exchange rate between any two currencies on the gold standard. In essence, currencies were pegged to gold. So suppose the British pound was pegged to gold at 5 pounds per ounce and the French franc was pegged at 10 pounds per ounce. The exchange rate between the pound and the franc would have been 2 francs per pound, or .5 pound per franc.

The simplicity of the gold standard was a large part of its appeal. When there were trade imbalances, they would be corrected by a flow of gold in the direction of the surplus. The money supply would rise or fall in direct relation to the gold flows. This automatic adjustment is known as the *price-specie-flow mechanism* (*specie* is another word for "coined money"), a concept developed by the Scottish philosopher David Hume. As early as 1758, Hume was making impressive attempts to illustrate that trade is not a zero-sum game but, rather, that all participants can benefit from trade. Until his arguments and those of his friend Adam Smith gained acceptance, mercantilism held sway, a belief that a nation's wealth is best measured by its money stocks and that richer nations are those that have trade surpluses. Hume argued in *Of the Jealousy of Trade* that the wealth of all nations is directly related to the total volume of trade, that a rising tide lifts all boats.[6]

Modern monetary arrangements assign no special role to gold. The Federal Reserve, the central bank of the United States, is not required to tie the dollar to anything. This gives the Federal Reserve flexibility that is helpful during economic crises. For example, the Fed can print money to pump into a recession. Economist Paul Krugman points out that this flexibility is why the 1987 stock market crash did not cause a depression similar to that of 1929.[7]

The international gold standard ended when the financial burdens of World War I forced Britain to sell a substantial portion of its gold. Other countries involved in the war, including Germany, France, and Russia, suspended the exchange of paper money for gold and stopped exports of gold. Between World War I and World War II there was a short-lived flirtation with a renewal of the gold standard, but it was not successfully reestablished.

An Iranian currency trader counts gold coins. One expert called gold coins "Iranians' political hedge fund."

Although the gold standard has not been the international monetary system for many years, it continues to have some ardent and influential advocates—most economists not among them[8]—who call for a return to the gold standard and fixed exchange rates. Among its advocates are the publisher of *Forbes* and twice presidential candidate Steve Forbes, politician and vice-presidential candidate Jack Kemp, and *The Wall Street Journal* editor and Pulitzer Prize editorialist Robert Bartley. One of the staunchest supporters of a return to the gold standard was the French economist Jacques Rueff, a member of the French Academy and an adviser to the French government. The heart of Rueff's argument is expressed in one word: *discipline*. Under the gold standard, a government cannot create money that is not backed by gold. Therefore, no matter how great the temptation to create more money for political advantage, a government cannot do so without the required amount of gold.[9] Unfortunately, this discipline sacrifices the flexibility of a freely floating monetary system.

Yet gold remains a refuge for people who fear inflation. For example, in Iran, with tension escalating over its nuclear program and the economy stalling, the demand for gold has risen dramatically. "Gold coins are Iranians' political hedge fund. We keep them at home and they make us feel secure," observes Heydar Pourian, editor of *Iqtisad Iran* (Iran Economics).[10] With official reports of inflation at 14 percent in Iran, gold's value has gained 21 percent. Refugees, from Hitler's Germany of World War II to today's terror-based regimes, can attest that the small bars of bullion they managed to smuggle out can be credited with their survival. There is no question that the world's interest in gold remains high, especially when considering its other applications in industrial uses and jewelry. Figure 5.1 is an advertisement in the *Financial Times* (of London) of gold bullion, coins, and bars for sale.

BRETTON WOODS

During World War II, the countries of the world were much too involved with the hostilities to consider the gold standard or any other monetary system. However, many officials realized some system had to be established to operate when peace returned. In 1944, representatives of the 44 allied nations met at the Mount Washington Hotel in **Bretton Woods,** New Hampshire, to plan for the future. This was a historic undertaking: It resulted in the first negotiated agreement to support trade through the establishment of monetary institutions among independent nations.

There was a consensus among the Bretton Woods representatives that (1) stable exchange rates were desirable but experience might dictate adjustments, (2) floating or fluctuating exchange rates had proved unsatisfactory, though the reasons for this opinion were little discussed, and (3) the government controls of trade, exchange, production, and so forth, that had developed from 1931 through World War II were wasteful, discriminatory, and detrimental to expansion of world trade and investment. To achieve its goals, the Bretton Woods Conference established two international monetary institutions, the International Monetary Fund (IMF) and the International Bank for Reconstruction and Development (IBRD), also called the World Bank. The IMF Articles of Agreement contained the rules for international monetary policies and their enforcement. The agreement went into effect in December 1945

Bretton Woods
The New Hampshire town where treasury and central bank representatives met near the end of World War II; they established the IMF, the World Bank, and the gold exchange standard

and served as the basis of the international monetary system until 1971. The World Bank's function was to lend money for development projects.

International Monetary Fund

International Monetary Fund (IMF) Institution that coordinates multilateral monetary rules and their enforcement

The premise of the **International Monetary Fund (IMF)** is that the common interest of all nations in a workable international monetary system far transcends conflicting national interests.[11] The first article of the IMF Articles of Agreement outlines the institution's purpose in six points:[12]

• To promote international monetary cooperation.

• To facilitate the expansion and balanced growth of international trade.

• To promote exchange stability and orderly exchange arrangements among members.

• To assist in the establishment of a multilateral system of payments.

• To make the fund's resources available for balance-of-payments corrections.

• To shorten the duration and lessen the disequilibrium of members' balances of payments.

Although the International Monetary Fund deals solely with governments, its policies and actions have a profound impact on businesses and people worldwide because they set the framework for trade. The IMF has become much more visible in recent years as its policies and actions routinely make world headlines.

The IMF Articles of Agreement, the center of the Bretton Woods system, set up fixed exchange rates among member-nations' currencies, with **par value** based on gold and the U.S. dollar, which was valued at $35 per ounce of gold. For example, the British pound's par value was US$2.40, the French franc's was US$0.18, and the German mark's was US$0.2732. There was an understanding that the U.S. government would redeem dollars for gold and that the dollar was the only currency to be redeemable for gold. The Bretton Woods meetings resulted in a dollar-based gold exchange standard, and thus the U.S. dollar became both a means of international payment and a reserve currency.

This system supported substantial international trade growth during the 1950s and 1960s. Other countries changed their currency's value against the dollar and gold, but the U.S. dollar remained fixed. This meant that the United States, in order to satisfy the growing demand for reserves, since countries would hold dollars as a proxy for gold, had to run a balance-of-payments deficit. That is, in the United States the flow of dollars out was greater than the flow in; the demand on dollars for holding outside the country was greater than the dollars that they were making through exports. From 1958 through 1971, the United States ran up a cumulative deficit of $56 billion. The deficit was financed partly by use of the U.S. gold reserves, which shrank from $24.8 billion to $12.2 billion,[13] and partly by incurring liabilities to foreign central banks. During this period, those liabilities increased from $13.6 billion to $62.2 billion.[14] By 1971, the Treasury held only 22 cents' worth of gold for each US$ held by those banks.

Such a deficit would eventually inspire a lack of confidence in the reserve currency and lead to a financial crisis. Known as the **Triffin paradox,**[15] that is exactly what happened when, after trade deficits in the late 1960s, President Charles De Gaulle pushed the Bank of France to redeem its dollar holdings for gold. Eventually, in 1971, President Nixon suspended the dollar's convertibility into gold. Bretton Woods had tried to make adjustments by creating Special Drawing Rights (SDRs) in 1969, an international reserve asset we'll review later in this chapter, whose value was based on a basket of currencies, to save the fixed rate system. The Smithsonian Agreement was a further attempt to restructure the monetary system, but by 1973, Japan and Europe had allowed their currencies to float, bringing an end to the Bretton Woods system.

The IMF operates as a collaboration of nations. Each of the 184 members contributes funds, known as its quota, which is determined based on relative size in the world economy. The aggregate quotas, which as of March 2006 totaled $308 billion, form a pool of money from which the IMF can lend to countries. As of 2006, the IMF's outstanding loans totaled $34 billion to 65 countries. Of that total, $6 billion was loaned on special concessions to 56 heavily indebted poor countries.[16] The quota also is used as a basis to determine how much a nation can borrow from the IMF, how much its SDR allocation is, and how many votes it has.[17] For example, the United States has 17.08 percent of the total votes and its quota is 17.1, while the United Kingdom has 4.95 percent of the total, China 2.94, and Japan 6.13.[18]

The IMF was begun before the United Nations, and when the UN was formed, the IMF was brought into relationship with the UN. This relationship preserved the IMF's independence, which was justified by the need for independent control of monetary management. Presently the IMF is addressing economic and exchange rate policies of countries with the largest trade imbalances. Causes of these imbalances include low levels of savings in the United States, high levels of savings in China, inflexibility of the Chinese currency, and continued balance of payment surpluses in Japan, Germany, and oil-producing countries. From a U.S. perspective, this is a welcome development because it suggests a recognition that the increasing U.S. trade deficit is caused by global forces in addition to its own budget deficit. The focus on trade issues by the IMF is welcomed because it comes at a time when the World Trade Organization's latest attempts in the Doha Round seem to have failed.[19]

The economist Jeffrey Sachs, director of the Earth Institute, observes that the IMF has been able to reinvent itself as challenges have evolved on the economic, monetary, and

par value
Stated value

Triffin paradox
The concept that a national currency that is also a reserve currency will eventually run a deficit, which eventually inspires a lack of confidence in the reserve currency and leads to a financial crisis

financial levels. He sees five major challenges facing today's IMF and the international monetary system. The first is that the rise of Asian economies will make the U.S.-centric approach of the IMF obsolete. As he puts it, "The U.S. will no longer be conductor of the global monetary orchestra."[20] The IMF needs to play a valuable role in convincing the rising economies to accept multilateral responsibilities that reach beyond their own economies. Second, as Asia rises, so will the temptation toward protectionism in the United States and Europe. These countries will exert pressure on China to manipulate its currency to meet their objectives, and the IMF can help to make certain that China's monetary policy is managed both for China and for long-term multilateral stability.

The third challenge Sachs foresees for the IMF is that financial crises will become more global and more intricate. That suggests that the IMF will have to become more action-prone. The African debt cancellation came 20 years after the African debt crisis. Such time lags won't work in a fast-paced, global, evolving economy. Debtor liquidity will need to be maintained, and the IMF can ensure that it is by developing institutional debtor-creditor workout schemes. Meanwhile, as global trade continues to increase, Sachs sees fewer currencies in circulation, both because smaller economies will adopt major currencies such as the dollar or the euro and because regional trading groups will develop regional currencies on the euro model. The IMF can support this process, its fourth challenge, in political, economic, and technical ways.

The fifth challenge has to do with an increasing number of ecological shocks, such as the recent Southeast Asian tsunami, earthquakes in Pakistan and Indonesia, and hurricanes in the United States. Such shocks also include an increasing number of diseases, such as HIV/AIDS and the bird flu. The IMF challenge here is to develop a way for global financial markets to spread these risks through insurance against such ecological disasters for governments.

The IMF has had many successes. It has developed and maintained a system of currency exchange that makes global trade possible. It has supported governments in their noninflationary monetary management, and it has helped the world trading system avoid financial disasters. The five challenges Sachs outlines for the IMF represent possible next steps in its evolution as a global monetary institution and are a result of its past successes. That is not to suggest that the IMF has not had enormous failures, because it certainly has. Most of these failures involve the mismanagement of crises in developing countries.

In early 2006, Brazil and Argentina surprised the IMF by paying off their loans ahead of schedule. Brazil, Argentina, Turkey, and Indonesia account for 70 percent of the IMF loans, so these early repayments raised some concerns.[21] Does the IMF need a new business model? In addition to the early repayments, the number of new loans is the lowest it has been since 1970. Reduced demand for loans from the IMF is due to the solid economic performance of the economies of emerging markets, so this can be seen as a positive development. Yet IMF interest rates cover the fund's operating costs, close to $1 billion in 2005, so when the IMF books fewer loans, their income falls. They do have a reserve, though. More information about the IMF can be found at its Web site, www.imf.org.

The World Bank

World Bank

Institution that focuses on funding of development projects

The **World Bank**, also known as the International Bank for Reconstruction and Development (IBRD), was established along with the IMF at Bretton Woods with the purpose of addressing development issues in a postwar world. Today the World Bank Group, made up of five institutions, is the world's largest source of development assistance, providing nearly $16 billion in loans a year to its client countries.[22] The World Bank itself focuses on projects in middle-income and creditworthy poor countries, while the International Development Association (IDA) loans to the poorest countries. Together they provide low-interest loans and grants for projects designed to help countries develop infrastructure, health and education, and other areas connected to development. The World Bank Group is owned by its 184 member nations.

The International Finance Corporation (IFC), the private sector arm of the World Bank, invests in companies and financial institutions in developing countries. IFC is the World Bank's investment banker, arranging private risk ventures in developing countries.

IFC is helping to build domestic capital markets so that local entrepreneurs in developing countries will have access to funding. Such funding is especially important to entrepreneurs in segments traditionally excluded from the formal economy—women, indigenous groups, and people in rural areas. In 2005, IFC invested $15 million in a Mexican microfinance institution, Financiera Compartamos, in the form of a structured bond. The proceeds of the transaction are being used to fund some 400,000 Mexican small businesses, of which more than 99 percent are owned by women in rural areas. Compartamos provides microloans through village banking, solidarity group loans, and individual loans. Loans provide working capital for the company's clients to build small businesses.

Emma Acosta Salazar is a manufacturer of straw hats who is financed by Compartamos. She started her business because she needed a fixed job and so that her husband would not have to emigrate to the United States. Emma began by buying a machine and subcontracting to people who bought hats. As she made money, she bought more machines. She has been with Compartamos for two years, and has used her loans to purchase material and close good business deals. Emma is teaching the trade to her children while making a way for them to continue their studies and one day go to college.

Source: www.ifc.org (accessed June 23, 2006).

The last two organizations that constitute the World Bank Group are the Multilateral Investment Guarantee Agency (MIGA) and the International Centre for the Settlement of Investment Disputes (ICSID). MIGA guarantees private sector investment in developing countries through political risk insurance, technical assistance, and dispute mediation. ICSID helps to resolve disputes between governments and foreign investors and, in that way, helps build direct foreign investment. As of 2006, 155 nations had signed the dispute resolution convention established by ICSID.

In addition to the World Bank Group, there are several other multilateral development banks that provide support and advice for investment activities in the developing world. They include the African Development Bank, the Asian Development Bank, the European Bank for Reconstruction and Development, and the Inter-American Development Bank. The Bank for International Settlements also merits a brief focus here, because it offers central bankers a forum for their discussions on the global financial system. Its role has become increasingly important in a floating exchange environment.

Bank for International Settlements

The **Bank for International Settlements (BIS)** is an international organization of central banks that exists to "foster cooperation among central banks and other agencies in pursuit of monetary and financial stability."[23] Central bankers of major industrial countries meet at least seven times a year at the BIS to discuss the global financial system. Its clients are governments and international agencies, not private individuals or corporations. BIS is the oldest international financial institution in the world, having been founded in 1930 to address war reparations imposed on Germany by the Treaty of Versailles. Today the BIS has four main functions. It serves as a banker for central banks, as a forum for international monetary

Bank for International Settlements
Institution for central bankers; operates as their bank

BIS is known as the most discreet financial institution in the world. Although its round tower stands out as a distinctive landmark in Basel, Switzerland, there is no sign identifying the building.

cooperation, as a center for research, and as an agent or trustee for governments in various international financial arrangements.

BIS is known as the most discreet financial institution in the world. In fact, although the round tower of the bank is the first landmark in Basel, Switzerland, for anyone leaving the main railway station and heading toward the city center, there is no sign identifying the building.

Now that we have reviewed the role of Bretton Woods in establishing two of the major international monetary institutions, the IMF and the World Bank, and briefly looked at the Bank for International Settlements, our attention can move on to what happened after the gold exchange system of Bretton Woods ceased to function.

The Emergence of a Floating Currency Exchange Rate System

When, in response to De Gaulle's push for France to redeem its dollar holdings for gold, President Nixon announced in 1971 that the United States would no longer exchange gold for the paper dollars held by foreign central banks, he was said to have "closed the gold window." The shock caused currency exchange markets to remain closed for several days, and when they reopened, they began developing a new system for which few rules existed. Currencies were floating, and the stated US$ value of 35 dollars per ounce of gold was now meaningless because the United States would no longer exchange any of its gold for dollars.

fixed currency exchange rates
Rates that governments agree on and undertake to maintain

floating currency exchange rates
Rates that are allowed to float against other currencies and are determined by market forces

Jamaica Agreement
The 1976 IMF agreement that allows flexible exchange rates among members

Two attempts were made to agree on durable, new sets of **fixed currency exchange rates,** one in December 1971 and the other in February 1973. Both times, however, banks, businesses, and individuals felt that the central banks had pegged the rates incorrectly, and the speculators were correct each time. In March 1973 the major currencies began to float in the foreign exchange markets, and the system of **floating currency exchange rates** still prevails. The agreement that established the rules for the floating system was accepted by IMF members after the fact, at a meeting in Jamaica in 1976. Known as the **Jamaica Agreement**, it allows for flexible exchange rates among IMF members, while condoning central bank operations in the money markets to smooth out volatile periods. Gold was demonetized, as well; it was abandoned as a reserve currency. The Jamaica Agreement also gives less developed countries greater access to IMF funds, while quotas for developed countries were increased.

CURRENT CURRENCY ARRANGEMENTS

Initially the IMF recognized three types of currency exchange arrangements, but it later extended the categories to eight. First, we'll look at the three original categories—a free float, a managed float, and a fixed peg—and then we'll look more closely at the variations that have developed. The *free (clean) float* is one of the world's closest approaches to perfect competition, because there is no government intervention and large amounts of various monies are being traded by thousands of buyers and sellers. Buyers and sellers may change sides on short notice as information, rumors, or moods change or as their clients' needs differ. In the *managed (dirty) float,* governments intervene in the currency markets as they perceive their national interests to be served. Nations may explain their interventions in the currency market in terms of "smoothing market irregularities" or "ensuring orderly markets." In a *fixed peg,* a country pegs the value of its currency at a fixed rate to another currency.

Money is central to business, international or domestic. Currencies, currency fluctuations, exchange rates, and the mechanics of buying and selling foreign currency are fundamental tools of the international business professional and are used daily in the practice of international trade. In fact, foreign currency trading is growing into an increasingly profitable commodity market in banks and financial institutions worldwide. The information in this box will help you understand how to follow the international money trail.

How to Designate Currencies

Almost every country in the world has its own currency, and the euro is the now the single currency of most EU countries. Some countries like Japan, with the yen (¥), and Great Britain, with the pound sterling (£), use symbols to identify their currencies. Most world currencies use the first letter of the currency name, such as *P*, but globally this can be confusing. Does "P20" mean 20 pesetas, pesos, pounds, pataca, or pa'anga or 20 of another currency? And if it means 20 pesos, are they pesos from Mexico, Bolivia, Argentina, Chile, Colombia, or some other country? To address this confusion, the international banking community developed the ISO 4217 set of currency abbreviations, which standardizes how currencies are identified.

ISO 4217 uses three-letter abbreviations, such as *USD* for "United States dollar." When currencies are defined by supranational entities, the ISO system assigns two-letter entity codes starting with *X* to be used instead of country codes, as in the case of *XCD* for "Central Caribbean dollar."

Depending on whether you are using e-mail, news or the Web, some currency symbols may be used but many others should *not* be used. In e-mail and news, the only currency symbol that may be used safely is the dollar symbol ($). To express a value in any other currency, you should use the ISO 4217 abbreviation. For "£10," *GBP 10* should be used. In HTML, the only currency symbols that may be used safely are $ for "dollar," ¢ for "cent," £ for "pound," ¥ for "yen," and ¤ for a generic currency. To show the value of any other currency, the ISO 4217 abbreviation should be used.

World Fact: According to the *CIA World Factbook,* there were 178 currencies in the world until February 28, 2002, when European national bank notes and currencies were taken out of circulation and replaced by the euro, which added one new currency and eliminated 12.

Culture Cue: Bosque Real is the world's largest country club and is located near Mexico City. See www.bosquereal.com.

World Wide Resource:
- www.oanda.com/convert/classic
- www.x-rates.com/
- www.banknotes.com/images.htm
- http://fx.sauder.ubc.ca/currency_table.html

Source: www.jhall.demon.co.uk/currency (accessed July 13, 2006).

The eight categories of exchange rate arrangements that the IMF now uses to describe how countries position their currencies in relation to other currencies are explained below, from not having any legal tender to having fixed and then freely floating exchange rate arrangements:

- *Exchange arrangements with no separate legal tender* describe one country's adopting the currency of another or a group of countries adopting a common currency. An example of the first is the U.S. dollar's use in Panama, El Salvador, and Ecuador. An example of the second is the European Union's euro being used as shared currency in 12 of the EU countries (soon to be joined by the 13th, Slovenia).

- *Currency board arrangements* describe a legislated commitment to exchange domestic currency for a specific foreign currency at a fixed rate. The currency board arrangement commits the government to hold foreign reserves equal to its domestic currency supply. In Estonia, for example, the rise and fall of the kroon (EEK) is tied to the euro. In Hong Kong, the Hong Kong dollar (HKD) is tied to the U.S. dollar.

- *Other conventional fixed peg arrangements* describe a peg in which there is a fixed rate relationship and exchange rate fluctuations are allowed within a narrow band of less than 1 percent. The peg could be to one currency or to a basket of currencies. The Saudi Riyal is pegged in this way to the U.S. dollar.

- *Pegged exchange rates within horizontal bands* describe pegged arrangements in which the exchange rate fluctuations are allowed to be greater than 1 percent around a central rate. Denmark's krone is pegged in this way to the euro.

- *Crawling pegs* describe arrangements in which the currency is readjusted periodically at a fixed, preannounced rate or in response to changes in indicators. Bolivia, Costa Rica, and Tunisia operate crawling peg arrangements.

- *Exchange rates within crawling bands* describe fluctuating margins around a central rate within which the currency is maintained and adjusted periodically. Romania is an example of this arrangement.

- *Managed floating with no preannounced path for the exchange rate* describes a monetary authority that actively intervenes on the exchange market without specifying or making public its goals and targets. Algeria, India, Malaysia, and Singapore are examples of this approach.

- *Independently floating exchange rates* is an approach that relies on the market. There may be interventions, yet they are conducted to moderate the rate of change rather than to establish the currency's level. Examples of countries following this approach are the United States, Mexico, Canada, and the United Kingdom.

Below is a summary of the number of countries that presently follow each approach:[24]

Exchange arrangements with no separate legal tender	41 countries
Currency board arrangements	7 countries
Other conventional fixed peg arrangements	40 countries
Pegged exchange within horizontal bands	5 countries
Crawling pegs	6 countries
Exchange rates within crawling bands	2 countries
Managed floating with no preannounced path	50 countries
Independently floating	36 countries

The floating exchange rate system, with its various approaches, seems to be meeting its challenges. Admittedly, economic policy coordination as practiced by the G7 and, with the recent addition of Russia, the G8, has emerged as a key factor in the foreign exchange (Fx) markets. And although there is little doubt the G8 central banks have become more adept at influencing currency movements, another development challenges their efforts. That is the explosive growth in the volume of currencies being traded in the world's foreign exchange markets. From an annual volume of roughly $18 billion in 1979, foreign exchange transactions are now estimated at $1.9 trillion daily.[25] Even the richest countries have government reserves of "only" a few billion dollars available to influence exchange rates. For example, if the foreign exchange market players believe the Japanese yen should be stronger in US$ terms, the yen will strengthen in spite of any government market intervention. The floating system seems to be able to respond to market movements with flexibility and relative order.

Floating currencies can move against one another quickly and in large swings. Such changes have many causes, including political events, expectations, and government economic policies, such as allowing trade imbalances and deficits. Relative inflation becomes a significant issue for international businesspeople. One means of measuring relative inflation is *purchasing power parity (PPP)*, the theory of which is that an exchange rate between the currencies of two countries is in equilibrium when it equates the prices of a basket of goods and services in both countries.

The review of floating currency arrangements is important for international business managers as it brings attention to the fact that currencies can change value in terms of each other in large amounts. These changes create major uncertainties. Managers protect their organizations and themselves through a process called *hedging,* which is explained in Chapter 21.

THE EURO

euro (€)
Currency of the
European Monetary
Union

In January 1999, a new major currency, the **euro** (€), joined the world markets. It began trading at 1 euro for US$1.14. Despite forecasts that the euro would be a strong currency, it fell to as low as $0.8455 in 2001, but by May 31, 2002, it had rebounded to $0.93.[26] In the fall of 2002, the euro and the U.S. dollar were trading at par, and by January 2004 the euro had strengthened to a record high of $1.3625. In late May 2006, the rate was at $1.2739.[27]

The agreement to move to a common currency, the Maastricht Treaty, was signed by the European Union members in 1991, with a target date of 1999. To prepare for such cooperation, EU members had to first coordinate their monetary policies to achieve a harmonization of their economies. Budget deficits, public debt, and exchange rates all had to be carefully controlled. Then these countries had to cede monetary control of their economies to a central EU institution, the European Central Bank. On January 1, 1999, for the first time since the Roman Empire, 11 of the original 15 EU countries shared a common currency, the Euro. Those countries were Austria, Belgium, Finland, France, Germany, Ireland, Italy, Luxembourg, the Netherlands, Portugal, and Spain. Greece joined in 2001, to make 12 EU countries committed to European Monetary Union (EMU). Sweden, Denmark, and the United Kingdom chose to remain outside the euro zone. The euro was used for pricing in local markets, along with the traditional script, until January 1, 2002, when the euro script was introduced and, gradually, the local currency withdrawn. Although there were many forecasts of doom, such as ATM chaos, loss of savings, and counterfeiting, in actuality, the conversion from local currencies to the euro went smoothly. Slovenia will be joining the euro zone in 2007.

"May I have my allowance in euros, Dad?"

Source: From the *Wall Street Journal* — Permission, Cartoon Features Syndicate.

The effect of the euro on business has been largely positive, both for members of the euro zone and for those trading into the euro zone. There are two main benefits: The euro's use reduces transaction costs for conducting business within the zone and eliminates exchange rate fluctuation risk. No longer does a business need to take the time and pay banking fees to change Greek drachma into French francs. In addition, corporate finance managers no longer need to hedge their exposure across the 12 replaced currencies. Establishment of the euro is also one step closer to an integrated, single market, which will allow greater efficiencies. For European business, the euro also has encouraged a transition from a local or national market focus to a European focus. That means a rethinking of production and distribution systems. In terms of financing business ventures, the capital markets are now more extensive, as well.

We began our discussion of the international monetary system with a focus on its development, the gold standard, the Bretton Woods system, the transition from fixed to floating exchange rates, and the establishment of a new currency, the euro. These monetary institutions and arrangements are important to the conduct of international business for they establish the rules and processes that give shape to the way international business is conducted. Now we adjust our focus to the methods governments use to track and record their and their citizens' participation in international trade, the balance-of-payments accounts. These accounts are also used by economists and businesspeople to analyze a country's level of participation in international trade.

Balance of Payments

The **balance of payments (BOP)** is a record of a country's transactions with the rest of the world. BOP data are of interest to international businesspeople for several reasons. First, the balance of payments reveals demand for the country's currency. If a country is exporting more than it imports, there will be a high demand for the currency in other countries in order to pay for the exported goods. This demand may well create pressure on the exporter's currency, in which case it might be expected to strengthen. Another value of the BOP is that its trend helps managers predict what sort of economic environment may develop in the country. This impacts their choice of strategic risks to take in specific countries. For example, if there are BOP difficulties, a country may not be able to increase its imports. It may well

balance of payments (BOP)

Record of a country's transactions with the rest of the world

institute measures to decrease imports and to limit repatriation of funds. Businesses active in such markets would want to develop strategies to address such possible constraints.

BOP ACCOUNTS

Each international transaction is an exchange of assets with a debit and a credit side. Payments *to* other countries, funds flowing out, are tracked as debits (–), while transactions that are payments *from* other countries, funds flowing in, are tracked as credits (+). The BOP is presented as a double-entry accounting statement in which total credits and debits are always equal. The statement of a country's BOP is divided into several accounts and many subaccounts. A sample of these subaccounts is included in Table 5.1, and the more significant ones are reviewed below.

current account
Record of a country's exports and imports in goods and services

goods or merchandise account
Record of tangible exports and imports

trade balance
The balance on the merchandise account

services account
Record of intangibles that are exchanged internationally

unilateral transfer
A transfer with no matched return flow, no reciprocity

Current Account   The **current account** tracks the net changes in exports and imports of goods and services, sometimes called *tangibles* and *intangibles*. Three subaccounts are included in the current account: (*a*) goods or merchandise, (*b*) services, and (*c*) unilateral transfers. The first two subaccounts are sometimes treated together, and they include the real (as opposed to the financial) international transactions, that is, exports and imports.

a. The **goods or merchandise account** deals with tangibles, such as autos, grain, clothing, and machinery, which can be seen and felt as they are exported or imported. The net balance on merchandise transactions is referred to as the **trade balance**.

b. The **services account** deals with intangibles that are exchanged internationally. Examples include insurance, banking, dividends or interest on foreign investments, royalties on patents or trademarks held abroad, travel, and transportation.

c. **Unilateral transfers** are transactions with no reciprocity, that is, no return flow. Some of these transfers are made by private persons or institutions and some by governments. Some private unilateral transfers are for charitable, educational, or missionary purposes; others are gifts from migrant workers to their families in their home countries and bequests or the transfer of capital by people migrating from one country to another. The largest government unilateral transfers are aid—which may be in money or in kind—from developed countries to developing countries. Pension payments to nonresidents and tax receipts from nonresidents are two other government-related unilateral transfers. To satisfy the needs of double-entry recording, an entry is made that treats the aid or gift as if it were a purchase of goodwill.

capital account
Record of the net changes in a nation's international financial assets and liabilities

Capital Account   The **capital account** records the net changes in a nation's international financial assets and liabilities over the BOP period, usually one year, with quarterly reports. A capital inflow—a credit entry—occurs when a resident sells stock, bonds, or other financial assets to nonresidents. Money flows to the resident, while at the same time the resident's long-term international liabilities (debit entry) are increased, because dividends (profit) may be paid on the stock, rent will be paid on other assets, and interest must be paid on the bonds. And at maturity the bonds' face amounts must be repaid.

Subaccounts under the capital account are (*a*) direct investment, (*b*) portfolio investment, and (*c*) international movements of short-term capital:

direct investments
Investments located in one country that are effectively controlled by residents of another country

a. **Direct investments** are investments in enterprises or properties located in one country that are effectively controlled by residents of another country. Effective control is assumed for BOP purposes (1) when residents of one country own 50 percent or more of the voting stock of a company in another country or (2) when one resident or an organized group of residents of one country own 25 percent or more of the voting stock of a company in another country.

portfolio investments
Long-term investments that do not give the investors control over the investment

b. **Portfolio investments** include all long-term—more than one year—investments that do not give the investors effective control over the object of the investment. Such transactions typically involve the purchase of stocks or bonds of foreign issuers for investment—not control—purposes, and they also include long-term commercial credits to finance trade.

	2004	2005
Current account		
Exports of goods and services and income receipts	**1,530,975**	**1,740,897**
Exports of goods and services	1,151,448	1,272,223
Goods, balance-of-payments basis	807,536	892,619
Services	343,912	379,604
Income receipts	379,527	468,674
Income receipts on U.S.-owned assets abroad	376,489	465,631
Compensation of employees	3,038	3,043
Imports of goods and services and income payments	**−2,118,119**	**−2,462,946**
Imports of goods and services	−1,769,031	−1,995,839
Income payments	−349,088	−467,107
Income payments on foreign-owned assets in the United States	−340,255	−458,225
Compensation of employees	−8,833	−8,882
Unilateral current transfers, net	**−80,930**	**−82,896**
U.S. government grants	−23,317	−30,362
U.S. government pensions and other transfers	−6,264	−6,312
Private remittances and other transfers	−51,349	−46,222
Capital account		
Capital account transactions, net	**−1,648**	**−5,647**
Financial account		
U.S.-owned assets abroad, net [increase/financial outflow (−)]	**−855,509**	**−491,729**
U.S. official reserve assets, net	2,805	14,096
Gold	. . . .	. . . .
Special drawing rights	−398	4,511
Reserve position in the International Monetary Fund	3,826	10,200
Foreign currencies	−623	−615
U.S. government assets, other than official reserve assets, net	1,215	7,580
U.S. credits and other long-term assets	−3,044	−2,217
Repayments on U.S. credits and other long-term assets	4,221	5,720
U.S. foreign currency holdings and U.S. short-term assets, net	38	4,077
U.S. private assets, net	−859,529	−513,405
Direct investment	−252,012	−21,481
Foreign securities	−102,383	−155,244
U.S. claims on unaffiliated foreigners reported by U.S. nonbanking concerns	−149,001	−118,522
U.S. claims reported by U.S. banks, not included elsewhere	−356,133	−218,158
Foreign-owned assets in the United States, net [increase/financial inflow (+)]	**1,440,105**	**1,292,695**
Foreign official assets in the United States, net	394,710	220,676
U.S. government securities	311,133	177,179
Other U.S. government liabilities	488	−134
U.S. liabilities reported by U.S. banks, not included elsewhere	70,329	24,272
Other foreign official assets	12,760	19,359
Other foreign assets in the United States, net	1,045,395	1,072,019
Statistical discrepancy (sum of above items with sign reversed)	**85,126**	**9,626**
Memoranda:		
Balance on goods	−665,390	−781,642
Balance on services	47,807	58,026
Balance on goods and services	−617,583	−723,616
Balance on income	30,439	1,567
Unilateral current transfers, net	−80,930	−82,896
Balance on current account	−668,074	−804,945

Source: U.S. Dept. of Commerce Bureau of Economic Analysis, International Economic Accounts, http://www.bea.gov/bea/international/bp_web/simple.cfm?anon = 71& table_id = 1 & area_id = 3.

c. **Short-term capital flows** involve changes in international assets and liabilities with an original maturity of one year or less. Some of the fastest-growing types of short-term flows are for currency exchange rate and interest rate hedging in the forward, futures, option, and swap markets. (These subjects have to do with risk coverage and will be addressed in Chapter 20, "Financial Management.") Among the more traditional types of short-term capital flows are payments and receipts for international finance and trade, short-term borrowings from foreign banks, exchanges of foreign notes or coins, and purchases of foreign commercial paper or foreign government bills or notes. The volatility, private nature, and wide varieties of short-term capital flows make them the most difficult BOP items to measure and, therefore, predictably the least reliable measurement in the BOP. Wide fluctuations of currency exchange rates and interest rates from the 1980s forward due to the floating exchange system have led to the surge in hedging activities.

Official Reserves Account   The **official reserves account** deals with (*a*) gold imports and exports, (*b*) increases or decreases in foreign exchange (foreign currencies) held by the government, and (*c*) decreases or increases in liabilities to foreign central banks. Because some BOP figures are inaccurate and incomplete (for example, the short-term capital flows item or time lags), the statistical discrepancy item is used to bring total credits and debits into accounting balance.

DEFICITS AND SURPLUSES IN BOP ACCOUNTS

The BOP current account and capital account add up to the total account, which, given the double-entry approach, is balanced. So a deficit in the current account is always accompanied by an equal surplus in the capital account, and vice versa. Let's see how this works. If you purchase a case of French wine in the United States for $200, your payment, as it heads out of the United States and to the French winery, will be recorded as a debit in the U.S. current account. Once the winery receives your dollars, it has to do something with them. If the treasurer of the winery decides to deposit your payment in a dollar account at a U.S. bank, the amount will show up as a credit in the U.S. capital account. If the winery exchanges your dollar payment for euros, then the bank receiving the dollars will have to make a decision about how to spend or invest the dollars. Sooner or later, these dollars will show up as a credit on the U.S. account.

Contrary to the commonly held belief, a current account deficit is not, in itself, a sign of bad economic conditions. What it means is that the country is importing capital. This is no more unnatural or dangerous than importing wine or cheese. The deficit is a response to conditions in the country. Among these conditions could be excessive inflation, low productivity, or inadequate saving. In the case of the United States, a current account deficit could occur because investments in the United States are secure and profitable. If there is a problem, it is in the underlying conditions and not in the deficit per se.[28] Countries with relatively high price levels, gross national products, interest rates, and exchange rates, as well as relatively low barriers to imports and attractive investment opportunities, are more likely to have current account deficits than are other countries.[29]

Right now the United States has a substantial deficit in its current account, $804.9 billion in 2005.[30] Citizens of the United States are importing more goods and services than they are exporting. At the same time, there is a surplus in the U.S. capital account. Those dollars that leave the United States to pay for imported goods come back into the United States in the form of foreign-owned investments, for example, Treasury bills and investment property in New York City. So let's remember that a deficit or surplus in the current account cannot be explained or evaluated without simultaneously examining an equal surplus or deficit in the capital account.[31]

When the U.S. current account balance shifted from a surplus of $8 billion in 1981 to a deficit of $147 billion in 1987, there was much concern. The shift was cited as the cause of unemployment in the United States. Herbert Stein points out, though, that "between 1981 and 1987, the number of people employed rose by over 12 million, and employment as a percent of population rose from 60 percent to 62.5 percent."[32]

As is to be expected, the capital accounts showed a parallel surplus, which was interpreted as a danger to the country. The popular fear was that the United States was becoming owned by foreigners. In particular, Arab investment in commercial agriculture and Japanese trophy real estate investments such as Rockefeller Center (now owned by a wealthy Chicago

Central Reserve/National Currency Conflict

Every member of the IMF keeps a *reserve account,* a bit like a savings account, with holdings the country can draw on when needed to finance trade or investments or to intervene in currency markets. As of March 2006, the countries with the largest reserve accounts are China ($875 billion), Japan ($852 billion), Taiwan (Republic of China, $257 billion), Russia ($231 billion), Korea ($223 billion), India ($148 billion), and Hong Kong ($125 billion). The reserve assets are gold, foreign exchange, SDRs, and reserve positions in the IMF. The U.S. dollar has been the most used central reserve asset in the world since the end of World War II, and at the end of the first quarter of 2005, roughly 60 percent of the world's $3.8 trillion reserve assets were held in dollars and 25 percent in euros. The dollars, held in the form of U.S. Treasury bonds, earn interest, so the more dollars held in the central reserve account, the better. But the countries holding those U.S. dollars in their foreign reserve accounts don't want their central reserve asset to lose value, and therein lies a contradiction: At some point, holding large numbers of U.S. dollars (or any other product) in supply causes them to lose value—the law of supply and demand.

At the same time, the U.S. dollar is the national currency of the United States of America, whose government must deal with inflation, recession, interest rates, unemployment, and other national, internal problems. The U.S. government uses fiscal and monetary policies to meet those problems—higher or lower taxes, decisions on how to spend available revenue, growth or contraction of the money supply, and rate of its growth or contraction.

It would be only accidental if the national interests of the United States in dealing with its internal problems were to coincide with the interests of the multitude of countries holding U.S. dollars in their central reserve asset accounts. For example, the United States may be slowing money supply growth and raising taxes to combat U.S. inflation, while the world needs more liquidity, in the form of U.S. dollars, to finance growth, trade, or investment. Or the United States may be stimulating its economy through faster money supply growth and lower taxes at a time when so many U.S. dollars are already outstanding that their value is dropping—not a happy state of affairs for countries holding U.S. dollars.

It was a quirk of history that thrust the currency of the United States into this conflicting role. The IMF hoped that a nonnational asset, the SDR, would rescue the US$ and the world from this conflict.

Source: Remarks by Chairman Alan Greenspan, November 14, 2005. See www.federalreserve.gov/BOARDDOCS/Speeches/2005/20051114/default.htm.

---

family and a New York real estate developer) scared many Americans. The fact is, though, that the foreign capital did not reduce the assets owned by Americans. Instead, it added to the capital stock within the country.[33]

SPECIAL DRAWING RIGHT (SDR)

The IMF created the **special drawing right (SDR)** in 1969 as a reserve asset, in an attempt to support the Bretton Woods fixed exchange rate system. We have seen already that Bretton Woods' fixed exchange rate regime did not hold. A country participating in this system had to have official government reserves that could be used to purchase its currency in world foreign exchange markets in order to maintain the exchange rate. As trade and international finance volumes expanded, the two main reserve assets, the U.S. dollar and gold, could no longer meet the need. Therefore, the IMF created this new international reserve asset—not a currency but, rather, an accounting transaction, a ledger entry. The objective was to make the SDR the principal reserve asset in the international monetary system.[34] The SDR also may be a step toward a truly international currency, albeit a small step.

The SDR's value is based on a basket of the following four currencies (with the percentage of each currency in parentheses): U.S. dollar (44), euro (34), Japanese yen (11), and British pound sterling (11). The weights broadly reflect the relative importance of the currencies in trade and payments, based on the value of the exports of goods and services by the member-countries issuing these currencies, reevaluated every five years. The dollar value of the SDR is posted daily on the IMF site at www.imf.org/external/np/fin/rates/rms_sdrv.cfm. Actually, because four currencies are involved in determining its value, the SDR remains more stable than any of the single currencies. That stability has made the SDR increasingly attractive as a unit for denominating international transactions. Future payment under a contract, for example, may be negotiated to be in a specified national currency at its rate in terms

special drawing right (SDR)
An international reserve asset established by the IMF; the unit of account for the IMF and other international organizations

of the SDR on the payment date, and some Swiss and British banks now accept accounts denominated in SDRs. The Bank for International Settlements also uses the SDR as its unit of account, as does the IMF, its 184 members, and 15 other official international institutions.

Yet today the SDR has limited use as a reserve asset. When the Bretton Woods system collapsed, the major currencies shifted to a floating exchange rate regime. In addition, the growth in international capital markets facilitated borrowing by creditworthy governments. Both of these developments lessened the need for SDRs. The ability of the SDR to serve as a safety net should the international monetary system run into serious difficulty has yet to be tested.

Summary

Explain the functioning of the gold standard.

Since ancient times, gold has been trusted as a way for people to store value, to exchange value, and to measure value. Under a gold standard, each country set a certain number of units of its currency per ounce of gold, and the ratios of their gold equivalence would establish the exchange rate between any two currencies. In essence, currencies were pegged to gold.

Describe the purposes of the IMF.

The basic idea of the IMF is that a workable international monetary system is in the interests of all nations. Its Articles of Agreement outline the purpose of the fund in six points: to promote international monetary cooperation, to facilitate the expansion and balanced growth of international trade, to promote exchange stability and orderly exchange arrangements among members, to assist in the establishment of a multilateral system of payments, to make the fund's resources available for balance-of-payments corrections, and to shorten the duration and lessen the disequilibrium of members' balance of payments.[35]

Appreciate the accomplishments of the Bretton Woods system and the developments shaping the world monetary system from the end of World War II to the present.

The gold exchange standard, established at Bretton Woods after World War II, worked until the 1970s, when it collapsed due to inflation and the surplus of U.S. dollars held outside the United States. Until then, the Bretton Woods system provided monetary stability that supported the growth of international trade.

Describe the purpose of the World Bank.

The World Bank lends money for development projects in middle-income and creditworthy poor countries. It provides low-interest loans and grants for projects designed to help countries develop infrastructure, health and education, and other areas connected to development.

Discuss the purpose of the Bank for International Settlements.

The Bank for International Settlements operates as a central bankers' bank. In addition, it serves as a forum for central bankers' discussions, leading to international monetary cooperation; as a center for research; and as an agent or trustee for governments in various international financial arrangements.

Discuss the floating exchange rate system.

There are three basic arrangements found in the floating exchange rate system: a free float, a managed float, and a fixed peg. Under a free (clean) float, market demand and supply regulate the exchange rate. In the managed (dirty) float, governments may intervene in the currency markets as they perceive their national interests to be served. In a fixed peg, the value of a currency is set at a fixed rate to another currency. There are other modifications of these three basic approaches, including having no currency and using that of another country; using different approaches to the peg, including operating it within a band or allowing it to crawl; having a currency board; and managing a floating exchange.

Describe the development of the common currency area for the euro.

The euro zone, established by the Maastricht treaty, began trading only in euros in 2002. There are presently 12 members in the euro zone, and many of the newly acceding countries want to join. Slovenia will be joining in 2007.

Explain the role of the balance of payments (BOP).

The balance of payments is a statistical record of a country's transactions with the rest of the world. From a business perspective, the BOP helps businesspeople predict what sort of economic environment might develop in the country.

Discuss the major BOP accounts.

The major BOP accounts are the current account, which tracks the net changes in exports and imports of goods and services; the capital account, which records the net changes in a nation's international financial assets and liabilities; and the official reserves account, which deals with the government's holdings of foreign currency, gold, and, possibly, SDRs.

Explain the uses of special drawing rights (SDRs).

SDRs were established by the IMF to replace the U.S. dollar as the main central reserve asset. They have not yet done so. SDRs do not circulate; they are an accounting entry.

gold standard (p. 140)

Bretton Woods (p. 141)

Interntional Monetary Fund (p. 142)

par value (p. 143)

Triffin paradox (p. 143)

World Bank (p. 144)

Bank for International Settlements
(p. 145)

fixed currency exchange rates (p. 146)

floating currency exchange rates (p. 146)

Jamaica Agreement (p. 146)

euro (p. 148)

balance of payments (BOP) (p. 149)

current account (p. 150)

goods or merchandise account (p. 150)

trade balance (p. 150)

services account (p. 150)

unilateral transfer (p. 150)

capital account (p. 150)

direct investment (p. 150)

portfolio investment (p. 150)

short term capital flows (p. 152)

official reserves account (p. 152)

special drawing right (SDR) (p. 153)

Questions

1. Explain the appeal gold holds for people. Discuss the pros and cons of a gold standard.

2. What is the Bretton Woods system?

3. Explain the role of the IMF.

4. Given the purpose of the IMF and World Bank, why do you think they are the target of considerable criticism? In your opinion, is this criticism justified?

5. Explain the current exchange rate arrangements.

6. The euro has now replaced 12 national currencies. What are some of the resulting advantages and savings for EU members?

7. What advantages does the euro zone offer to businesses outside the EU?

8. The European Central Bank now sets monetary policy for 12 European countries. What sorts of difficulties might that cause?

9. Why should managers monitor the BOP of the country in which their business operates?

10. Why were SDRs created? Discuss their success in their original mission and their current uses.

Research Task

globalEDGE globalEDGE.msu.edu

Use the globalEDGE site (http://globalEDGE.msu.edu/) to complete the following exercises:

1. The international reserves set aside is one way that countries attempt to maintain financial stability in times of economic turbulence. As such, the United Nations Conference on Trade and Development (UNCTAD) maintains international finance statistics on many developing countries. Using the *UNCTAD Handbook*, determine the international reserves for Costa Rica, Indonesia, Lebanon, Nigeria, and South Africa for 2004. Which country has the highest reserves? Which country has the lowest reserves? Do you think

these statistics provide any indication as to the level of protection each economy may have in light of unforeseen economic turbulence? Why or why not?

2. The Biz/ed Web site presents a "Trade Balance and Exchange Rate Simulation" which helps one understand how a change in exchange rates influences a country's trade balance. Locate the online simulator (check under the Academy section of globalEDGE) and identify what the trade balance is assumed to be a function of. Run the simulation to identify how exchange rate changes affect the exports, imports, and trade balance.

SDR Exchange Risk Minicase 5.1

The Asian Development Bank has made loans denominated in SDRs to several of its MNE customers in Southeast Asia. It has built up a portfolio to the amount of SDR 8 million.

Management decides to hedge by selling in the forward market the currencies that make up the SDR basket. How much of each currency must be hedged?

section three

International Environmental Forces

In Chapter 1, we stated that many practices followed at home can be transferred intact to other countries. However, we also mentioned that because of the differences in environmental forces, some ways of doing business must be adapted to local conditions or changed completely.

In Section Three, we shall examine these forces to see how they differ from those we encounter at home.

We begin Section Three with Chapter 6, which discusses cultural forces and points out that the variety of attitudes and values among cultures affects managers of all the business functions.

Next we look at the physical forces—location, topography, and climate (Chapter 7). The importance of natural resources and environmental sustainability is emphasized.

In Chapter 8, we explore economic and socioeconomic forces, including the underground economy. Management must know how land, labor, and capital are allocated to production and distribution.

In Chapter 9, we investigate the political forces that affect the success or failure of a foreign venture. Some of these are nationalism, terrorism, unstable governments, international organizations, and government-owned businesses.

Legal forces, the subject of Chapter 10, set the constraints within which managers must operate.

We continue with a discussion of the financial forces in Chapter 11. Some of these forces are currency exchange risks, taxation, tariffs, monetary and fiscal policies, inflation, and national accounting rules.

Finally, the composition, skills, and attitudes of an area's labor pool must be investigated because these forces affect productivity and, ultimately, the firm's profitability. Chapter 12 discusses these forces.

6

Sociocultural Forces

Speaking about cultural differences among Europeans . . . it is no good focusing on similarities and common interests and hoping things will work out. We have to recognize the differences and work with them.

—*Dr. Allan Hjorth, Copenhagen Business School, trainer in cross-cultural behavior*

Six Rules of Thumb for Doing Business across Cultures

Knowing your customer is just as important anywhere in the world as it is at home, whether one is aiming to sell computers in Abidjan or soft drinks in Kuala Lumpur. Each culture has its logic, and within that logic are real, sensible reasons for the way foreigners do things. If the businessperson can figure out the basic pattern of the culture, he or she will be more effective interacting with foreign clients and colleagues. The following six rules of thumb are helpful:

1. *Be prepared.* Whether traveling abroad or selling from home, no one should approach a foreign market without doing his or her homework. A mentor is most desirable, complemented by lots of reading on social and business etiquette, history and folklore, current affairs (including relations between your two countries), the culture's values, geography, sources of pride (artists, musicians, sports), religion, political structure, and practical matters such as currency and hours of business. Mimi Murphy, an exporter who trades primarily in Indonesia, says, "Whenever I travel, the first thing I do in any town is read the newspaper. Then when I meet my customer, I can talk about the sports or the news of the day. He knows that I am interested in the things he is interested in, and he will want to do business with me." The Internet can be helpful here as a source of information.

2. *Slow down.* Americans are clock watchers. In many countries, Americans are seen to be in a rush—in other words, unfriendly, arrogant, and untrustworthy. In other countries, the Japanese and Germans are considered to be somewhat time-obsessed. As current "mobile culture" teenagers become businesspeople, however, we may more and more tend to self-organize "on the fly."

3. *Establish trust.* Often American-style crisp business relationships will get you nowhere. Product quality, pricing, and clear contracts compete with the personal *relationship and trust* that are developed carefully and sincerely over time. The marketer must be established as *simpatico,* worthy of the business, and dependable in the long run.

4. *Understand the importance of language.* Obviously, translations must be done by a professional who speaks both languages fluently, who has a vocabulary sensitive to nuance and connotation, and who has talent with the idioms and imagery of each culture. An interpreter is often critical and may be helpful even when one of the parties speaks the other's language.

5. *Respect the culture.* Manners are important. The traveling representative is a guest in the country and must respect the host's rules. As a Saudi-Arabian official states in one of the *Going International* films, "Americans in foreign countries have a tendency to treat the natives as foreigners, and they forget that actually it is *they* who are the foreigners themselves!"

6. *Understand components of culture.* Any region is a sort of cultural iceberg with two components: *surface culture* (fads, styles, food, etc.) and *deep culture* (attitudes, beliefs, values). Less than 15 percent of a region's culture is visible, and strangers to the culture must look below the surface. Consider the British habit of automatically lining up on the sidewalk when

CONCEPT PREVIEWS
After reading this chapter, you should be able to:

explain the significance of culture for international business

identify the sociocultural components of culture

discuss the significance of religion to businesspeople

explain the cultural aspects of technology

discuss the pervasiveness of the information technology era

explain the importance of the ability to speak the local language

discuss the importance of unspoken language in international business

discuss the two classes of relationships within a society

discuss Hofstede's four cultural value dimensions

Gli Affari Internazionali

onales Geschäft Παγοσμιο Business

Negócios Internacionais   Los Negócios Internacionais

ernacionales   Affaires Internationales 国際商務 Παγοσμιο Business

waiting for a bus. This surface cultural trait seems to reflect a deep cultural desire to lead neat and controlled lives. Knowledge about other cultures and how they affect the way people do business may show businesspeople working in a culture different from their own that their solutions are not always the appropriate ones for a given task. Understanding this is the first step in learning to use cultural differences to gain a strategic advantage. Mishandling or ignoring cultural differences can cause numerous problems, such as lost sales, the departure of competent employees, and low morale that contributes to low productivity. When these differences are blended successfully, however, they can result in innovative business practices superior to those that either culture could produce by itself. ■

Source: Lisa Hoecklin, "Managing Cultural Differences," www .latinsynergy.org/strategicjointventure.htm#CHILE (December 27, 2000); "How to Negotiate European Style," *Journal of European Business,* July–August 1993, p. 46; and "Japanese Punctuality," http://joi.ito.com/ archives/2005/04/28/japanese_punctuality.html (August 4, 2006).

The national characteristics you encounter in this chapter and elsewhere are generalizations. They are broadly true, but there are always exceptions. Furthermore, characteristics change over time. The Scandinavians were considered by a 10th-century writer to be "the filthiest race God ever created," and a noted 18th-century writer was amazed at the lack of German military spirit and how easygoing Germans were compared to the French.[1] Before we examine the significance of culture for international businesspeople, let us first define culture.

What Is Culture?

culture

Sum total of beliefs, rules, techniques, institutions, and artifacts that characterize human populations

Although there are countless definitions of culture, most anthropologists view **culture** as the *sum total of the beliefs, rules, techniques, institutions, and artifacts that characterize human populations.*[2] In other words, culture consists of the "individual worldviews, social rules, and interpersonal dynamics characterizing a group of people set in a particular time and place."[3] Most anthropologists also agree that:

1. Culture is *learned,* not innate.

2. The various aspects of culture are *interrelated.*

3. Culture is *shared.*

4. Culture *defines the boundaries* of different groups.[4]

Because society is composed of people and their culture, it is virtually impossible to speak of one without referring to the other. Anthropologists often use the terms interchangeably or combine them into one word—*sociocultural.*[5] This is the term we shall use, because the variables in which businesspeople are interested are both social and cultural.

When people work in societies and cultures different from their own, the problems they encounter in dealing with a single set of cultures are multiplied by the number of cultural sets they find in each of their foreign markets. All too often, unfortunately, people who are familiar with only one cultural pattern may believe they have an awareness of cultural differences elsewhere, when in reality they do not. Unless they have had occasion to make comparisons with other cultures, they are probably not even aware of the important features of their own. They are probably also oblivious to the fact that many societies consider their culture superior to all others (**ethnocentricity**) and that their attempts to introduce the "German way" or the "American way" may be met with stubborn resistance.

ethnocentricity

Belief in the superiority of one's own ethnic group (see the *self-reference criterion* in Chapter 1)

How do international businesspeople learn to live with other cultures? The first step is to realize that there are cultures different from their own. Then they must go on to learn the characteristics of those cultures so that they may adapt to them. E. T. Hall, a famous anthropologist, claims this can be accomplished in only two ways: (1) Spend a lifetime in a country, or (2) undergo an extensive, highly sophisticated training program that covers the main characteristics of a culture, including the language. The program he mentions must be more than a briefing on a country's customs. It should be a study of what culture is and what it does, imparting some knowledge of the various ways in which human behavior has been institutionalized in a country.[6]

Culture Affects All Business Functions

MARKETING

In marketing, the wide variation in attitudes and values requires that many firms use diffferent marketing mixes in different markets.

> *In Japan, Procter & Gamble (P&G) used an advertisement for Camay soap in which a man meeting a woman for the first time compared her skin to that of a fine porcelain doll. Although the ad had worked well in South America and Europe, it insulted the Japanese. "For a Japanese man to say something like that to a Japanese woman means he's either unsophisticated or rude," said an advertising man who worked on the account. Interestingly, P&G used the ad despite the warning from the advertising agency.*
>
> *Another Camay ad that failed in Japan showed a Japanese woman bathing when her husband walks into the bathroom. She begins to tell him about her new beauty soap, but the husband, stroking her shoulder, hints that suds are not what are on his mind. Although it was well received in Europe, it failed badly in Japan, where it is considered bad manners for a husband to intrude on his wife.*
>
> *P&G also erred because it lacked knowledge about the business culture. The company introduced Cheer detergent by discounting its price, but this lowered the soap's reputation. Said a competitor, "Unlike in Europe and the United States, once you discount your product here, it's hard to raise the price again." Wholesalers were alienated because they made less money due to lower margins. Moreover, apparently P&G didn't realize that Japanese housewives shop in the 50,000 or more neighborhood convenience stores close to home. These small retailers, who sell 30 percent of all the detergent bought in Japan, have limited shelf space and thus do not like to carry discounted products because of the lower profit earned.[7]*

Although acquiring knowledge about Japanese culture was both time-consuming and expensive, evidently P&G was a good learner. Eight years after its difficulties with Cheer detergent, the company reentered the soap market, which was then controlled by two powerful Japanese consumer products concerns, Kao and Lion Corporation. Just two years later P&G held 20 percent of the market. What did it do differently this time?

When the home office told the Japanese affiliate to find new markets for products in which the firm was strong elsewhere in the world, P&G–Japan sent researchers to study Japanese dishwashing habits. They found that Japanese homemakers used much more detergent than was needed. This indicated that consumers wanted a more powerful soap, which P&G's laboratory created. The marketing message was simple: A little bit of Joy cleans better yet is easier on the hands. This message hit home. Said a Japanese homemaker who, after seeing the pilot commercials, rushed to buy a bottle, "Grease on Tupperware, that's the toughest thing to wash off. I had to try it."

Retailers wanted the product because P&G did the things it hadn't done with Cheer. For example, this time the profit margins for the retailers were high. P&G also exploited a weakness in the competing Japanese products: Their long-necked bottles wasted space, but Joy bottles were compact cylinders that took up less space in stores, warehouses, and delivery trucks. A buyer for a large Japanese store chain estimated that the bottle improved the efficiency of the store's distribution by 40 percent.

The P&G ad campaign also delighted Japanese retailers. Its agency designed a TV commercial in which a famous comedian dropped in on homemakers unannounced with a camera crew to test Joy on dirty dishes in the home. The camera focused on a patch of oil in a pan full of water. After a drop of Joy, the oil dramatically disappeared. Japanese soapmakers found that over 70 percent of Joy users had begun using it after seeing the commercial. "We mistakenly assumed Japanese didn't care much about grease-fighting power in dish soaps," the Kao dish-soap brand manager said. P&G, which had studied this part of Japanese culture, did know.[8]

Cultural Success and Failure in Disneyland

Why is it that Disneyland Paris had problems with falling attendance and losses while Tokyo Disneyland had steadily increasing attendance and is the most profitable Disney park? The experts who predicted that Tokyo Disneyland attendance would peak in the first year and then taper off were wrong; it has increased steadily. The park owes some of its success to its location in a metropolitan area of 30 million people, but a cultural change is believed to be a major reason for its success. Some say that Walt Disney Productions has written a new chapter in Japanese social history by popularizing the idea that family outings can be fun. Families now account for half of the park's visitors. An executive of Disney states, "Leisure was not always a part of the Japanese lifestyle. Fathers used to see family outings as a duty."

The early staggering losses at Disneyland Paris stemmed from the high interest costs and high overheads, many of which were caused by cultural errors. To cover the project's $4 billion cost, Disney put up just $170 million for 49 percent of the operation and public shareholders paid $1 billion for the 51 percent they own. The $2.9 billion balance was borrowed at interest rates of up to 11 percent. Disney management expected to reduce the debt by selling the six big hotels it had built, but the $340-per-night price it charged had kept them about half full. Moreover, the guests weren't staying as long or spending as much as Disney had planned.

Disney executives believed, incorrectly, that they could change the French attitude of not wanting to take their children from school during the school year, as Americans do, or not wanting to take more short breaks during the year, instead of one long vacation during the month of August. This would have given Euro Disney steady, high attendance all year rather than for just one month. One reason the visitors didn't spend more was the extremely high prices. Almost two years passed before Disney lowered them. Another reason the guests didn't spend more, even though in this case they wanted to, was also due to a cultural problem: the breakfast debacle. Apparently, a decision involving millions of dollars in revenue was based not on research but only on what someone told Disney. One executive said, "We were told that Europeans don't take breakfast, so we downsized the restaurants." However, when the park opened, everyone wanted breakfast and wouldn't settle for just croissants and coffee; they wanted bacon and eggs. Disney tried to serve 2,500 breakfasts in hotel restaurants seating 350 people. The Disney solution for the French public, known worldwide as connoisseurs of good eating: prepackaged breakfasts delivered to hotel rooms.

After 1995, Disneyland Paris worked to correct the cultural and financial errors that kept attendance down and losses up. The park cut admission prices by 22 percent and hotel rates by one-third. In addition to the original expensive, sit-down restaurants that Disney mistakenly believed all Europeans would demand, cheaper fast food is now available in self-service restaurants. Instead of marketing the park to Europe as if it were a single country, Disneyland Paris has offices in all the main European capitals, and each office tailors tour packages to fit its own market. By 1998 Disneyland Paris was France's biggest tourist attraction.

Disney is also continuing to build in Asia. A second park near Tokyo—DisneySea—opened in late 2001. In China, Disney has opened Hong Kong Disneyland. Again, Disney stumbled early, with low attendance and confusion among guests as to what to expect. Disney responded with a new marketing campaign and dozens of changes inside the park, including more seats because Chinese guests take an average of 10 minutes longer to eat than Americans. Management has also taken steps to see that Mandarin speakers don't accidentally get in the lines to hear English-speaking guides. Disney has a second Chinese Disney site planned for Shanghai, to open in 2010, which will be four times larger than the Hong Kong attraction.

Source: "Euro Disney's Fortunes Turn as Number of Visitors Rises," *Financial Times*, November 14, 1997, p. 13; "The Kingdom inside a Republic," *The Economist*, April 13, 1996, pp. 66–67; "Tokyo Disney Shifts Japanese Ideas on Leisure," *The Columbian*, May 1, 1994, p. F7; "Mickey n'est pas fini," *Forbes*, February 14, 1994, p. 42; "Euro Disney's Wish Comes True," *The Economist*, March 19, 1994, p. 83; http://hongkongdisneyland.com/eng (Sept. 22, 2004); and Merissa Marr and Geoffrey A. Fowler, "Chinese Lessons for Disney," *The Wall Street Journal*, June 12, 2006, pp. A1, A5.

It's important that each element of marketing be considered for its cultural relevance. For example, studies show that background music in ads that isn't consistent with the rest of the ad—say, traditional Chinese music in an ad for a modern shampoo product featuring blond models—will increase recall of the ad but will probably produce an overall negative response.[9]

Unlike P&G, Disney seemed to have an ideal global product and global promotion. According to the *Tokyo Disneyland Guidebook*, the Tokyo theme park is the same as those in California and Florida. Disneyland Paris is also similar, although, because of the French insistence on protecting their language and culture, Mickey and Donald developed French

MUSIC AND FOLKLORE

Musical commercials are generally popular worldwide, but tastes vary and the marketer must know what kind of music each market prefers. Thus, a commercial that used a ballad in the United States might be better received to the tune of a bolero in Mexico or a samba in Brazil. However, if the advertiser is looking to the youth market with a product that is patently American, then American music will help reinforce its image. And singers like Shakira appeal to both markets.

Those who wish to steep themselves in a culture find it useful to study its folklore, which can disclose much about a society's way of life. The incorrect use of folklore can sometimes cost the firm a share of the market. For example, associating a product with the cowboy would not obtain the same results in Chile or Argentina as in the United States, because in those countries the cowboy is a far less romantic figure—it's just a job. On the other hand, Smirnoff's use of an image of late revolutionary leader Ernesto "Che" Guevara in an advertisement for spicy vodka sparked controversy in Cuba, where Guevara is a national hero.[15] As another instance, a U.S. company might be paying handsome royalties to use American cartoon characters in its promotion, only to find they are considerably less important in foreign markets. In Mexico, songs of the "Singing Cricket" are known to all youngsters and their mothers, and a commercial tie-in with that character would be as advantageous to the firm as its use of Peanuts or Mickey Mouse. In many areas, especially where nationalistic feeling is strong, local firms have been able to compete successfully with foreign affiliates by making use of indigenous folklore in the form of slogans and proverbs. Tales and folklore are valuable in maintaining a sense of group unity.[16] Knowing them is an indication that one belongs to the group, which recognizes that an outsider is unfamiliar with its folklore.

Attitudes and Beliefs

Every culture has a set of attitudes and beliefs that influence nearly all aspects of human behavior and help bring order to a society and its individuals. The more managers can learn about certain key attitudes, the better prepared they will be to understand why people behave as they do, especially when their reactions differ from those that the managers have learned to expect in dealing with their own people.

Among the wide variety of cultural attitudes and beliefs, some are of prime importance to the businessperson, especially attitudes toward time, toward achievement and work, and toward change.

ATTITUDES TOWARD TIME

The attitudes-toward-time cultural characteristic may present more adaptation problems for Americans overseas than does any other. Time is important in the United States, and if we must wait past the appointed hour to see an individual, we may assume this person is not giving our meeting the importance it deserves. Yet the wait could mean just the opposite elsewhere. Latin American or Middle Eastern executives may be taking care of the minor details of their business so that they can attend to their important visitor without interruption.

> *An American who has worked in the Middle East for 20 years explains the Middle Eastern concept of time this way: "At worst, there is no concept at all of time in the Middle East. At best, there is a sort of open-ended concept." The head of Egypt's Industrial Design Center, an Egyptian, states, "The simple wristwatch is, in some respects, much too sophisticated an instrument for the Middle East. One of the first things a foreigner should learn in Egypt is to ignore the second hand. The minute hand can also be an obstacle if he expects Egyptians to be as conscious as he of time ticking away."[17]*

Probably even more critical than short-term patience is long-term patience. American preoccupation with monthly profit and loss is a formidable barrier to the establishment of successful business relationships with Asian and Middle Eastern executives, especially during the development of joint ventures and other business relationships that have good potential in the long run—precisely the factors in which these people are most interested.[18]

accents, and the Sleeping Beauty castle is called *Le Chateau de la Belle au Bois Dormant.* The Worldview box illustrates the problems a global firm can have when its management makes culturally insensitive decisions.

HUMAN RESOURCE MANAGEMENT

The national culture is also a key determinant for the evaluation of managers. In Great Britain, an American general manager complained, people were promoted because of the school they had attended and their family background but not for their accomplishments. School ties are important in France, too. In fact, this phenomenon extends elsewhere—an example is the elite Bishop Cotton Boys School in India.

PRODUCTION AND FINANCE

Personnel problems can result from differences in attitudes toward authority, another sociocultural variable. Latin Americans have traditionally regarded the manager as the *patron,* an authoritarian figure responsible for their welfare. When American managers accustomed to a participative leadership style are transferred to Latin America, they must become more authoritarian, or their employees will consider them weak and incompetent.

> *A production manager who had been sent to Peru from the United States was convinced that he could motivate the workers to achieve higher productivity by instituting a more democratic decision-making style. He brought in trainers from the home office to teach the supervisors how to solicit suggestions and feedback from the workers. Shortly after the new management style was introduced, the workers began quitting their jobs. When asked why, they replied that the new production manager and his supervisors apparently didn't know what to do and were therefore asking the workers for advice. The workers thought the company wouldn't last long with that kind of management, and they wanted to quit before the collapse, because then everyone would be hunting for a job at the same time.*

Production managers have found that attitudes toward change can seriously influence the acceptance of new production methods; even treasurers realize the strength of the sociocultural forces when, armed with excellent balance sheets, they approach local banks, only to find that the banks attach far more importance to who they are than to how strong their companies are.[10] One reason for Disney's financial problems in Paris was the insensitive attitude of Disney executives toward European business culture. A top French banker involved in the negotiations to restructure the park's debt claimed, "The Walt Disney group is making a major error in thinking it can impose its will once more."[11] These are just a few examples to show that sociocultural differences do affect all the business functions. As we examine the components of the sociocultural forces, we shall mention others.

Sociocultural Components

It should be apparent that to be successful in their relationships with people in other countries, international businesspeople must be students of culture. They must have factual knowledge, which is relatively easy to obtain, but they must also become sensitive to cultural differences, and this is more difficult. Hall, as we saw, recommended spending a lifetime in a country or, in lieu of this, undergoing an extensive program to study what the culture is and what it does. But most newcomers to international business do not even have the opportunity for area orientation. They can, however, take the important first step of realizing that there *are* other cultures. In this chapter we cannot do more than point out some of the important sociocultural differences as they concern businesspeople in the hope that you will become more aware of the need to be culturally sensitive—to know that there are cultural differences for which you must look. Remember that the more you know about another person's culture, the better your predictions of that person's behavior will be.

The concept of culture is so broad that even ethnologists (cultural anthropologists) have to break it down into topics to facilitate its study. A listing of such topics will give us a better understanding of what culture is and may also serve as a guide for international managers when they are analyzing a particular problem from the sociocultural viewpoint.

Experts' opinions on the components of culture vary, but the following list is representative of their thinking. Culture is:

1. Aesthetics
2. Attitudes and beliefs
3. Religion
4. Material culture
5. Language
6. Societal organization
7. Education
8. Legal characteristics
9. Political structures[12]

We shall examine the first six components in this chapter and leave educational issues, legal characteristics, and political structures for later chapters.

Aesthetics

aesthetics
A culture's sense of beauty and good taste

Aesthetics pertains to a culture's sense of beauty and good taste and is expressed in its art, drama, music, folklore, and dances.

ART

Of particular interest to international businesspeople are the formal aspects of art, color, and form because of the symbolic meanings they convey. Colors, especially, can be deceptive because they mean different things to different cultures. The color of mourning is black in the United States and Mexico, black and white in the Far East, and purple in Brazil. Green is a propitious color in the Islamic world, and any ad or package featuring green is looked at favorably there. While in the United States mints are packaged in blue or green paper, in Africa the wrapper is red. So marketers must be careful to check whether colors have any special meanings before using them for products, packages, or advertisements.

Be careful of symbols, too. The number seven signifies good luck in the United States but the opposite in Singapore, Ghana, and Kenya. In Japan, the number four is unlucky. If you are giving a Japanese client golf balls, make sure there are more or less than four in the package. Also, in general, avoid using a nation's flag or any symbols connected with religion.

> *Nike, the athletic shoe marketer, recalled 38,000 pairs of shoes carrying the word* air *written in flaming letters because, according to Muslims, it resembles the word* Allah *in Arabic. Another 30,000 pairs were diverted from Arabian countries to less sensitive countries. Recently, protests in Europe followed the publication in Denmark of cartoons showing Mohammed wearing a turban shaped like a bomb.*[13]

It is also important to learn whether there are local aesthetic preferences for form that could affect the design of products, packaging, or even the building in which the firm is located. The American style of steel and glass in the midst of oriental architecture will be a constant reminder to the local population of the outsider's presence.

Feng Shui   In Asia, it is often believed that if buildings, furniture, roads, and other human-made objects are placed in harmony with nature, they can bring good fortune. If they are not, they will cause a disaster. Before building a house, scheduling a funeral, or making an investment, a master of *feng shui* (pronounced "fung shway") is called in to give a seal of approval.

> *Occupancy in a five-star hotel in Shanghai was down to just 5 percent. Desperate to find a remedy, the management called in a master of* feng shui *to examine the hotel. His analysis—very bad*

Kelty McRae is a human resources business partner and vice president at Wachovia Securities in Charlotte, North Carolina, where she consults with senior leaders in the Corporate and Investment Banking Division to develop and drive the planning and execution of the human capital business plan. She partners with business leaders to build a culture that minimizes risk, maximizes diversity, and enhances business performance, resulting in improved efficiency, employee retention and utilization, and human capital ROI. Kelty serves as a coach to leaders on both personal development and the development of leaders' direct reports, as well as practices that reinforce a high-performance culture. Kelty works with clients who conduct business in India, China, Korea, Taiwan, Singapore, Germany, France, England, and Ireland. For her first international business experience, Kelty traveled to India in the spring of 2006. Here are Kelty's comments about the impacts of a foreign culture as experienced on her first-time international business trip:

My most memorable first-time international business experience occurred while delivering stand-up training to newly hired Genpact employees in Gurgaon, India. Wachovia partners with Genpact Corporation in support of its offshoring and outsourcing efforts. Learning about social norms prior to my arrival prepared me for how to interact with business leaders from another culture and what to expect in the classroom. For example, many of the students initially avoided direct eye contact, which is a sign of respect in India for one's elders. In America, a teacher might assume lack of eye contact as a lack of interest in learning; however, in the Genpact training room this proved to be far from reality. The seemingly "shy" Genpact employees absorbed and conquered knowledge aggressively. Initially, there were many times throughout the course of training that we felt compelled to check for understanding of the material, as there didn't seem to be an uninhibited openness of the students to ask questions as you might see in an American training class. We determined after a period of time that silence to "Are you familiar with XXX" definitely meant that we needed to provide more information. The culture calls for "saving face," and although Indians are voracious learners with a strong achievement orientation, the norm seemed to be to not cause embarrassment to any individual for lack of knowledge.

I found India to differ dramatically from any other place I have been, and the experience invigorating while at times energy zapping. The sheer increase in the number of people around you, social norms about personal space, and various styles of interpersonal communication absorb your attention. There is extreme poverty and what may appear to an American as a lack of residential vs. commercial zoning. Migrant workers line all streets with tent villages. Cars and trucks, mopeds and bikes, donkeys and an occasional camel or elephant share the road with sacred cows. Orderly chaos is the best description. The system seems crazy, ineffective, and light years behind America, but amazingly it works!

You cannot pick up a Newsweek, Time, or other business magazine without hearing about "Incredible India." India's advancement and economical potential is and will increasingly be a powerful worldly force. It is clear that India has infrastructure issues to address; however, a magical underlying energy waits to slowly make its mark on society. In my view, regardless of political party alignments associated with outsourcing/offshoring efforts, Americans should seek to learn about the impact India is having on the world's economy and how their culture offers a unique and important lesson for us all.

Kelty's advice on how to get a job in international business:

- "Target positions in multinational organizations and or organizations involved in the offshoring and outsourcing of work to foreign countries."
- "Choose internship opportunities that will allow you to work with a diverse population."

Kelty's advice on succeeding in international business:

- "Cultural awareness, exceptional interpersonal/communication skills, ability to be nimble, flexible in approach to problem solving."
- "Openness to new experiences/change and foreign language skills."
- "Assume nothing, be open to learning. Seek to understand the source of difference. Do your homework—proactively learn about other countries' cultural values."

World Wide Resources:

www.wachoviasecurities.com

www.eweek.com/article2/0,1895,1853721,00.asp

www.kwintessential.co.uk/etiquette/doing-business-in.html

feng shui *because the building was at the end of a very long street, "like a river rushing toward the hotel." To overcome this, he had them change the color of the roof, put reflective material over the main entrance, and dig up the flagpoles outside and put them at an angle to the street instead of being parallel to it. This, he claimed, was done "to diversify the energy flow." He also asked management to put a fountain in front of the hotel, nine dragons and nine turtles in the fountain, and a pair of lions in the front garden. The hotel's occupancy rate shot up to 80 percent.*[14]

accents, and the Sleeping Beauty castle is called *Le Chateau de la Belle au Bois Dormant.* The Worldview box illustrates the problems a global firm can have when its management makes culturally insensitive decisions.

HUMAN RESOURCE MANAGEMENT

The national culture is also a key determinant for the evaluation of managers. In Great Britain, an American general manager complained, people were promoted because of the school they had attended and their family background but not for their accomplishments. School ties are important in France, too. In fact, this phenomenon extends elsewhere—an example is the elite Bishop Cotton Boys School in India.

PRODUCTION AND FINANCE

Personnel problems can result from differences in attitudes toward authority, another sociocultural variable. Latin Americans have traditionally regarded the manager as the *patron,* an authoritarian figure responsible for their welfare. When American managers accustomed to a participative leadership style are transferred to Latin America, they must become more authoritarian, or their employees will consider them weak and incompetent.

> *A production manager who had been sent to Peru from the United States was convinced that he could motivate the workers to achieve higher productivity by instituting a more democratic decision-making style. He brought in trainers from the home office to teach the supervisors how to solicit suggestions and feedback from the workers. Shortly after the new management style was introduced, the workers began quitting their jobs. When asked why, they replied that the new production manager and his supervisors apparently didn't know what to do and were therefore asking the workers for advice. The workers thought the company wouldn't last long with that kind of management, and they wanted to quit before the collapse, because then everyone would be hunting for a job at the same time.*

Production managers have found that attitudes toward change can seriously influence the acceptance of new production methods; even treasurers realize the strength of the sociocultural forces when, armed with excellent balance sheets, they approach local banks, only to find that the banks attach far more importance to who they are than to how strong their companies are.[10] One reason for Disney's financial problems in Paris was the insensitive attitude of Disney executives toward European business culture. A top French banker involved in the negotiations to restructure the park's debt claimed, "The Walt Disney group is making a major error in thinking it can impose its will once more."[11] These are just a few examples to show that sociocultural differences do affect all the business functions. As we examine the components of the sociocultural forces, we shall mention others.

Sociocultural Components

It should be apparent that to be successful in their relationships with people in other countries, international businesspeople must be students of culture. They must have factual knowledge, which is relatively easy to obtain, but they must also become sensitive to cultural differences, and this is more difficult. Hall, as we saw, recommended spending a lifetime in a country or, in lieu of this, undergoing an extensive program to study what the culture is and what it does. But most newcomers to international business do not even have the opportunity for area orientation. They can, however, take the important first step of realizing that there *are* other cultures. In this chapter we cannot do more than point out some of the important sociocultural differences as they concern businesspeople in the hope that you will become more aware of the need to be culturally sensitive—to know that there are cultural differences for which you must look. Remember that the more you know about another person's culture, the better your predictions of that person's behavior will be.

The concept of culture is so broad that even ethnologists (cultural anthropologists) have to break it down into topics to facilitate its study. A listing of such topics will give us a better understanding of what culture is and may also serve as a guide for international managers when they are analyzing a particular problem from the sociocultural viewpoint.

Experts' opinions on the components of culture vary, but the following list is representative of their thinking. Culture is:

1. Aesthetics
2. Attitudes and beliefs
3. Religion
4. Material culture
5. Language
6. Societal organization
7. Education
8. Legal characteristics
9. Political structures[12]

We shall examine the first six components in this chapter and leave educational issues, legal characteristics, and political structures for later chapters.

Aesthetics

aesthetics

A culture's sense of beauty and good taste

Aesthetics pertains to a culture's sense of beauty and good taste and is expressed in its art, drama, music, folklore, and dances.

ART

Of particular interest to international businesspeople are the formal aspects of art, color, and form because of the symbolic meanings they convey. Colors, especially, can be deceptive because they mean different things to different cultures. The color of mourning is black in the United States and Mexico, black and white in the Far East, and purple in Brazil. Green is a propitious color in the Islamic world, and any ad or package featuring green is looked at favorably there. While in the United States mints are packaged in blue or green paper, in Africa the wrapper is red. So marketers must be careful to check whether colors have any special meanings before using them for products, packages, or advertisements.

Be careful of symbols, too. The number seven signifies good luck in the United States but the opposite in Singapore, Ghana, and Kenya. In Japan, the number four is unlucky. If you are giving a Japanese client golf balls, make sure there are more or less than four in the package. Also, in general, avoid using a nation's flag or any symbols connected with religion.

> *Nike, the athletic shoe marketer, recalled 38,000 pairs of shoes carrying the word* air *written in flaming letters because, according to Muslims, it resembles the word* Allah *in Arabic. Another 30,000 pairs were diverted from Arabian countries to less sensitive countries. Recently, protests in Europe followed the publication in Denmark of cartoons showing Mohammed wearing a turban shaped like a bomb.*[13]

It is also important to learn whether there are local aesthetic preferences for form that could affect the design of products, packaging, or even the building in which the firm is located. The American style of steel and glass in the midst of oriental architecture will be a constant reminder to the local population of the outsider's presence.

Feng Shui In Asia, it is often believed that if buildings, furniture, roads, and other human-made objects are placed in harmony with nature, they can bring good fortune. If they are not, they will cause a disaster. Before building a house, scheduling a funeral, or making an investment, a master of *feng shui* (pronounced "fung shway") is called in to give a seal of approval.

> *Occupancy in a five-star hotel in Shanghai was down to just 5 percent. Desperate to find a remedy, the management called in a master of* feng shui *to examine the hotel. His analysis—very bad*

Kelty McRae is a human resources business partner and vice president at Wachovia Securities in Charlotte, North Carolina, where she consults with senior leaders in the Corporate and Investment Banking Division to develop and drive the planning and execution of the human capital business plan. She partners with business leaders to build a culture that minimizes risk, maximizes diversity, and enhances business performance, resulting in improved efficiency, employee retention and utilization, and human capital ROI. Kelty serves as a coach to leaders on both personal development and the development of leaders' direct reports, as well as practices that reinforce a high-performance culture. Kelty works with clients who conduct business in India, China, Korea, Taiwan, Singapore, Germany, France, England, and Ireland. For her first international business experience, Kelty traveled to India in the spring of 2006. Here are Kelty's comments about the impacts of a foreign culture as experienced on her first-time international business trip:

My most memorable first-time international business experience occurred while delivering stand-up training to newly hired Genpact employees in Gurgaon, India. Wachovia partners with Genpact Corporation in support of its offshoring and outsourcing efforts. Learning about social norms prior to my arrival prepared me for how to interact with business leaders from another culture and what to expect in the classroom. For example, many of the students initially avoided direct eye contact, which is a sign of respect in India for one's elders. In America, a teacher might assume lack of eye contact as a lack of interest in learning; however, in the Genpact training room this proved to be far from reality. The seemingly "shy" Genpact employees absorbed and conquered knowledge aggressively. Initially, there were many times throughout the course of training that we felt compelled to check for understanding of the material, as there didn't seem to be an uninhibited openness of the students to ask questions as you might see in an American training class. We determined after a period of time that silence to "Are you familiar with XXX" definitely meant that we needed to provide more information. The culture calls for "saving face," and although Indians are voracious learners with a strong achievement orientation, the norm seemed to be to not cause embarrassment to any individual for lack of knowledge.

I found India to differ dramatically from any other place I have been, and the experience invigorating while at times energy zapping. The sheer increase in the number of people around you, social norms about personal space, and various styles of interpersonal communication absorb your attention. There is extreme poverty and what may appear to an American as a lack of residential vs. commercial zoning. Migrant workers line all streets with tent villages. Cars and trucks, mopeds and bikes, donkeys and an occasional camel or elephant share the road with sacred cows. Orderly chaos is the best description. The system seems crazy, ineffective, and light years behind America, but amazingly it works!

You cannot pick up a Newsweek, Time, or other business magazine without hearing about "Incredible India." India's advancement and economical potential is and will increasingly be a powerful worldly force. It is clear that India has infrastructure issues to address; however, a magical underlying energy waits to slowly make its mark on society. In my view, regardless of political party alignments associated with outsourcing/offshoring efforts, Americans should seek to learn about the impact India is having on the world's economy and how their culture offers a unique and important lesson for us all.

Kelty's advice on how to get a job in international business:

- "Target positions in multinational organizations and or organizations involved in the offshoring and outsourcing of work to foreign countries."
- "Choose internship opportunities that will allow you to work with a diverse population."

Kelty's advice on succeeding in international business:

- "Cultural awareness, exceptional interpersonal/communication skills, ability to be nimble, flexible in approach to problem solving."
- "Openness to new experiences/change and foreign language skills."
- "Assume nothing, be open to learning. Seek to understand the source of difference. Do your homework—proactively learn about other countries' cultural values."

World Wide Resources:

www.wachoviasecurities.com

www.eweek.com/article2/0,1895,1853721,00.asp

www.kwintessential.co.uk/etiquette/doing-business-in.html

feng shui *because the building was at the end of a very long street, "like a river rushing toward the hotel." To overcome this, he had them change the color of the roof, put reflective material over the main entrance, and dig up the flagpoles outside and put them at an angle to the street instead of being parallel to it. This, he claimed, was done "to diversify the energy flow." He also asked management to put a fountain in front of the hotel, nine dragons and nine turtles in the fountain, and a pair of lions in the front garden. The hotel's occupancy rate shot up to 80 percent.*[14]

MUSIC AND FOLKLORE

Musical commercials are generally popular worldwide, but tastes vary and the marketer must know what kind of music each market prefers. Thus, a commercial that used a ballad in the United States might be better received to the tune of a bolero in Mexico or a samba in Brazil. However, if the advertiser is looking to the youth market with a product that is patently American, then American music will help reinforce its image. And singers like Shakira appeal to both markets.

Those who wish to steep themselves in a culture find it useful to study its folklore, which can disclose much about a society's way of life. The incorrect use of folklore can sometimes cost the firm a share of the market. For example, associating a product with the cowboy would not obtain the same results in Chile or Argentina as in the United States, because in those countries the cowboy is a far less romantic figure—it's just a job. On the other hand, Smirnoff's use of an image of late revolutionary leader Ernesto "Che" Guevara in an advertisement for spicy vodka sparked controversy in Cuba, where Guevara is a national hero.[15] As another instance, a U.S. company might be paying handsome royalties to use American cartoon characters in its promotion, only to find they are considerably less important in foreign markets. In Mexico, songs of the "Singing Cricket" are known to all youngsters and their mothers, and a commercial tie-in with that character would be as advantageous to the firm as its use of Peanuts or Mickey Mouse. In many areas, especially where nationalistic feeling is strong, local firms have been able to compete successfully with foreign affiliates by making use of indigenous folklore in the form of slogans and proverbs. Tales and folklore are valuable in maintaining a sense of group unity.[16] Knowing them is an indication that one belongs to the group, which recognizes that an outsider is unfamiliar with its folklore.

Attitudes and Beliefs

Every culture has a set of attitudes and beliefs that influence nearly all aspects of human behavior and help bring order to a society and its individuals. The more managers can learn about certain key attitudes, the better prepared they will be to understand why people behave as they do, especially when their reactions differ from those that the managers have learned to expect in dealing with their own people.

Among the wide variety of cultural attitudes and beliefs, some are of prime importance to the businessperson, especially attitudes toward time, toward achievement and work, and toward change.

ATTITUDES TOWARD TIME

The attitudes-toward-time cultural characteristic may present more adaptation problems for Americans overseas than does any other. Time is important in the United States, and if we must wait past the appointed hour to see an individual, we may assume this person is not giving our meeting the importance it deserves. Yet the wait could mean just the opposite elsewhere. Latin American or Middle Eastern executives may be taking care of the minor details of their business so that they can attend to their important visitor without interruption.

> An American who has worked in the Middle East for 20 years explains the Middle Eastern concept of time this way: "At worst, there is no concept at all of time in the Middle East. At best, there is a sort of open-ended concept." The head of Egypt's Industrial Design Center, an Egyptian, states, "The simple wristwatch is, in some respects, much too sophisticated an instrument for the Middle East. One of the first things a foreigner should learn in Egypt is to ignore the second hand. The minute hand can also be an obstacle if he expects Egyptians to be as conscious as he of time ticking away."[17]

Probably even more critical than short-term patience is long-term patience. American preoccupation with monthly profit and loss is a formidable barrier to the establishment of successful business relationships with Asian and Middle Eastern executives, especially during the development of joint ventures and other business relationships that have good potential in the long run—precisely the factors in which these people are most interested.[18]